Handbook on Poverty and Inequality

Handbook on Poverty and Inequality

Jonathan Haughton
Shahidur R. Khandker

THE WORLD BANK
Washington, DC

© 2009 The International Bank for Reconstruction and Development/The World Bank
1818 H Street, NW
Washington, DC 20433
Telephone: 202-473-1000
Internet: www.worldbank.org
E-mail: feedback@worldbank.org

ISBN: 978-0-8213-7613-3
eISBN: 978-0-8213-7614-0
DOI: 10.1596/978-0-8213-7613-3

Library of Congress Cataloging-in-Publication Data

Haughton, Jonathan Henry.
    Handbook on poverty and inequality / Jonathan Haughton and Shahidur R. Khandker.
        p. cm.
    Includes bibliographical references and indexes.
    ISBN 978-0-8213-7613-3—ISBN 978-0-8213-7614-0 (electronic)
    1. Poverty—Statistical methods. 2. Poverty—Econometric models. 3. Equality—Economic aspects—Econometric models. I. Khandker, Shahidur R. II. Title.
    HC79.P6H344 2009
    339.4'60727—dc22
                                                                                    2009000849

Cover design: Patricia Hord.Graphik Design

Contents

Contents

Contents

Boxes

Figures

Tables

Contents

Preface

The *Handbook on Poverty and Inequality* provides tools to measure, describe, monitor, evaluate, and analyze poverty. It provides background materials for designing poverty reduction strategies. This book is intended for researchers and policy analysts involved in poverty research and policy making. The *Handbook* began as a series of notes to support training courses on poverty analysis and gradually grew into a 16-chapter book. Now the *Handbook* consists of explanatory text with numerous examples, interspersed with multiple-choice questions (to ensure active learning) and combined with extensive practical exercises using Stata statistical software.

The *Handbook* has been thoroughly tested. The World Bank Institute has used most of the chapters in training workshops in countries throughout the world, including Afghanistan, Bangladesh, Botswana, Cambodia, India, Indonesia, Kenya, the Lao People's Democratic Republic, Malawi, Pakistan, the Philippines, Tanzania, and Thailand, as well as in distance courses with substantial numbers of participants from numerous countries in Asia (in 2002) and Africa (in 2003), and online asynchronous courses with more than 200 participants worldwide (in 2007 and 2008). The feedback from these courses has been very useful in helping us create a handbook that balances rigor with accessibility and practicality. The *Handbook* has also been used in university courses related to poverty.

The *Handbook* is designed to be accessible to people with a university-level background in science or social sciences. It treats the material at a Master's-degree level, with an emphasis on intuitive explanations and practical examples. It also provides the skills needed to be able to work on poverty analysis straightaway, and gives a solid foundation for those headed toward a research career in the subject.

With sufficient self-discipline, it is possible to master the material in the *Handbook* without a formal course, by working through all the Stata-based exercises in detail and by taking advantage of the multiple-choice questions at the end of the chapters. But in our experience, most people find it easier to commit themselves to a structured training course—10 intensive days suffice—whether face-to-face or online. Either route should prepare one well to undertake relatively sophisticated poverty analyses.

In preparing the *Handbook*, we have drawn heavily on the extensive and excellent work by Martin Ravallion of the World Bank's Development Research Group; the discussion in the World Bank's *World Development Report 2000/2001: Attacking Poverty*; as well as background papers or presentations by Kevin Carey, Shaohua Chen, and Zeynep Orhun; and contributions from José Ramon ("Toots") Albert, Kathleen Beegle, Nidhiya Menon and Celia Reyes. Zeynep Orhun thoroughly reviewed the first 10 chapters, and Peter Lanjouw gave us very useful comments. Hussain Samad, Changqing Sun, and Ngo Viet Phuong contributed to the preparation of the Stata exercises, and Lassana Cissokho helped with the bibliographic work. We would like to express our sincere gratitude to all for their contributions.

We are deeply indebted to Roumeen Islam for her encouragement and support throughout the development of the book. We also thank Denise Bergeron, Stephen McGroarty, and Dina Towbin for editorial assistance, and Dulce Afzal and Maxine Pineda for support toward the production of the book.

Questions, comments, and suggestions related to the *Handbook* are most welcome, because they allow us to improve the *Handbook* as we update and extend it; they should be directed to Shahidur Khandker at skhandker@worldbank.org. Our goal is to increase the capacity to undertake poverty analysis everywhere. We hope that the *Handbook* represents a useful step in this direction.

Jonathan Haughton
Suffolk University, Boston

Shahidur R. Khandker
World Bank, Washington, DC

Foreword

Over one hundred years have passed since 1899, when Seebohm Rowntree undertook his path-breaking study of poverty in his hometown of York, in the north of England. A single paid enumerator, along with several volunteers, interviewed 11,560 households in the span of about six months, collecting information on housing conditions, rent, and employment. Income was imputed from wage data obtained from employers. Rowntree established a poverty line based on the cost of a basic diet that would provide 3,478 Calories per day for men, to which he added an allowance for clothing and fuel.

The data were compiled, by hand of course, into tables and graphs, and the resulting study, *Poverty: A Study of Town Life*, was published in 1901. The book has been called the first quasi-scientific empirical study of the subject. Not only did it inspire many subsequent studies, but it had an enormous influence on public policy, in large part because it showed that much poverty was structural in the sense that even working people were unable to earn enough to meet their needs. This finding implied that government might need to play a role in tackling poverty, which is what happened in Britain with the introduction of the Old Age Pensions Act in 1908 and the National Insurance Act in 1911. Both reforms were influenced by Rowntree's work and introduced by his friend, David Lloyd George.

Much has remained the same since Rowntree's study. We still need to collect survey information to analyze poverty; those data must be compiled, analyzed, and presented as input into policy making; and we still wrestle with many of the same issues Rowntree faced—how to define an appropriate poverty line, how to measure income, and how to judge well-being.

Much has changed, too. The easy availability of computing power and statistical software has made the job of the poverty analyst both easier and harder—easier because much of the grunt work of data compilation and presentation can be handled quickly, and harder because much more is now expected of the analyst. Putting together a few tabulations is no longer sufficient; now the analyst must consider the robustness and representativeness of the results, justify the decisions made about the choice of welfare indicator and poverty line, know about the construction of price indexes, be able to handle panel data, have the competence to make and understand international comparisons of poverty, and apply increasingly sophisticated statistical techniques.

It is in meeting these expectations that you will find this book useful. It grew out of lecture notes prepared to accompany courses on poverty analysis and it balances a discussion of theory and principles with numerous examples and exercises. After working through the *Handbook* you will be able to do solid work on poverty analysis, and you will find that the specialized literature on the subject has become accessible. You will become part of a growing cadre of analysts who bring rigor and good sense to bear on one of humanity's most persistent problems. Rowntree would approve.

Martin Ravallion
Director
Development Research Group
World Bank

About the Authors

Jonathan Haughton (PhD, Harvard University, 1983) is a professor of economics at Suffolk University in Boston and senior economist at the Beacon Hill Institute for Public Policy. A prize-winning teacher, he has authored more than 30 articles in refereed journals, penned more than 20 book chapters, coedited three books on Vietnam, and written at least 100 reports on policy issues. He has taught or conducted research in more than two dozen countries on five continents. Recent projects include an impact evaluation of the Thailand Village Fund, a study of tax incidence in Vietnam, and the use of a computable general equilibrium model to assess the economic effects of a switch from taxing income to taxing consumption in the United States.

Shahidur R. Khandker (PhD, McMaster University, Canada, 1983) is a lead economist in the Development Research Group of the World Bank. When this *Handbook* was written, he was a lead economist at the World Bank Institute. He has authored more than 30 articles in peer-reviewed journals, including the *Journal of Political Economy, The Review of Economic Studies*, and the *Journal of Development Economics*; has published several books, including *Fighting Poverty with Microcredit: Experience in Bangladesh*, published by Oxford University Press; and has written several book chapters and more than two dozen discussion papers at the World Bank on poverty, rural finance and microfinance, agriculture, and infrastructure. He has worked in close to 30 countries. His current research projects include seasonality in income and poverty, and impact evaluation studies of rural energy and microfinance in countries in Africa, Asia, and Latin America.

Abbreviations

CSES	Cambodian Socio-Economic Survey
FGT	Foster-Greer-Thorbecke
GE	generalized entropy
HBS	household budget survey
ICP	International Comparison Project
MDGs	Millennium Development Goals
OECD	Organisation for Economic Co-operation and Development
P_0	headcount index of poverty
P_1	poverty gap index
P_2	poverty severity index
PPP	purchasing power parity
PWT	Penn World Tables
SESC	Socio-Economic Survey of Cambodia
SST	Sen-Shorrocks-Thon
SUSENAS	National Socioeconomic Survey (Indonesia)
VHLSS06	Vietnam Household Living Standards Survey of 2006
VLSS93	Vietnam Living Standards Survey of 1993

All dollar amounts are U.S. dollars unless otherwise specified.

Chapter 1

What Is Poverty and Why Measure It?

Summary

Poverty is "pronounced deprivation in well-being." The conventional view links well-being primarily to command over commodities, so the poor are those who do not have enough income or consumption to put them above some adequate minimum threshold. This view sees poverty largely in monetary terms.

Poverty may also be tied to a specific type of consumption; for example, people could be house poor or food poor or health poor. These dimensions of poverty often can be measured directly, for instance, by measuring malnutrition or literacy.

The broadest approach to well-being (and poverty) focuses on the capability of the individual to function in society. Poor people often lack key capabilities; they may have inadequate income or education, or be in poor health, or feel powerless, or lack political freedoms.

There are four reasons to measure poverty:

- To keep poor people on the agenda

- To be able to identify poor people and so to be able to target appropriate interventions

- To monitor and evaluate projects and policy interventions geared to poor people

- To evaluate the effectiveness of institutions whose goal is to help poor people.

To help countries think systematically about how the position of poor people may be improved, and to act accordingly, the World Bank favors the Poverty Reduction Strategy Paper (PRSP) process. Countries are expected to measure and analyze domestic poverty, and to identify and operationalize actions to reduce poverty. The PRSP process requires strong technical support. A central purpose of this *Handbook* is to impart the requisite technical and analytical skills.

Learning Objectives

After completing the chapter on *What Is Poverty and Why Measure It?*, you should be able to

1. Define poverty.

2. Summarize the three main views of poverty.

3. State four justifications for measuring poverty.

4. Summarize the role of the Poverty Reduction Strategy Paper process.

5. Explain why technical and analytical training in poverty analysis are needed.

Introduction: The Concepts of Well-Being and Poverty

According to the World Bank (2000), "poverty is pronounced deprivation in well-being." This of course begs the questions of what is meant by *well-being* and of what is the reference point against which to measure deprivation.

One approach is to think of well-being as the command over commodities in general, so people are better off if they have a greater command over resources. The main focus is on whether households or individuals have enough resources to meet their needs. Typically, poverty is then measured by comparing individuals' income or consumption with some defined threshold below which they are considered to be poor. This is the most conventional view—poverty is seen largely in monetary terms—and is the starting point for most analyses of poverty.

A second approach to well-being (and hence poverty) is to ask whether people are able to obtain a *specific* type of consumption good: Do they have enough food? Or shelter? Or health care? Or education? In this view the analyst goes beyond the more traditional monetary measures of poverty: Nutritional poverty might be measured by examining whether children are stunted or wasted; and educational poverty might be measured by asking whether people are literate or how much formal schooling they have received.

Perhaps the broadest approach to well-being is the one articulated by Amartya Sen (1987), who argues that well-being comes from a capability to function in society. Thus, poverty arises when people lack key capabilities, and so have inadequate income or education, or poor health, or insecurity, or low self-confidence, or a sense of powerlessness, or the absence of rights such as freedom of speech. Viewed in this way, poverty is a multidimensional phenomenon and less amenable to simple solutions. For instance, while higher average incomes will certainly help reduce poverty, these may need to be accompanied by measures to empower the poor, or insure them against risks, or to address specific weaknesses such as inadequate availability of schools or a corrupt health service.

Poverty is related to, but distinct from, inequality and vulnerability. *Inequality* focuses on the distribution of attributes, such as income or consumption, across the whole population. In the context of poverty analysis, inequality requires examination if one believes that the welfare of individuals depends on their economic position relative to others in society. *Vulnerability* is defined as the risk of falling into poverty in the future, even if the person is not necessarily poor now; it is often associated with the effects of "shocks" such as a drought, a drop in farm prices, or a financial crisis. Vulnerability is a key dimension of well-being since it affects individuals' behavior in terms of investment, production patterns, and coping strategies, and in terms of the perceptions of their own situations.

The concepts, measures, and analytical tools covered in this *Handbook* are mainly introduced in the context of the monetary measures of poverty, especially consumption. However, they frequently are, and should be, applied to other dimensions of poverty.

Why Measure Poverty?

It takes time, energy, and money to measure poverty, since it can only be done properly by gathering survey data directly from households. Why, then, do we need to go to the trouble of measuring poverty? At least four good reasons come to mind.

Keeping Poor People on the Agenda

Perhaps the strongest justification is that provided by Ravallion (1998), who argues, "[A] credible measure of poverty can be a powerful instrument for focusing the attention of policy makers on the living conditions of the poor." Put another way, it is easy to ignore the poor if they are statistically invisible. The measurement of poverty is necessary if it is to appear on the political and economic agenda.

Targeting Domestic and Worldwide Interventions

A second reason for measuring poverty is to target interventions. Clearly, one cannot help poor people without knowing who they are. This is the purpose of a poverty profile, which sets out the major facts on poverty (and, typically, inequality), and then examines the pattern of poverty to see how it varies by geography (for example, by region, urban/rural, mountain/plain), by community characteristics (for example, in communities with and without a school), and by household characteristics (for example, by education of household head, by size of household). A well-presented poverty profile is invaluable, even though it typically uses rather basic techniques such as tables and graphs. (For a straightforward example, see Nicholas Prescott and Menno Pradhan 1997).

Probably the most important operational use of the poverty profile is to support efforts to target development resources toward poorer areas. However, which regions should command priority in targeting? This question can only be answered at a highly aggregate level by most survey data (like the Socio-Economic Survey of Cambodia (SESC) of 1993–94 or the Cambodia Socio-Economic Survey (CSES) of 1999) because of the limited number of geographic domains that are typically sampled. For example, in the CSES 1999, poverty is lowest in Phnom Penh, where the headcount poverty rate was 15 percent compared to the national poverty rate of 51 percent. The survey data can sometimes be combined with more detailed census data to allow for much finer geographic targeting.

A good poverty profile also makes employment targeting possible. The ability of the vast majority of households in Cambodia to escape poverty will depend on their earnings from employment. The highest poverty rate was found among people living in households headed by farmers (46 percent in 1993–94 in Cambodia). By contrast, households headed by someone working in the government are least likely to be poor; in these occupations the poverty rate was 20 percent (1993–94). This would suggest that policies that aim to reduce poverty through enhancing income-generating capabilities should be targeted toward the agricultural sector.

The relationship between poverty and education is particularly important because of the key role played by education in raising economic growth and reducing poverty. The better educated have higher incomes and thus are much less likely to be poor. Cambodians living in households with an uneducated household head are more likely to be poor, with a poverty rate of 47 percent in 1993–94. With higher levels of education, the likelihood of being poor falls considerably. Raising education attainment is clearly a high priority to improve living standards and reduce poverty.

The relationship between gender and poverty may also indicate another targeting strategy for poverty reduction. In Cambodia, about 25 percent of the population lives in households headed by women. Perhaps surprisingly, the CSES 1999 data show that the poverty rate was slight *lower* among female-headed households (48 percent) than among male-headed households (52 percent). In this case, targeting interventions based on the gender of the head of household would not help to distinguish the poor from the nonpoor.

Targeting is also important at a worldwide level. Institutions, including the World Bank and aid agencies, have limited resources, and would like to know how best to deploy those resources to combat poverty. For this, they need to know where in the world poor people are located, and this in turn requires viable information on poverty in every country. All developed countries, and about two-thirds of developing countries, have undertaken nationally representative household surveys to collect information on consumption and/or income; in many cases, these surveys have been repeated over time.

Successful efforts to target policies and programs to help poor people also require an understanding of why they are poor. This is not simply academic curiosity: it is integral to the process of finding workable solutions and managing tradeoffs. For instance, does a tax on rice exports help the poor? We know it will favor urban residents who eat rice and will hurt rice farmers, but more information is needed before we can conclude that the policy would help poor people. Or will providing outboard motors help poor fishermen? It might simply lead to overfishing and so be of no long-term help. Will providing sewers in slums help the poor residents, or might it worsen their lot as higher rents force them to move and provide a windfall to landowners? Questions such as these cannot be answered adequately without viable information that measures poverty, even if this is only the first step toward developing solutions.

Monitoring and Evaluating Projects and Policy Interventions

More generally, the third reason for measuring poverty is to be able to predict the effects of, and then evaluate, policies and programs designed to help poor people. Policies that look good on paper—new opportunities for microcredit for the poor, for instance—may in practice not work as well as expected. To judge the effects, one would ideally like to monitor the effects of a policy on poor people and evaluate the outcomes in comparison with a control group. Rigorous analysis of this kind is needed both to improve the design of projects and programs and to weed out ones that are not working.

Information on poverty is also helpful in understanding the politics of many government policies. By collecting information on households and their economic status, one can assess who uses public services and who gains from government subsidies. If programs are cut or there is retrenchment of the public sector, poverty data provide information on the effects of these plans. Using information on poverty, one can simulate the impact of different policies. The identification of the gainers and losers goes a long way toward determining who will support, or oppose, a given policy.

Evaluating the Effectiveness of Institutions

The fourth reason for measuring poverty is to help evaluate institutions. One cannot tell if a government is doing a good job of combating poverty unless there is solid information on poverty. This does not only apply to governments. "Our dream is a world free of poverty," writes the World Bank,[1] and its first mission statement is "to fight poverty with passion and professionalism for lasting results."[2] The institution's success in pursuing this goal can only be judged if there are adequate measures of poverty.

When evaluating projects, policies, and instruments, our concern is with poverty comparisons, the title of Martin Ravallion's influential monograph (Ravallion 1992). In this context, we typically want to know whether poverty has fallen (a qualitative measure) and by how much (a quantitative measure). Such comparisons are surprisingly difficult to do well—often they are not robust—and require close attention to issues of measurement, which is one of the major themes of this *Handbook*.

Thinking Systematically: Poverty Reduction Strategy Papers

Measurement is necessary but not sufficient. It is also important to think clearly and systematically about how the position of poor people may be improved, and to act accordingly.

To do this, the World Bank favors the Poverty Reduction Strategy Paper process. First introduced for Highly Indebted Poor Countries (HIPC) in 1999, this approach begins with a country-driven policy paper setting out a long-term strategy for fighting poverty and rooted in the latest available data and analysis.

The idea is that leaders, administrators, analysts, and others from within a country should take the lead in developing a PRSP, so that the process is "owned" locally and not imposed from the outside—although the World Bank typically insists that the process be followed. This begins with the measurement of poverty, followed by an analysis of its dimensions and causes. Based on this foundation, the expectation is that there will be extensive dialogue about what needs to be done to reduce the number of poor people. Thus, once poverty is measured and the poor are identified, the next steps in the PRSP process are to choose public actions and programs that have the greatest impact on poverty, identify indicators of progress, and monitor change in a systematic manner. Poverty measurement and diagnostics are therefore central to informing policy making for poverty reduction in many countries.

The creation of a good PRSP requires strong technical support. A central purpose of this *Handbook* is to impart the requisite technical and analytical skills.

Review Questions

1. Poverty is
○ A. A lack of command over commodities in general
○ B. A pronounced deprivation in well-being
○ C. Lack of capability to function in society
○ D. All of the above

2. Which of the following is *not* a reason to go to the trouble and expense of measuring poverty?

- A. To evaluate the impact of policy interventions geared toward the poor
- B. To keep poor people on the agenda of public policy
- C. To measure the distributional effects of economic growth
- D. To target interventions designed to reduce poverty

3. Is the following statement true or false? "The World Bank promotes the Poverty Reduction Strategy Paper process in order to determine to which countries it should lend money."

- True
- False

Notes

1. See http://go.worldbank.org/4DO5SXV2H0 (accessed June 7, 2008). More recently, the World Bank has begun to use a new slogan, "Working for a World Free of Poverty"; see http://www.worldbank.org/ (accessed June 7, 2008).
2. http://go.worldbank.org/DM4A38OWJ0 (accessed June 7, 2008).

References

Prescott, Nicholas, and Menno Pradhan. 1997. "A Poverty Profile of Cambodia." Discussion Paper No. 373, World Bank, Washington, DC.

Ravallion, Martin. 1992. "Poverty Comparisons: A Guide to Concepts and Methods." Living Standards Measurement Surveys Working Paper No. 88, World Bank, Washington, DC.

————. 1998. "Poverty Lines in Theory and Practice." Living Standards Measurement Surveys Working Paper No. 133, World Bank, Washington, DC.

Sen, Amartya. 1987. *Commodities and Capabilities*. Amsterdam: North-Holland.

World Bank. 2000. *World Development Report 2000/2001: Attacking Poverty*. Washington, DC: World Bank.

Chapter 2

Measuring Poverty

Summary

The first step in measuring poverty is defining an indicator of welfare such as income or consumption per capita. Information on welfare is derived from survey data. Good survey design is important. Although some surveys use simple random sampling, most use stratified random sampling. This requires the use of sampling weights in the subsequent analysis. Multistage cluster sampling is also standard; it is cost-effective and unbiased, but it lowers the precision of the results, which calls for some adjustments when analyzing the data.

The World Bank-inspired Living Standards Measurement Surveys (LSMS) feature multitopic questionnaires and strict quality control. The flexible LSMS template is widely used.

Income, defined in principle as *consumption + change in net worth*, is generally used as a measure of welfare in developed countries, but it tends to be seriously understated in less-developed countries. Consumption is less understated and comes closer to measuring *permanent income*. However, it requires one to value durable goods (by assessing the implicit rental cost) and housing (by estimating what it would have cost to rent).

While consumption per capita is the most commonly used measure of welfare, some analysts use consumption per adult equivalent, in order to capture differences in need by age, and economies of scale in consumption. The Organisation for Economic Co-operation and Development (OECD) scale ($= 1 + 0.7 \times (N_A - 1) + 0.5 \times N_C$) is popular, but such scales are controversial and cannot be estimated satisfactorily.

Other popular measures of welfare include calorie consumption per person per day, food consumption as a proportion of total expenditure, and nutritional status as measured by stunting or wasting. However, there is no ideal measure of well-being, and analysts need to be aware of the strengths and limitations of any measure they use.

Learning Objectives

After completing the chapter on *Measuring Poverty*, you should be able to

1. Summarize the three steps required to measure poverty.

2. Recognize the strengths and limitations arising from the need to use survey data in poverty analysis, including the choice of sample frame, unit of observation, time period, and choice of welfare indicators.

3. Describe the main problems that arise with survey data, including:

   • survey design (sampling frame/coverage, response bias)

   • stratification

   • multistage cluster sampling.

4. Explain why weighting is needed when surveys use stratified random sampling.

5. Describe and evaluate the use of equivalence scales, including the OECD scale.

6. Define consumption and income as measures of welfare, and evaluate the desirability of each in the context of measuring well-being in less-developed countries.

7. Summarize the problems that arise in measuring income and consumption, and explain how to value durable goods and housing services.

8. Identify measures of household welfare other than consumption and income, including calorie consumption per capita, nutritional status, health status, and food consumption, as a proportion of total expenditure.

9. Argue the case that there is no ideal measure of welfare.

Introduction: Steps in Measuring Poverty

The goal of this chapter is to set out a method for measuring poverty. Given the enormous literature available on the subject, we simply set out the main practical issues, with suggestions for further reading for those interested in pursuing the subject more.

Three steps need to be taken in measuring poverty (for further discussion, see Ravallion 1998):

• Defining an indicator of welfare

• Establishing a minimum acceptable standard of that indicator to separate the poor from the nonpoor (the poverty line)

• Generating a summary statistic to aggregate the information from the distribution of this welfare indicator relative to the poverty line.

This chapter defines an indicator of welfare; chapter 3 discusses the issues involved in setting a poverty line; chapter 4 deals with measuring aggregate welfare and its distribution.

Household Surveys

All measures of poverty rely on household survey data, so it is important to recognize the strengths and limitations of such data and to set up and interpret them with care.

Key Survey Issues

Ravallion (1992) lists a number of issues related to surveys that require attention before one even attempts to measure or analyze poverty:

- *The sample frame*: The survey may represent a whole country's population, or some more narrowly defined subset, such as workers or residents of one region. The appropriateness of a survey's particular sample frame will depend on the inferences one wants to draw from it. Thus, a survey of urban households would allow one to measure urban poverty, but not poverty in the country as a whole.

- *The unit of observation*: This is typically the household or occasionally the individuals within the household. A household is usually defined as a group of persons eating and living together.

- *The number of observations over time*: Most surveys are single cross-sections, covering a sample of households just once. *Longitudinal surveys*, in which the same households or individuals are resurveyed one or more times (also called *panel data sets*) are more difficult to do, but these have been undertaken in a several countries (for example, the Vietnam Living Standards Surveys of 1992–93 and 1997–98, or parts of the Thailand Socioeconomic Surveys of 2002 and 2004).

- *The principal living standard indicator collected*: Most measures of welfare are based on household consumption expenditure or household income. Many surveys collect both, although this typically requires two interviews per household: to save on costs, some surveys gather data on either income or expenditure. Given budget constraints, there are always tradeoffs: Since a more detailed and complex questionnaire takes longer to administer, the sample size will have to be smaller, which reduces the precision of the statistics based on these data and limits the amount of disaggregation (for example, to the provincial level) that is possible.

Common Survey Problems

Several common problems arise when using and interpreting household survey data. We review these, organizing our thoughts largely along the lines set out in Ravallion (1992).

Survey Design. If the sample on which a survey is based is not random, then the resulting estimates of poverty are almost impossible to interpret. They are likely to be biased, but we do not know by how much.

A simple national random sample would create a list of everyone in the country and then randomly choose subjects to be interviewed, with each person having an equal chance of being selected. In practice, sampling always falls short of this ideal for three reasons. First, some people or households may be hard to find; for instance, most surveys interview people at their homes, but this completely overlooks homeless persons, a group that is likely to be poor.

Second, some of the surveys that have been used to measure poverty were not designed for this purpose in that their sample frames were not intended to span the entire population.

> **Examples:** This is true of labor force surveys, which have been widely used for poverty assessments in Latin America; the sample frame is typically restricted to the "economically active population," which precludes certain subgroups of the poor. To take another example, household surveys in the Republic of Korea have typically excluded one-person households from the sample frame, which renders the results unrepresentative.

Key questions to ask about any survey are the following:

- Does the sample frame (the initial listing of the population from which the sample was drawn) span the entire population?

- Is there likely to be a response bias? This may take one of two forms: *unit nonresponse*, which occurs when some households do not participate in the survey, and *item nonresponse*, which occurs when some households do not respond fully to all the questions in the survey.

Third, it is very often cost-effective deliberately to oversample some small groups (for example, minority households in remote areas) and to undersample large and homogeneous groups. Such *stratified random sampling*—whereby different subgroups of the population have different (but known) chances of being selected but all have an equal chance in any given subgroup—can increase the precision in poverty measurement obtainable with a given number of interviews. When done, it is necessary to use weights when analyzing the data, as explained more fully in the following section.

Sampling. Two important implications flow from the fact that measures of poverty and inequality are always based on survey data.

First, it means that actual measures of poverty and inequality are *sample statistics*, and so estimate the true population parameters with some error. Although it is standard practice to say that, for instance, "the poverty rate is 15.2 percent," it would be more accurate to say something like "We are 99 percent confident that the true poverty rate is between 13.5 percent and 16.9 percent; our best point estimate is that it is 15.2 percent." Outside of academic publications, such caution is, unfortunately, rather rare.

The second implication is that it is essential to know how the sampling was done, because the survey data may need to be weighted in order to get the right estimates of such measures as mean income or poverty rates. In practice, most household surveys oversample some areas (such as low-density mountainous areas, or regions with small populations), to get adequately large samples to compute tolerably accurate statistics for those areas. Conversely, areas with dense, homogeneous populations tend to be undersampled. For instance, the Vietnam Living Standards Survey of 1997/98 (VLSS98) oversampled the sparsely populated central highlands and undersampled the dense and populous Red River delta (Vietnam 2000).

In cases such as this, it is not legitimate to compute simple averages of the sample observations such as per capita income to make inferences about the whole population. Instead, weights must be used, as the following example shows.

> *Example:* Consider the case of a country with 10 million people who have a mean annual per capita income of $1,200. Region A is mountainous and has 2 million people with average per capita incomes of $500; region B is lowland and fertile and has 8 million people with an average per capita income of $1,375.
>
> Now suppose that a household survey samples 2,000 households, picked randomly from throughout the country. The mean income per capita of this sample is the best available estimator of the per capita income of the population, and so we may calculate this and other statistics using the simplest available formulae (which are generally the ones shown in this *Handbook*). For example, the Vietnam Living Standards Survey of 1992–93 (VLSS93) essentially chose households using a simple random sample, using the census data from 1989 to determine where people lived; thus, the data from the VLSS93 are easy to work with, because no special weighting procedure is required.
>
> Further details are set out in table 2.1. If 400 households are surveyed in Region A (one household per 5,000 people) and 1,600 in Region B (one household per 5,000 people), then each household surveyed effectively "represents" 5,000 people; a simple average of per capita income ($1,215.60), based on the survey data, would then generally serve as the best estimator of per capita income in the population at large, as shown in the "case 1" panel in table 2.1.

Table 2.1 Illustration of Why Weights Are Needed to Compute Statistics Based on Stratified Samples

	Region A	Region B	Whole country
Population (million)	2.0	8.0	10.0
True income/capita ($/year)	500	1,375	1,200
Case 1. Simple random sampling. *Use simple average*.			
Sample size (given initially)	400	1,600	2,000
Estimated total income, $	196,000	2,235,200	2,431,200
	= 400 × 490	= 1,600 × 1,397	= 196,000 + 2,235,200
Estimated income/capita, ($/year)*	490	1,397	**1,215.6**
			= 2,431,200/2,000
Case 2. Stratified sampling.			
Sample size (given initially)	1,000	1,000	2,000
Estimated total income, $	490,000	1,397,000	1,887,000
	=1,000 × 490	= 1,000 × 1,397	= 490,000 + 1,397,000
Case 2a. Stratified sample, using simple average. *This is incorrect, so don't do this!*			
Estimated income/capita ($/year)	490	1,397	**943.5**
			=1,887,000/2000
Case 2b. Stratified sampling, using weighted average. *This is the correct approach*.			
Weight (Based on population)	0.2	0.8	
	= 2.0/10.0=	= 8.0/10.0	
Estimated income/capita ($/year)	490	1,397	**1,215.6**
			= (0.2 × 490) + (0.8 × 1,397)

Source: Example created by the authors.

* Estimated income per capita is likely to differ from true income per capita, due both to sampling error (only a moderate number of households were surveyed) and nonsampling error (for example, underreporting, poorly worded questions, and the like).

But now suppose that 1,000 households were surveyed in Region A (one per 2,000 people) and another 1,000 in Region B (one per 8,000 people). If weights were not used, the estimated income per capita would be $943.50 (see the "case 2a" panel in table 2.1), but this would be incorrect. Here, a weighted average of observed income per capita is needed in order to compute the national average. Intuitively, each household sampled in Region A should get a weight of 2,000 and each household in Region B should be given a weight of 8,000 (see table 2.1). The mechanics are set out in the "case 2b" panel in table 2.1 and yield an estimated per capita income of $1,215.60.

In picking a sample, most surveys use the most recent population census numbers as the sample frame. Typically, the country is divided into regions, and a sample is picked from each region (referred to as a *stratum* in the sampling context). Within each region, subregional units such as towns, counties, districts, and communes are usually chosen randomly, with the probability of being picked being in proportion to population size. Such multistage sampling may even break down the units further, for example, to villages within a district.

At the basic level (the *primary sampling unit* such as a village, hamlet, or city ward), it is standard to sample households in clusters. Rather than picking individual households randomly throughout a whole district, the procedure is typically to pick several villages and then randomly sample 15 to 20 households within each chosen village. The reason for doing cluster sampling, instead of simple random sampling, is that it is far cheaper to survey several households in a small area than to have to find households scattered widely over a potentially very large area.

But the use of cluster sampling, which is now almost ubiquitous, has an important corollary: The information provided by sampling clusters is less reliable as a guide to conditions in the overall area than pure random sampling would be. To see this, compare figure 2.1.a (simple random sampling) with figure 2.1.b (cluster sampling). Although, on average, cluster sampling will give the correct results (for per capita income, for instance), so the expected mean values are unaffected—it is less reliable because we might, by chance, have chosen two particularly poor clusters, or two rich ones. Thus, cluster sampling produces larger standard errors for the estimates of population parameters. This needs to be taken into account when programming the statistical results of sample surveys. Not all statistical packages handle clustering; however, Stata deals with it well using the *svyset* commands (see appendix 3 for details).

Most living standards surveys sample households rather than individuals. If the variable of interest is household-based—for instance, the value of land owned per household or the educational level of the household head—then the statistics should be computed using household weights.

But a survey that samples households will give too little weight to *individuals* in large households. To see this, consider the realistic case of a survey that, at the village

Figure 2.1a Simple Random Sample

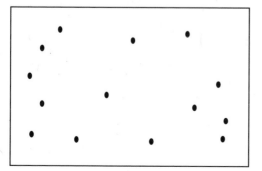

Figure 2.1b Cluster Sampling

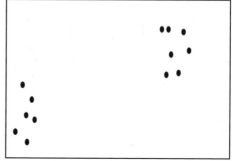

Source: Authors.

level, randomly chooses 15 households for its sample. Perhaps one of these households consists of five persons; and another has just a single individual. In effect, the large household represents five times as many people as the small household, and if we are interested in individual-level measures—such as income per capita, or the age or gender of individuals—then we should put five times as much weight on the large household as the small. This calls for the use of *individual weights*, which are usually computed as the household weights times the size of the household. Most, but not all, statistical packages handle this easily, but the analyst still has to provide the appropriate instructions.

Goods Coverage and Valuation. It has been widely observed that the more detailed the questions about income and expenditure, the higher are the reported levels of income and expenditure. It follows that if economic welfare is to be measured satisfactorily, these questions must be comprehensive; to ensure comparability, they should not change over time. It is important to collect information on the volume and value of "own consumption"—such as food from the family farm that the household eats—since this is a component both of income and of expenditure ("in kind"). Such in-kind income/expenditure will typically have to be valued at local prices. It is also essential to collect enough information on housing (rent or current capital value if the household owns its residence), and the main durable goods (age, purchase price, current value), in order to be able to quantify these important components of expenditure and income.

Variability and the Time Period of Measurement. Income and consumption vary from month to month, year to year, and over a lifetime. But income typically varies more significantly than consumption. This is because households try to smooth their consumption over time, for instance by managing their savings, or through risk-sharing arrangements such as using remittances. In less-developed countries, most analysts prefer to use current consumption than current income as an indicator of living standards in poor countries for the following reasons:

- In the short run it reflects more accurately the resources that households control.

- Over the long term, it reveals information about incomes at other dates, in the past and future.

- In poor countries, income is particularly difficult to measure accurately, especially in agriculture and for pastoralists.

This does not mean that consumption is a perfect measure of well-being. Any household that is credit-constrained—and this is likely to be especially true of poorer households—will be limited in the extent to which it can smooth consumption over its lifecycle.

Comparisons across Households at Similar Consumption Levels. Households vary not only in their income or expenditure levels, but in size, in the prices they face, in the publicly provided goods (such as roads and schools) to which they have access, in the amount of leisure time they enjoy, and in the agreeableness of the environment in which they live (some areas are too hot or too cold or too dry or too flood-prone). This makes it difficult to compare household welfare across households. Thus an annual income of US$1,000 might suffice for a couple living in a rural area, where food and housing are cheap, but it would be utterly inadequate for a family of four in an urban setting.

In practice, it is impossible to take all such factors fully into account, so all comparisons across households remain imperfect. However, some corrections are easier than others: It is relatively straightforward, data permitting, to correct for differences in the cost of living faced by households; and income or expenditure can be expressed in per capita (or per adult equivalent) terms, an issue to which we return in the following section. But researchers rarely include the value of publicly provided goods and services, mainly because these are hard to value and it is difficult to attribute usage. However, an attempt is made in benefit-incidence analysis, a topic addressed in chapter 15.

Review Questions

1. Which of the following is *not* one of the three steps involved in measuring poverty?

   - A. Generating a summary statistic to reflect the degree of poverty.
   - B. Computing a Gini coefficient.
   - C. Defining an indicator of well-being.
   - D. Establishing a minimum acceptable standard of well-being.

2. To measure poverty, one needs data based on surveys of individuals or households, and data from all such surveys are useful in measuring poverty.

   - True.
   - False.

3. You have information based on a regionally stratified random sample of households chosen with clustering.

   - A. This means that regions in the country were first grouped together and then a simple random sample of households was chosen from each of these groupings.
   - B. This implies that any measures of poverty will need to be computed using household or individual weights.
   - C. This means that the standard error of measures of income will be smaller than would be the case with simple random sampling.
   - D. The result is that one cannot generally break down poverty rates by region.

Key features of Living Standards Measurement Surveys

Motivated by the need to measure poverty more accurately, the World Bank has taken the lead in the development of relatively standard, reliable household surveys, under its Living Standards Measurement Surveys (LSMS) project. The electronic version of the books edited by Grosh and Glewwe (2000) includes an extensive sample questionnaire—best thought of as a template, not an off-the-shelf survey—and detailed chapters that deal with the design and implementation of such surveys. The LSMS surveys have two key features: multitopic questionnaires and considerable attention to quality control.

Multitopic Questionnaires. The LSMS surveys ask about a wide variety of topics, not simply demographic characteristics or health experience or some other narrow issue.

- The most important single questionnaire is the *household questionnaire*, which often runs to 100 pages or more. Although there is an LSMS template, each country needs to adapt and test its own version. The questionnaire is designed to ask questions of the best informed household member. The household questionnaire asks about household composition; consumption patterns, including food and nonfood; assets including housing; landholding and other durables; income and employment in agriculture/nonagriculture and wage/self-employment; sociodemographic variables, including education, health, migration, and fertility; and anthropometric information, especially the height and weight of each household member.

- There is also a *community questionnaire*, which asks community leaders (teachers, health workers, village officials) for information about the whole community, such as the number of health clinics, access to schools, tax collections, demographic data, and agricultural patterns. Sometimes there are separate community questionnaires for health and education.

- The third part is the *price questionnaire*, which collects information about a large number of commodity prices in each community where the survey is undertaken. This is useful because it allows analysts to correct for differences in price levels by region and over time.

Quality Control. The LSMS surveys are distinguished by their attention to quality control. Key features include the following:

- Most important, they devote a lot of attention to obtaining a representative national sample (or regional sample, in a few cases). Thus, the results can usually be taken as nationally representative. It is surprising how many other surveys are undertaken with less attention to sampling, so one does not know how well they really represent conditions in the country.

- The surveys make extensive use of screening questions and associated skip patterns. For instance, a question might ask whether a family member is currently attending school; if yes, one jumps to page x and asks for details; if no, then the interviewer jumps to page y and asks other questions. This reduces interviewer errors.

- Numbered response codes are printed on the questionnaire, so the interviewer can write a numerical answer directly on the questionnaire. This makes subsequent computer entry easier, more accurate, and faster.

- The questionnaires are designed to be easy to change and to translate, which makes it straightforward to modify them in the light of field tests.

- The data are collected by decentralized teams. Typically each team has a supervisor, two interviewers, a driver/cook, an anthropometrist, and someone who does the data entry onto a laptop computer. The household questionnaire is so long that it requires two visits for collecting the data. After the first visit, the data are entered; if errors arise, they can be corrected on the second visit, which is typically two weeks after the first visit. In most cases the data are entered onto printed questionnaires and then typed into a computer, but some surveys now enter the information directly into computers.

- The data entered are subject to a series of range checks. For instance, if an age variable is greater than 100, then it is likely that there is an error that needs to be corrected.

This concern with quality has some important implications, notably the following:

- The LSMS data are usually of high quality, with accurate entries and few missing values.

- Since it is expensive to maintain high quality, the surveys are usually quite small; the median LSMS survey covers just 4,200 households. This is a large enough sample for accurate information at the national level, and at the level of half a dozen regions, but not at a lower level of disaggregation, such as a province, department, or county.

- The LSMS data have a fairly rapid turnaround time, with some leading to a statistical abstract (at least in draft form) within two to six months of the last interview.

Even when surveys are based on the LSMS template, it is still difficult to compare measures of consumption or income or poverty either across countries or within a country over time. This is because small differences in the way questions are phrased, or in the detail requested in the household interview, can have a substantial impact on the reported results. Seemingly minor changes—such as adding a few questions on tobacco use, or asking for more details about durable goods—can have effects on the measurement of the variables that are large enough to swamp the underlying trends. At a minimum, before presenting comparative results, the analyst should examine the underlying questionnaires for comparability and should be cautious about the way in which any comparative results are presented and interpreted.

Review Questions

> 4. Living Standards Measurement Surveys are generally characterized by all of the following *except*:
>
> o A. Large sample sizes.
> o B. Multiple questionnaires.
> o C. Close attention to quality control.
> o D. Extensive questions.

Measuring Poverty: Choosing an Indicator of Welfare

There are a number of ways to measure well-being. The welfarist approach (Sen 1979) seeks to measure household *utility*, which in turn is usually assumed to be approximated by household consumption expenditure or household income; these may be considered as *inputs* into generating utility. Given enough income, the household is assumed to know best how to deploy these resources, whether on food, clothing, housing, or the like. When divided by the number of household members, this gives a per capita measure of consumption expenditure or income. Of course, even household expenditure or income is an imperfect proxy for utility; for instance, it excludes potentially important contributors to utility such publicly provided goods or leisure.

A more paternalistic, or nonwelfarist, approach might focus on whether households have attained certain minimal levels of, say, nutrition or health. Thus, while the welfarist approach focuses on per capita consumption expenditure or income, other (nonwelfarist) measures of individual welfare might include indicators such as infant mortality rates in the region, life expectancy, the proportion of spending devoted to food, housing conditions, or child schooling; these may be thought of as measures of *output*, reflections of utility rather than inputs into the generation of utility.

Such measures are useful in fleshing out a multidimensional portrait of poverty, but they rest on a somewhat different philosophical foundation from the welfarist approach, and this can make interpretation difficult. For instance, if people have enough income to feed, clothe, and house themselves adequately, how concerned should we then be if they do not in fact do so? In some cases there may be informational problems—perhaps no one in the household knows how to cook—but in the absence of such imperfections, to what extent are we justified in trying to save people from themselves? This age-old dilemma does not have a simple solution.

If we choose to assess poverty based on household consumption or expenditure per capita, it is helpful to think in terms of an expenditure function, which shows the minimum expense required to meet a given level of utility u, which is derived from a vector of goods x, at prices p. It can be obtained from an optimization problem in which the objective function (expenditure) is minimized subject to a set level of utility, in a framework where prices are fixed.

Let the consumption measure for the household i be denoted by y_i. Then an expenditure measure of welfare may be denoted by:

$$y_i = p \cdot q = e(p, x, u), \qquad (2.1)$$

where p is a vector of prices of goods and services, q is a vector of quantities of goods and services consumed, $e(.)$ is an expenditure function, x is a vector of household characteristics (number of adults, number of young children, and so on), and u is the level of "utility" or well-being achieved by the household. Put another way, given the prices (p) that it faces, and its demographic characteristics (x), y_i measures the spending that is needed to reach utility level u.

Typically, we compute the actual level of y_i from household survey data that include information on consumption. Once we have computed yi, we can construct *per capita* household consumption for every individual in the household, which implicitly assumes that consumption is shared equally among household members. For this approach to make sense, we must also assume that all individuals in the household have the same needs. This is a strong assumption, for in reality, different individuals have different needs based on their individual characteristics.

Several factors complicate the process of estimating per capita consumption. Table 2.2 reports estimates of both nominal and inflation-adjusted ("real") per capita consumption from three different household surveys in Cambodia. Using the 1997 Cambodia Socioeconomic Survey (CSES), for example, nominal and real per

Table 2.2 Summary of per Capita Consumption from Cambodian Surveys

Surveys	Nominal	Real (inflation adjusted)
SESC 1993–94	1,833	2,262
CSES 1997 (adjusted)	2,223	2,530
CSES 1997 (unadjusted)	1,887	2,153
CSES 1999 (Round 1)	2,037	1,630
CSES 1999 (Round 2)	2,432	1,964
CSES 1999 (both rounds)	2,238	1,799

Source: Gibson 1999.

Note: CSES = Cambodia Socio-Economic Survey. SESC = Socio-Economic Survey of Cambodia. All values are in riels per person per day. Real values are estimated in 1993–94 Phnom Penh prices, as deflated by the value of the food poverty lines. Adjusted figures from 1997 incorporate corrections for possible underestimation of certain types of consumption (see Knowles [1998] and Gibson [1999] for details). Differences between Rounds 1 and 2 in 1999 are detailed in Gibson (1999).

capita consumption were 2,223 and 2,530 riels, respectively (Gibson 1999). However, across years the estimates of consumption in real terms for 1993–94 may not be directly comparable with the 1999 estimates because the surveys did not have exactly the same set of questions regarding consumption. For example, real consumption per capita was measured as 2,262 riels for 1993–94, but was only 1,799 in 1999, despite robust economic growth during the interval; this may merely be an artifact of the different ways in which questions were asked.

Traditionally, we use a monetary measure to value household welfare. The two most obvious candidates are income and expenditure.

Candidate 1: Income

It is tempting to measure household welfare by looking at household income. Practical problems arise immediately: What is income? Can it be measured accurately? The most generally accepted measure of income is the one formulated by Haig and Simons (Haig 1921, Simons 1938):

$$\text{Income} \equiv \text{consumption} + \text{change in net worth}.$$

> *Example:* Suppose I had assets of $10,000 at the beginning of the year. During the year I spent $3,000 on consumption. And at the end of the year I had $11,000 in assets. Then my income was $4,000, of which $3,000 was spent, and the remaining $1,000 added to my assets.

The first problem with this definition is that it is not clear what time period is appropriate. Should we look at someone's income over a year? Five years? A lifetime? Many students are poor now, but have good lifetime prospects, and we may not want to consider them as being truly poor. On the other hand, if we wait until we have information about someone's lifetime income, it will be too late to help him or her in moments of poverty.

The second problem is measurement. It is easy enough to measure components of income such as wages and salaries. It may be possible to get adequate (if understated) information on interest, dividends, and income from some types of self-employment. But it is likely to be hard to get an accurate measure of farm income; or of the value of housing services; or of capital gains (for example, the increase in the value of animals on a farm, or the change in the value of a house that one owns).

For instance, the Vietnam Living Standards Surveys undertaken in 1992–93 (Vietnam 1994) and again in 1997–98 (Vietnam 2000) collected information on the value of farm animals at the time of the survey, but not the value a year before. Thus, it was not possible to measure the change in the value of animal assets. Many farmers that reported negative cash income may in fact have been building up assets, and they actually had positive income.

It is typically the case, particularly in societies with large agricultural or self-employed populations, that income is seriously understated. This certainly appears to be the case for Vietnam. Table 2.3 shows income per capita for households in 1993 for each of five expenditure quintiles: a quintile is a fifth of the sample, and quintile 1 contains the poorest fifth of individuals, and so on. For every quintile, households on average reported less income than expenditure, which is simply not plausible. This would imply that households must be running down their assets, or taking on much more debt, which was unlikely in a boom year like 1993.

Income tends to be understated for several reasons:

- People forget, particularly when asked in a single interview, about items they may have sold, or money they may have received, up to a year before.

- People may be reluctant to disclose the full extent of their income, lest the tax collector or a neighbor get wind of the details.

- People may be reluctant to report income earned illegally, for instance, from smuggling, corruption, poppy cultivation, or prostitution.

- Some parts of income are difficult to calculate, for example, the extent to which the family buffalo has risen in value.

Research based on the 1969–70 socioeconomic survey in Sri Lanka estimated that wages were understated by 28 percent; business income by 39 percent; and rent, interest, and dividends by 78 percent (Visaria 1980, 18). It is not clear how much these figures are applicable elsewhere, but they do give a sense of the potential magnitude of the understatement problem.

Candidate 2: Consumption Expenditure

Consumption includes both goods and services that are purchased and those that are provided from one's own production (in-kind).

Table 2.3 Income and Expenditure by per Capita Expenditure Quintiles, Vietnam

(In thousands of dong per capita per year, 1992/93)

	Lowest	Lower-mid	Middle	Mid-upper	Highest	Overall
Income/capita	494	694	956	1,191	2,190	**1,105**
Expenditure/capita	518	756	984	1,338	2,540	**1,227**
Memo						
Food spending/capita	378	526	643	807	1,382	**747**
Food as % of expenditure	73	70	65	60	54	**61**

Source: Vietnam 1994.

Note: In 1993, exchange rate was about 10,000 dong/US$.

In developed countries, a strong case can be made that consumption is a better indicator of lifetime welfare than is income. Income typically rises and then falls in the course of one's lifetime, in addition to fluctuating somewhat from year to year, whereas consumption remains relatively stable. This smoothing of short-term fluctuations in income is predicted by the permanent income hypothesis, under which transitory income is saved while long-term (permanent) income is largely consumed.

The lifecycle of income and consumption is captured graphically in figure 2.2. While the available evidence does not provide strong support for this *lifecycle hypothesis* in the context of less-developed countries, households there do appear to smooth out the very substantial seasonal fluctuations in income that they typically face during the year (see Alderman and Paxson 1994; Paxson 1993). Thus, information on consumption over a relatively short period, such as one a month, as typically collected by a household survey is more likely to be representative of a household's general level of welfare than equivalent information on income, which is more volatile.

A more practical case for using consumption, rather than income, is that households may be more able, or willing, to recall what they have spent rather than what they earned. Even so, consumption is likely to be systematically understated for the following reasons:

• Households tend to underdeclare what they spend on luxuries or illicit items. For instance, the amount that households said they spent on alcohol, according to the 1972–73 household budget survey in the United States was just half the amount that companies said they sold (Carlson 1974).

Figure 2.2 Lifecycle Hypothesis: Income and Consumption Profile over Time

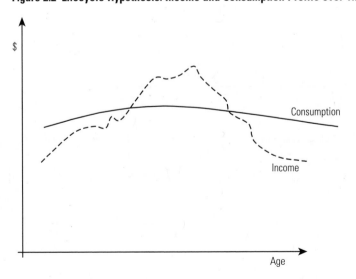

Source: Authors.

- Questions matter. According to VLSS93, Vietnamese households devoted 1.7 percent of their expenditure to tobacco; the VLSS98 figures showed that this had risen to 3 percent. An increase of this magnitude is simply implausible and not in line with sales reported by the cigarette and tobacco companies. A more plausible explanation is that VLSS98 had more detailed questions about tobacco use. When the questions are more detailed, respondents are likely to remember in more detail and to report higher spending.

The understatement of both income and consumption means that poverty rates are overstated. It also means that the estimates of total income and consumption that are based on the survey data invariably fall short of the levels observed in national accounts data—and in some countries this gap is growing. It is tempting to gross up the survey results—for instance, raising everybody's income by 10 percent if this is the size of the gap between the survey data and national accounts—before computing poverty rates. Some countries do this, but it is not a satisfactory solution, since understatement seems to be a smaller problem for the poor than the rich, at least in absolute terms. We address this issue in more detail in chapter 10.

Measuring Durable Goods. In measuring poverty it might be argued that only food, the ultimate basic need (which constitutes seven-tenths of the spending of poor households), should be included. On the other hand, even households that cannot afford adequate quantities of food devote some expenditures to other items, such as clothing, and shelter. It is reasonable to suppose that if these items are getting priority over food purchases, then they must represent very basic needs of the household, and so should be included in the poverty line. This argument also applies to durable goods.

The problem is that durable goods, such as bicycles and televisions, are bought at a point in time, and then consumed over a period of several years. Consumption should only include the amount of a durable good that is eaten up during the year, which can be measured by the change in the value of the asset during the year, plus the cost of locking up one's money in the asset.

> *Example:* For instance, if my watch was worth $25 a year ago, and is worth $19 now, then I used $6 worth of watch during the year; I also tied up $25 worth of assets in the watch, money that could have earned me $2.50 in interest (assuming 10 percent) during the year. Thus, the true cost of the watch during the year was $8.50. This is essentially the amount that I would have to pay if I were to try to rent the watch for a year.

A comparable calculation needs to be done for each durable good that the household owns. Clearly the margin of potential measurement error is large, since the price of each asset may not be known with much accuracy, and the interest rate used is somewhat arbitrary. The Vietnamese VLSS surveys asked for information about when each good was acquired, and at what price, and the estimated current value of the good.[1] This suffices to compute the current consumption of the durable item, as the illustration in box 2.1 shows.

One might wonder why attention needs to be paid to calculating the value of durable goods consumption when the focus is on poverty—in practice, first and foremost the ability to acquire enough food. The answer is that when expenditure is used as a yardstick of welfare, it is important to achieve comparability across households. If the value of durable goods were not included, one might have the impression that a household that spends $100 on food and $5 on renting a bicycle is better off than a household that spends $100 on food and owns a bicycle (that it could rent out for $5), when in fact both households are equally well off , all else being equal.

Box 2.1   Calculating the Value of Durable Goods Consumption: An Illustration

A Vietnamese household surveyed in April 1998 says that it bought a television two years earlier for 1.1 m dong (about US$100). The television is now believed to be worth 1m dong. Overall prices rose by a total of 10 percent over the past two years. How much of the television was consumed over the year prior to the survey?

a. Recompute the values in today's prices. Thus, the TV, purchased for 1.1 m dong in 1996, would have cost 1.21 m dong (= 1.1 m dong × (1+10 percent)) now.

b. Compute the depreciation. The television lost 0.21 m dong in value in two years, or 0.105 m dong per year (about US$7).

c. Compute the interest cost. At today's prices, the television was worth 1.105 m dong a year ago (1.21 m dong less this past year's depreciation of 0.105 m dong), and this represents the value of funds locked up during the year prior to the survey. At a real (inflation-adjusted) interest rate of 3 percent, the cost of locking up these resources was 0.03315 m dong over the course of the year.

Thus the total consumption cost of the television was 0.138 m dong (= 0.105 + 0.033), or about US$10.

This computation is only possible if the survey collects information on the past prices of all the durables used by the household. Where historical price data are not available, researchers in practice typically apply a depreciation + interest rate to the reported value of the goods; so if a television is worth 1 m dong now, is expected to depreciate by 10 percent per annum, and the real interest rate is 3 percent, then the imputed consumption of the durable good is measured as 1 m ((10 percent + 3 percent) = 0.13 m dong). Deaton and Zaidi (1998) recommend that one use average depreciation rates derived from the sample, rather than the rates reported by each individual household.

Measure the Value of Housing Services. If you own your house or apartment, it provides housing services that should be considered as part of consumption. The most satisfactory way to measure the values of these services is to ask how much you would have to pay if, instead of owning your home, you had to rent it, although this question is seldom asked in practice.

The standard procedure is to estimate, for those households that rent their dwellings, a function that relates the rental payment to such housing characteristics as the size of the house (in square feet of floor space), the year in which it was built, the type of roof, and whether there is running water. This gives the following:

Rent = f(area, running water, year built, type of roof, location, number of bathrooms…)

The estimates based on this "hedonic" regression then are used to impute the value of rent for those households that own, rather than rent, their housing. For all households that own their housing, this imputed rental, along with the costs of maintenance and minor repairs, represents the annual consumption of housing services.[2] In the case of households that pay interest on a mortgage, it is appropriate to count the imputed rental and costs of maintenance and minor repairs in measuring consumption, but not the mortgage interest payments as well, because this would represent double-counting.[3]

In the case of Vietnam there is a problem with this approach: almost nobody rents housing. Of those that do, most pay a nominal rent for a government apartment. Only 13 of the 5,999 households surveyed in VLSS98 paid private sector rental rates.[4] On the other hand the VLSS surveys did ask each household to put a capital value on their house or apartment. In computing consumption expenditure, the Vietnam General Statistics Office assumed that the rental value of housing was 3 percent of the capital value of the housing. This is, of course, a somewhat arbitrary procedure.

Weddings and Funerals. Families spend money on weddings. Such spending is often excluded when measuring household consumption expenditure. The logic is that the money spent on weddings mainly gives utility to the guests, not the spender. Of course if one were to be strictly correct, then expenditure should include the value of the food and drink that one enjoys as a guest at other people's weddings, although in practice this is rarely included. Alternatively, one might think of wedding expenditures as rare and exceptional events, which shed little light on the living standard of the household. Similar considerations apply to other large and irregular spending, on items such as funerals and dowries.

Accounting for Household Composition Differences. Households differ in size and composition, and so a simple comparison of aggregate household consumption can be quite misleading about the well-being of individuals in a given household. Most researchers recognize this problem and use some form of normalization. The most straightforward method is to convert from household consumption to individual consumption by dividing household expenditures by the number of people in the household. Then, total household expenditure per capita is the measure of welfare assigned to each member of the household. Although this is by far the most common procedure, it is not very satisfactory for two reasons:

- First, different individuals have different needs. A young child typically needs less food than an adult, and a manual laborer requires more food than an office worker.

- Second, there are economies of scale in consumption, at least for such items as housing. It costs less to house a couple than to house two individuals separately.

> *Example:* Suppose we have a household with two members and monthly expenditure of $150 in total. We would then assign each individual $75 as their monthly per capita expenditure. If we have another household with three members, it would appear that each member is worse off, with only $50 per capita per month. However, suppose we know that the two-person household contains two adult males age 35, whereas the second household contains one adult female and two young children. This added information may change our interpretation of the level of well-being in the second household, since we suppose that young children may have much lower costs (at least for food) than adults.

In principle, the solution to this problem is to apply a system of weights. For a household of any given size and demographic composition (such as one male adult, one female adult, and two children), an equivalence scale typically measures the number of adult males to which that household is deemed to be equivalent. Each member of the household counts as some fraction of an adult male. Effectively, household size is the sum of these fractions and is not measured in numbers of persons but in numbers of *adult equivalents*. Economies of scale can be allowed for by transforming the number of adult equivalents into effective adult equivalents.

In the abstract, the notion of equivalence scale is compelling. It is much less persuasive in practice, because of the problem of picking an appropriate scale. How these weights should be calculated and whether it makes sense even to try is still subject to debate, and there is no consensus on the matter. However, equivalence scales are not necessarily unimportant. For example, take the observation that in most household surveys, per capita consumption decreases with household size. It is probably more appropriate to interpret this as evidence that there are economies of scale to expenditure, and not necessarily as proof that large households have a lower standard of living.

The commonest solution to this problem is to pick a scale that seems reasonable, on the grounds that even a bad equivalence scale is better than none at all, and explore the robustness of the results (for example, estimates of the poverty rate) to different equivalence scales. Often the equivalence scales are based on the different calorie needs of individuals of different ages.

OECD scale   The OECD scale is widely used, and may be written as

$$AE = 1 + 0.7\,(N_{adults} - 1) + 0.5\,N_{children} \qquad (2.2)$$

where *AE* refers to "adult equivalent." A one-adult household would have an adult equivalent of 1, a two-adult household would have an *AE* of 1.7, and a three-adult household would have an *AE* of 2.4. Thus the 0.7 reflects economies of scale; the smaller this parameter, the more important economies of scale are considered to be. In developing countries, where food constitutes a larger part of the budget, economies of scale are likely to be less pronounced than in rich countries. The 0.5 is the weight given to children, and presumably reflects the lower needs (for food, housing space, and so forth) of children. Despite the elegance of the formulation, there are real problems in obtaining satisfactory measures of the degree of economies of scale and even of the weight to attach to children.

Other scales   Many other scales have been used. For instance, a number of researchers used the following scale in analyzing the results of the LSMS that were undertaken in the Côte d'Ivoire, Ghana, and Peru (Glewwe and Twum-Baah 1991):

Age (years)	0–6	7–12	13–17	>17
Weight (i.e., adult equivalences)	0.2	0.3	0.5	1.0

An elegant formulation is as follows:

$$AE = (N_{adults} + \alpha\,N_{children})^{\theta}$$

where α measures the cost of a child relative to an adult, and $\theta \leq 1$ is a parameter that captures the effects of economies of scale. Consider a family with two parents and two children. For $\alpha = \theta = 1$, AE = 4 and our welfare measure becomes expenditure per capita. But if $\alpha = 0.7$ and $\theta = 0.8$, then AE = 2.67, and the measure of expenditure per adult equivalent will be considerably larger.

Estimate an equivalence scale   Several researchers have tried to estimate the extent to which there are economies of scale in consumption, essentially by looking at how aggregate household consumption of goods, such as food, varies with household size and composition (for example, Pendakur 1999; see, too, Jenkins and

Cowell 1994). There are a number of problems here. First, it assumes that resources like food are equitably distributed within the household, although in practice the intrahousehold allocation is likely to reflect the distribution of power among household members. And second, there is a very basic identification problem: If children provide utility to parents, then how can we say that a couple with a child, earning $10,000, is necessarily worse off than a childless couple with the same income? (Pollack and Wales 1979). The consensus view is summed up by Deaton and Zaidi (1998), who argue, "there are so far no satisfactory methods for estimating economies of scale."

Income or Expenditure? Most rich countries measure poverty using income, while most poor countries use expenditure. There is a logic to this; in rich countries, income is comparatively easy to measure (much of it comes from wages and salaries), while expenditure is complex and hard to quantify. On the other hand, in less-developed countries income is hard to measure (much of it comes from self employment), while expenditure is more straightforward and hence easier to estimate. The arguments for and against income and consumption as the appropriate welfare measures for poverty analysis are summarized in table 2.4; further discussion may be found in Hentschel and Lanjouw (1996), Blundell and Preston (1998), and Donaldson (1992).

Table 2.4 Which Indicator of Welfare: Income or Consumption?

Income ("potential")

Pro:	Con:
• Easy to measure, given the limited number of sources of income.	• Likely to be underreported.
• Measures degree of household "command" over resources (which they could use if they so wish).	• May be affected by short-term fluctuations (for example, the seasonal pattern of agriculture).
• Costs only a fifth as much to collect as expenditure data, so sample can be larger.	• Some parts of income are hard to observe (for example, informal sector income, home agricultural production, self-employment income).
	• Link between income and welfare is not always clear.
	• Reporting period might not capture the "average" income of the household.

Consumption ("achievement")

Pro:	Con:
• Shows current actual material standard of living.	• Households may not be able to smooth consumption (for example, via borrowing, social networks).
• Smoothes out irregularities, and so reflects long-term average well-being.	• Consumption choices made by households may be misleading (for example, if a rich household chooses to live simply, that does not mean it is poor).
• Less understated than income, because expenditure is easier to recall.	• Some expenses are not incurred regularly, so data may be noisy.
	• Difficult to measure some components of consumption, including durable goods.

Source: Adapted from Albert (2004).

Review Questions

5. One commonly used measure of household welfare is income, which ideally is defined as

- A. Wages plus salaries.
- B. Earnings plus remittances.
- C. Wages plus profits plus transfer income.
- D. Consumption plus change in net worth.

6. Especially in less-developed countries, income as reported in household surveys is typically understated, even by poor people, because

- A. People forget how much income they made over the past year or even month.
- B. Income taxes are high.
- C. Most households rent their homes in the informal market.
- D. Illegal income is a large proportion (typically at least a quarter) of household income.

7. Expenditure is widely believed to reflect welfare better than incomes, in less-developed countries, because

- A. Annual expenditure is more closely related to lifetime ("permanent") income than is annual income.
- B. Households understate their spending on luxuries.
- C. Household surveys tend to ask more questions about expenditure than about income.
- D. The imputed value of durables (including housing) is included in expenditure but not income.

8. A household owns a bicycle that it bought two years ago for $40 and is now worth $28. It faces an interest rate of 10%. Then the true economic value of the services of the bicycle over the past year was closest to

- A. $12.
- B. $9.40.
- C. $6.60.
- D. $4.00.

9. For households that rent their homes, expenditure on housing is given by the rent they pay; and for households that own their homes, there is no need to count expenditure on housing because it is already counted as part of income.

- True.
- False.

> 10. The OECD scale measures adult equivalents as follows:
>
> $$AE = 1 + 0.7 (N_{adults} - 1) + 0.5\, N_{children}.$$
>
> Based on this scale, a household consisting of two parents, a grandmother, two teenagers, and an infant would:
>
> o A. Have a lower adult equivalent expenditure than it would have expenditure per capita.
> o B. Have an adult equivalent of 3.4.
> o C. Have a higher adult equivalent than a household with five adults.
> o D. Become better off when the eldest teenager becomes an adult.

Candidate 3. Other Measures of Household Welfare

Even if they were measured perfectly, neither income nor expenditure would be an ideal measure of household well-being. For instance, neither measure puts a value on the leisure time enjoyed by the household; neither measures the value of publicly provided goods (such as education, or public health services); and neither values intangibles such as peace and security.

Other possible measures of well-being include the following:

- *Calories consumed per person per day.* If one accepts the (nonwelfarist) notion that adequate nutrition is a prerequisite for a decent level of well-being, then we could just look at the quantity of calories consumed per person. Anyone consuming less than a reasonable minimum—often set at 2,100 Calories per person per day—would be considered poor.[5] Superficially, this is an attractive idea, and we will return to it in chapter 3. However, at this point we just note that it is not always easy to measure calorie intake, particularly if one wants to distinguish between different members of a given household. Nor is it easy to establish the appropriate minimum number of calories per person, as this will depend on the age, gender, and working activities of the individual.

- *Food consumption as a fraction of total expenditure.* Over a century ago, Ernst Engel observed in Germany that as household income per capita rises, spending on food rises too, **but less quickly**. This relationship is shown in figure 2.3. As a result, the proportion of expenditure devoted to food falls as per capita income rises. One could use this finding, which is quite robust, to come up with a measure of well-being and hence a measure of poverty. For instance, households that devote more than (say) 60 percent of their expenditures to food might be considered to be poor. The main problem with this measure is that the share of spending going to food also depends on the proportion of young to old family members (more children indicates a higher proportion of spending on food), and on the relative price of food (if food is relatively expensive, the proportion of spending going to food will tend to be higher).

Figure 2.3 Engel Curve: Food Spending Rises Less Quickly Than Income

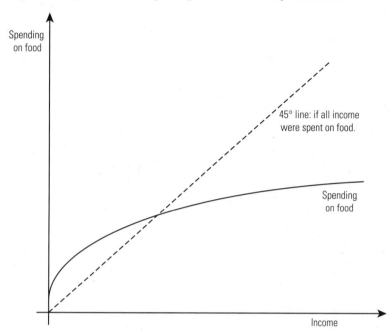

- *Measures of outcomes rather than inputs.* Food is an input, but nutritional status (being underweight, stunting or wasting) is an output. So one could measure poverty by looking at malnutrition.

  Of course, this requires establishing a baseline anthropometric standard against which to judge whether someone is malnourished. This is a controversial issue; generally, less stunting (as measured by height for age) is found in Sub-Saharan Africa than in Southeast Asia, although there is no reason to believe that the latter region is poorer than Africa. On the other hand, anthropometric indicators have the advantage that they can reveal living conditions within the household (rather than assigning the overall household consumption measure across all members of the household without really knowing how consumption expenditure is divided among household members).

- *Peer or observer assessments.* In Vietnam, very poor households are eligible for some subsidies, to cover health care and educational fees, for instance. The decision about who qualifies as being sufficiently poor is taken at the village level, where the local People's Committee typically knows enough about individual households to make the determination. Krishna et al. (2004) have made use of villager assessments in rural Kenya to validate observations about the degree of household poverty and its evolution over a generation. And Lanjouw and Stern (1991) classified villagers in a village in northern India into categories of poverty and wealth, based on discussions with villagers themselves.

33

The main problem with such assessments is that, because they are based on perceptions formed on imperfect information, they may be biased. Lanjouw and Stern found that in their survey village, landless agricultural laborers were almost all deemed by their peers to be poor; yet based on income information, only about half fell below the poverty line used.

When one is looking at a community (province, region) rather than individual households, it might make sense to judge the poverty of the community by life expectancy, or the infant mortality rate, although these are not always measured very accurately. School enrollments (a measure of investing in the future generation) represent another outcome that might indicate the relative well-being of the population. Certainly, none of these other measures of well-being are replacements for consumption per capita; nor does consumption per capita fully replace these measures. Rather, when taken together they allow us to get a more complete and multidimensional view of the well-being of a population, although this does not guarantee greater clarity. Consider the statistics in table 2.5, which refer to 11 different countries. How countries are ranked in terms of living standards clearly depends on which measure or indicator is considered.

In sum, there is no ideal measure of well-being: all measures of poverty are imperfect. That is not an argument for avoiding measuring poverty, but rather for approaching all measures of poverty with a degree of caution, and for asking in some detail about how the measures are constructed.

Table 2.5 Poverty and Quality of Life Indicators

Countries	GNP per capita (1999 dollars)	% population below poverty line	Female life expectancy at birth, years (1998)	Prevalence of child malnutrition, % children <5 years (1992–98)	Female adult illiteracy rate, % of people 15+ years, (1998)
Algeria	1,550	22.6 (1995)	72	13	46
Bangladesh	370	35.6 (1995/96)	59	56	71
Cambodia	260	36.1 (1997)	55	—	80
Colombia	2,250	17.7 (1992)	73	8	9
Indonesia	580	20.3 (1998)	67	34	20
Jordan	1,500	11.7 (1997)	73	5	17
Morocco	1,200	19.0 (1998/99)	69	10	66
Nigeria	310	34.1 (1992/93)	55	39	48
Peru	2,390	49.0 (1997)	71	8	16
Sri Lanka	820	35.3 (1990/91)	76	38	12
Tunisia	2,100	14.1 (1990)	74	9	42

Source: World Bank 2000.

Note: — = Not available.

Review Question

11. Which of the following is *not* a popular measure of welfare at the house-
    hold level:

    ○ A. The percentage of its spending that a household devotes to food.
    ○ B. The average height of children given their age, relative to a well-fed population.
    ○ C. The consumption of calories per capita.
    ○ D. Life expectancy at birth.

Notes

1. The questionnaires for the VLSS surveys are available from the Environmental and Social Statistics Department of the General Statistics Office, Hanoi.

2. This assumes that renters are responsible for maintenance and repair costs, so that the rental paid does not include a provision for these items. In some countries the owner, rather than the renter, would bear these costs, in which case the imputed rental also includes the costs, and no further adjustment would be called for.

3. However, if we want to measure income (rather than consumption), then we should use the imputed rental for households that own their property free and clear, and rental less mortgage interest payments for those who have borrowed against their housing.

4. Computation by the authors using the data from the Vietnam Living Standards Survey of 1997/98. The data are available from the General Statistics Office, Hanoi.

5. A calorie is the energy required to heat 1 gram of water by 1°C. A kilocalorie, also referred to as a Calorie, represents 1,000 calories.

References

Albert, José Ramon. 2004. "Measuring Poverty." Presentation (PowerPoint) at course on Introduction to Poverty Measurement and Analysis, Ministry of Economic Planning and Development, Blantyre, Malawi, January 19–20.

Alderman, Harold, and Chris Paxson. 1994. "Do the Poor Insure? A Synthesis of the Literature on Risk and Consumption in Developing Countries." In *Economics in a Changing World, Vol. 4: Development, Trade, and Environment*, ed. E. L. Bacha. London: Macmillan.

Blundell, R., and I. Preston. 1998. "Consumption Inequality and Income Uncertainty." *Quarterly Journal of Economics* 113: 603–40.

Carlson, Michael D. 1974. "The 1972–73 Consumer Expenditure Survey." *Monthly Labor Review* December, 16–23.

Deaton, Angus. 1997. *The Analysis of Household Surveys: A Macroeconomic Approach to Development Policy*. Baltimore: Johns Hopkins University Press.

    An essential volume for any graduate student working with survey data.

Deaton, Angus, and Salman Zaidi. 1999. "Guidelines for Constructing Consumption Aggregates for Welfare Analysis." Woodrow Wilson School of Public and International Affairs, Princeton University, Princeton, NJ. http://www.wws.princeton.edu/%7Erpds/down loads/deaton_zaidi_consumption.pdf Subsequently issued in 2002 as Living Standards Measurement Study Working Paper No. 135, World Bank, Washington, DC.

A clear, sensible discussion of the practical issues that arise in measuring a consumption indicator of welfare. Includes a sample questionnaire and some useful Stata code.

Donaldson, D. 1992. "On the Aggregation of Money Measures of Well-Being in Applied Welfare Economics." *Journal of Agricultural and Resource Economics* 17: 88–102.

Duclos, Jean-Yves, and Abdelkrim Araar. 2006. *Poverty and Equity: Measurement, Policy and Estimation with DAD.* New York: Springer, and Ottawa: International Development Research Centre.

An excellent, but technically rather advanced, treatment of poverty and inequality, with a very complete discussion of measurement and estimation. The authors have developed their own (free) software, DAD, that is one of the most accurate and comprehensive tools for reporting and graphing measures of poverty and inequality.

Gibson, John. 1999. "A Poverty Profile of Cambodia, 1999." Report to the World Bank and the Ministry of Planning, Phnom Penh.

Glewwe, Paul, and Kwaku A. Twum-Baah. 1991. "The Distribution of Welfare in Ghana, 1987–88." Living Standards Measurement Study Paper No. 75, World Bank, Washington, DC.

Grosh, Margaret, and Paul Glewwe, eds. 2000. *Designing Household Survey Questionnaires for Developing Countries: Lessons from 15 Years of Living Standard Measurement Study.* Volumes 1, 2, and 3. Washington, DC: World Bank and Oxford University Press.

Every statistics office should have a copy of this pair of volumes, or better still the CD-ROM version. This reference work includes sample questionnaires as well as detailed chapters on all aspects of designing, implementing, and using living standard measurement surveys.

Haig, Robert M. 1921. "The Concept of Income: Economic and Legal Aspects." In *The Federal Income Tax*, 1–28. New York: Columbia University Press.

Hentschel, J., and P. Lanjouw. 1996. "Constructing an Indicator of Consumption for the Analysis of Poverty: Principles and Illustrations with Reference to Ecuador." Working Paper No. 124, Living Standards Measurement Study, World Bank, Washington, DC.

Jenkins, S., and F. Cowell. 1994. "Parametric Equivalence Scales and Scale Relativities." *Economic Journal* 104: 891–900.

Knowles, James C. 1998. "An Updated Poverty Profile for Cambodia–1997: Technical Report." Ministry of Planning, Phnom Penh.

Krishna, Anirudh, Patricia Kristjanson, Maren Radeny, and Wilson Nindo. 2004. "Escaping Poverty and Becoming Poor in Twenty Kenyan Villages." *Journal of Human Development*, 5 (2): 211–26.

Lanjouw, Peter, and Nicholas Stern. 1991. "Poverty in Palanpur." *World Bank Economic Review* 5 (1): 23–55.

Paxson, Christina. 1993. "Consumption and Income Seasonality in Thailand." *Journal of Political Economy* 101 (1): 39–72.

Pendakur, K. 1999. "Semiparametric Estimates and Tests of Base-Independent Equivalence Scales." *Journal of Econometrics* 88: 1–40.

Pollack, R., and T. Wales. 1979. "Welfare Comparisons and Equivalence Scales." *American Economic Review* 69: 216–21.

Ravallion, Martin. 1998. "Poverty Lines in Theory and Practice." LSMS Working Paper No. 133, World Bank, Washington, DC.

———. 1992. "Poverty Comparisons: A Guide to Concepts and Methods." LSMS Working Paper No. 88, World Bank, Washington, DC.

A very useful survey, with an emphasis on comparing poverty across time and space. In writing chapters 2 and 3, we have drawn heavily on the ideas in this paper.

Rowntree, S. 1901. *Poverty: A Study of Town Life*. London: Macmillan.

Sen, Amartya. 1979. "Personal Utilities and Public Judgements: Or What's Wrong with Welfare Economics?" *The Economic Journal* 89: 537–58.

Simons, Henry. 1938. *Personal Income Taxation: The Definition of Income as a Problem of Fiscal Policy*. Chicago: University of Chicago Press.

Vietnam, General Statistical Office. 2000. *Vietnam Living Standards Survey 1997–1998*. Hanoi: Statistical Publishing House.

Vietnam, State Planning Committee and General Statistical Office. 1994. *Vietnam Living Standards Survey 1992–1993*. Hanoi.

Visaria, Pravin (with Shyamalendu Pal). 1980. "Poverty and Living Standards in Asia." Living Standards Measurement Study Working Paper No. 2, World Bank, Washington, DC.

World Bank. 2000. *World Development Report 2000/2001: Attacking Poverty*. Washington, DC: World Bank.

Chapter 3

Poverty Lines

Summary

The poor are those whose expenditure (or income) falls below a poverty line. This chapter explains how poverty lines are constructed and discusses the strengths and weaknesses of defining poverty lines based on three methods: the cost of basic needs, food energy intake, and subjective evaluations. The construction of a poverty line is the most difficult step in the practical measurement of poverty.

The *cost of basic needs approach* is most commonly used. It first estimates the cost of acquiring enough food for adequate nutrition—usually 2,100 Calories per person per day—and then adds the cost of other essentials such as clothing and shelter. When price information is unavailable, the *food energy intake method* can be used. This method plots expenditure (or income) per capita against food consumption (in calories per person per day) to determine the expenditure (or income) level at which a household acquires enough food. *Subjective poverty lines* are based on asking people what minimum income level is needed just to make ends meet.

An absolute poverty line remains fixed over time, adjusted only for inflation, as in the United States. It allows the evolution of poverty over time to be tracked, and is also useful when evaluating the effects of policies and programs on the incidence of poverty. However, in most countries, poverty lines are revised from time to time, reflecting the evolution of social consensus about what constitutes poverty. Poverty lines that are revised in this way allow relative poverty to be measured, but not absolute poverty.

The choice of poverty line depends on the use to which it will be put: thus, for international comparisons, the $1/day standard is helpful, while for targeting programs or policies to the poor a relative poverty line suffices. The appropriate choice of poverty line is a matter of judgment, and will therefore vary from country to country.

Learning Objectives

After completing the chapter on *Poverty Lines*, you should be able to

1. Explain what a poverty line is, why it is needed, and how countries adjust their poverty lines over time.

2. Distinguish between absolute and relative poverty lines, and identify the conditions under which one might be preferred to the other.

3. Identify the steps required to construct a poverty line using the cost of basic needs method, and justify the choices made at each step.

4. Show how to construct a poverty line using the food energy intake method, and explain the serious weaknesses of this method.

5. Explain how subjective poverty lines are constructed and critically appraise their usefulness.

6. Construct a poverty line using real survey data, using

   • the cost of basic needs method

   • the food energy intake method.

Introduction: Defining a Poverty Line

Assume we have chosen a measure of household well-being, say, consumption expenditure. The next step is to choose a poverty line. Households whose consumption expenditure falls below this line are considered poor.

The choice of poverty line depends in large measure on the intended use of the poverty rates. If the goal is to identify "the poor" for a targeted system of food subsidies, a line that generates a poverty rate of 60 percent, or of 2 percent, is unlikely to be helpful. In this sense, the poverty rate is indeed a social and policy construct, and appropriately so.

However, it is common practice to define the poor as those who lack command over basic consumption needs, including food and nonfood components. In this case the poverty line is obtained by specifying a consumption bundle considered adequate for basic consumption needs, then estimating the cost of these basic needs. The poverty line may be thought of as the minimum expenditure required by an individual to fulfill his or her basic food and nonfood needs.

Once we have computed a household's consumption, we need to determine whether that amount places the household in poverty, or defines the household as poor. The threshold used for this is the poverty line. The poverty line defines the level of consumption (or income) needed for a household to escape poverty.

It is sometimes argued that the notion of a poverty line implies a distinct turning point in the welfare function. That is, by rising from just below to just above the poverty line, households (and individuals therein) move from considerable misery to an adequate minimum amount of well-being. However, given that well-being follows a continuum, and given how arbitrary the choice of poverty line is, the notion of such a turning point is not compelling.

A corollary is that it usually makes sense to define more than one poverty line. For example, one common approach is to define one poverty line that marks households that are poor, and another lower level that marks those that are extremely poor. Another approach is to construct a food poverty line, which is based on some notion of the minimum amount of money a household needs to purchase some basic-needs food bundle and nothing more. If the cost of basic nonfood needs is estimated, the food poverty line added to the nonfood needs will equal the overall poverty line.

Review Questions

1. A poverty line is
○ A. The minimum expenditure required to fulfill basic needs.
○ B. The threshold consumption needed for a household to escape poverty.
○ C. Somewhat arbitrary because the line between poor and nonpoor can be hard to define.
○ D. All of the above.

More formally, following Ravallion (1998), the poverty line for a household, z_i, may be defined as the minimum spending or consumption (or income, or other measure) needed to achieve at least the minimum utility level u_z, given the level of prices (p) and the demographic characteristics of the household (x), so

$$zi = e(p, x, u_z). \tag{3.1}$$

In practice, we cannot measure u_z, or even $e(\cdot)$, so a more pragmatic solution is needed.

There are two approaches. One is to compute a poverty line for each household, adjusting it from household to household to take into account differences in the prices they face and their demographic composition. For example, a small household in a rural area may face low housing costs and relatively modest food prices. Thus, their z_i may be low compared with a large household in a city where housing is more expensive and food prices are perhaps higher. This gives a different poverty line for each household.

A second and more widely used approach is to construct one per capita poverty line for all individuals, but to adjust per capita expenditure (or income) y_i for differences in prices and household composition. The adjusted per capita y_i is then compared with the poverty line to determine if the individual is living below the poverty line. With this approach, it is easier to talk of "the poverty line" and present it as a single number.

The approach taken for Cambodia in 1999 is somewhere between these two extremes. Separate poverty lines were constructed for each of three major regions, based on the prices prevailing in those areas; whether a household in any given region is poor is then determined by comparing its expenditure per capita with the appropriate regional poverty line. These poverty lines are shown in table 3.1, based on Gibson's (1999) poverty profile of Cambodia using the Cambodia Socio-Economic Survey (CSES) 1999 data, and Prescott and Pradhan's (1997) profile using the Socio-Economic Survey of Cambodia (SESC) 1993–94 data. We discuss the construction of these poverty lines in more detail later in the chapter.

As shown in table 3.1, the money value of poverty lines for Phnom Penh, the capital of Cambodia, are higher than for other areas. This is consistent with experience in other countries. For example, in Vietnam, Duong and Trinh (1999) noted that the World Bank concluded that households would need to spend at least 1,071,000 Vietnamese dong (about $81) per person per year in 1998 to be out of poverty. However, for urban areas, the amount was estimated to be 1,342,000 dong ($101); in rural areas it was just 1,054,000 dong ($79). This reflects the fact that costs are higher in cities.

Over time, we expect nominal poverty lines to change for a population. This is due to two factors. First, poverty lines reflect the costs of purchasing food and nonfood items. As prices rise—inflation is typical—nominal poverty lines increase. This is what underlies the rising nominal poverty lines in Cambodia, shown in table 3.1. It is also reflected in the poverty line for Thailand, shown in table 3.2.

Table 3.1 Summary of Poverty Lines for Cambodia

| | (riels per person per day) | | | |
| | 1993/94 SESC | | 1999 CSES | |
Area	Food poverty line	Poverty line	Food poverty line	Poverty line
Phnom Penh	1,185	1,578	1,737	2,470
Other urban	995	1,264	1,583	2,093
Rural	881	1,117	1,379	1,777

Sources: Prescott and Pradhan 1997; Gibson 1999.

Note: Average exchange rate was 2,617 riels/US$ in 1993–94 and 3,808 riels/US$ in 1999. SESC = Socio-Economic Survey of Cambodia; CSES = Cambodia Socio-Economic Survey.

Table 3.2 Average Poverty Line of Thailand

Year	Poverty line (baht/person/month)
1988	473
1990	522
1992	600
1994	636
1996	737
1998	878
1999	886

Source: Kakwani 2000.

Note: The mid-year exchange rate was 37 baht/$ in 1999, 42.4 baht/$ in 1998, and 25 baht/$ in all previous years.

Second, the poverty line could change if the real poverty threshold were revised over time. This raises the question of whether we should look at relative, or absolute, poverty lines. We now consider each in turn.

Review Question

2. In measuring poverty in Cambodia, researchers used

   ○ A. One poverty line for the country, and adjusted household spending for price differences.
   ○ B. Separate poverty lines for each individual.
   ○ C. Separate poverty lines for each household.
   ○ D. Separate poverty lines for each major region.

Relative Poverty

Sometimes we are interested in focusing on the poorest segment (for example, poorest one-fifth or two-fifths) of the population; these are the relatively poor. When defined in this way, it is a truism that "the poor are always with us." It is often helpful to have a measure such as this to target programs geared to helping the poor.

In practice, rich countries have higher poverty lines than do poor countries, as shown clearly in figure 3.1, which is from Chen and Ravallion (2008). This explains why, for instance, the official poverty rate in the early 1990s was close to 15 percent in the United States and also close to 15 percent in much poorer Indonesia. Many of those counted as poor in the United States would be considered comfortably well-off by Indonesian standards.

Figure 3.1 Poverty Lines across Countries

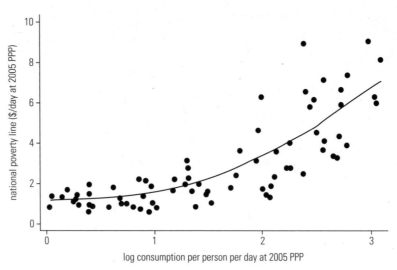

Source: Chen and Ravallion 2008.

As countries become better off, they have a tendency to revise the poverty line upward—with the notable exception of the United States, where the line has (in principle) remained unchanged for four decades. For instance, the European Union typically defines the poor as those whose per capita income falls below 50 percent of the median. As the median income rises, so does the poverty line, so this is more properly viewed as a crude measure of inequality rather than of absolute poverty.

Based on a sample of 36 countries, Ravallion, Datt, and van de Walle (1991) estimated the following relationship:

$$\ln Z_i = 6.704 - 1.773 \ln(C/cap) + 0.228 \, [\ln (C/cap)]^2 + v_i \qquad (3.2)$$
$$t = 5.1 \quad t = -3.6 \qquad\qquad t = 5.1$$

where $R^2 = 0.89$; all three coefficients are statistically significant at the 1 percent level or better. They found that at the mean value of per capita consumption (which they measured in purchasing power parity terms), the elasticity of the official poverty line (z_i) with respect to consumption per capita (C/cap) was 0.71. This means that if per capita consumption were to rise 10 percent, the official poverty line would rise 7.1 percent on average. But the nonlinear relationship implies that the elasticity of the poverty line with respect to consumption per capita was close to 0 in low-income countries, and was almost 1 in high-income countries. Using more recent data, Chen and Ravallion (2008) find very similar results.

To the extent that one's goal is to identify and target today's poor, then a relative poverty line is appropriate, and needs to be tailored to the overall level of development of the country. For instance, a $1/day poverty line might be useful in Vietnam, where 27 percent of the population would be considered poor by this standard in 1998 (Haughton 2000), but would be of little relevance in the United States, where almost nobody would fall below that poverty line.

Review Question

3. According to Ravallion, Datt, and van de Walle (1991), as countries become richer, they adjust their real poverty lines upward

- A. A little, if they are poor, and a lot if they are rich.
- B. A little, if they are rich, and a lot if they are poor.
- C. To maintain poverty at 27 percent.
- D. To adjust for inflation.

Absolute Poverty. An absolute poverty line is "fixed in terms of the standards indicator being used, and fixed over the entire domain of the poverty comparison" (Ravallion 1992, 25). In other words, the poverty line is set so that it represents the same purchasing power year after year, but this fixed line may differ from country to country or region to region (the "domain" of the relevant comparison). For example, the U.S. poverty line does not change over time (except to adjust for inflation), so that the poverty rate today may be compared with the poverty rate of a decade ago, knowing that the definition of what constitutes poverty has not changed.

An absolute poverty line is essential if one is trying to judge the effect of antipoverty policies over time, or to estimate the impact of a project (for example, microcredit) on poverty. Legitimate comparisons of poverty rates between one country and another can only be made if the same absolute poverty line is used in both countries. Thus, the World Bank needs absolute poverty lines to be able to compare poverty rates across countries. Such comparisons are useful in determining where to channel resources, and in assessing progress in the war on poverty.

The World Bank has recently revised its measurement of world poverty; Chen and Ravallion (2008) use a poverty rate of US$1.25 a day (in 2005 U.S. dollars), and by this standard there were 1.38 billion poor in 2005 (see box 3.1). If the poverty line is set at US$2.00 a day, this number rises to 2.09 billion. These are absolute poverty lines. There is a vigorous controversy about whether world poverty is indeed falling; this issue is addressed more completely in chapter 10. In this context, the focus is on absolute poverty.

| Box 3.1 | The "$1/Day" Standard |

Cross-country comparisons of poverty rates are notoriously difficult (see chapter 10), but Shao-hua Chen and Martin Ravallion (2008) of the World Bank have tried to get around this problem by computing the proportion of the population in different countries living on less than US$1.25 per person per day (in 2005 U.S. dollars). This line refers to the poverty line used by the 15 poorest countries in their sample, converted to U.S. dollars using the most recent measures of purchasing power parity. The numbers shown in the table below suggest that the poverty rate in Vietnam compares favorably with that of India and is falling rapidly, but lags behind (more affluent) China.

Country	Percentage of population living on less than $1.25/day	Year	Country	Percentage of population living on less than $1/day	Year
China, rural	26	2005	Indonesia, rural	24	2005
China, urban	2	2005	Indonesia, urban	19	2005
India, rural	44	2004/05	Philippines	23	2006
India, urban	36	2004/05	Vietnam	50	1998
Nigeria	64	2003	Vietnam	22	2006

Source: PovCalNet (accessed November 11, 2008).

Review Question

| 4. An absolute poverty line is needed for all of the following *except* |

    o A. To make international comparisons of poverty rates..
    o B. To evaluate the effects of projects, such as irrigation investments, on poverty.
    o C. To target antipoverty measures to the poorest quintile of the population.
    o D. To measure the success of government policies in combating poverty.

Issues in Choosing an Absolute Poverty Line

In choosing an absolute poverty line, one first has to determine how to measure the standard of living, and then pick an appropriate level to serve as a poverty line.

Decide the Standard of Living

An important conceptual problem arises when working with absolute poverty lines—the issue of what is meant by "the standard of living" (Ravallion [1998], on which much of this discussion is based).

In practice, almost all absolute poverty lines are set by measuring the cost of buying a basket of goods (the "commodity-based poverty line," which we denote by z). If we assume that

$$u = f(y), \tag{3.3}$$

which says that utility or "standard of living" (u) depends on income or expenditure (y), then

$$y = f^{-1}(u). \tag{3.4}$$

Equation (3.4) says that for any given level of utility, there is some income (or expenditure) level that is needed to achieve it. If u_z is the utility that just suffices to avoid being poor, then

$$z = f^{-1}(u_z). \tag{3.5}$$

In other words, given a poverty line that is absolute in the space of welfare (that is, gives u_z) there is a corresponding absolute commodity-based poverty line.

But suppose we make a different but equally plausible assumption, which is that utilities are interdependent. My well-being may depend not just on what I consume, but also on how my consumption stacks up against that of the rest of society. Thus, a household of four with an income of $12,000 per year would not be considered poor in Indonesia, but when this household compares its position with average incomes in the United States, it may feel very poor. We may capture this idea by assuming

$$u = g\left(y, \frac{y}{\bar{y}}\right), \tag{3.6}$$

where $\bar{y}$ is the mean income in the society. In this case

$$u_z = g\left(z, \frac{z}{\bar{y}}\right) \tag{3.7}$$

and making the standard assumption of invertibility,

$$z = g^{-1}(\bar{y}, u_z). \tag{3.8}$$

Equation (3.8) means that for a poverty line to be absolute in the space of welfare (that is, to yield u_z), the commodity-based poverty line (z) may have to rise as $\bar{y}$ rises. The commodity-based poverty line would then look more like a relative poverty line. The key idea here is that the poverty line should be set at a level that enables individuals to achieve certain capabilities, including healthy and active lives and full participation in society. In practice, this almost certainly would imply that the commodity-based poverty line would rise as a country becomes more affluent, because the minimum resources needed to participate fully in society probably rise over time. In Sen's prose, "an absolute approach in the space of capabilities translates into a relative approach in the space of commodities" (Sen 1983, 168). However, in what follows, we simplify the analysis by assuming that utilities are not interdependent, so the commodity-based poverty line is given in absolute terms.

Review Question

5. Is the following statement true or false? If my well-being depends on where I stand relative to others, then the dollar absolute poverty line needs to change as a country becomes richer.

  o True
  o False

Decide u_z and $g(\cdot)$

Even if we assume that the commodity-based poverty line remains constant, we are still left with two problems.

- *The referencing problem.* What is the appropriate value of u_z—that is, what is the value of the utility of the poverty line? The choice is arbitrary, of course, but "a degree of consensus about the choice of the reference utility level in a specific society may well be crucial to mobilizing resources for fighting poverty" (Ravallion 1998, 6).

- *The identification problem.* Given u_z, what is the correct value of z—that is, what is the correct commodity value of the poverty line? This problem arises for two reasons: the size and demographic composition of households vary—an issue raised in the discussion of equivalence scales in chapter 2—and "the view that we can measure welfare by looking solely at demand behavior is untenable" (Ravallion 1998, 7).

The implication is that external information and judgments will be required to answer the referencing and identification problems, and hence, to determine the absolute poverty line. But how is this to be done in practice?

Table 3.3 presents absolute and relative poverty headcount rates for different regions in the world. How regions compare with each other depends on which poverty measure is used. For example, by the absolute measure of less than $1/day, Sub-Saharan Africa has the highest portion of the population living in poverty. However, countries in Latin America and the Caribbean have the highest portion of their population living below one-third of the average national consumption; in effect, these Latin American and Caribbean countries are the most unequal societies, an issue that is addressed directly in chapter 6.

Table 3.3 Absolute and Relative Poverty Rates

Region	Percentage of population living on less than $1/day (in 1998)	Percentage of population living on less than one-third of average national consumption for 1993 (in 1998)
East Asia and Pacific	15.3	19.6
East Asia and Pacific excluding China	11.3	24.6
Europe and Central Asia	5.1	25.6
Latin America and the Caribbean	15.6	51.4
Middle East and North Africa	1.9	10.8
South Asia	40.0	40.2
Sub-Saharan Africa	46.3	50.5
Total	**24.0**	**32.1**
Total excluding China	26.2	37.0

Source: World Bank 2000.

Review Question

6. The poverty line will vary depending on the domain of comparison because

- ○ A. Of the referencing problem.
- ○ B. Of the identification problem.
- ○ C. Of the purpose of the comparison.
- ○ D. The $1/day standard is too low.

Solution A: Objective Poverty Lines

How then are we to determine poverty lines? One possibility is to pick an "objective" poverty line. A common and fairly satisfactory method of approaching capabilities is to begin with nutritional requirements. The most common way of making this operational is the cost of basic needs approach, while the food energy intake method has been suggested as an alternative when the data are more limited.

The Cost of Basic Needs Method

The most satisfactory approach to building up a poverty line, while remaining in the spirit of trying to ensure that the line covers basic needs, proceeds as follows:

- Stipulate a consumption bundle that is deemed to be adequate, with both food and nonfood components.

- Estimate the cost of the bundle for each subgroup (urban or rural, each region, and so forth).

This is essentially the approach taken by Seebohm Rowntree in his seminal studies of poverty in York, undertaken in 1901 and 1936 (Rowntree 1941). Note that although we begin with a consumption bundle—so much food, so much housing space, so much electricity, and so forth—the poverty line is measured in money. We are therefore not insisting that each basic need be met by each person (a nonwelfarist position), only that it *could* be met (a welfarist position). Operationally, the steps to follow are these:

- Pick a nutritional requirement for good health, such as 2,100 Calories per person per day. This standard is widely used, and has been proposed by the Food and Agricultural Organization of the United Nations. It is also an approximation, given that food needs vary across individuals, by climate, by the level of an individual's activity, and seasonally.

- Estimate the cost of meeting this food energy requirement, using a diet that reflects the habits of households near the poverty line (for example, those in the lowest, or second-lowest, quintile of the income distribution; or those consuming between 2,000 and 2,200 calories). This may not be easy if diets vary widely across the country. Call this food component z^F.

- Add a nonfood component (z^{NF}). There is a lot of disagreement about how to do this; we offer some more thoughts on this issue below; for U.S. practice, see box 3.2, below.

- Then the basic needs poverty line is given by

$$z^{BN} = z^F + z^{NF}. \tag{3.9}$$

Review Question

7. Is the following statement true, false, or uncertain? The cost of basic needs approach requires that households meet their basic needs of food and essential nonfood spending.

○ True
○ False
○ Uncertain

Box 3.2   The U.S. Poverty Line

In 1963 and 1964, Mollie Orshansky of the U.S. Social Security Administration computed the cost of an "adequate" amount of food intake, to get z^F. She then multiplied this number by 3 to get z^{BN}. Why? Because at the time, consumers in the United States devoted a third of their spending to food. This line is still used, updated regularly for price changes.

Source: Dalaker and Naifeh 1998.

To illustrate how this might work, suppose, following common practice, that we use a food energy threshold of 2,100 Calories per day. Suppose that there are only three foodstuffs: rice, corn, and eggs. For this hypothetical example, imagine that table 3.4 shows the expenditure on each item, and the amount consumed per person by a household in the second (from bottom) quintile; because such a household consumes, we suppose, just 2,000 Calories per day, the figures here have to be grossed up to give the cost of purchasing 2,100 Calories. In this example the cost comes to 105 pesos per day.

The choice of which diet to use when estimating the cost of obtaining 2,100 Calories is not a trivial one, a point emphasized in the context of Indonesia by Pradhan et al. (2000).[1] To illustrate, consider the information in table 3.5, drawn from the Vietnam Living Standards Survey of 1992–93 (World Bank 1994). Households in the

Table 3.4 Illustration of Construction of Cost-of-Food Component of Poverty Line

	Expenditure per day (pesos)	Calories	Calories, adjusted to give 2,100 Calories	Expenditure, adjusted to cover 2,100 Calories
Rice	60	1,400	1,470	63
Corn	20	400	420	21
Eggs	20	200	210	21
Total	**100**	**2,000**	**2,100**	**105**

Source: Authors.

Table 3.5 Food Consumption by Expenditure Quintile, Vietnam, 1992–93

Quintile	Expenditure per capita, thousand dong/year	Percentage of expenditure devoted to food	Calories per capita per day	Dong per Calorie
Lowest	562	70	1,591	0.68
Low-mid	821	65	1,855	0.79
Middle	1,075	60	2,020	0.87
Mid-upper	1,467	54	2,160	1.00
Upper	2,939	47	2,751	1.38

Source: World Bank 1994.

Review Question

8. In constructing a cost of basic needs poverty line in Vietnam, the poverty line will be

   o A. Lower if the food price of the lowest quintile is used.
   o B. Higher if one uses the calorie per capita level of the lowest quintile.
   o C. Lower if one uses the percentage of spending on nonfood from the top expenditure quintile.
   o D. Higher if one uses a threshold of 2,020 Calories per capita per day.

poorest quintile paid 0.68 dong per Calorie; those in the richest expenditure quintile paid almost twice as much (1.38 dong/Calorie). Depending on which cost per calorie one uses, the poverty line could vary widely.

An application. In practice, researchers in this case used the price of food for households in the middle quintile, on the grounds that those households were close to the poverty line because they were consuming almost 2,100 Calories per day. The annual food expenditure of the middle quintile, grossed up to pay for 2,100 Calories per day, came to 750,228 dong per capita in 1993; the nonfood expenditure of this same group of households was taken to be adequate for those at the poverty line (after a similar grossing up). This gave an overall poverty line of 1,160,842 dong. Individual households lived in regions with different prices, so their expenditure per capita was first deflated, then compared with this poverty line. The result was an estimated headcount poverty rate in Vietnam of 58 percent (World Bank 1999).

To compare poverty over time, this poverty line was updated to 1998. The cost of each item in the poverty-line diet of 1993 was recomputed using 1998 prices (as taken from the price questionnaire component of the Vietnam Living Standards Survey, mainly); nonfood expenditure was inflated using data from the Vietnam General Statistical Office's price index. This yielded a poverty line of 1,793,903 dong, and an associated poverty rate of 37 percent. The details are summarized in table 3.6.

There is no wholly satisfactory way to measure the nonfood component of the poverty line, and the procedures followed tend to be case specific. We saw above that for Vietnam, researchers essentially used the (slightly adjusted) level of nonfood spending by households that were in the middle expenditure quintile in 1993. The poverty lines developed for the Republic of Korea measure the cost of food plus the cost of housing that meets the official minimum apartment size plus the cost of nonfood items as measured by average spending by households in the poorest two-fifths of the income distribution.

Table 3.6 Poverty Lines and Headcount Measures of Poverty, Vietnam

	Poverty line (thousand dong/capita/year)	Headcount poverty rate (percent)
Poverty overall		
1993	1,160 ($109)	58
1998	1,790 ($135)	37
Food poverty		
1993	750 ($70)	25
1998	1,287 ($97)	15

Sources: Vietnam General Statistical Office 2000; World Bank 1994.

Note: The food poverty rate excludes any provision for nonfood items; it sets the poverty line at z^F.

Is there a better way to proceed? Probably not. Even the theory calls for compromise. Consider the food expenditure function shown in figure 3.2. Generally, $b = f(y)$, where b is food purchases and y is total expenditure. Following Ravallion (1998), let b^F be the cost of buying 2,100 Calories. Then an upper poverty line might be given by

$$f^{-1}(b^F) = z^f,\qquad(3.10)$$

which measures the income level at which the household would buy 2,100 Calories of food; this is essentially the poverty line used in Vietnam. The nonfood component is given by A (in figure 3.2).

A lower poverty line might be given by

$$z_L^F = b^F,\qquad(3.11)$$

which measures the per capita expenditure level at which the household could just buy enough food, but would not have any money left over to buy anything else; in Vietnam this is referred to as the food poverty line. But even in this case, households will typically buy nonfood items, as shown by C in figure 3.2. Ravallion suggests that one might want to compromise, and measure nonfood at the midpoint between these two extremes, giving B. In each case, the poverty line would be given by

$$z = b^F + 0\ (or\ A\ or\ B').\qquad(3.12)$$

Figure 3.2 Food Expenditure Function

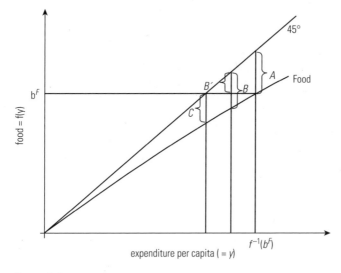

Review Question

<table>
<tr><td>9. The nonfood component of the poverty line, under the cost of basic needs approach, may be obtained as</td></tr>
</table>

  ○ A. The cost of basic housing and services.
  ○ B. Nonfood consumption of a household with just enough income to buy 2,100 Calories of food per capita per day along with other necessary goods and services.
  ○ C. Nonfood consumption of a household with just enough income to buy 2,100 Calories of food per capita per day.
  ○ D. All of the above.

As one might expect, when there is potential disagreement about the best approach to take, practice varies widely from one analyst to the next. Table 3.7 summarizes the approaches used to measure poverty in Africa, based on World Bank poverty assessments undertaken up to 1998. Based on a list of 40 cases of poverty measurement compiled by Hanmer, Pyatt, and White (1999), 23 measured relative poverty; most of these set the poverty line as a share of mean income or expenditure (11 cases) or identified the poor using some percentage (for example, 20 percent, 25 percent) of the income or expenditure distribution. The remaining 17 cases used an absolute measure of poverty, with most of them beginning with a calorie requirement (12 cases), sometimes adding a nonfood component (5 cases). In a further five cases, the analysts specified a basket of goods (including food) that was intended to measure the cost of basic needs but did not begin by identifying a calorie requirement. The heterogeneity of these measures makes it difficult to compare poverty across countries, although if one's interest is in assessing poverty within a country, these differences are of secondary importance.

Food Energy Intake Method

The basic needs approach outlined above requires information on the prices of the goods that the poor consume, especially when making comparisons across regions or over time. When price data are not available, a number of researchers have used an alternative method to construct the poverty line—the *food energy intake method*. As before, the goal here is to find the level of consumption expenditure (or income) that allows the household to obtain enough food to meet its energy requirements. Note that consumption will include nonfood as well as food items; even underfed households typically consume some clothing and shelter, which means that at the margin these "basic needs" must be as valuable as additional food.

The basic idea is captured in figure 3.3, which shows a *calorie income function*; as income (or expenditure) rises, food energy intake also rises, although typically

Table 3.7 Typology of Poverty Lines in World Bank Poverty Assessments for Africa

Absolute (17 cases)	
Calorie requirement (12)	Calories only
	Calorie cost/food share (1)
	Calories + basket of goods (5)
Basket of goods (including food) (5)	
Relative (23 cases)	
Relative to income base	Multiple of wage
	Share of mean income or expenditure (11)
Specified percentage of income distribution (11)	

Source: Hanman, Pyatt, and White 1999.

Figure 3.3 Calorie Income Function

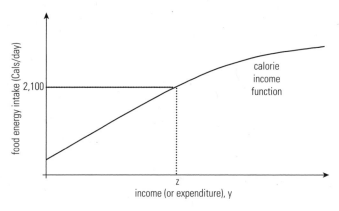

Source: Authors.

more slowly. Given some level of just-adequate food energy intake *k*, one may use this curve to determine the poverty-line level of expenditure, *z*. Formally, the function shows

$$k = f(y) \qquad (3.13)$$

So, given monotonicity,

$$y = f^{-1}(k), \qquad (3.14)$$

or, given a minimum adequate level of calorie k_{min}, we have

$$z = f^{-1}(k_{min}), \qquad (3.15)$$

where *z* is the poverty line. This approach is parsimonious in that it does not require any information about the prices of goods consumed.

First one needs to determine the amount of food that is adequate. Vietnam pegs this level at 2,100 calories per person per day, in line with UN Food and Agriculture

Organization recommendations, but it is recognized that individuals may need more or less food than this. Clearly, the needs of young children, growing teenagers, manual workers, pregnant women, or sedentary office workers may differ quite markedly; physical stature also plays a role. Not all countries have set the same cutoff point, as table 3.8 shows.

A variant of this approach was used to measure poverty in Vietnam, using data from the Vietnam Living Standards Survey of 1993 (World Bank 2004). Separate food expenditure lines were estimated for urban and rural areas in each of seven provinces; the cost of obtaining 2,100 Calories of food per person per day was then computed, as were the associated poverty lines—one for each rural and urban area in each province. This gave a headcount index of 55 percent (Dollar and Litvack 1998).

Table 3.8 Per Capita Daily Calorie Intake Used in Poverty Line Construction

	Years	Urban	Rural
Bangladesh	1996–99	2,112	2,122
India	1993–95	2,100	2,400
Indonesia	1990, 1999	2,100	2,100
Laos	1995	2,100	2,100
Pakistan	1992–93, 1996–97	2,295	2,550
Thailand	1990, 1998	2,100	2,100
Vietnam	1993, 1998	2,100	2,100

Source: www.idrc.ca/uploads/user-S/10282146370mimap60.doc [accessed July 16, 2008].

Note: Thailand now uses Calorie levels that are differentiated by age and gender; for instance, for adults ages 31–50, 2,100 Calories for men and 1,750 Calories for women.

Review Question

10. Is the following statement true, false, or uncertain? The food energy intake approach sets the poverty line at the level of expenditure at which the household buys just enough calories (for example, 2,100 Calories per capita per day).

○ True
○ False
○ Uncertain

Unfortunately, the food energy intake method is seriously flawed, and should not be used for comparisons across time, or across regions, or between urban and rural areas, unless the alternatives are infeasible. Ravallion and Bidani (1994) computed headcount poverty measures for Indonesia using the SUSENAS (Indonesia's National Socioeconomic Survey) data for 1990, using both the cost of basic needs and the food energy intake methods. Their results are shown in table 3.9. The most striking finding is that while the overall poverty rates are designed to be relatively

Table 3.9 Headcount Measures of Poverty in Indonesia, 1990

| | Percentage of individuals who are poor | | |
| | Cost of basic needs method | | Food energy intake method |
	Food	Food + nonfood	
Indonesia overall	7.9	19.6	15.1
Urban	2.8	10.7	16.8
Rural	10.2	23.6	14.3

Source: Ravallion and Bidani 1994.

similar, the disaggregated results are very different: the cost of basic needs method shows rural poverty to be more than twice as great as urban poverty, while the food energy intake method indicates (implausibly) that poverty is higher in urban than in rural areas. Ravallion and Bidani also computed poverty rates using these two measures for each of the main regions of Indonesia, and found almost no correlation between the two measures.

Why is the food energy intake method potentially unreliable? The weaknesses of the method were pointed out in an important article by Ravallion and Bidani (1994); in the next few paragraphs we summarize their approach and findings. The method also failed in a recent analysis of data from Vietnam, for slightly different reasons, also summarized below.

The Urban-Rural Problem. The problem begins when one recognizes that food energy, typically shown on the calorie income function, depends on other factors as well as income. The other influences include the tastes of the household (for example, urban tastes in food may differ from rural tastes); the level of activity of household members; the relative prices of different foods, and of food to nonfood items; and the presence of publicly provided goods.

Figure 3.4 shows hypothetical (but plausible) calorie income functions for urban and rural households. Rural households can obtain food more cheaply, both because food is typically less expensive in rural areas and also because they are more willing to consume foodstuffs that are cheaper per calorie (such as cassava rather than rice); urban consumers are more likely to buy higher quality foodstuffs, which raises the cost per calorie. It follows that the calorie income function for rural households will typically be higher than that for urban households. The implication is that for a given level of food energy intake, the poverty line in the rural area will be lower than in the urban area, as figure 3.4 makes clear. To the extent that this reflects differences in the cost of living, it is not a problem to have two poverty lines of this kind.

The key finding of Ravallion and Bidani (1994), based on 1990 data from the SUSENAS household survey in Indonesia, was that the urban poverty line (Indonesian rupiah [Rp] 20,614/person/month) was much higher than the rural

Figure 3.4 **Calorie Income Functions for Urban and Rural Indonesia**

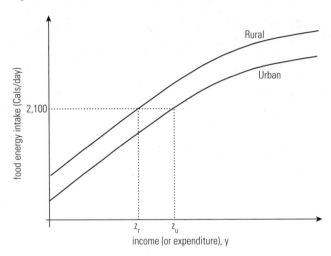

Source: Authors.

one (Rp 13,295/person/month) and, most important, this gap far exceeded the difference in the cost of living between urban and rural areas. Using these poverty lines, Ravallion and Bidani (1994) found that poverty in Indonesia appeared to be higher in the urban than in the rural areas (table 3.10), a completely implausible result. The point is also illustrated in figure 3.5, which shows the cumulative distribution of consumption per capita for rural and urban areas and marks the poverty lines and headcount poverty rates.

Review Question

11. Ravallion and Bidani found, using the food energy intake method, that the urban poverty line in Indonesia exceeded the rural poverty line by more than a simple comparison of living costs would lead one to expect, because

    ○ A. Urban households eat more.
    ○ B. Urban households eat better-quality food.
    ○ C. Urban food prices are much higher than rural food prices.
    ○ D. Urban housing costs more than rural housing.

The Relative Price Problem. When researchers tried to apply the food energy intake approach to data from the Vietnam Living Standards Survey of 1998, the method failed. As with the 1993 data, the idea was to compute food expenditure functions, find the cost of 2,100 Calories of food, and calculate the related level of expenditure per capita, which would then serve as a poverty line. After undertaking this exercise, researchers found a higher level of poverty in 1998 than in 1993, an

Table 3.10 Poverty Lines in Indonesia Using Food Energy Intake Method, 1990

Poverty measure	Indonesia overall	Urban areas	Rural areas
P_0 (%)	15.1	16.8	14.3
P_1 (%)	2.42	3.23	1.06
P_2 (x 100)	0.66	0.94	0.53

Source: Ravallion and Bidani 1994.

Figure 3.5 Cumulative Distribution Functions for Consumption, Indonesia, 1990

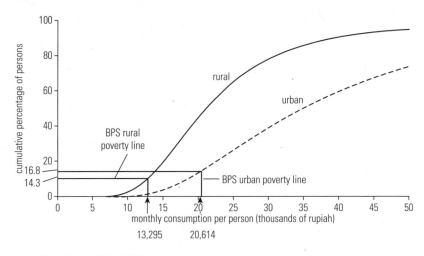

Source: Ravallion and Bidani 1994.

Note: BPS = Biro Pusat Statistik (the Indonesian Central Bureau of Statistics).

implausible result in an economy whose real GDP grew by 9 percent annually between 1993 and 1998, and where there was a general sense that the benefits of this growth had spread widely.

What went wrong? Figure 3.6 shows the situation. The food expenditure function shifted down between 1993 and 1998; for a given (real) income, households in 1998 would buy less food than in 1993. The main reason was that the price of food rose 70 percent between 1993 and 1998, while the price of nonfood items rose by just 25 percent; thus, food became *relatively* much more expensive. As a result, consumers shifted away from food to nonfood consumption. This meant that the poverty line rose from z_{93} to z_{98} (see figure 3.6), a jump that turned out to be implausibly large. As noted above, the cost of basic needs method proved much more satisfactory in this case, because it tracked the cost of the components of spending (rice, other food, and nonfood items) between 1993 and 1998, and thus was able to inflate the poverty line so that it tracked the evolution of the cost of living (for the poor) correctly over time.

This is a serious indictment of the food energy intake method. But it should also be clear that every measure of poverty can be faulted because each rests in part on arbitrary assumptions. In measuring poverty, there is no single truth.

Figure 3.6 The Determination of Poverty Lines for Vietnam, 1993 and 1998

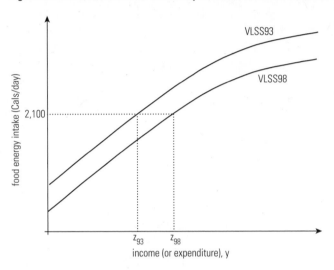

Source: Authors.

Review Question

12. Is the following statement true or false? The food energy intake method showed that the real poverty line in Vietnam rose rapidly between 1993 and 1998, because of inflation.

   ○ True
   ○ False

Solution B: Subjective Poverty Lines

We could measure poverty by asking people to define a poverty line, and using this to measure the extent of poverty. For instance, in a survey one might ask

> *What income level do you personally consider to be absolutely minimal? That is to say, with less you could not make ends meet.*

The answers will vary from person to person (and by size of household), but they could be plotted, and a line fitted through them, to get a subjective poverty line such as z^* in figure 3.7. It may also be possible to get adequate results by asking "do you consider your current consumption to be adequate to make ends meet?"

Mahar Mangahas has amassed extensive information on subjective poverty in the Philippines as part of the social weather stations project. Collected biannually since 1985, and quarterly since 1992, the surveys poll about 1,200 households. Each household is shown a card with a line running across it; below the line is marked "poor" (*mahirap*) and above the line "nonpoor," and each household is asked to mark on the card where it fits. Separately, households are also asked to define a poverty line. Figure 3.8 reproduces a graph that tracks the evolution of this poverty rate from 1983 to 2008. Here are the comments of Mahar Mangahas that accompany the graph:

Figure 3.7 Estimating a Subjective Poverty Line

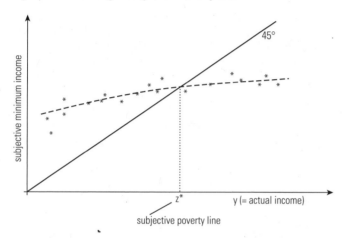

Source: Authors.

Figure 3.8 Self-Rated Poverty: Households That Are "Mahirap," April 1983 to Second Quarter 2008

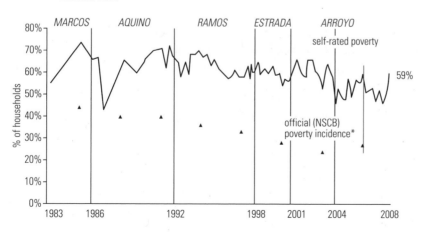

Source: Mangahas 2008 (http://www.sws.org.ph/), reprinted with permission.
Note: NSCB = National Statistical Coordination Board of the Philippines.

Fifty-nine percent of Filipino families, or about 10.6 million, rate themselves as *Mahirap* or Poor, 24% put themselves on the Borderline, and 17% rate themselves as *Hindi Mahirap* or Not Poor, according to the Second Quarter 2008 Social Weather Survey, fielded over June 27-30, 2008.

The new Self-Rated Poverty rate is 9 points higher than the 50% (estimated 9.0 million) in the First Quarter, and 13 points above the previous low of 46% (est. 8.1 million) in December 2007, thus wiping out the decline in Self-Rated Poverty "to its 20-year low in 2007" mentioned in President Gloria Macapagal-Arroyo's State of the Nation Address last July 28th. (Mangahas 2008)[2]

Gaurav Datt of the World Bank has analyzed the Filipino data in some detail. Here are some of his more interesting findings (Datt 2002):

- *Self-rated poverty lines are high.* In 1997, the median poverty line was about 10,000 pesos per month for a "typical" household; this compares with the government's "basic needs" poverty line, which at that time stood at 4,495 pesos/month. The implication is that self-rated poverty rates are high—60 percent of all households in 1997, compared with 25 percent using the basic needs line.

- *The self-rated poverty line has risen rapidly over time,* by about 60–70 percent between 1985 and 1997. One consequence is that there is no trend in self-rated poverty over time. Another implication is that even when there is an economic slowdown, as occurred in 1997–98, the self-rated poverty rate hardly changes: it rose from 59 percent in 1996–97 to 61 percent in 1998.

- Perhaps a surprise, the *self-rated poverty line given by poor households is only slightly lower* than that for nonpoor households, and in fact, the difference is not statistically significant. One might have expected poor households to have a less generous measure of the poverty line.

- There is a *clear urban/rural difference in perceptions* of the poverty line, with urban households setting a (money) poverty line at about twice the level of rural households, giving

$$z^{u}_{self-rated} \approx 2z^{r}_{self-rated}. \tag{3.16}$$

The cost of living is certainly higher in urban areas, but by a factor of 1.2 to 1.5 rather than by a factor of 2. Thus, the urban self-rated poverty line is, in real terms, higher than its rural counterpart. Why?

- One possibility is that there is more inequality in the urban areas, and that this raises expectations.

- Another plausible explanation is that households in urban areas may have more exposure to the media, and may have been affected more thoroughly by consumerism.

- A third explanation is that urban households may be more attuned to political processes, and their estimates of the poverty line may include an element of strategic behavior—trying to influence policy makers.

Self-rated measures of poverty are rarely collected. If the Filipino experience is at all representative, it is clear that self-rated measures may complement, but cannot fully supplant, the more traditional "objective" measures of poverty.

The question of the reliability of self-rated measures of satisfaction continues to be debated. Angus Deaton (2008) finds a measure of "life satisfaction," as collected in 123 countries in 2006 by the Gallup organization, is highly correlated with real per capita income. More specifically, life satisfaction is measured on a scale of 0 (dissatisfied) through 10 (satisfied), in response to a question that asks, "All things considered, how satisfied are you with your life as a whole these days?" This, notes Deaton, is not synonymous with "happiness," which is a more short-term phenomenon. Using a measure of GDP per capita in 2000 international dollars, Deaton (2008) estimated the following regression:

$$\text{Average life satisfaction} = 0.845 \ln(\text{GDP/capita}) - 3.25 \text{ GDP growth rate, 2003–05} + \alpha$$
$$\text{SE} = 0.050 \qquad\qquad \text{SE} = 1.46$$

Here, α refers to the intercept. This equation has an R^2 of 0.71. The strong link between real income and life satisfaction is clear; more surprising, perhaps, is that after controlling for the level of per capita GDP, faster GDP growth is associated with *lower* life satisfaction, perhaps because of the psychological and other adjustment costs associated with rapid economic growth.

Deaton concludes that, "reports of life satisfaction, at least on average, may provide a useful summary of the different components of people's capabilities" (2008, 12), but he considers that more objective measures of poverty are still needed, because people may simply have adapted to misery and hardship. The dilemma is this: if a poor slave says he is happy, should we take that assertion at face value? But if not, then a subjective measure of life satisfaction is an incomplete measure of well-being.

Review Question

> 13. Based on experience in the Philippines, which of the following statements is *not* true?
>
> - A. Subjective poverty lines are not absolute over time.
> - B. Self-rated poverty lines show high poverty rates.
> - C. The rich report markedly higher poverty lines than the poor.
> - D. Urban households set poverty lines higher than rural households, by more than the price differential between urban and rural areas would imply.

Notes

1. Pradhan et al. (2000) favor an interactive procedure: pick a reference population that is relatively poor and compute their cost of calories; now recompute the poverty line; take as the new reference population those households close to this poverty line and recalculate the cost of calories; compute the poverty line again; and so on, until the poverty line stabilizes.
2. The exchange rate in mid-September 2003 was P54.75 per U.S. dollar.

References

Chen, Shaohua, and Martin Ravallion. 2008. "The Developing World Is Poorer Than We Thought, But No Less Successful in the Fight against Poverty." Policy Research Working Paper No. 4703, World Bank, Washington, DC.

Dalaker, Joseph, and Mary Naifeh. 1998. *Poverty in the United States: 1997*. U.S. Bureau of the Census, Current Population Reports, Series P60-201, U.S. Government Printing Office, Washington, DC.

Datt, Gaurav. 2002. "Implementation Completion Report. Philippines: Enhanced Poverty Monitoring – Studies Component." World Bank, Washington, DC.

Deaton, Angus. 2008. "Income, Health, and Well-Being around the World: Evidence from the Gallup World Poll." *Journal of Economic Perspectives* 22 (2): 53–72.

Dollar, David, Paul Glewwe, and Jennie Litvack, eds. 1998. *Household Welfare and Vietnam's Transition*. World Bank Regional and Sectoral Studies. Washington, DC: World Bank.

Dollar, David, and Jennie Litvack. 1998. "Macroeconomic Reform and Poverty Reduction in Vietnam." In *Household Welfare and Vietnam's Transition*, ed. D. Dollar, P. Glewwe, and J. Litvack, 1–28. Washington, DC: World Bank.

Duong, Nguyen Binh, and Dinh Tien Trinh. 1999. "Identification of Poverty in Vietnam." In *Health and Wealth in Vietnam: An Analysis of Household Living Standards*, ed. Dominique Haughton, Jonathan Haughton, Sarah Bales, Truong Thi Kim Chuyen, and Nguyen Nguyet Nga. Singapore: Institute of Southeast Asian Studies Press.

Gibson, John. 1999. "A Poverty Profile of Cambodia, 1999." Report to the World Bank and the Ministry of Planning, Phnom Penh.

Hanmer, Lucia C., Graham Pyatt, and Howard White. 1999. "What Do the World Bank's Poverty Assessments Teach Us about Poverty in Sub-Saharan Africa?" *Development and Change* 30 (4): 795–823.

Haughton, Jonathan. 2000. "Ten Puzzles and Surprises: Economic and Social Change in Vietnam, 1993–1998." *Comparative Economic Studies* 42 (4): 67–92.

Kakwani, Nanak. 2000. "Growth and Poverty Reduction: An Empirical Analysis." *Asian Development Review* 18 (2): 74–84.

Mangahas, Mahar. 2008. "Second Quarter 2008 Social Weather Survey: Self-Rated Poverty jumps to 59%." Social Weather Stations project, the Philippines. http://www.sws.org.ph/.

Pradhan, Menno, Asep Suryahadi, Sudarno Sumarto, and Lant Pritchett. 2000. "Measurements of Poverty in Indonesia, 1996, 1999, and Beyond." Policy Research Working Paper Series No. 2438, World Bank, Washington, DC.

Prescott, Nicholas, and Menno Pradhan. 1997. "A Poverty Profile of Cambodia." Discussion Paper No. 373, World Bank, Washington, DC.

Ravallion, Martin. 1992. "Poverty Comparisons: A Guide to Concepts and Methods." LSMS Working Paper No. 88, World Bank, Washington, DC.

———. 1996. "How Well Can Method Substitute for Data? Five Experiments in Poverty Analysis." *The World Bank Research Observer* 11 (2): 199–221.

———. 1998. *Poverty Lines in Theory and Practice*. Washington, DC: World Bank.

Ravallion, Martin, and Benu Bidani. 1994. "How Robust Is a Poverty Profile?" *World Bank Economic Review* 8 (1): 75–102.

Ravallion, Martin, Gaurav Datt, and Dominique van de Walle. 1991. "Quantifying Absolute Poverty in the Developing World." *Review of Income and Wealth* 37 (4): 345–61.

Rowntree, Benjamin Seebohm. 1941. *Poverty and Progress: A Second Social Survey of York*. London: Longmans, Green.

Sen, Amartya. 1983. "Development: Which Way Now?" *The Economic Journal* 93 (372): 742–62.

Vietnam General Statistical Office. 2000. Viet Nam Living Standards Survey 1997-1998, Statistical Publishing House, Hanoi.

World Bank. 1994. "Viet Nam Living Standards Survey (VNLSS) 1992–93." Poverty and Human Resources Division, World Bank, Washington, DC.

———. 1999. *Entering the 21st Century: World Development Report 1999/2000*. Washington, DC: World Bank.

———. 2000. *World Development Report 2000/2001: Attacking Poverty*. Washington, DC: World Bank.

Chapter 4

Measures of Poverty

Summary

Assume that information is available on a welfare measure, such as income per capita, and on a poverty line, for each household or individual. This chapter explains how one may then construct summary measures of the extent of poverty.

The *headcount index* (P_0) measures the proportion of the population that is poor. It is popular because it is easy to understand and measure. But it does not indicate how poor the poor are.

The *poverty gap index* (P_1) measures the extent to which individuals fall below the poverty line (the poverty gaps) as a proportion of the poverty line. The sum of these poverty gaps gives the minimum cost of eliminating poverty, if transfers were perfectly targeted. The measure does not reflect changes in inequality among the poor.

The squared poverty gap index (also known as the *poverty severity index*, P_2) averages the squares of the poverty gaps relative to the poverty line. It is one of the Foster-Greer-Thorbecke (FGT) class of poverty measures that allow one to vary the amount of weight that one puts on the income (or expenditure) level of the poorest members in society. The FGT poverty measures are additively decomposable. It is also possible to separate changes in the FGT measures into a component resulting from rising average incomes, and a component resulting from changes in the distribution of income.

The *Sen-Shorrocks-Thon index* combines measures of the proportion of poor people, the depth of their poverty, and the distribution of welfare among the poor. This measure allows one to decompose poverty into three components and to ask: Are there more poor? Are the poor poorer? Is there higher inequality among the poor?

Other measures of poverty are available. The *time taken to exit* measures the average time it would take for a poor person to get out of poverty, given an assumption about the economic growth rate; it may be obtained as the *Watts Index* divided by the growth rate of income (or expenditure) of the poor.

Learning Objectives

After completing the chapter on *Measures of Poverty*, you should be able to

1. Describe and explain the headcount index, indicate why it is popular, and explain why it is an imperfect measure of poverty.

2. Describe and compute the poverty gap and poverty severity indexes, and evaluate their adequacy as measures of poverty.

3. Explain and evaluate the FGT (Foster-Greer-Thorbecke) family of poverty measures.

4. Compute the Sen and Sen-Shorrocks-Thon indexes of poverty, and show how the latter may be decomposed to identify the sources of changes in poverty.

5. Compute the Watts index and the related time taken to exit measure.

6. Argue that there is no single best measure of poverty.

Introduction

Given information on a welfare measure such as per capita consumption, and a poverty line, the next issue is deciding on an appropriate summary measure of aggregate poverty. A number of aggregate measures of poverty can be computed. The formulas presented in this chapter are all based on the assumption that the survey represents a simple random sample of the population, which makes them relatively easy to understand. Where the sampling is more complex—the typical situation in practice—weighting is needed, and the relevant formulas and associated programming are somewhat more difficult, but can be handled fairly easily by most major statistical packages such as Stata, SPSS, and SAS.

Headcount Index

By far, the most widely used measure is the *headcount index*, which simply measures the proportion of the population that is counted as poor, often denoted by P_0. Formally,

$$P_0 = \frac{N_p}{N},$$

(4.1)

where N_p is the number of poor and N is the total population (or sample). If 60 people are poor in a survey that samples 300 people, then $P_0 = 60/300 = 0.2 = 20$ percent. For reasons that will be clearer below, it is often helpful to rewrite (4.1) as

$$P_0 = \frac{1}{N} \sum_{i=1}^{N} I(y_i < z). \qquad (4.2)$$

Here, $I(\cdot)$ is an indicator function that takes on a value of 1 if the bracketed expression is true, and 0 otherwise. So if expenditure (y_i) is less than the poverty line (z), then $I(\cdot)$ equals 1 and the household would be counted as poor.

The greatest virtues of the headcount index are that it is simple to construct and easy to understand. These are important qualities. However, the measure has at least three weaknesses:

First, the headcount index does not take the intensity of poverty into account. Consider the following two income distributions:

Headcount Poverty Rates in A and B, Assuming Poverty Line of 125				
	Expenditure for each individual in country			Headcount poverty rate (P_0)
Expenditure in country A	100	100	150	150	50%
Expenditure in country B	124	124	150	150	50%

Clearly, there is greater poverty in country A, but the headcount index does not capture this. As a welfare function, the headcount index is unsatisfactory in that it violates the transfer principle, an idea first formulated by Dalton (1920) that states that transfers from a richer to a poorer person should improve the measure of welfare. With the headcount index, if a somewhat poor household were to give to a very poor household, the index would be unchanged, even though it is reasonable to suppose that poverty overall has lessened.

Some argue that if it is to be meaningful, the headcount index should imply that there is a "jump" or discontinuity in the distribution of welfare at about the poverty line, so it makes sense to speak of the poor and the nonpoor. In practice, such a jump is not found (Ravallion 1996).

Second, the headcount index does not indicate how poor the poor are, and hence does not change if people below the poverty line become poorer. Indeed, the easiest way to reduce the headcount index is to target benefits to people just below the poverty line, because they are the ones who are cheapest to move across the line. But by most normative standards, people just below the poverty line are the least deserving of the poor.

Third, the poverty estimates should be calculated for individuals, not households. If 20 percent of households are poor, it may be that 25 percent of the population is poor (if poor households are large) or 15 percent is poor (if poor households are small); the only relevant figures for policy analysis are those for individuals.

But survey data are almost always related to households, so to measure poverty at the individual level we must make a critical assumption that all members of a given household enjoy the same level of well-being. This assumption may not hold in many situations. For example, some elderly members of a household, or girls, may be much poorer than other members of the same household. In reality, consumption is not always evenly shared across household members.

Poverty Gap Index

A moderately popular measure of poverty is the *poverty gap index*, which adds up the extent to which individuals on average fall below the poverty line, and expresses it as a percentage of the poverty line. More specifically, define the poverty gap (G_i) as the poverty line (z) less actual income (y_i) for poor individuals; the gap is considered to be zero for everyone else. Using the index function, we have

$$G_i = (z - y_i) \times I(y_i < z) \tag{4.3}$$

Then the poverty gap index (P_1) may be written as

$$P_1 = \frac{1}{N} \sum_{i=1}^{N} \frac{G_i}{z}. \tag{4.4}$$

This table shows how the poverty gap is computed, divided by the poverty line, and averaged to give P_1, the poverty gap index.

Calculating the Poverty Gap Index, Assuming Poverty Line of 125					
	Expenditure for each individual in country				Poverty gap index (P_1)
Expenditure in country C	100	110	150	160	
Poverty gap	25	15	0	0	
G_i/z	0.20	0.12	0	0	0.08 [= 0.32/4]

This measure is the mean proportionate poverty gap in the population (where the nonpoor have zero poverty gap). Some people find it helpful to think of this measure as the minimum cost of eliminating poverty (relative to the poverty line), because it shows how much would have to be transferred to the poor to bring their incomes or expenditures up to the poverty line (as a proportion of the poverty line). The minimum cost of eliminating poverty using targeted transfers is simply the sum of all the poverty gaps in a population; every gap is filled up to the poverty line. However, this interpretation is only reasonable if the transfers could be made perfectly efficiently, for instance, with lump sum transfers, which is implausible. Clearly, this assumes that the policy maker has a lot of information; one should not be surprised to find that a very "pro-poor" government would need to spend far more than this in the name of poverty reduction.

At the other extreme, one can consider the maximum cost of eliminating poverty, assuming that the policy maker knows nothing about who is poor and who is not. From the form of the index, it can be seen that the ratio of the minimum cost of eliminating poverty with perfect targeting (that is, G_i) to the maximum cost with no targeting (that is, z, which would involve providing everyone with enough to ensure they are not below the poverty line) is simply the poverty gap index. Thus, this measure is an indicator of the potential savings to the poverty alleviation budget from targeting: the smaller the poverty gap index, the greater the potential economies for a poverty alleviation budget from identifying the characteristics of the poor—using survey or other information—so as to target benefits and programs.

The poverty gap index still violates Dalton's transfer principle. To see this, consider the following example:

Poverty Gap Poverty Rates in A and B, Assuming Poverty Line of 125

	Expenditure for each individual in country				Poverty gap rate (P_1)	Headcount index (P_0)
Expenditure in country A	99	101	150	150	0.10	50%
Expenditure in country B	79	121	150	150	0.10	50%

For both of these countries, the poverty gap rate is 0.10, but most people would argue that country B has more serious poverty because it has an extremely poor member. One could think of the distribution in B as being generated from that in A by transferring 20 from the poorest person to the next poorest person—hardly an improvement in most people's eyes, yet one that has no effect on the poverty gap rate.

Squared Poverty Gap (Poverty Severity) Index

To construct a measure of poverty that takes into account inequality among the poor, some researchers use the squared poverty gap index. This is simply a weighted sum of poverty gaps (as a proportion of the poverty line), where the weights are the proportionate poverty gaps themselves; a poverty gap of, say, 10 percent of the poverty line is given a weight of 10 percent while one of 50 percent is given a weight of 50 percent; this is in contrast with the poverty gap index, where the gaps are weighted equally. Hence, by squaring the poverty gap index, the measure implicitly puts more weight on observations that fall well below the poverty line. Formally,

$$P_2 = \frac{1}{N} \sum_{i=1}^{N} \left(\frac{G_i}{z} \right)^2.$$ (4.5)

This table shows how the poverty gap is computed, divided by the poverty line, squared, and averaged to give P_2, the squared poverty gap index.

Calculating the Poverty Gap Index, Assuming Poverty Line of 125					
	Expenditure for each individual in country				Squared poverty gap index (P_2)
Expenditure in country C	100	110	150	160	
Poverty gap	25	15	0	0	
G_i/z	0.20	0.12	0	0	
$(G_i/z)^2$	0.04	0.0144	0	0	0.0136 [= 0.0544/4]

The measure lacks intuitive appeal, and because it is not easy to interpret it is not used very widely. It may be thought of as one of a family of measures proposed by Foster, Greer, and Thorbecke (1984), which may be written, quite generally, as

$$P_\alpha = \frac{1}{N}\sum_{i=1}^{N}\left(\frac{G_i}{z}\right)^\alpha, \quad (\alpha \geq 0), \tag{4.6}$$

where α is a measure of the sensitivity of the index to poverty and the poverty line is z, the value of expenditure per capita for the ith person's household is x_i, and the poverty gap for individual i is $G_i = z - x_i$ (with $G_i = 0$ when $x_i > z$). When parameter $\alpha = 0$, P_0 is simply the headcount index. When $\alpha = 1$, the index is the poverty gap index P_1, and when α is set equal to 2, P_2 is the poverty severity index. For all $\alpha > 0$, the measure is strictly decreasing in the living standard of the poor (the higher one's standard of living, the less poor one is deemed to be). Furthermore, for $\alpha > 1$ the index also has the property that the increase in measured poverty because of a fall in one's standard of living will be deemed greater the poorer one is. The measure is then said to be "strictly convex" in incomes (and "weakly convex" for $\alpha = 1$).

Another convenient feature of the FGT class of poverty measures is that they can be disaggregated for population subgroups and the contribution of each subgroup to national poverty can be calculated.

> *Example:* Suppose that the headcount poverty rate in the urban areas, where 40 percent of the population lives, is 8 percent, and that the rural poverty rate is 35 percent. Then the national poverty rate may be obtained as the weighted average of these subnational poverty rates, as
> $P_0 = P_{0,urban}(N_{urban}/N) + P_{0,rural}(N_{rural}/N) = .08(0.4) + 0.35(0.6) = 0.242$, or 24.2 percent.

Although the FGT measure provides an elegant unifying framework for measures of poverty, it leaves unanswered the question of the best value of α.

The measures of poverty depth and poverty severity provide information complementary to the incidence of poverty. It might be the case that some groups have a high poverty incidence but low poverty gap (when numerous members are just below the poverty line), while other groups have a low poverty incidence but a high poverty gap for those who are poor (when relatively few members are below the poverty line but with extremely low levels of consumption). Table 4.1 provides an example from Madagascar. According to the headcount measure (P_0), unskilled workers show the third highest poverty rate, while the group is ranked fifth according to the poverty severity index (P_2). Compared to herders, unskilled workers have a higher risk of being in poverty, but their poverty tends to be less severe. The types of interventions needed to help the two groups are therefore likely to be different.

Table 4.1 Poverty Indexes By Subgroups, Madagascar, 1994

	Headcount $[P_0]$ (percent)	Rank	Poverty gap $[P_1]$ (percent)	Rank	Poverty severity × 100 $[P_2]$	Rank
Small farmers	81.6	1	41.0	1	24.6	1
Large farmers	77.0	2	34.6	2	19.0	2
Unskilled workers	*62.7*	*3*	*25.5*	*4*	*14.0*	*5*
Herders and fishermen	51.4	4	27.9	3	16.1	3
Retirees and the handicapped	50.6	5	23.6	5	14.1	4

Source: Coudouel, Hentschel, and Wodon 2001.

Review Questions

1. In a sample of 5,000 households, 800 households have expenditure levels below the poverty line. This means that the headcount poverty rate

   o A. Was 16 percent.
   o B. Was 0.0625.
   o C. Cannot be computed from these numbers.
   o D. Is too small to be computed accurately.

2. A society consists of four individuals with the following incomes: 200, 220, 300, and 320. The poverty line is 250. The poverty gap index is then

   o A. 0.5.
   o B. 0.08.
   o C. 0.16.
   o D. 20.

3. The squared poverty gap index (sometimes referred to as the poverty severity index) is obtained by computing the square of the poverty gap index, which puts more weight on the very poor.

   o True
   o False

Sen Index

Sen (1976) proposed an index that seeks to combine the effects of the number of
poor, the depth of their poverty, and the distribution of poverty within the group.
The index is given by

$$P_s = P_0\left(1-\left(1-G^P\right)\frac{\mu^P}{z}\right), \tag{4.7}$$

where P_0 is the headcount index, μ^P is the mean income (or expenditure) of the poor,
and G^P is the Gini coefficient of inequality among the poor. The Gini coefficient
ranges from 0 (perfect equality) to 1 (perfect inequality), and is discussed in chapter
5 in the context of measuring inequality. The Sen index can also be written as the
average of the headcount and poverty gap measures, weighted by the Gini coefficient
of the poor, giving

$$P_s = P_0 G^P + P_1(1 - G^P). \tag{4.8}$$

It can be shown (Xu and Osberg 2002) that the Sen index may also be written as

$$P_S = P_0 P_1^P (1 + G^{PP}), \tag{4.9}$$

where G^{PP} is the Gini coefficient of the poverty gap ratios of only the poor and P_1^P
is the poverty gap index *calculated over poor individuals only*.

The Sen index has been widely discussed, and has the virtue of taking the income
distribution among the poor into account. However, the index is almost never used
outside of the academic literature, perhaps because it lacks the intuitive appeal of
some of the simpler measures of poverty, but also because it "cannot be used to
decompose poverty into contributions from different subgroups" (Deaton 1997, 147).

The Sen-Shorrocks-Thon Index

The Sen index has been modified by others, and one of the more attractive versions
is the Sen-Shorrocks-Thon (SST) index, defined as

$$P_{SST} = P_0 P_1^P (1 + \hat{\mathbf{G}}^P), \tag{4.10}$$

which is the product of the headcount index, the poverty gap index (applied to the poor only), and a term with the Gini coefficient of the poverty gap ratios (that is, of the G_n's) for the whole population. This Gini coefficient typically is close to 1, indicating great inequality in the incidence of poverty gaps.

> *Example:* In 1996, 12.4 percent of the population of Quebec province (Canada) was in poverty. The poverty gap index, *applied to the poor only*, stood at 0.272. And the Gini coefficient of the poverty gap ratios was 0.924. Thus the SST index was $0.065 = (0.124 \times 0.272 \times (1 + 0.924))$.

Osberg and Xu (1999) used the SST index to compare poverty in the United States and Canada over time. Figure 4.1 shows that while poverty was similar in the two countries a generation ago, it is now clearly higher in the United States than in Canada.

One strength of the SST index is that it can help give a good sense of the sources of change in poverty over time. This is because the index can be decomposed into

Figure 4.1 Comparison of Canada and the United States Using the SST Index, 1971–94

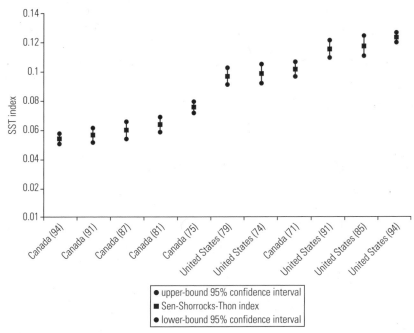

Source: Osberg and Xu 1999, reproduced with permission from *Canadian Public Policy—Analyse de Politiques.*

Note: Poverty line based on half of median equivalent income. The 95% confidence interval is the mean ± 2 standard deviations, based on 300 bootstraps.

$$\Delta \ln P_{SST} = \Delta \ln P_0 + \Delta \ln P_1^P + \Delta \ln(1 + G^P),\qquad(4.11)$$

which may be interpreted as, percentage change in SST index = percentage change in headcount index + percentage change in poverty gap index (among poor) + percentage change in (1 + Gini coefficient of poverty gaps). In plain English, this allows us to decompose poverty into three aspects: Are there more poor? Are the poor poorer? And is there higher inequality among the poor?

> *Example:* The information in table 4.2 comes from Osberg and Xu (1999), and traces the evolution of poverty in the Canadian province of Newfoundland between 1984 and 1996. It is clear that most of the change in the poverty rate over time was due to variations in the number of people in poverty (P_1), rather than in the size of the poverty gap per poor person (P_1^P) or the distribution of poverty among the poor (G^P).

Note that the values of the SST index provided by Osberg and Xu in figure 4.1 do not give just a single point estimate for each observation; the authors also provide a confidence interval. Because the SST index is complex, it is not possible to compute these confidence intervals analytically. Instead, they are computed artificially using *bootstrapping*. The basic idea behind the bootstrap is straightforward and clever. Suppose we have a survey sample of 2,000 households. Now pick a sample of 2,000 from this sample *with replacement*—that is, pick a household, then put it back into the sample, pick another household, put it back into the sample, and so on, until you have picked 2,000 households. Some households will be chosen more than once, but that is fine. Now compute the SST index using this artificial sample. Then repeat the process many times; Osberg and Xu used 300 repetitions. The result is a distribution of values of the SST from which it is easy to find, say, the 95 percent confidence interval. Sample Stata code to generate confidence intervals for the SST index is given in appendix 3, in the exercises associated with chapter 5.

Table 4.2 Decomposition of Poverty and Changes in Poverty in Newfoundland, 1984–96

	SST index	P_0	P_1^P	$1 + G^P$	$\Delta \ln$SST index	$\Delta \ln P_0$	$\Delta \ln P_1^P$	$\Delta \ln (1 + G^P)$
1984	0.137	0.245	0.304	1.844				
1989	0.095	0.169	0.296	1.897	−0.370*	−0.372*	−0.027	0.028
1994	0.105	0.184	0.304	1.884	0.104	0.086	0.026	−0.007
1995	0.125	0.212	0.316	1.864	0.168	0.141	0.038	−0.010
1996	0.092	0.164	0.294	1.897	−0.307	−0.254	−0.071	0.018

Source: Osberg and Xu 1999.

Note: Poverty line is half of median equivalent income, using the "Organisation for Economic Co-operation and Development scale"—that is, equivalent income = 1 + 0.7(Nadults − 1) + 0.5(Nchildren).

* denotes statistically significant at the 95 percent level.

The Watts Index

The first distribution-sensitive poverty measure was proposed in 1968 by Watts (see Zheng 1993), and in its discrete version takes the form

$$W = \frac{1}{N}\sum_{i=1}^{q}[\ln(z) - \ln(y_i)] = \frac{1}{N}\sum_{i=1}^{q}\ln\left(\frac{z}{y_i}\right), \qquad (4.12)$$

where the N individuals in the population are indexed in ascending order of income (or expenditure), and the sum is taken over the q individuals whose income (or expenditure) y_i falls below the poverty line z.

The following table shows how the Watts index is computed, by dividing the poverty line by income, taking logs, and finding the average over the poor. Although it is not a particularly intuitive measure, the Watts index is increasingly used by researchers because it satisfies all the theoretical properties that one would want in a poverty index. Ravallion and Chen (2001) argue that three axioms are essential to any good measure of poverty. Under the *focus axiom*, the measure should not vary if the income of the nonpoor varies; under the *monotonicity axiom*, any income gain for the poor should reduce poverty; and under the *transfer axiom*, inequality-reducing transfers among the poor should reduce poverty. The Watts index satisfies these three axioms, but the headcount (P_0) and poverty severity (P_1) measures do not.

Calculating the Watts Index, Assuming Poverty Line of 125					Watts index
	Expenditure for each individual in country				
Case 1 (poor)					
Expenditure in country C	100	110	150	160	
z/y_i	1.25	1.14	0.83	0.78	
log (z/y_i)	0.223	0.128	−0.182	−0.247	*0.088*
Case 2 (less poor)					
Expenditure in country C	110	120	150	160	
z/y_i	1.14	1.04	0.83	0.78	
log (z/y_i)	0.128	0.041	−0.182	−0.247	*0.042*
Case 3 (deeper poverty)					
Expenditure in country C	90	120	150	160	
z/y_i	1.25	1.10	0.83	0.78	
log (z/y_i)	0.329	0.041	−0.182	−0.247	*0.092*

Table 4.3 presents a variety of poverty measures for a selection of 13 countries using the $2/day standard (actually, US$60.8 per month in 2005 prices). These were computed by the World Bank's PovcalNet program (http://iresearch.worldbank.org/PovcalNet/povcalNet.html), which first fits a Lorenz curve to available data (which are typically grouped) on the distribution of per capita income (or expenditure), and

Table 4.3 Measures of Poverty (with a $2/day Poverty Line) and Inequality for Selected Countries and Regions

	Year	Mean per month[a]	P_0 (%)	P_1 (%)	$P_2 \times 100$	Watts	Gini	Mean log deviation
Nigeria	2003	39	83.9	46.9	30.78	0.838	0.429	0.320
India, rural	2004/5	50	79.5	30.9	14.66	0.429	0.305	0.160
Uganda	2005	53	75.6	36.4	21.12	0.581	0.426	0.305
India, urban	2004/5	62	65.8	26.0	12.90	0.378	0.376	0.233
Haiti	2001	64	72.1	41.8	28.98	0.812	0.595	0.675
Senegal	2005	67	60.3	24.6	12.96	0.374	0.392	0.259
China, rural	2005	71	55.6	19.5	8.92	0.274	0.359	0.213
Vietnam	2006	83	48.4	16.2	7.04	0.223	0.378	0.234
Armenia	2003	84	43.4	11.3	4.13	0.143	0.338	0.198
South Africa	2000	153	42.9	18.3	9.66	0.273	0.578	0.605
China, urban	2005	162	9.4	2.1	0.81	0.029	0.348	0.209
Guatemala	2006	200	24.3	8.9	4.43	0.129	0.537	0.525
Peru	2005	224	19.4	6.3	2.68	0.088	0.520	0.484
Paraguay	2005	257	18.4	7.3	4.06	0.108	0.539	0.546
Mexico	2006	330	4.8	1.0	0.31	0.012	0.481	0.405

Source: World Bank, PovcalNet, accessed November 4, 2008.

Note: P_0 is the headcount poverty rate; P_1 is the poverty gap index; and P_2 is the poverty severity index. The poverty line is set at US$2 per day ($60.8 per month).

a. Mean monthly expenditure (or income) per capita in 2005 purchasing power parity US$.

then applies the chosen poverty line to estimate the poverty rates; further details about PovCalNet are given in chapter 10. All of our admonitions about the pitfalls of comparing poverty rates across countries must be borne in mind here, but the purpose of this tabulation is not so much to rank countries but rather to ask whether the different measures of poverty tell a consistent story. By and large, countries with lower mean levels of per capita expenditure (or income) have higher headcount poverty rates, and also have higher poverty gaps, poverty severity, and Watts indexes. The exceptions are interesting: Haiti has an unexpectedly high level of poverty as measured by the headcount rate, and South Africa has an unusually high amount of poverty as measured by the poverty severity index; these are a consequence of the very high levels of inequality in those countries. In passing, we might note that the Watts index tracks P_2 more closely than it tracks the headcount poverty rate.

Time Taken to Exit

Most poverty profiles for Cambodia, and indeed for most countries, rely on the three basic classes of FGT poverty statistics discussed above. But when thinking about poverty reduction strategies, it may be useful to show how long it would take, at different potential economic growth rates, for the average poor person to exit poverty. A poverty statistic with this property was derived by Morduch (1998); the statistic is decomposable by population subgroups and is also sensitive to the distribution of expenditure (or income) among the poor. For the *j*th person below the poverty line, the expected time to exit poverty (that is, to reach the poverty line), if consumption per capita grows at positive rate *g* per year, is

$$t_g^j \approx \frac{\ln(z) - \ln(x_j)}{g} = \frac{W}{g}. \qquad (4.13)$$

Thus, the time taken to exit is the same as the Watts index divided by the expected growth rate of income (or expenditure) of the poor.

What effect can economic growth have on the elimination of poverty? Figure 4.2 shows the average time it would take to raise the consumption level of a poor person in Cambodia to the poverty line, for various hypothetical growth rates. It is assumed that this growth rate is continuous, is in real terms, and is distributionally neutral among the poor. If the economic growth rate enjoyed by the poor were only 1 percent per year, it would take over 20 years for the average poor person to exit poverty. But at a growth rate of 4 percent per year it would take less than six years for the average poor person to exit poverty. Hence, economic growth that acts to raise the real consumption levels of the poor can have a powerful effect on the elimination of poverty.

Despite the potency of economic growth, it will generally take more than just growth to rapidly improve the lives of the very poor. The expected time to exit poverty for those people who are so poor that they are below the food poverty line in Cambodia—that is, they cannot afford enough food, even if they were to devote all their consumption spending to food—is more than 15 years, even at a 3 percent

Figure 4.2 Average Exit Time from Poverty

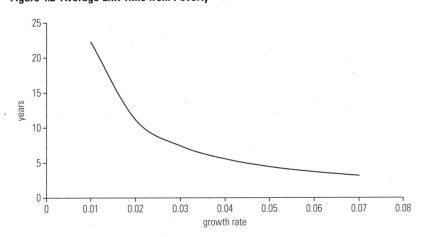

Source: Authors, based on Morduch (1998).

continuous annual growth rate. Thus, targeted programs are likely to be needed to deliver benefits to the poor, for instance, in the form of improvements in their human and physical assets or through interventions (for example, infrastructure and markets) that improve the returns they get from those assets.

Other Measures

There are other additive poverty measures that are distribution-sensitive. Following Atkinson (1987), one can characterize a general class of additive measures, encompassing the Watts index, the FGT class of measures, and some other measures (such as the second measure proposed by Clark, Hemming, and Ulph [1981]), as taking the following form:

$$P = \frac{1}{N} \sum_{i=1}^{N} p(z, y_i), \qquad (4.14)$$

where $p(z, y_i)$ is the individual poverty measure, taking the value zero for the non-poor ($y_i > z$) and some positive number for the poor, the value of which is a function of both the poverty line and the individual living standard, nondecreasing in the former and nonincreasing in the latter.

Given the wide variety of aggregate measures of poverty that are available, which ones should be used? We turn to this question in chapter 5.

Review Questions

5. An important strength of the Sen-Shorrocks-Thon index of poverty is that it allows one to decompose changes in poverty into changes in the head-count index, changes in the poverty gap index (for the poor), and changes in the distribution of the poverty gap.

   o True
   o False

6. The Watts index of poverty is

   o A. Computed by dividing the poverty line by income for all individuals and taking the average of the log of this ratio over the sample.
   o B. Computed by dividing the poverty line by income for all individuals below the poverty line and taking the average of the log of this ratio over the sample.
   o C. Computed by dividing the poverty line by income for all individuals and taking the log of the average of this ratio over the sample.
   o D. Computed by dividing the poverty line by income for all individuals below the poverty line and taking the log of the average of this ratio over the sample.

7. It can be shown that the average time taken to exit from poverty (t) is given by W/g, where W is the Watts index and g is

- A. The size of the sample (that is, the number of households surveyed).
- B. The average age of individuals in the sample.
- C. The growth rate of real income (or consumption) per capita per year.
- D. The percentage of households that are poor.

References

Atkinson, Anthony. 1987. "On the Measurement of Poverty." *Econometrica* 55: 749–64.

Clark, Stephen, Richard Hemming, and David Ulph. 1981. "On Indices for the Measurement of Poverty." *Economic Journal* 91 (361): 515–26.

Coudouel, A., J. S. Hentschel, and Q. D. Wodon. 2002. "Poverty Measurement and Analysis." In *A Sourcebook for Poverty Reduction Strategies*, ed. J. Klugman, 29–69. Washington, DC: World Bank.

Dalton, Hugh. 1920. "The Measurement of the Inequality of Incomes." *Economic Journal* 30: 384–61.

Deaton, Angus. 1997. *The Analysis of Household Surveys: A Microeconometric Approach to Development Policy*. Baltimore, MD: Johns Hopkins University Press for the World Bank.

Foster, James, J. Greer, and Eric Thorbecke. 1984. "A Class of Decomposable Poverty Measures." *Econometrica* 52 (3): 761–65.

Morduch, Jonathan. 1998. "Poverty, Economic Growth, and Average Exit Time." *Economics Letters* 59: 385–90.

Osberg, Lars, and Kuan Xu. 1999. "Poverty Intensity: How Well Do Canadian Provinces Compare?" *Canadian Public Policy—Analyse de Politiques* 25 (2):179–95.

Ravallion, Martin. 1996. "How Well Can Method Substitute for Data? Five Experiments in Poverty Analysis." *The World Bank Research Observer* 11 (2): 199–221.

Ravallion, Martin, and Shaohua Chen. 2001. "Measuring Pro-Poor Growth." Policy Research Working Paper No. 2666, World Bank, Washington, DC.

Sen, Amartya K. 1976. "Poverty: An Ordinal Approach to Measurement." *Econometrica* 44 (2): 219–31.

Xu, Kuan, and Lars Osberg. 2002. "On Sen's Approach to Poverty Measures and Recent Developments." Working Paper, Department of Economics, Dalhousie University, Halifax, Nova Scotia.

Zheng, B. 1993. "An Axiomatic Characterization of the Watts Poverty Index." *Economics Letters* 42 (1): 81–6.

Chapter 5

Poverty Indexes: Checking for Robustness

Summary

There are four main reasons why measures of poverty may not be robust.

Sampling error occurs because measures of poverty are based on sample data, which gives the true poverty rate only with some degree of uncertainty. It is good practice to report standard deviations and confidence intervals for poverty measures; this can be done by *bootstrapping*. Because household surveys tend to be relatively small, it is not possible to disaggregate the results to units smaller than relatively broad regions.

Measurement error occurs in all survey data; we know, for instance, that households underreport income and expenditure, which tends to overstate the degree of poverty. The effect can be large: in some cases a 5 percent understatement of consumption can translate into a 10 percent overstatement of the headcount poverty rate.

Poverty rates vary depending on the equivalence scale used, although the variation is typically fairly modest. Equivalence scales are not widely used because of the difficulty of agreeing on an appropriate set of weights.

The choice of a poverty line and associated poverty rate (for example, headcount index, poverty gap index) is arbitrary. Sometimes, although not always, these choices matter. By comparing the cumulative distribution function of expenditure (or income) per capita—sometimes called the *poverty incidence curve*—between two situations, one may judge whether the choice of poverty line affects the conclusion about the change in poverty. If there is first order stochastic dominance, the choice of poverty line is not crucial; otherwise it is often possible to use higher-order tests (for example, second-order stochastic dominance) to help reach a clear conclusion about whether poverty differs between two time periods (or regions or countries).

No study of poverty is complete without some discussion of the robustness of the findings.

Learning Objectives

After completing the chapter on *Poverty Indexes: Checking for Robustness*, you should be able to

1. Explain what is meant by robustness and why poverty measures might not be robust.

2. Describe sampling error, and argue the case for presenting standard deviations and confidence intervals along with poverty rates.

3. Explain what bootstrapping is and how it may be used to generate confidence intervals and sample standard deviations.

4. Enumerate the sources of measurement error.

5. Define the elasticity of the headcount index with respect to errors in mean expenditure (or income) per capita, and explain how this translates an understatement of expenditure (or income) into an overstatement of poverty.

6. Explain what an adult equivalence scale is and describe some common equivalence scales.

7. Explain why equivalence scales are not widely used in practice.

8. Define, and show how to graph, the poverty incidence curve and the poverty deficit curve.

9. Explain what is meant by first-order stochastic dominance, and why it is useful when assessing how robust a poverty comparison is to the choice of poverty line or poverty measure.

Introduction

Between 1998 and 2003, the poverty rate in Vietnam, as measured by the headcount index, fell from 37 percent to 29 percent. Good news indeed! But before celebrating, it is important to ask how robust this conclusion is.

The problem is the pervasive uncertainty about four possibly crucial aspects of a poverty comparison.

- First is *sampling error*, which arises because we are trying to measure the poverty rate for the country as a whole on the basis of information from a relatively modest number of households.

- Second, there is likely to be *measurement error*, so that our measures of poverty are inherently imprecise.

- Third, there are unknown *differences in needs* between households at similar consumption levels, yet considerable arbitrariness in the way in which equivalence scales are used to address this problem.

- Fourth is *uncertainty and arbitrariness about both the poverty line and the precise poverty measures* used.

Given these problems, how robust are poverty comparisons? Would they change if we made alternative assumptions? These are the questions addressed in this chapter.

Sampling Error

Suppose one wants to determine the average per capita expenditure level in a country. It is unrealistic to measure everyone's expenditure, so pick a simple random sample of individuals and measure their expenditure. The average expenditure for those sampled (the sample mean, $\bar{x}$) is found to be $652 per year. For now, this is the best estimate of the average per capita expenditure for all people in the population. But if another simple random sample were to be taken, it would almost certainly yield a slightly different sample mean, $655 for instance. In other words, the sample mean is a random variable; to the extent that it only approximates the true mean expenditure per capita of the population, we have a degree of sampling error.

Let $\hat{s}^2$ be the sample variance of expenditure, which is to say, the variance as estimated based on the sample, given by $\hat{s}^2 = (1/n-1)\sum_{i=1}^{n}(x_i - \bar{x})^2$. Then the estimated variance *of the sample mean* is given by

$$\hat{v}(\bar{x}) = \frac{\hat{s}^2}{n},\qquad(5.1)$$

where n is the number of observations in the sample. For instance, in our example, if we have 400 observations, and the sample variance is $590, then the variance of the sample mean is 590/400 = 1.475, and the standard error of the sample mean is 1.21. Note that as the sample becomes larger, the standard error of the sample mean decreases—the estimate becomes more precise and sampling error decreases. However, it takes a quadrupling of the sample size to halve the standard error of the sample mean. There is a 95 percent probability that the interval 655 ± 1.96 × 1.21 = (652.6, 657.4) contains the population mean.

The headcount poverty rate is a proportion, $\hat{p}$, and the variance of the sample proportion takes the form $\hat{v}(\hat{p}) = \hat{p}(1-\hat{p})/(n-1)$. Thus, if the estimated poverty rate were 0.252 and the sample size 400, we have $\hat{v}(\hat{p}) = 0.000472$. Taking the square root gives the standard error of the sample proportion, which in this case is 0.022. There is a 95 percent probability that the true poverty rate is in the interval $\hat{p} \pm 1.96 \times \sqrt{\hat{v}(\hat{p})}$, which here means a poverty rate somewhere between 0.209 and 0.295. This is a relatively wide interval; if the estimate had been based on 1,000 observations the 95 percent confidence interval for the poverty rate would run from 0.225 to 0.279, and we could say (loosely) that our estimate of the poverty rate is 25.2 percent, plus or minus 2.25 percentage points. This is more useful, and more honest, than simply saying "the poverty rate is 25.2 percent." Unfortunately, it is not yet common practice to report confidence intervals with estimates of the poverty rate.

It follows from this discussion that acceptably accurate measures of poverty rates generally require a sample size of close to 1,000; thus, a national survey of 6,000 households only allows the results to be disaggregated into about six to eight regions.

In practice, the computation of the standard error of the estimated poverty rate is complicated by the fact that most household surveys are not simple random samples, but instead typically use stratified cluster sampling. As explained in chapter 2, most surveys sample clusters of households (for example, groups of 10 to 20 households living in a given village or ward) because it is less expensive. Although this does not affect the estimate of the mean, it does increase the variance, relative to simple random sampling.

When measuring sampling error it is vital to correct for clustering. For the purposes of illustrating this point, consider the case of the Vietnam Living Standards Survey of 1993 (VLSS93), which used simple random sampling with clustering; there is relevant information on 4,799 households, representing 23,838 individuals. The headcount poverty rate at the time, using a cost of basic needs approach, was 58.0 percent. If there were no clustering we could apply the formulas given above to find a standard error for this estimate of 0.79 percent and hence a 95 percent confidence interval of 56.4 percent to 59.6 percent.

However, there was clustering. To compute the standard error of the estimated poverty rate in this case, it is helpful to use *bootstrapping*. As explained in chapter 4, one computes the poverty rate many times by sampling with replacement from the survey data; when there is clustering, one samples clusters of observations (rather than individual observations). From the distribution of these computed poverty rates it is possible to measure the standard deviation and create confidence intervals. Some sample Stata code for bootstrapping is given in appendix 3; Deaton (1997) provides further code; Biewen (2002) discusses additional applications. The bootstrapped standard error of the estimated poverty rate for the VLSS93 is 1.50 percent, which in this case is almost twice as big as the estimate that ignores clustering, and yields a 95 percent confidence interval that is relatively broad at (55.0 percent, 61.0 percent).

Stratification further complicates the computation because it typically requires that each observation be weighted using sampling weights. Let $\bar{x}_w$ be the estimated mean value of the variable of interest (which could be the poverty rate, or per capita income, for instance). Assuming that there is no clustering, then the variance of this estimate may be obtained using

$$\hat{v}(\bar{x}_w) = \frac{n}{n-1} \sum_{i=1}^{n} w_i^2 (x_i - \bar{x}_w)^2,\qquad(5.2)$$

where the w_i are sampling weights normalized so that they sum to 1 (see Deaton [1997, 47] who notes that this generally needs to be programmed explicitly). For instance, in the Vietnam Household Living Standards Survey of 2006 (VHLSS06), the headcount poverty rate is estimated at 16.6 percent; if one measures the standard error of this estimate correctly (that is, using the square root of $\hat{v}(\bar{x}_w)$ from equation (5.2)), one obtains a value of 0.45 percent and hence a 95 percent confidence interval of (15.7 percent, 17.5 percent).[1]

The most common situation is where we have sampling weights *and* clustering. In the Stata statistical package, this is handled by first using the `svyset` command to identify the strata and clusters, and then applying the `svy: mean` command, which generates a linearized standard error of the sample mean. Using this command in the VHLSS06 case yields a standard error of the estimated poverty rate of 0.69 percent. This is our preferred estimate, and allows us to conclude that "we estimate the headcount poverty rate in Vietnam to have been 16.6 percent in 2006, and are 95 percent confident that it was more than 15.2 percent but less than 18.0 percent."

Measurement Error

We know that measures of welfare, such as expenditure per capita, are measured with error; it follows that statistics based on these measures, such as the headcount poverty rate, are also estimated with some degree of error. These errors in measurement would occur even if everyone in the population were surveyed, which is why this problem is quite distinct from sampling error (which would disappear if everyone were included in the survey).

The problem, of course, is that by definition we do not know how large the errors in measurement are, or even what form they take. So the best we can do is try to think through the implications of the different types of errors that might be plausible.

Suppose, for example, that our welfare indicator is measured with an additive random error with a mean of zero. This means that, on average, our measure is correct; however, the value that we actually observe for almost every individual observation will be either a bit too large or a bit too small. This adds noise to the distribution.

The situation is shown in the panels in figure 5.1; the distribution of the log of expenditure per capita in Vietnam in 2006, as observed in the VHLSS06, is shown by the thin line in every case. In the top left panel, the heavy curve shows the distribution of the log of expenditure per capita after adding a random error (from a uniform distribution with mean 0 and running from –0.75 to 0.75)—the "distribution with measurement error." The new curve is still centered at the same mean, but it is now lower and fatter. If the poverty line is set below the peak (the mode), as will commonly be the case, then the measured headcount poverty rate (using the heavy curve) will be higher than the true poverty rate (using the light curve). In other words, *under plausible conditions, even a measurement error with zero mean will lead to an overstatement of the poverty rate.* Ravallion (1988) sets out the necessary and sufficient conditions for greater variability in the welfare indicator ("measurement error") to increase the expected value of a poverty measure defined on that indicator. In the case of Vietnam in 2006, the measured headcount poverty rate (for the poverty line used in Vietnam) would be 16.6 percent if there were no measurement error, but would rise to 24.3 percent in the presence of the measurement error used here.

The top right panel also shows the effect of adding zero-mean measurement error, but in this case the errors come from a normal distribution (with the same standard deviation as the uniform distribution used in the top left panel). Again, the distribution with measurement error is squatter; here the measured poverty rate would be 22.6 percent (against the actually observed rate of 16.6 percent). The normal distribution has thinner tails than the uniform distribution, which is why the overstatement of the poverty rate is slightly more modest in this case.

Another plausible case is when the welfare measure is systematically underestimated; this is typical, resulting from incomplete recall, deliberate omissions, or the exclusion from the survey of poor but hard-to-reach groups such as the homeless. In the bottom left panel of figure 5.1, we assume that everyone's log expenditure per capita is understated by 0.4 (compared to a mean level of 8.66); in the bottom right panel we suppose that the true log expenditure per capita should be 5 percent higher than what is actually observed. These are simply variants on the basic idea that survey-based measures of variables such as expenditure per capita are frequently understated.

Clearly, the measured poverty rate will overstate true poverty if, in fact, expenditure is understated. In the examples here, the "true" poverty rate would be 5.0 percent (bottom left panel), or 4.7 percent (bottom right panel) in the absence of this type of measurement error, compared with the observed rate of 16.6 percent. These are large differences. Ravallion (1988) argues that a θ percent underestimation of mean consumption at all consumption levels is commonly associated with a reduction in the poverty rate of $2 \times \theta$ percent; in the jargon of poverty analysis, the elasticity of the headcount index to errors in the mean, holding the income distribution (as measured by the Lorenz curve) constant, is often close to two; for

Figure 5.1 Distribution of Log of Expenditure per Capita with and without Measurement Error, for Vietnam in 2006

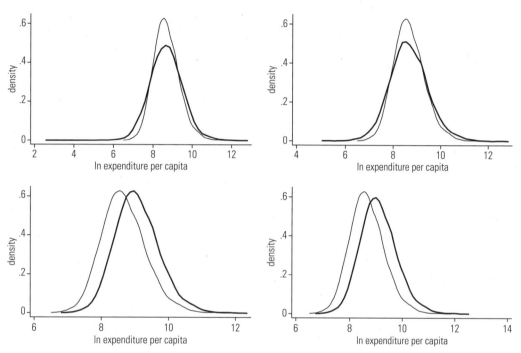

Source: Authors' compilation based on VHLSS06.

Note: Light line shows actual distribution; heavy line shows distribution with perturbations, including measurement errors with zero mean distributed uniformly (top left) and normally (top right), and with a fixed positive shock (bottom left) and proportionate shock (bottom right).

higher-order Foster-Greer-Thorbecke poverty measures, such as the poverty gap index, the elasticities are usually even higher.

In the context of measurement, it is worth noting that in practice, inflation—defined as a substantial, sustained increase in the general level of prices—raises the nominal value both of expenditure and of the poverty line, so has no net effect on the measures of poverty. However, when relative prices change, for instance, if the price of food rises more than other prices, then there will generally be an effect on the level of poverty, as well as on the pattern of who is poor.

Equivalence Scales

Poverty studies usually measure living standards using expenditure (or income) per capita. As discussed in chapter 2, because needs vary among household members, and because there are economies of scale in consumption, poverty measures based on per capita welfare indicators may not be good estimates. An alternative is to base our poverty measures on expenditure (or income) per adult equivalent. If poverty estimates are not affected by the adult equivalence weights that we choose, it is safe to say that those poverty estimates are not biased as a consequence of the weighting procedure used.

Kathleen Short and her colleagues investigated the sensitivity of the U.S. 1997 poverty rate to a number of variations on the Organisation for Economic Co-operation and Development (OECD) equivalence scales (Short et al. 1999). The results are summarized in table 5.1. While different definitions of adult equivalence do change the measured poverty rate in the United States, the most striking feature of table 5.1 is how small these differences are. In other words, the choice of adult equivalence scale may not matter very much.

Table 5.2 displays adult equivalence weights that have been used in India and in Taiwan, China. A study by Visaria (1980) of living standards in Asia includes a discussion of the importance of weights, and reports the correlation coefficient between (unweighted) expenditure per capita and expenditure per adult equivalent using these weights, using data from Sri Lanka (1969–70), Taiwan, China (1974), and Peninsular Malaysia (1973). All the correlation coefficients were 0.96 or higher; they are shown in table 5.3. Because the equivalence scales give similar rankings of households to those using expenditure per capita, the case for using adult equivalence scales (rather than the much simpler expenditure per capita) is not compelling. This helps explain why adult equivalence scales are not used more often in practical poverty analysis.

However, it is good practice to explore the sensitivity of one's results—especially when measuring poverty rates—to differences in the choice of equivalence scale. By

Table 5.1 Sensitivity of Headcount Poverty Rate (P_0) to Different Specifications of Adult Equivalence Scales, United States, 1999

Adult equivalence scale used	Headcount poverty rate, %
$N_a + N_c$ (that is, use income per capita)	13.3
$(N_a + 0.7\ N_c)^{0.65}$	13.1
$(N_a + 0.7\ N_c)^{0.70}$	12.3
$(N_a + 0.7\ N_c)^{0.75}$	12.7
$(N_a + 0.7\ N_c)^{0.5}$	13.4
$(N_a + 0.7\ N_c)^{0.6}$	12.7
$(N_a + 0.85\ N_c)^{0.65}$	12.7
$1 + 0.4(N_a - 1) + 0.4(\text{child } 1) + 0.3(N_c - 1)$ (Canadian scale)	13.8
One adult: 1. Two adults: 1.41. Single parents: $(N_a + 0.8 + 0.5N_c - 1)$. All other families: $(N_a + 0.5N_c)^{0.7}$	13.1

Source: Short et al. 1999.

Note: N_a = Number of adults. N_c = Number of children.

Table 5.2 Adult Equivalents, India and Taiwan, China

India: Adult equivalents			Taiwan, China: Adult equivalents		
Age	Male	Female	Age	Male	Female
0	0.43	0.43	0–1	0.3	0.3
1–3	0.54	0.54	2–4	0.4	0.4
4–6	0.72	0.72	5–7	0.5	0.5
7–9	0.87	0.87	8–10	0.7	0.7
10–12	1.03	0.93	11–14	0.8	0.8
13–15	0.97	0.80	15–20	0.9	0.9
16–19	1.02	0.75	21+	1.0	0.9
20–39	1.00	0.71			
40–49	0.95	0.68			
20–59	0.90	0.64			
60–69	0.80	0.51			
70+	0.70	0.50			

Source: Visaria 1980, 200.

**Table 5.3 Correlation Coefficients, Expenditure per Capita with Expenditure per
Adult Equivalent**

Survey	Years	India weights	Taiwan, China weights
Sri Lanka	1969–70	0.99	0.96
Taiwan, China	1974	0.98	0.96
Peninsular Malaysia	1973	0.99	0.97

Source: Visaria 1980, 201.

way of illustration, we perform such an exercise using data from the Vietnamese
VHLSS06. Suppose that we are interested in identifying the poorest 20 percent of the
population, on the basis of one of three possible measures of welfare:

- Expenditure per capita

- Expenditure per adult equivalent using the OECD scale ("OECD expenditure");
  the number of adult equivalents is given by $1 + 0.7(N_a - 1) + 0.5N_c$, where N_a is
  the number of adults and N_c the number of children in the household

- Expenditure per adult equivalent using a measure that reflects economies of scale
  in consumption ("economies of scale expenditure"); in this case, the number of
  adult equivalents is measured by $(N_a + 0.7N_c)^{0.7}$.

The three measures move closely together; the correlation between expenditure
per capita and OECD expenditure is 0.986, and between expenditure per capita and
economies of scale expenditure is 0.967.

Although the measures are closely correlated, it is possible that they would classify people differently. For instance, measures of expenditure per capita routinely

identify large households as being disproportionately poor; however, if there are economies of scale in consumption, this measure would overstate poverty among large households. Indeed, a measure of adult equivalence that makes a strong allowance for economies of scale might find that large households are less poor than average. In the Vietnamese case, the poverty rate for households with five or more members is 27 percent using expenditure per capita, and 23 percent using economies of scale expenditure; but for households with just one or two members, the poverty rate is 11 percent if one uses expenditure per capita, and 28 percent using the economies of scale expenditure measure. In every case the mean poverty rate over the whole sample is, by construction, 20 percent.

Table 5.4 identifies the 20 percent poorest Vietnamese using our three measures of welfare. About a tenth of those identified as poor using expenditure per capita would not be poor using the other measures; and about a tenth of those identified as poor using OECD expenditure or economies of scale expenditure would not be poor using expenditure per capita. This is a relatively modest level of disagreement, suggesting that measures of poverty in Vietnam in 2006 were fairly robust to the choice of method used for dealing with adult equivalence, assuming the goal is to identify who is poor.

Choice of Poverty Line and Poverty Measure

The choice of a poverty line, and the associated poverty measure (for example, the headcount index P_0 or the poverty gap index P_1), is arbitrary. However, if the various measures of poverty (introduced in chapter 4) tell the same story, it does not much matter which measure one chooses because they are close substitutes for one another.

There are times, especially when we are comparing poverty over time, when the choice of poverty measure might matter. For instance, suppose there is a change—an increase in the price of a staple crop, for example—that has the effect of making

Table 5.4 Classifying the Poor Using Alternative Measures of Welfare, Vietnam, 2006

	Percentages					
	OECD expenditure		Economies of scale expenditure		Total	Number of observations
	Not poor	Poor	Not poor	Poor		
Expenditure per capita						
Not poor	78.4	1.6	77.8	2.2	80.0	7,351
Poor	1.6	18.4	2.2	17.8	20.0	1,838
Total	80.0	20.0	80.0	20.0	100.0	
Number of observations	7,351	1,838	7,350	1,839		

Source: VHLSS06.

the poorest worse off, but raising the barely poor out of poverty. This could lower poverty as measured by P_0 and raise it as measured by, say, P_2. Such cases may be the exception rather than the rule, but they suggest that it is important to look at higher-order poverty measures and not rely on the headcount poverty rate alone.

Just as the choice of poverty measure can matter, so too can the poverty line itself. In the case of the rise in the price of the staple crop, where the very poor lost out but the barely poor gained, we might have picked up the effect if we used two poverty lines: a low poverty line might have shown more people becoming worse off, while a high poverty line could have shown the opposite.

One useful practical exercise, which should be done routinely in poverty analysis, is to vary the poverty line and examine the associated poverty rates. This both shows how sensitive poverty is to changes in the poverty line, and allows one to pick up changes that have occurred in the distribution of welfare among people near the poverty line. The ADePT 2.0 program, which helps automate the production of tables for poverty profiles, computes this as a matter of course (see chapter 7). Table 5.5 shows the poverty rates for Vietnam for 2006, for the official poverty line and also for poverty lines that are somewhat above and below the official line. A 5 percent increase in the poverty line is associated with a 13 percent increase in the poverty rate, representing an elasticity of 2.6; this shows that poverty in Vietnam is, in fact, quite sensitive to the choice of poverty rate.

A Single Measure of Standard of Living

A natural extension of the idea of checking the effect of different poverty lines on the poverty rate is to look at the entire distribution, using the theory of stochastic dominance. Ravallion (1998) provides a clear exposition, and we draw on his work in organizing the ideas in the following paragraphs.

The first step is to imagine the curve that is traced out as one plots the headcount index (P_0) on the vertical axis and the poverty line on the horizontal axis, allowing

Table 5.5 Sensitivity of Poverty Rate in Vietnam to Changes in the Poverty Line, 2006

	Poverty rate (%)	Standard error of estimate of the poverty rate (%)
Poverty line + 10 percent	21.2	0.76
Poverty line + 5 percent	18.9	0.74
Poverty line	16.6	0.69
Poverty line − 5 percent	14.6	0.65
Poverty line − 10 percent	12.6	0.60

Source: VHLSS06.

Note: Based on observations of 9,189 households. The poverty rates have been adjusted for stratification (64 provinces and cities) and clustering (630 primary sampling units).

the latter to vary from zero to the maximum consumption. This is simply the cumulative distribution function, and may also be thought of as the *poverty incidence curve*, F(z). Each point on the curve gives the proportion of the population consuming less than the amount given on the horizontal axis, as in figure 5.2. Thus, the poverty incidence curve for year 1 in figure 5.2 shows that if the poverty line is $600, the poverty rate is 24 percent; if the poverty line is $900, the poverty rate is 53 percent; and so on.

One can go further. Calculating the area under the poverty incidence curve up to each point—the shaded area in figure 5.2, for example—and then plotting it against the poverty line traces out the *poverty deficit curve*, D(z), shown in figure 5.3. Each point on the curve in figure 5.3 is the total value of the poverty gap (or, equivalently, the poverty gap index multiplied by the poverty line z).

From figure 5.2 we see that for every possible choice of poverty line, the poverty rate in year 2 is below that of year 1. Thus, there is *first-order stochastic dominance*: the precise choice of poverty line is unimportant (at least up to the maximum conceivable poverty line z^{max}, which is the relevant range), because no matter what poverty line is chosen, we still conclude that poverty fell between year 1 and year 2. For a more formal treatment of stochastic dominance, see box 5.1, below.

In figure 5.2 the ranking was unambiguous, but not so in figure 5.4: using a poverty line of $600, poverty is higher in year 1; but with a poverty line of $1,000, poverty is higher in year 2 (as measured by the headcount index). In this case it is not at all clear whether poverty has risen or fallen.

Figure 5.2 Poverty Incidence Curves with First-Order Stochastic Dominance

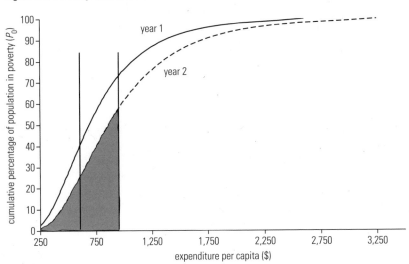

Source: Authors.

Figure 5.3 Poverty Deficit Curves

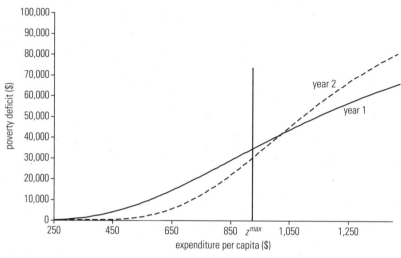

Source: Authors.

Figure 5.4 Poverty Incidence Curves Showing Ambiguous Ranking

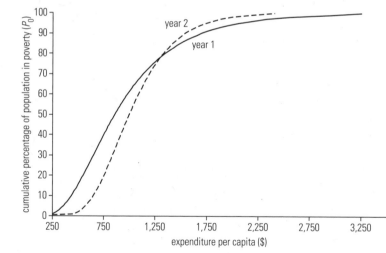

Source: Authors.

It is sometimes possible to resolve this issue by appealing to second- (or higher-) order stochastic dominance. To do this, one must exclude the headcount index and consider only additive measures that reflect the depth of poverty, such as the poverty gap index (P_1) and the squared poverty gap index (P_2). A fall in poverty then requires that the poverty deficit curve, given by the area under the cumulative distribution, be nowhere lower for year 1 at all points up to the maximum poverty line, and at least somewhere higher. What happens above z^{max} is not relevant, for the study of poverty at least.

In the example in figure 5.3, there is *second-order dominance in the relevant range*, and we may consider that poverty has indeed fallen. Intuitively, using the poverty gap index as the measure of poverty is equivalent to saying that the sum of the poverty gaps (that is, the poverty deficit) is smaller in year 2 than in year 1, no matter what poverty line is used, provided it is below z^{max}.

> *Example:* To illustrate the two dominance tests, consider an initial state in which four people have consumption in amounts (100, 110, 140, 150) in year 1 and these change to (110, 112, 128, 150) in year 2. Has poverty changed between year 1 and year 2?
>
> To help answer this question, consider the numbers in table 5.6. If the poverty line is 100, a quarter of the population is poor in year 1 and none are poor in year 2. It would appear that poverty has fallen. But if the poverty line is set at 130, the poverty rate was 0.5 in year 1 and actually rose to 0.75 in year 2. In other words, whether poverty (as measured by the headcount rate) has risen or fallen turns out to be sensitive to the choice of poverty line. Formally, the poverty incidence curves cross, so we do not have first-order stochastic dominance.

Now consider the poverty deficit curve. If the poverty line is 120, the value of the poverty deficit curve is 1.25, obtained by summing the values of the poverty incidence curves (that is, 0.25 + 0.50 + 0.50 in this case). The poverty deficit was unambiguously higher (or at least not lower) in year 1 than in year 2 (see table 5.6, final three columns), no matter what poverty line was chosen. In this case there is second-order stochastic dominance, and we have a moderately robust finding that poverty has fallen. This makes some intuitive sense: between year 1 and year 2, average

Table 5.6 Comparison of Poverty Incidence and Poverty Deficit Curves Using Different Poverty Lines

Poverty line (z)	Poverty incidence curve, $F(z)$[a]			Poverty deficit curve, $D(z)$[b]		
	Year 1		Year 2	Year 1		Year 2
100	0.25	>	0	0.25	>	0
110	0.50	=	0.50	0.75	>	0.50
120	0.50	=	0.50	1.25	>	1.00
130	0.50	<	0.75	1.75	=	1.75
140	0.75	=	0.75	2.50	=	2.50
150	1.00	=	1.00	3.50	=	3.50

Source: Example designed by the authors.

Note: Assumes a society of four people with consumption of (100, 110, 140, 150) in year 1 and (110, 112, 128, 150) in year 2.

a. Poverty incidence curves cross.

b. Poverty deficit curves do not cross.

income did not change, but the incomes of the poorest members of society rose (albeit at the expense of one of the moderately well-off individuals). Such a redistribution would widely be considered to have reduced poverty. Similar comparisons can be made using other poverty measures, although this is not done often.

In figure 5.2 the poverty incidence curve for year 2 was everywhere below that for year 1. It is possible that this is due to sampling error, and that if we had chosen different samples in the two years, the curves might have intersected. This raises the question of how we might test whether the difference between the two curves is statistically significant. One approach that appears to be relatively efficient (Tse and Zhang 2003) is to divide the horizontal axis (up to the maximum plausible poverty line) into perhaps 10 or 12 segments, and test the statistical significance of the difference between the two cumulative density functions at the edge of each interval; Davidson and Duclos (2000) set out the theory in some detail. An easier but less complete approach to measuring first order dominance is to use the Kolmogorov-Smirnov test, which is based on the largest vertical distance between the two cumulative frequency curves. Most textbooks on statistics explain how to do this test, and provide tabulations of critical values. The syntax in Stata may be found by typing "help ksmirnov" or "search kolmogorov."

Robustness: More Than One Dimension

Until now we have assumed that the poverty line applicable to each household is measured correctly, so that we have an accurate appreciation of the needs of different people. However, these needs may themselves vary in an unknown way—some

---

Box 5.1 First-Order Stochastic Dominance, Formally

A more formal statement of first-order stochastic dominance runs as follows: Consider two income distributions y_1 and y_2 with cumulative distribution functions $F(y_1)$ and $F(y_2)$. If $F(y_1)$ lies nowhere above and at least somewhere below $F(y_2)$ then distribution y_1 displays first-order stochastic dominance over distribution y_2: $F(y_1) \leq F(y_2)$ for all y. Hence, in distribution y_1 there are no more individuals with income less than a given income level than in distribution y_2, for all levels of income. We can express this in an alternative way using the inverse function $y = F^{-1}(p)$ where p is the share of the population with income less than a given income level: first-order dominance is attained if $F_1^{-1}(p) \geq F_2^{-1}(p)$ for all p. The inverse function $F^{-1}(p)$ simply plots incomes against cumulative population, usually using ranked income percentiles. First-order stochastic dominance of distribution y_1 over y_2 implies that any social welfare function that is increasing in income will record higher levels of welfare in distribution y_1 than in distribution y_2.

people need more food, or special medicine, which would increase the resources they would need to avoid being poor. We may think of this as equivalent to knowing the poverty line only imperfectly, and ask what would happen if the poverty line itself were subject to error.

When the poverty line is best considered as a random variable, the true poverty rate will, under plausible conditions, likely be higher than the rate that is measured based on the survey data. Returning to the data for Vietnam for 2006, suppose that the log of the poverty line consists of the log of the official poverty line plus a random component (with mean zero, uniformly distributed over the interval –0.5 to 0.5). While the poverty rate with the fixed poverty line is 16.6 percent, it rises to 19.3 percent when this randomized poverty line is used.

Unfortunately, we do not generally know the distribution of the poverty line; if we did, we could and would have incorporated that information already. However, if we can assume that the distribution of the poverty lines is the same for the situations we are comparing—for example, two points in time, or two regions of a country—and the distribution is unrelated to our measure of welfare, we can still apply our tests (visual and otherwise) for first order dominance, no matter the underlying distribution of the poverty lines.

Sometimes we might recognize that needs differ in some systematic way—for instance, we might believe that rural households need more food than urban households—but are not sure how to compare needs between these groups. In this case, it is difficult to apply a test for first-order dominance globally. However, we may be able to apply the test separately for rural and for urban households; if first-order dominance applies for each group separately, it turns out that it will also hold in the aggregate, as long as we are using additive poverty measures (such as the headcount or poverty gap measures).

More general tests can be devised for a large variety of situations, but many are difficult to explain nonmathematically and so are unlikely to be convincing to policy makers. However, the key message of this chapter is that when making poverty comparisons, or even when reporting on poverty at a single time, it is important to examine the robustness of the results; sometimes estimated poverty rates can be surprisingly fragile.

Review Questions

1. Because of sampling error

- ○ A. Measures of poverty are sample statistics.
- ○ B. If one were to undertake the same survey again with a different sample, the results would be different.
- ○ C. It is desirable to present measures of poverty with their confidence intervals (which may require bootstrapping to compute).
- ○ D. All of the above.

2. Measurement error is inevitable in survey data, and indeed expenditure and especially income are typically substantially understated. This usually implies that

  o A. Poverty rates are understated, especially the poverty severity measure.
  o B. Poverty rates are overstated, especially the poverty severity measure.
  o C. Poverty rates are understated, especially if based on income.
  o D. Poverty rates are overstated, especially if based on expenditure.

3. Information on expenditure per capita has been gathered for year 1 and year 2. The poverty rate appears to be lower in year 2. First-order stochastic dominance means that

  o A. The poverty incidence curve for year 1 is everywhere above the poverty incidence curve for year 2.
  o B. The headcount poverty rate in year 2 is lower than the headcount poverty rate in year 1, for any poverty line.
  o C. For any level of expenditure per capita, the cumulative percentage of the population below the poverty line is lower in year 2 than in year 1.
  o D. All of the above.

4. Based on a sample of 180 observations you find that income has a mean of 920 and a variance of 300. Then the 95 percent confidence interval for the sample mean is

  o A. (902.7, 937.3)
  o B. (917.5, 922.5)
  o C. (919.9, 920.1)
  o D. (916.7, 923.3)

5. When observations are derived from clustering this implies, compared with simple random sampling, that

  o A. The expected mean is the same but the expected variance is narrower.
  o B. The expected mean is the same but the expected variance is wider.
  o C. The expected mean is higher but the expected variance is the same.
  o D. The expected mean is lower but the expected variance is the same.

6. Second-order stochastic dominance tests cannot be applied to the headcount poverty rate

  o True
  o False

> 7. When the official poverty line is used, the headcount poverty rate is 31.5 percent. But if the poverty line is raised by 10 percent, then the poverty rate would be 38.1 percent. This represents an elasticity of poverty with respect to the poverty line of about
>
> ○ A. 2.0
> ○ B. 0.7
> ○ C. 3.8
> ○ D. 3.2

Note

1. Note that the estimate of the population variance in the presence of sampling weights is given by $\hat{s}_w^2 = n/n - 1 \sum_{i=1}^{n} w_i (x_i - \overline{x}_w)^2$, and unlike in the case of simple random sampling (see equation (5.1)), we cannot simply divide this by n to obtain $\hat{v}(\overline{x}_w)$. If we were to do this we would obtain a standard error of 0.39 percent, which is incorrect and would, in this case, give a spurious sense of precision.

References

Biewen, Martin. 2002. "Bootstrap Inference for Inequality, Mobility and Poverty Management." *Journal of Econometrics* 108 (2): 317–42.

Davidson, Russell, and Jean-Yves Duclos. 2000. "Statistical Inference for Stochastic Dominance and for the Measurement of Poverty and Inequality." *Econometrica* 68 (6): 1435–64.

Deaton, Angus. 1997. *The Analysis of Household Surveys: A Microeconometric Approach to Development Policy.* Baltimore: Johns Hopkins University Press for the World Bank.

Ravallion, Martin. 1998. *Poverty Lines in Theory and Practice.* Living Standards Measurement Study Series. Washington, DC: World Bank.

Short, Kathleen, Thesia Garner, David Johnson, and Patricia Doyle. 1999. "Experimental Poverty Measures: 1990 to 1997." U.S. Census Bureau, Current Population Reports, Consumer Income, P60–205, U.S. Government Printing Office, Washington, DC.

Tse, Y. K., and Xibin Zhang. 2003. "A Monte Carlo Investigation of Some Tests for Stochastic Dominance." Department of Econometrics and Business Statistics, Monash University, Clayton, Victoria, Australia.

Visaria, Pravin (with Shyamalendu Pal). 1980. "Poverty and Living Standards in Asia: An Overview of the Main Results and Lessons of Selected Household Surveys." Living Standards Measurement Study Working Paper No. 2, World Bank, Washington, DC.

Chapter 6

Inequality Measures

Summary

Inequality is a broader concept than poverty in that it is defined over the entire population, and does not only focus on the poor.

The simplest measurement of inequality sorts the population from poorest to richest and shows the percentage of expenditure (or income) attributable to each fifth (quintile) or tenth (decile) of the population. The poorest quintile typically accounts for 6–10 percent of all expenditure, the top quintile for 35–50 percent.

A popular measure of inequality is the Gini coefficient, which ranges from 0 (perfect equality) to 1 (perfect inequality), but is typically in the range of 0.3 to 0.5 for per capita expenditures. The Gini coefficient is derived from the Lorenz curve, which sorts the population from poorest to richest, and shows the cumulative proportion of the population on the horizontal axis and the cumulative proportion of expenditure (or income) on the vertical axis. While the Gini coefficient has many desirable properties—mean independence, population size independence, symmetry, and Pigou-Dalton Transfer sensitivity—it cannot easily be decomposed to show the sources of inequality.

The best known entropy measures are Theil's T and Theil's L, both of which allow one to decompose inequality into the part that is due to inequality within areas (for example, urban and rural) and the part that is due to differences between areas (for example, the rural-urban income gap), as well as the sources of changes in inequality over time. Typically, at least three-quarters of inequality in a country is due to within-group inequality, and the remaining quarter to between-group differences.

Atkinson's class of inequality measures is quite general, and is sometimes used. The decile dispersion ratio, defined as the expenditure (or income) of the richest decile divided by that of the poorest decile, is popular but a very crude measure of inequality.

A Pen's Parade graph can be useful in showing how incomes, and income distribution, change over time. Microsimulation exercises are increasingly used to identify the sources of changes in income distribution, and to identify changes resulting from changes in prices, in endowments, in occupational choice, and in demographics.

Learning Objectives

After completing the chapter on *Inequality Measures*, you should be able to

1. Explain what inequality is and how it differs from poverty.

2. Compute and display information on expenditure (or income) quintiles.

3. Draw and interpret a Lorenz curve.

4. Compute and explain the Gini coefficient of inequality.

5. Argue that the Gini coefficient satisfies mean independence, population size independence, symmetry, and Pigou-Dalton Transfer sensitivity, but is not easily decomposable.

6. Draw a Pen's Parade for expenditure per capita, and explain why it is useful.

7. Compute and interpret generalized entropy measures, including Theil's T and Theil's L.

8. Compute and interpret Atkinson's inequality measure for different values of the weighting parameter ε.

9. Compute and criticize the decile dispersion ratio.

10. Decompose inequality using Theil's T to distinguish between-group from within-group components of inequality, for separate geographic areas and occupations.

11. Identify the main sources of changes in inequality using Theil's L.

12. Explain how microsimulation techniques can be used to quantify the effect on income distribution of changes in prices, endowments, occupational choice, and demographics.

Introduction: Definition of Inequality

Much of this handbook focuses on poverty—the situation of individuals or households who find themselves at the bottom of the income distribution. Typically, analyzing poverty requires information both about the mean level of, say, expenditure

Table 6.1 Breakdown of Expenditure per Capita by Quintile, Vietnam, 1993

Indicator	Expenditure quintiles					
	Lowest	Low-mid	Middle	Mid-upper	Upper	Overall
Per capita expenditure (thousand dong/year)	518	756	984	1,338	2,540	1,227
Percentage of expenditure	8.4	12.3	16.0	21.8	41.4	100.0
Memo: Cumulative percentage of expenditure	8.4	20.7	36.7	58.5	100.0	
Memo: Cumulative percentage of population	20.0	40.0	60.0	80.0	100.0	

Source: Authors' computations, based on the Vietnam Living Standards Survey 1993.

Note: Totals may not add up due to slight rounding errors.

per capita, as well as its distribution at the lower end. But sometimes we are more interested in measuring inequality than poverty, which is why we have included this chapter.

Inequality is a broader concept than poverty in that it is defined over the entire population, not just for the portion of the population below a certain poverty line. Most inequality measures do not depend on the mean of the distribution; this property of mean independence is considered to be a desirable feature of an inequality measure. Of course, inequality measures are often calculated for distributions other than expenditure—for instance, for income, land, assets, tax payments, and many other continuous and cardinal variables.

The simplest way to measure inequality is by dividing the population into fifths (quintiles) from poorest to richest, and reporting the levels or proportions of income (or expenditure) that accrue to each level. Table 6.1 shows the level of expenditure per capita, in thousand dong per year, for Vietnam in 1993, based on data from the Vietnam Living Standards Survey. A fifth of the individuals (not households) included in the survey were allocated to each expenditure quintile. The figures show that 8.4 percent of all expenditures were made by the poorest fifth of individuals, and 41.4 percent by the top fifth. Quintile information is easy to understand, although sometimes a summary measure is needed rather than a whole table of figures.

Commonly Used Summary Measures of Inequality

Several summary measures of inequality have been developed, and in this section we present the most important of these. For further details, see the classic book by Atkinson (1983); Duclos and Araar (2006) provide a more technical treatment, and Araar and Duclos (2006) summarize the details of DAD, a very useful software package they developed specifically for the accurate measurement of inequality and poverty.

Decile Dispersion Ratio

A simple and popular measure of inequality is the decile dispersion ratio, which presents the ratio of the average consumption (or income) of the richest 10 percent of the population to the average consumption (or income) of the poorest 10 percent. This ratio can also be calculated for other percentiles (for instance, dividing the average consumption of the richest 5 percent, the 95th percentile, by that of the poorest 5 percent, the 5th percentile).

The decile dispersion ratio is readily interpretable, by expressing the income of the top 10 percent (the "rich") as a multiple of that of those in the poorest decile (the "poor"). However, it ignores information about incomes in the middle of the income distribution, and does not even use information about the distribution of income within the top and bottom deciles.

Gini Coefficient of Inequality

The most widely used single measure of inequality is the Gini coefficient. It is based on the Lorenz curve, a cumulative frequency curve that compares the distribution of a specific variable (for example, income) with the uniform distribution that represents equality. To construct the Gini coefficient, graph the *cumulative* percentage of households (from poor to rich) on the horizontal axis and the *cumulative* percentage of expenditure (or income) on the vertical axis. The Lorenz curve shown in figure 6.1 is based on the Vietnamese data in table 6.1. The diagonal line represents perfect equality. The Gini coefficient is defined as A/(A + B), where A and B are the areas shown in the figure. If A = 0, the Gini coefficient becomes 0, which means perfect equality, whereas if B = 0, the Gini coefficient becomes 1, which means complete inequality. In this example, the Gini coefficient is about 0.35. Some users, including the World Bank, multiply this number by 100, in which case it would be reported as 35.

Formally, let x_i be a point on the x-axis, and y_i a point on the y-axis. Then

$$Gini = 1 - \sum_{i=1}^{N} (x_i - x_{i-1})(y_i + y_{i-1}).$$ (6.1)

When there are N equal intervals on the x-axis, equation (6.1) simplifies to

$$Gini = 1 - \frac{1}{N} \sum_{i=1}^{N} (y_i + y_{i-1}).$$ (6.2)

Figure 6.1 Lorenz Curve

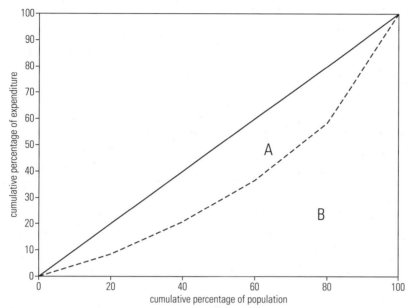

Source: Authors' illustration.

For users of Stata, there is a "fastgini" command that can be downloaded and used directly (see appendix 3). This command also allows weights to be used, a capability not incorporated into equations (6.1) and (6.2). This Stata routine also allows the standard error of the Gini coefficient to be computed using a jackknife procedure.[1] The free, stand-alone DAD software (Araar and Duclos 2006) allows one to measure a wide array of measures of poverty and inequality, including the Gini coefficient.

Table 6.2 shows that the value of the Gini coefficient for expenditure per capita in Vietnam rose from 0.313 in 1993 to 0.350 in 1998. The jackknife standard errors for these estimates are small, and the 95 percent confidence intervals do not overlap; therefore, we can say with some confidence that inequality—as measured by the Gini coefficient, at least—rose during this period. Similarly, it is clear that inequality within the urban areas of Vietnam in 1998 was substantially greater than within rural areas, and this difference is highly statistically significant.

The Gini coefficient is not entirely satisfactory. To see this, consider the criteria that make a good measure of income inequality:

- *Mean independence.* If all incomes were doubled, the measure would not change. The Gini satisfies this.

- *Population size independence.* If the population were to change, the measure of inequality should not change, all else equal. The Gini satisfies this, too.

Table 6.2 Inequality in Vietnam, as Measured by the Gini Coefficient for Expenditure per Capita, 1993 and 1998

Year and area	Gini	Standard error	95% confidence interval	
			Lower bound	Upper bound
1993	0.3126	0.0045	0.3039	0.3213
1998	0.3501	0.0042	0.3419	0.3584
1998, urban	0.3372	0.0068	0.3238	0.3505
1998, rural	0.2650	0.0037	0.2578	0.2721

Source: Authors' calculations based on Vietnam Living Standards Surveys of 1992–93 and 1998.

- *Symmetry.* If any two people swap incomes, there should be no change in the measure of inequality. The Gini satisfies this.

- *Pigou-Dalton Transfer sensitivity.* Under this criterion, the transfer of income from rich to poor reduces measured inequality. The Gini satisfies this, too.

It is also desirable to have

- *Decomposability.* Inequality may be broken down by population groups or income sources or in other dimensions. The Gini index is not easily decomposable or additive across groups. That is, the total Gini of society is not equal to the sum of the Gini coefficients of its subgroups.

- *Statistical testability.* One should be able to test for the significance of changes in the index over time. This is less of a problem than it used to be because confidence intervals can typically be generated using bootstrap techniques.

Generalized Entropy Measures

There are a number of measures of inequality that satisfy all six criteria. Among the most widely used are the Theil indexes and the mean log deviation measure. Both belong to the family of generalized entropy (GE) inequality measures. The general formula is given by

$$GE(\alpha) = \frac{1}{\alpha(\alpha-1)}\left[\frac{1}{N}\sum_{i=1}^{N}\left(\frac{y_i}{\bar{y}}\right)^{\alpha} - 1\right],$$ (6.3)

where $\bar{y}$ is the mean income per person (or expenditure per capita). The values of GE measures vary between zero and infinity, with zero representing an equal distribution and higher values representing higher levels of inequality. The parameter α in the GE class represents the weight given to distances between incomes at different parts of the income distribution, and can take any real value. For lower values of α, GE is more sensitive to changes in the lower tail of the distribution, and for higher values GE is more sensitive to changes that affect the upper tail. The most common values of α used are 0, 1, and 2. GE(1) is Theil's T index, which may be written as

$$GE(1) = \frac{1}{N} \sum_{i=1}^{N} \frac{y_i}{\bar{y}} \ln\left(\frac{y_i}{\bar{y}}\right).$$

(6.4)

GE(0), also known as Theil's L, and sometimes referred to as the mean log deviation measure, is given by

$$GE(0) = \frac{1}{N} \sum_{i=1}^{N} \ln\left(\frac{\bar{y}}{y_i}\right).$$

(6.5)

Once again, users of Stata do not need to program the computation of such measures from scratch; the "ineqdeco" command," explained in appendix 3, allows one to obtain these measures, even when weights need to be used with the data.

Atkinson's Inequality Measures

Atkinson (1970) has proposed another class of inequality measures that are used from time to time. This class also has a weighting parameter ε (which measures aversion to inequality). The Atkinson class, which may be computed in Stata using the "ineqdeco" command, is defined as

$$A_\varepsilon = 1 - \left[\frac{1}{N} \sum_{i=1}^{N} \left(\frac{y_i}{\bar{y}}\right)^{1-\varepsilon}\right]^{1/(1-\varepsilon)}, \quad \varepsilon \neq 1$$

$$= 1 - \frac{\prod_{i=1}^{N}(y_i^{(1/N)})}{\bar{y}}, \qquad \varepsilon = 1.$$

(6.6)

Table 6.3 sets out in some detail the steps involved in the computation of the GE and Atkinson measures of inequality. The numbers in the first row give the incomes of the 10 individuals who live in a country, in regions 1 and 2. The mean income is 33. To compute Theil's T, first compute $y_i/\bar{y}$, where $\bar{y}$ is the mean income level; then compute $\ln(y_i/\bar{y})$, take the product, add up the row, and divide by the number of people. Similar procedures yield other GE measures, and the Atkinson measures, too.

Table 6.4 provides some examples of different measures of inequality (Dollar and Glewwe 1998, 40); Gottschalk and Smeeding (2000) summarize evidence on inequality for the world's "industrial" countries. All three measures agree that inequality is lowest in Vietnam, followed closely by Ghana, and is highest in Côte d'Ivoire. This illustrates another point: in practice, the different measures of inequality typically tell the same story, so the choice of one measure over another is not of crucial importance in the discussion of income (or expenditure) distribution.

Table 6.3 Computing Measures of Inequality

Measure		Region 1					Region 2				
Incomes (y_i)		10	15	20	25	40	20	30	35	45	90
Mean income $(\bar{y})$	33.00										
$y_i/\bar{y}$		0.30	0.45	0.61	0.76	1.21	0.61	0.91	1.06	1.36	2.73
$\ln(y_i/\bar{y})$		−0.52	−0.34	−0.22	−0.12	0.08	−0.22	−0.04	0.03	0.13	0.44
Product		−0.16	−0.16	−0.13	−0.09	0.10	−0.13	−0.04	0.03	0.18	1.19
GE(1), Theil's T	**0.080**										
$\ln(\bar{y}/y_i)$		0.52	0.34	0.22	0.12	−0.08	0.22	0.04	−0.03	−0.13	−0.44
GE(0), Theil's L	**0.078**										
$(y_i/\bar{y})^2$		0.09	0.21	0.37	0.57	1.47	0.37	0.83	1.12	1.86	7.44
GE(2)	**0.666**										
$(y_i/\bar{y})^{0.5}$		0.55	0.67	0.78	0.87	1.10	0.78	0.95	1.03	1.17	1.65
Atkinson, $^\varepsilon=0.5$	**0.087**										
$(y_i)^{1/n}$		1.26	1.31	1.35	1.38	1.45	1.35	1.41	1.43	1.46	1.57
Atkinson, $^\varepsilon=1$	**0.164**										
$(y_i/\bar{y})^{-1}$		3.30	2.20	1.65	1.32	0.83	1.65	1.10	0.94	0.73	0.37
Atkinson, $^\varepsilon=2$	**0.290**										

Source: Authors' compilation.

Table 6.4 Expenditure Inequality in Selected Developing Countries

Country	Gini coefficient	Theil's T	Theil's L
Côte d'Ivoire, 1985–86	0.435	0.353	0.325
Ghana, 1987–88	0.347	0.214	0.205
Jamaica, 1989	—	0.349	0.320
Peru, 1985–86	0.430	0.353	0.319
Vietnam, 1992–93	0.344	0.200	0.169

Source: Reported in Dollar and Glewwe (1998, 40).

Note: — = Not available. The numbers for Vietnam differ from those shown in table 6.2 because a slightly different measure of expenditure per capita was used in the two cases.

One caveat is in order: income is more unequally distributed than expenditure. This is a consequence of household efforts to smooth consumption over time. It follows that when comparing inequality across countries it is important to compare either Gini coefficients based on expenditure, or Gini coefficients based on income, but not mix the two.

Inequality Comparisons

Many of the tools used in the analysis of poverty can be similarly used for the analysis of inequality. Analogous to a poverty profile (see chapter 7), one could draw a profile of inequality, which, among other things, would look at the extent of inequality among certain groups of households. This profile provides information on the homogeneity of the various groups, an important element to take into account when designing policy interventions.

The nature of changes in inequality over time can also be analyzed. One could focus on changes for different groups of the population to show whether inequality changes have been similar for all or have taken place, say, in a particular sector of the economy. In rural Tanzania, average incomes increased substantially between 1983 and 1991—apparently tripling over this period—but inequality increased, especially among the poor. Although the nationwide Gini coefficient for income per adult equivalent increased from 0.52 to 0.72 during this period, the poverty rate fell from 65 percent to 51 percent. Ferreira (1996) argues that a major cause of the rise in both rural incomes and rural inequality was a set of reforms in agricultural price policy; despite higher prices, poorer and less efficient farmers found themselves unable to participate in the growth experienced by wealthier, more efficient farmers.

In comparing distributions over time, one of the more useful graphs is a *Pen's Parade*, which is a form of *quantile graph*. On the horizontal axis, every person is lined up from poorest to richest, while the vertical axis shows the level of expenditure (or income) per capita. Often the graph is truncated toward the upper end of the distribution, to focus on changes at the lower end, including the zone in which people are in poverty. If the axes were flipped, this graph would simply be a cumulative density

Figure 6.2 Pen's Parade (Quantile Function) for Expenditure per Capita, Vietnam, 1993 and 1998

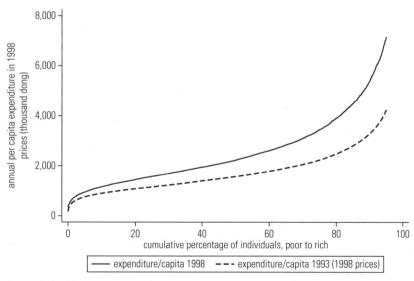

Source: Created by the authors, based on data from the Vietnam Living Standards Surveys of 1992–93 and 1998.

Note: This function is truncated at the 95th percentile.

function. The Pen's Parade is most helpful when comparing two different areas or periods. This is clear from figure 6.2, which shows the graphs for expenditure per capita for Vietnam for 1993 and 1998; over this five-year period, incomes (and spending) rose across the board, and although inequality increased, wages were still higher at the bottom of the distribution in 1998 than in 1993. There is nothing inevitable about this; Ferreira and Paes de Barros (2005) show an interesting quantile graph of income per person in urban Brazil; between 1976 and 1996 incomes on average rose slightly and inequality on average was reduced, yet the position of those at the very bottom actually worsened—a feature that appears very clearly on their Pen's Parade.

Measuring Pro-Poor Growth

As national income (or expenditure) rises, the expenditure of the poor may rise more or less quickly than that of the country overall. A visually compelling way to show this effect is with a *growth incidence curve*, which can be computed as long as data are available from surveys undertaken at two times. The procedure is as follows:

a. Divide the data from the first survey into centiles—for instance, using the `xtile` command in Stata—and compute expenditure per capita for each of the 100 centiles.

b. Divide the data from the second survey into centiles, and again compute expenditure per capita for each centile.

c. After adjusting for inflation, compute the percentage change in (real) expenditure per capita for each centile and graph the results.

Figure 6.3 shows just such a graph for Vietnam and compares the outcomes of the Vietnam Living Standards Surveys of 1992–93 and 1998; it uses the same data as figure 6.2. During this period, the mean increase in real expenditure per capita was 37 percent, and the median increase was 34 percent. It is clear from the graph that, with the exception of the very poorest centile, expenditure rose less quickly for those in the lower part of the expenditure distribution than for those who were better off.

Even so, expenditure rose substantially even for the poor. One way to measure the "rate of pro-poor growth," suggested by Ravallion and Chen (2003), is to compute the mean growth rate of expenditure per capita experienced by the poor. In 1992–93 the headcount poverty rate was 57 percent in Vietnam; averaging the growth in expenditure for this group using the data that underlie the growth incidence curve yields 32 percent. This means that, although expenditure per capita rose by 37 percent nationwide over the five-year interval between the two surveys, the increase was 32 percent for the poor.

Figure 6.3 Poverty Incidence Curve for Expenditure per Capita, Vietnam, 1993 and 1998

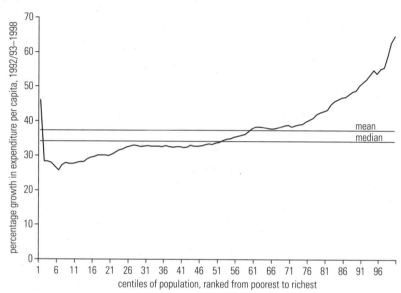

Source: Created by the authors, based on data from the Vietnam Living Standards Surveys of 1992–93 and 1998.

The growth incidence curve reflects averages. The incomes of the poor might rise on average, but some poor households might still find themselves worse off. The examination of poverty dynamics of this nature requires panel data; this topic is discussed in some detail in chapter 11.

Decomposition of Income Inequality

The common inequality indicators mentioned above can be used to assess the major contributors to inequality, by different subgroups of the population and by region. For example, average income may vary from region to region, and this alone implies some inequality "between groups." Moreover, incomes vary inside each region, adding a "within-group" component to total inequality. For policy purposes, it is useful to be able to decompose these sources of inequality: if most inequality is due to disparities across regions, for instance, then the focus of policy may need to be on regional economic development, with special attention to helping the poorer regions.

More generally, household income is determined by household and personal characteristics, such as education, gender, and occupation, as well as geographic factors including urban and regional location. Some overall inequality is due to

111

differences in such characteristics—this is the "between-group" component—and some occurs because there is inequality within each group, for instance, among people with a given level of education or in a given occupation. The generalized entropy (GE) class of indicators, including the Theil indexes, can be decomposed across these partitions in an additive way, but the Gini index cannot.

To decompose Theil's T index (that is, GE(1)), let Y be the total income of all N individuals in the sample, and $\bar{y} = Y/N$ be mean income. Likewise, Y_j is the total income of a subgroup (for example, the urban population) with N_j members, and $\bar{y}_j = Y_j/N_j$ is the mean income of this subgroup. Using T to represent GE(1),

$$
\begin{aligned}
T &= \sum_{i=1}^{N} \frac{y_i}{N\bar{y}} \ln\left(\frac{y_i N}{\bar{y} N}\right) \\
&= \sum_{i=1}^{N} \frac{y_i}{Y} \ln\left(\frac{y_i N}{Y}\right) \\
&= \sum_{j}\left(\frac{Y_j}{Y}\right) T_j + \sum_{j}\left(\frac{Y_j}{Y}\right)\ln\left(\frac{Y_j/Y}{N_j/N}\right),
\end{aligned}
\tag{6.7}
$$

where T_j is the value of GE(1) for subgroup j. Equation (6.7) separates the inequality measure into two components, the first of which represents within-group inequality while the second term measures the between-group inequality.

Exercise: Decompose Theil's T measure of inequality into "within" and "between" components, using the income data provided in table 6.2. (Hint: "Within" inequality should account for 69.1 percent of all inequality.)

A similar decomposition is possible for GE(0); this breakdown of Theil's L is given by

$$
L = \sum_{i=1}^{N} \frac{1}{N} \ln\left(\frac{\bar{y}}{Y_i}\right) = \sum_{j}\left(\frac{N_j}{N}\right) L_j + \sum_{j}\frac{N_j}{N}\ln\left(\frac{\bar{y}}{\bar{y}_j}\right).
\tag{6.8}
$$

When we have information on a welfare measure for two time points, we are often interested in identifying the components of the change in inequality. Defining $n_j = N_j/N$, which is the proportion of those in the sample who are in the jth subgroup, and adding the time subscripts 1 (for initial period) and 2 (for the second period), where appropriate, we have, for Theil's L

$$
\Delta L \approx \sum_{j} n_j\left[\ln\left(\frac{\bar{y}_{,2}}{\bar{y}_{,1}}\right) - \ln\left(\frac{\bar{y}_{j,2}}{\bar{y}_{j,1}}\right)\right] + \sum_{j}\left[L_j + \ln\left(\frac{\bar{y}}{\bar{y}_j}\right)\right]\Delta n_j + \sum_{j} n_j \Delta L_j.
\tag{6.9}
$$

This decomposition is accurate if the changes are relatively small, and if average values across the two periods (for example, of n_j or L_j) are used. The first term on the right-hand side measures the effect on inequality of changes in relative mean incomes; if the income of a small, rich group grows particularly rapidly, for instance, greater inequality is likely to result. The second term measures the effects of shifts in population from one group to another. Finally, the third term in equation (6.9) measures the size of changes in within-group inequality.

These decompositions may be illustrated with data on expenditure per capita for Vietnam, as set out in table 6.5. Using Theil's L, measured inequality rose appreciably between 1993 and 1998. In 1993, about a fifth of inequality was attributable to the urban-rural gap in expenditure levels (after correcting for price differences); by 1998, almost a third of inequality arose from the urban-rural gap, which widened considerably during this period. This shows up in the breakdown of the change in inequality; following equation 6.9 we have

0.039　　　　　 ≈ 0.050　　　　　　　 − 0.016　　　　　　 + 0.005.
[change in L] ≈ [effect of change in incomes] + [population shift effect] + [change in within-group inequality]

From this breakdown it appears that the rise in inequality in Vietnam between 1993 and 1998 was mainly due to a disproportionately rapid rise in urban, relative to rural, incomes. This increase was attenuated by a rise in the relative size of the urban population, but exacerbated by a modest increase in inequality within both urban and rural populations.

Similar results were found for Zimbabwe in 1995–96. A decomposition of Theil's T there showed that the within-area (within rural areas and within urban areas) contribution to inequality was 72 percent, while the between-area (between urban and

Table 6.5 Decomposition of Inequality in Expenditure per Capita by Area, Vietnam, 1993 and 1998

Area	Theil's L (GE(0))		
	1993	1998	Change
All Vietnam	0.160	0.199	**0.039**
Urban only	0.173	0.189	0.016
Rural only	0.118	0.120	0.002
Decomposition			
"Within" inequality	0.129	0.135	
"Between" inequality	0.031	0.064	
Memo: "Between" inequality as percentage of total inequality	20	32	

Source: Authors' calculations based on Vietnam Living Standards Surveys of 1992–93 and 1998.

rural areas) component was 28 percent. In many Latin American countries, the between-area component of inequality explains an even higher share of total inequality, reflecting wide differences in living standards between one region and another in countries such as Brazil and Peru.

We are often interested in which of the different income sources, or components of a measure of well-being, are primarily responsible for the observed level of inequality. For example, if total income can be divided into self-employment income, wages, transfers, and property income, the distribution of each income source can be examined. If one of the income sources were raised by 1 percent, what would happen to overall inequality? The simplest and most commonly used procedure is to compute the measure of inequality using the initial data, and then to simulate a new distribution (for instance, by raising wages by 1 percent) and recompute the measure of inequality.

Table 6.6 shows the results for the Gini coefficient for income sources in Peru (1997). As the table shows, self-employment income is the most equalizing income source. Thus, a 1 percent increase in self-employment income (for everyone that receives such income) would lower the Gini coefficient by 4.9 percent, which represents a reduction in overall inequality. However, a rise in property income would be associated with an increase in inequality.

Generally, results such as these depend on two factors:

- The importance of the income source in total income (for larger income sources, a given percentage increase will have a larger effect on overall inequality)

- The distribution of that income source (if it is more unequal than overall income, an increase in that source will lead to an increase in overall inequality).

Table 6.6 also shows the effect on the inequality of the distribution of *wealth* of changes in the value of different sources of wealth.

A final example, in the same spirit, comes from the Arab Republic of Egypt. In 1997, agricultural income represented the most important inequality-increasing source of income, while nonfarm income had the greatest inequality-reducing

Table 6.6 Expected Change in Income Inequality Resulting from a 1 Percent Change in Income (or Wealth) Source, 1997 (as Percentage of Change in Gini Coefficient), Peru

Income source	Expected change	Wealth sources	Expected change
Self-employment income	−4.9	Housing	1.9
		Durable goods	−1.5
Wages	0.6	Urban property	1.3
Transfers	2.2	Agricultural property	−1.6
Property income	2.1	Enterprises	0

Source: Rodriguez 1998.

Table 6.7 Decomposition of Income Inequality in Rural Egypt, 1997

Income source	Percentage of households receiving income from this source	Share in total income (%)	Concentration index for the income source	Percentage contribution to overall income inequality
Nonfarm	61	42	0.63	30
Agricultural	67	25	1.16	40
Transfer	51	15	0.85	12
Livestock	70	9	0.94	6
Rent	32	8	0.92	12
All sources	100	100		100

Source: Adams 1999, 32.

potential. Table 6.7 sets out this decomposition and shows that while agricultural income represents only 25 percent of total income in rural areas, it accounts for 40 percent of the inequality.

Income Distribution Dynamics

There is a longstanding, if inconclusive, debate about the links between income distribution and economic growth. Simon Kuznets (1966), based on his analysis of the historical experience of the United Kingdom and the United States, believed that in the course of economic development, inequality first rises and then falls. Although there are other cases where this pattern has been observed, it is by no means inevitable. There are many components of inequality, and they may interact very differently depending on the country. Bourguignon, Ferreira, and Lustig (2005, 2) emphasize this diversity of outcomes, and argue that changes in income distribution are largely due to three "fundamental forces":

- Changes in the distribution of assets and the personal characteristics of the population (for example, educational levels, gender, ethnicity, capital accumulation)— the *endowment effects*

- Changes in the returns to these assets and characteristics (for example, the wage rate, or profit rate)—the *price effects*

- Changes in how people deploy their assets, especially in the labor market (for example, whether they work, and if they do, in what kind of job)—the *occupational choice effects*.

To these three one might also add *demographic effects*; for instance, if households have fewer children, the earnings of working members will stretch further, and measured income per capita will rise.

In *The Microeconomics of Income Distribution Dynamics in East Asia and Latin America*, Bourguignon, Ferreira, and Lustig (2005) set out and apply an approach that is designed to allow quantification of the effects on the whole income distribution of the various changes in "fundamental forces" that occur between two time points. Over time, the way that households choose their jobs, the returns from different types of employment, and the assets (especially education) that households bring to the labor market, all change, and as they do, so does the distribution of income. Thus, the idea is to set up basic parametric models of occupational choice and earnings, to measure these at different times, and then to separate out the effects of changing returns from the effects of changing endowments.

To illustrate, consider the following simplified and stylized example. Suppose that in 1995 we find that wages are related to years of education as follows:

$$\text{In}(w_i) = 4 + 0.03ed_i - 0.00075(ed_i)^2 + \varepsilon_i. \tag{6.10}$$

Here ed_i measures years of schooling for individual i, w_i is the wage rate, and ε_i is an error term that picks up measurement error and the influences of unobserved variables (such as ability, for instance). In this case, an individual with six years of schooling could expect to earn a wage of 63.6; if the person were particularly vigorous and able, such that their actual wage were 85.9, this expression implies that for this person, the observed residual would be $e_i = 0.3$. Now suppose that in 2006 we find, on the basis of new survey data, that

$$\text{In}(w_i) = 3.9 + 0.027ed_i - 0.00085(ed_i)^2 + \varepsilon_i. \tag{6.11}$$

If the individual still has six years of schooling, and is as vigorous and able as before, we could expect his wage to be 76.1. This reflects a reduction in the return on education that appears to have occurred in this society between 1995 and 2006. However, if the individual now has nine years of education, the new wage could be expected to be 79.4. If we perform similar calculations for all individuals in a survey, we can simulate the effects on income distribution of the changes in the "fundamental forces."

The more sophisticated applications of income distribution dynamics are relatively intricate; Bourguignon, Ferreira, and Lustig (2005) provide more details. But the result of this extra effort is that one gains more insight into the factors that drive income distribution. Consider the numbers for urban Brazil shown in table 6.8. Between 1976 and 1996, inequality in income per capita fell very slightly—the Gini coefficient fell from 0.595 to 0.591—and incomes grew slightly. Yet, the incidence of severe poverty rose significantly. Ferreira and Paes de Barros (2005) argue that during this period a number of people were trapped at the bottom of the income distribution, excluded from labor markets (note the rise in the open unemployment rate), and not covered by formal safety nets. At the same time, the rate of return on education fell, but the average level of schooling rose sharply (from 3.2 to 5.3 years per person).

Table 6.8 Economic Indicators for Brazil, 1976 and 1996

Indicator	1976	1996
Gini, urban areas, income per capita	0.595	0.591
Poverty headcount rate: poverty line of 30 reais/month in 1976 prices	0.068	0.092
Poverty headcount rate: poverty line of 60 reais/month in 1976 prices	0.221	0.218
Household income per capita per month, in 1976 reais	265	276
Open unemployment rate (%)	1.8	7.0
Percentage employed in formal-sector jobs	58	32
Average years of schooling	3.2	5.3

Source: Ferreira and Paes de Barros 2005.

The net effect was to create greater equality of incomes in the middle and upper ends of the distribution, while those at the very bottom became worse off.

This type of microsimulation exercise allows one to ask questions such as how much would the Gini coefficient have changed if the only fundamental force to vary between 1976 and 1996 were a change in the return to education for wage earners? The answer in this particular case is that the Gini would have risen from 0.595 to 0.598. Or again, if the only change had been the rise in education, the Gini would have fallen from 0.595 to 0.571. By identifying effects such as these, it is possible to construct a fuller and clearer story about what has driven changes in the distribution of income over time.

Review Questions

1. You are provided with the following information:					
a. Quintile	20	20	20	20	20
b. % expenditure	7	12	15	20	46
c. Cumulative % expenditure	7	19	34	54	100
d. Expenditure/capita	350	600	750	1,00	2,300
The Lorenz curve graphs:					

    o A. a. on the horizontal axis, b. on the vertical axis.
    o B. a. on the horizontal axis, c. on the vertical axis.
    o C. a. on the horizontal axis, d. on the vertical axis.
    o D. None of the above.

2. If income is transferred from someone who is better off to someone who is less well off, the Gini coefficient always rises (Pigou-Dalton transfer sensitivity).

    o True
    o False

3. A country has five residents, whose incomes are as follows: 350, 600, 750, 1000, and 2300. Then

- ○ A. Theil's T is 0.114 and Theil's L is 0.344.
- ○ B. Theil's T is 0.444 and Theil's L is 0.344.
- ○ C. Theil's T is 0.114 and Theil's L is 0.113.
- ○ D. Theil's T is 0.444 and Theil's L is 0.344.

4. A Pen's Parade is used for comparing

- ○ A. Income distributions at two points in time.
- ○ B. Expenditure distributions at two points in time.
- ○ C. Income distributions in two different areas.
- ○ D. All of the above.

5. According to table 6.8, between 1976 and 1996 in Brazil, which did *not* occur:

- ○ A. Inequality rose (as measured by the Gini coefficient).
- ○ B. Deep poverty worsened.
- ○ C. The unemployment rate rose.
- ○ D. Income rose.

6. In decomposing inequality, which of the following is *not* true?

- ○ A. A change in Theil's L = the effect of a change in income + population shift effect + change in within-group inequality.
- ○ B. A change in Theil's L = the change in between group inequality + change in within-group inequality.
- ○ C. $L = \sum_{i-1}^{N} \frac{1}{N} \ln\left(\frac{\bar{y}}{Y_i}\right) = \sum_j \left(\frac{N_j}{N}\right) L_j + \sum_j \frac{N_j}{N} \ln\left(\frac{\bar{y}}{\bar{y}_j}\right).$
- ○ D. The change in the Gini coefficient equals $= \sum_j \left(\frac{Y_j}{Y}\right) T_j + \sum_j \left(\frac{Y_j}{Y}\right) \ln\left(\frac{Y_j/Y}{N_j/N}\right),$

7. Suppose that between 2005 and 2007, the urban-rural gap widened but inequality within urban areas stayed the same, and inequality within rural areas did not change either. This implies that between-group inequality rose relative to within-group inequality.

- ○ True
- ○ False

8. According to the Kuznets curve, in the course of economic development,

   o   A. Inequality first falls and then rises.
   o   B. Inequality first rises and then falls.
   o   C. Inequality begins high and then falls to a lower sustainable level.
   o   D. Inequality begins low and then rises to a higher sustainable level.

Note

1. Suppose that we have a statistic, θ, and would like to calculate its standard error. The statistic could be as simple as a mean, or as complex as a Gini coefficient. Using the full sample, our estimate of the statistic is $\hat{\theta}$. We could also estimate the statistic leaving out the ith observation, representing it as $\hat{\theta}_i$. If there are N observations in the sample, then the jackknife standard error of the statistic is given by $\widehat{se} = [(N-1/N)\sum_{i=1}^{N}(\theta_{(i)} - \theta)^2]^{1/2}$. Provided the statistic of interest is not highly nonlinear, the jackknife estimate typically gives a satisfactory approximation, and it is useful in cases, such as the Gini coefficient, where analytic standard errors may not exist.

References

Adams, Richard H., Jr. 1999. "Nonfarm Income, Inequality, and Land in Rural Egypt." Policy Research Working Paper No. 2178, World Bank, Washington, DC.

Araar, Abdelkrim, and Jean-Yves Duclos. 2006. "DAD: A Software for Poverty and Distributive Analysis." PMMA Working Paper 2006-10, Université Laval, Quebec.

Atkinson, A. B. 1970. "On the Measurement of Inequality." *Journal of Economic Theory* 2 (3): 244–63.

———. 1983. *The Economics of Inequality*, 2nd edition. Oxford: Clarendon Press.

Bourguignon, François, Francisco Ferreira, and Nora Lustig, eds. 2005. *The Microeconomics of Income Distribution Dynamics in East Asia and Latin America*. Washington, DC: World Bank and Oxford University Press.

Dollar, David, and Paul Glewwe. 1998. "Poverty and Inequality: The Initial Conditions." In *Household Welfare and Vietnam's Transition*, ed. David Dollar, Paul Glewwe, and Jennie Litvack. World Bank Regional and Sectoral Studies. Washington, DC: World Bank.

Duclos, Jean-Yves, and Abdelkrim Araar. 2006. *Poverty and Equity: Measurement, Policy and Estimation with DAD*. New York: Springer, and Ottawa: International Development Research Centre.

Ferreira, Francisco, and Ricardo Paes de Barros. 2005. "The Slippery Slope: Explaining the Increase in Extreme Poverty in Urban Brazil, 1976–1996." In *The Microeconomics of Income Distribution Dynamics in East Asia and Latin America*, ed. François Bourguignon, Francisco Ferreira, and Nora Lustig. Washington, DC: World Bank and Oxford University Press.

Ferreira, M. Luisa. 1996. "Poverty and Inequality during Structural Adjustment in Rural Tanzania." Policy Research Working Paper No. 1641, World Bank, Washington, DC.

Gottschalk, P., and T. Smeeding. 2000. "Empirical Evidence on Income Inequality in Industrial Countries." In *Handbook of Income Distribution. Volume 1. Handbooks in Economics, vol. 16,* ed. A. B. Atkinson and F. Bourguignon. Amsterdam, New York, and Oxford: Elsevier Science/North-Holland.

Kuznets, Simon. 1966. *Modern Economic Growth: Rate, Structure and Spread*. New Haven and London: Yale University Press.

Ravallion, Martin, and Shaohua Chen. 2003. "Measuring Pro-Poor Growth." *Economics Letters* 78 (1): 93–9.

Rodriguez, Edgard. 1998. "Toward a More Equal Income Distribution? The Case of Peru 1994-1997." Poverty Reduction and Economic Management Network, Poverty Group, World Bank, Washington, DC.

Vietnam General Statistical Office. 2000. *Viet Nam Living Standards Survey 1997–1998*. Hanoi: Statistical Publishing House.

World Bank. 1994. "Viet Nam Living Standards Survey (VNLSS) 1992–93." Poverty and Human Resources Division, World Bank, Washington, DC.

Chapter 7

Describing Poverty: Poverty Profiles

Summary

A poverty profile sets out the major facts on poverty and examines the pattern of poverty to see how it varies by

- Geography (region, urban or rural, mountain or plain, and so on)

- Community characteristics (for example, villages with and without a school)

- Household and individual characteristics (for example, educational level).

A well-presented poverty profile can be immensely useful in assessing how economic change is likely to affect aggregate poverty, even though the profile typically just uses basic techniques such as tables and graphs.

Some tables show the poverty rate for each group, for example, by level of education of household head, or by region of the country. It is good practice to show the confidence intervals of the poverty rates, which works especially well when the information is shown graphically. Alternatively, one may show what fraction of the poor have access to facilities (running water or electricity, for instance) or live in a given region, and compare this with the circumstances of the nonpoor. This chapter illustrates these concepts using a number of graphs and tables based on data from Cambodia and Indonesia.

The World Bank's *Poverty Reduction Handbook* (1992) has a long list of questions that a poverty profile should address. Provided the data are available, it is helpful to show how poverty has evolved over time. The change can often be linked to economic growth, and sometimes to specific government policies.

Most household surveys do not sample enough households to allow the analyst to break down the results at the subregional level. Yet, poverty targeting—building roads, providing grants to poor villages, and the like—typically requires such detail. One solution is to use poverty mapping: use the survey data to relate a household's poverty econometrically to a set of variables that are also available from the census; then apply the estimated regression equation to the census data to estimate whether a household is poor. This information can then be aggregated to give poverty rates for small areas.

A poverty profile is descriptive, but it serves as the basis for the analysis of poverty.

Learning Objectives

After completing the chapter on *Describing Poverty: Poverty Profiles*, you should be able to

1. Explain what a poverty profile is and why it is useful.

2. Design tables and graphs that clearly and effectively show the dimensions of poverty.

3. Show why the use of additive poverty measures, such as the Foster-Greer-Thorbecke class of measures (see chapter 4), can facilitate poverty comparisons.

4. Explain why, in making poverty comparisons over time, one must correct for differences in sampling frame and method, adjust for price differences, and ensure comparability in the measures of income or expenditure.

5. Compute the relative risk of being poor for different household groups.

6. Summarize the steps required to undertake a poverty mapping, and explain why such a mapping has practical value.

Introduction: What Is a Country Poverty Profile?

A country poverty profile sets out the major facts on poverty (and typically, inequality), and then examines the pattern of poverty to see how it varies by geography (by region, urban or rural, mountain or plain, and so on), by community characteristics (for example, in communities with and without a school), and by household characteristics (for example, by education of household head or by household size). Hence, a poverty profile is a comprehensive poverty comparison, showing how poverty varies across subgroups of society. A well-presented poverty profile can be immensely informative and extremely useful in assessing how the sectoral or regional pattern of economic change is likely to affect aggregate poverty, even though it typically uses basic techniques such as tables and graphs.

As an example, regional poverty comparisons are important for targeting development programs to poorer areas. A study of poverty in Cambodia showed that headcount poverty rates were highest in the rural sector and lowest in Phnom Penh in 1999. Figure 7.1 shows that approximately 40 percent of the rural population, 10 percent of the population of Phnom Penh, and 25 percent of other urban residents lived in households below the poverty line. Figure 7.1 also shows the 95 percent confidence interval that surrounds the estimates of the headcount index for each area. We interpret these confidence intervals to mean that we are 95 percent certain that they embrace the true poverty. They reflect sampling error; other things being equal, the larger the sample, the narrower the confidence interval.

These standard error bands can be especially helpful when the subpopulations include only a small number of observations, because the bar charts may otherwise give a misleading sense of confidence in the precision of the illustrated poverty comparison. In the Cambodian case, the sampling errors are sufficiently small to have full confidence in the conclusion that headcount poverty rates are lower in Phnom Penh than in other urban areas, which in turn are lower than in rural areas. As for

Figure 7.1 Headcount Poverty by Region, Cambodia, 1999

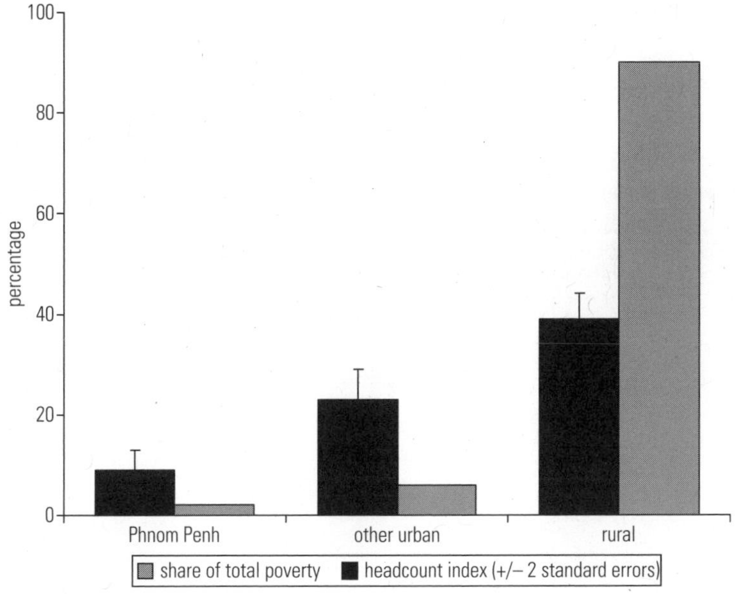

Source: Gibson 1999.

contribution to the total amount of poverty, 91 percent of people living below the poverty line live in rural areas, 7 percent live in other urban areas, and 2 percent live in Phnom Penh, as the shaded bars in figure 7.1 show.

For the next example, table 7.1 presents information on Ecuadoran households' access to services. The table shows, for instance, that 52 percent of the nonpoor have waste collection, compared with just 24 percent of poor households. On average, the poor have lower access to services. An interesting finding, however, is that *within* urban areas, the poor have almost as much access to electricity as the nonpoor; in this case, essentially all the differential between the poor and the nonpoor occurs in rural areas. Note that we have rounded the figures to the nearest percentage point to avoid giving an impression of spurious accuracy.

In a further illustration, table 7.2 shows poverty measures by household characteristics—gender and education level of household head—for Malawi in 1997–98. Clearly, the higher the education level that household heads achieve, the less likely that the household is poor. This is a standard finding, but tables such as table 7.2 help quantify the size of the effect.

Table 7.1 Selected Characteristics of the Poor in Ecuador, 1994

| | Percentage with access to basic services | | | | | |
| | Urban | | Rural | | Total | |
Service	Poor	Nonpoor	Poor	Nonpoor	Poor	Nonpoor
Sewerage connection	57	83	12	28	30	64
Electricity supply	98	100	62	76	76	91
Water from public network	61	79	18	23	35	59
Waste collection	60	77	1	6	24	52

Source: World Bank 1996.

Table 7.2 Poverty among Household Groups in Malawi, 1997–98

Household characteristics	Headcount (P_0) (percent)	Poverty gap (P_1) (percent)	Squared poverty gap (P_2)($\times$ 100)
Gender of head			
Male	58	22	11
Female	66	28	15
Education levels of head			
No education	71	31	17
Less than standard IV	63	25	13
Standard IV	58	22	11
Primary school	47	15	6
Secondary school	30	8	3
University	16	7	4

Source: Malawi National Economic Council 2000.

124

Note: Standard IV is the fourth year of primary school. Primary education follows an eight-year cycle, followed by four years of secondary school.

The World Bank's *Poverty Reduction Handbook* (1992) sets out some key questions that one may ask when preparing a poverty profile:

1. Does poverty vary widely between different areas in the country?

2. Are the most populated areas also the areas where most of the poor live?

3. How is income poverty correlated with gender, age, urban and rural, racial or ethnic characteristics?

4. What are the main sources of income for the poor?

5. On what sectors do the poor depend for their livelihoods?

6. What products or services—tradables and nontradables—do the poor sell? A tradable good is one that is, or easily might be, imported or exported. The prices of such goods are influenced by changes in the world price and the exchange rate.

7. To what extent are the rural poor engaged in agriculture? In off-farm employment?

8. How large a factor is unemployment? Underemployment?

9. What are the important goods in the consumption basket of the poor? How large are the shares of tradables and nontradables?

10. How is income poverty linked to malnutrition or educational outcomes?

11. What are the fertility characteristics of the poor?

12. To what public services do the poor have access? What is the quality of these services?

13. How important are private costs of education and health for the poor?

14. Can the poor access formal or informal credit markets?

15. What assets—land, housing, and financial—do the poor own? Do property rights over such assets exist?

16. How secure is their access to, and tenure over, natural resources?

17. Is environmental degradation linked to poverty?

18. How variable are the incomes of the poor? What risks do they face?

19. Are certain population groups in society at a higher risk of being poor than others? Households that are at high risk of being poor, but are not necessarily poor now, are considered to be vulnerable (see chapter 12 for more details about vulnerability).

A poverty profile that presents, in clear and readable form, answers to the above questions would be helpful. But the extent to which a detailed poverty profile can be constructed depends on what data are available. While certain variables, such as educational and health indicators and access to essential services, are the most basic components of a poverty profile, the relevance of many other variables depends on country circumstances. The general rule is that all variables that correlate with poverty and are relevant for policies under consideration should be included. By this rule, income-generating activities, asset positions, access to social and infrastructure services, and the composition of consumption are all of interest. Sometimes it is also helpful to compare monetary with nonmonetary measures of poverty, such as the link between per capita consumption and malnutrition.

Additive Poverty Measures

It is much easier to make poverty comparisons using an additive poverty measure, where poverty in different areas can be added up easily to get the overall poverty rate. The Foster-Greer-Thorbecke poverty measures (P_α see equation (4.6) of chapter 4) may be decomposed into the poverty rates by area. To see how this works, suppose the population can be divided into m mutually exclusive subgroups. Then a poverty profile presents poverty measures, $P_{\alpha,j}$, for $j = 1, \ldots , m$. Aggregate poverty can then be written as the population-weighted average of these subgroup poverty measures:

$$P_\alpha = \frac{1}{N} \sum_{j=1}^{m} P_{\alpha,j} N_j , \qquad (7.1)$$

where

$$P_{\alpha,j} = \frac{1}{N_j} \sum_{i=1}^{N_j} p_\alpha(z_j, y_i^j) \qquad (7.2)$$

is the poverty measure for subgroup j with population N_j. Here y_i^j is the welfare indicator of individual i who belongs to subgroup j, where $i = 1, \ldots , N_j$. The total population N is equal to $\sum_{j=1}^{m} N_j$.

An attractive feature of additive poverty measures is that they ensure "subgroup consistency." If poverty rises in any subgroup of the population, aggregate poverty will also increase, other things being equal. This makes good common sense.

Profile Presentation

There are two main ways of presenting a poverty profile. The first splits the sample by some characteristic—for instance, region of residence, or age of household head—then shows the poverty rate for each component, as in table 7.2. The second divides up the sample by poverty status (for example, poor vs. nonpoor, or by expenditure per capita quintile), then summarizes the incidence of characteristics, such as educational level, or access to piped water, for each group, as in the shaded columns in figure 7.1.

Both methods of presentation are useful, but their value also depends on the use to which they will be put. Suppose the government wants to provide cash grants to the poor, but in practice cannot identify which households are poor, and so plans to give grants only to those living in chosen target regions (indicator targeting). In this case, we would like to know which regions have the highest incidence of poverty—which we learn from the first type of profile—to minimize the amount of grants that end up in the hands of the nonpoor.

Poverty Comparisons over Time

If two or more rounds of household surveys are available, one may be able to measure the evolution of poverty over time. Ideally, such a measurement would use data from highly comparable questionnaires that use a similar sampling frame and research protocol and the same definitions of income or consumption.

One of the most difficult adjustments that has to be made when comparing monetary measures over time is for inflation. Deaton (2001) shows that the drop in the official poverty rate in India between 1993–94 and 1999–2000 was understated because the statistics office overstated inflation, and so raised the poverty line too quickly over time; we return to this case in more detail in chapter 16. If we have constructed a poverty line in the base year using the cost of basic needs approach, we just need to adjust this poverty line over time by applying the changes over time in the costs of each component of the poverty line (food, and nonfood items, typically).We can then compute the poverty rate in the second period. In practice, we might want to do this for each main region of the country, to take regional price variations into account. Alternatively, we could deflate income or expenditure from the second period and compare it with the original poverty line.

In practice, the lack of good price data, especially broken down by region over time, is a serious problem; indeed, it is the Achilles heel of intertemporal poverty comparisons. However, it is not the only problem, because household survey questionnaires tend to evolve. Such changes may adapt the surveys to better reflect the standard of living at a given time, but it makes intertemporal comparability more difficult.

But the demand for poverty comparisons over time is high, by governments, nongovernmental organizations, and others. So even if the comparisons are less than ideal, they are made nonetheless. In such cases, the analyst needs to be sure to

- Correct for major differences in the sampling frame and sampling method for the different surveys or the different rounds of a panel survey

- Use regional and temporal price indexes to ensure a similar definition of the poverty line over time and across regions (or to measure "real" income or expenditure over time)

- Adjust the definition of consumption or income aggregates over time to ensure that a similar definition is used. As noted in chapter 2, a significant problem is that more detailed questions about income or expenditure tend to yield higher values for overall income or expenditure.

To illustrate the construction and presentation of poverty rates over time, we again turn to the case of the Cambodian Socio-Economic Surveys of 1993/94 and 1997 (Gibson 1999). Table 7.3 compares the baseline poverty profile for Cambodia derived between these years. Note that the nominal value of the poverty line (consisting of the food poverty line plus a nonfood allowance equal to the level of nonfood consumption of persons whose per capita consumption just equals the food poverty line) increased by 15 percent in Phnom Penh, 11 percent in other urban areas, and 8 percent in rural areas.

The estimates in table 7.3 indicate that the incidence of poverty declined modestly in Cambodia as a whole (from 39 percent to 36 percent) during the period 1993/94 to June 1997. On a regional basis, poverty declined significantly in other urban areas (from 37 percent to 30 percent), modestly in rural areas (from 43 percent to 40 percent) and not at all in Phnom Penh (where it remained at 11 percent). During the same period, the estimates indicate that two other measures of poverty

Table 7.3 Poverty Measures for Cambodia, 1993/94 and June 1997

	Headcount index (P_0) (percent)		Poverty gap index (P_1) (percent)		Poverty severity index (P_2), × 100		Memo: Poverty line (riels/day)	
	1993/94	1997	1993/94	1997	1993/94	1997	1993/94	1997
Food poverty line								
Phnom Penh	6.2	3.4	1.3	0.5	0.4	0.1	1,578	1,819
Other urban	19.6	15.4	4.4	3.3	1.4	1.1	1,264	1,407
Rural	21.9	20.0	4.0	3.9	1.1	1.2	1,117	1,210
Total	20.0	17.9	3.7	3.5	1.1	1.1		
Poverty line								
Phnom Penh	11.4	11.1	3.1	2.2	1.2	0.6		
Other urban	36.6	29.9	9.6	7.5	3.6	2.7		
Rural	43.1	40.1	10.0	9.7	3.3	3.4		
Total	39.0	36.1	9.2	8.7	3.1	3.1		

Source: Gibson 1999.

Note: The official exchange rate was close to 2,500 riels/$ in 1993/94 and 3,000 riels/$ in 1997.

(the poverty gap and the poverty severity index) declined significantly, both in Phnom Penh and in other urban areas but not in rural areas.

Poverty measures are sometimes translated into the *relative risks* of being poor for different household groups. These risks indicate whether the members of a given group are poor in relation to the corresponding probability for all other households in society. So, for example, if the headcount poverty rate is 20 percent nationally, but 30 percent for rural households, then rural households are 50 percent more likely to be poor than the average household.

This concept can be applied to examine whether, over time, the relative poverty risk of specific population groups decreases or increases. Table 7.4 compares the relative poverty risk of various groups in Peru in 1994 and 1997. It shows, for instance, that households with seven persons or more were 71 percent more likely to be poor in 1994 than other households in society; and that this relative risk was 106 percent in 1997 (that is, they were more than twice as likely to be poor as other households in Peru). Or again, between 1994 and 1997, the relative risk of being poor for households where the spouse of the head was working diminished (from −11 percent to −21 percent).

Table 7.4 Poverty Risks for Selected Groups of Households, Peru
(percent)

Household characteristic	1994	1997
Households using house for business purposes	−28	−29
Rural households with at least one member in off-farm employment	−24	−23
Households where spouse of head was working	−11	−21
Households without water or sanitation	54	50
Households without electricity	63	69
Households where head had less than secondary education	73	72
Households of seven persons or more	71	106

Source: World Bank 1999.

Review Questions

1. A poverty profile describes the main facts on poverty and relates these to geographical, community, and household characteristics.

   o True
   o False

2. Which of the following is *not* one of the key questions that are typically addressed in a poverty profile?

   o A. How important are private costs of education for the poor?
   o B. On what sectors do the poor depend for their livelihoods?
   o C. How is income poverty correlated with gender, and with ethnic characteristics?
   o D. How has the distribution of income changed over time?

> 3. Subgroup consistency of a poverty measure means that if an individual moves into poverty, then measured poverty will increase.
>
> ○ True
> ○ False

> 4. In table 7.4, the relative risk of poverty for households without electricity was 63 percent in 1994 and 69 percent in 1997. This means that
>
> ○ A. 69 percent of poor households had no electricity in 1997.
> ○ B. Fewer poor people had electricity in 1997 than in 1994.
> ○ C. Poor households were 69 percent less likely to have electricity than nonpoor households, in 1997.
> ○ D. Households without electricity were 69 percent more likely to be poor than other households, in 1997.

Excerpts from Poverty Profiles for Indonesia and Cambodia

This section presents excerpts from poverty profiles for Indonesia and Cambodia. These give a flavor of the types of tables and figures that are typically constructed for poverty profiles, and that are well worth imitating.

Indonesia

Table 7.5 gives an example of a poverty profile in which the sampled households in Indonesia's 1987 SUSENAS (National Socioeconomic Survey) have been classified into 11 groups according to their principal income source. Results are given for the three main poverty measures discussed above. The following points are noteworthy:

- In the absence of adequate information on urban versus rural prices, Ravallion and Huppi (1991) assumed an urban-rural cost-of-living differential of 10 percent. Although this appears to be a reasonable assumption, their results are sensitive to this assumption.

- The poverty measures are based on the estimated population distributions of persons ranked by household consumption per person, where each person in a given household is assumed to have the same consumption. Household-specific sampling rates have been used in estimating the distributions.

- In forming the poverty profile, households have been grouped by their stated "principal income source." Many households have more than one income source. In principle, one could form subgroups according to the various interactions of primary and secondary income sources, but this would rapidly generate an

Table 7.5 Sectoral Poverty Profile for Indonesia, 1987

Principal sector of employment	Population share (percent)	Headcount index (P_0) (percent)	Poverty gap index (P_1) (percent)	Poverty severity index (P_2), × 100
Farming				
Self-employed	41.1	31.1	6.42	1.97
Laborer	8.6	38.1	7.62	2.21
Industry				
Urban	3.0	8.1	1.26	0.32
Rural	3.4	19.4	3.00	0.76
Construction	4.3	17.4	2.92	0.80
Trade				
Urban	6.3	5.0	0.71	0.17
Rural	7.6	14.7	2.42	0.61
Transport	4.1	10.7	1.53	0.34
Services				
Urban	7.6	4.2	0.61	0.14
Rural	7.3	11.6	1.84	0.49
Other	6.7	17.1	3.55	1.03
Total	**100.0**	**21.7**	**4.22**	**1.24**

Source: Huppi and Ravallion 1991.

unwieldy poverty profile; as a general rule, it is important to keep poverty profiles straightforward and uncluttered.

- The three measures are in close agreement on the poverty ranking of sectors. For example, the two farming subgroups are the poorest by all three measures.

Changes in the poverty profile may arise from the contributions of different subgroups to changes over time in aggregate poverty. Table 7.6 provides information on the relative contribution of various sectors to aggregate poverty alleviation in Indonesia between 1984 and 1987. These are the "intrasectoral effects," expressed as a percentage of the reduction in aggregate poverty for each poverty measure. For instance, 11 percent of the reduction in poverty (as measured by P_0) between 1984 and 1987 was due to the fall in poverty among farm laborers. The table also gives the aggregate contribution of shifts in population and the interaction effects between sectoral gains and population shifts.

The drop in poverty among self-employed farmers had the largest influence on aggregate poverty reduction, and most particularly on the reduction in the severity of poverty as measured by P_2. About 50 percent of the reduction in the national headcount index was due to gains in this sector, while it accounted for 57 percent of the gain in P_2. Note that the rural farm sector's impressive participation in the reduction of aggregate poverty is due to both significant declines in its poverty measures, and the large share of national poverty accounted for by this sector.

Furthermore, 13 percent of the decline in the national headcount index was due to population shifts between various sectors of employment, mainly because people

Table 7.6 Sectoral Decomposition of the Change in Poverty in Indonesia, 1984–87

Principal sector of employment	Population share,1984 (percent)	Contribution of sectoral change		
		Headcount index (P_0) (percent)	Poverty gap index (P_1) (percent)	Poverty severity index (P_2), × 100
Farming				
Self-employed	45.0	49.8	54.6	57.4
Laborer	9.0	11.2	14.8	16.5
Industry				
Urban	2.6	0.8	0.4	0.3
Rural	3.3	2.8	3.1	2.7
Construction	4.1	3.2	2.6	2.2
Trade				
Urban	5.4	2.2	1.6	1.4
Rural	6.6	7.2	5.6	4.7
Transport	3.8	3.6	2.7	2.2
Services				
Urban	6.5	1.0	1.0	0.9
Rural	5.8	2.9	2.4	2.0
Total sector effects (including omitted sectors)	n.a.	89.3	93.8	95.1
Contribution of population shifts	n.a.	13.2	10.4	9.4
Interaction effects	n.a.	–2.6	–4.3	–4.5
Total	**100.0**	**100.0**	**100.0**	**100.0**

Source: Adapted from Huppi and Ravallion (1991).

Note: n.a. = Not applicable. Minor sectors omitted.

moved out of high-poverty into low-poverty sectors. The sectors that gained in population share were almost all urban (Huppi and Ravallion 1991), and had initially lower poverty measures. The fact that population was moving out of the rural sector, where poverty was falling faster, accounts for the negative interaction effects in table 7.6.

Cambodia

A basic breakdown of Cambodian poverty rates by region in 1999 is given in figure 7.1. The figure shows that at least 85 percent of the poor are concentrated in rural areas. Some more detailed figures are shown in table 7.7, using data from the Cambodia Socio-Economic Survey of 1999. Data in 1999 were collected in two rounds, and table 7.7 contains estimates for each round (and the pooled sample) of the three main poverty statistics, and also reports the results from the previous surveys for comparison.

An interesting feature of these results is that there is substantial discrepancy in the poverty estimates from the two survey rounds in 1999. The headcount index is

Table 7.7 Comparisons of Poverty Estimates from Cambodian Surveys

	Headcount index (P_0) (percent)	Poverty gap index (P_1) (percent)	Poverty severity index (P_2), × 100
SESC 1993/94	39.0	9.2	3.1
1997 CSES (as adjusted by Knowles [1998])	36.1	8.7	3.1
1997 CSES (unadjusted)	47.8	13.7	5.3
	(1.5)	(0.7)	(0.3)
CSES 1999 (Round 1)	64.4	23.9	11.3
	(2.3)	(1.3)	(0.8)
CSES 1999 (Round 2)	35.9	6.5	2.0
	(2.4)	(0.7)	(0.4)
CSES 1999 (both rounds combined)	51.1	15.4	6.7
	(1.8)	(0.9)	(0.5)

Sources: Gibson 1999; Knowles 1998.

Note: The exchange rate was close to 3,000 riels/$ in 1997 and 3,800 riels/$ in 1999. SESC = Socio-Economic Survey of Cambodia; CSES = Cambodian Socio-Economic Survey. No sampling errors (reported in parentheses for the other years) are reported by the first two poverty profiles, but the relative errors for SESC 1993/94 and the adjusted 1997 CSES would likely be higher than the relative error in 1999 because the sampling scheme used previously was not as efficient (fewer clusters and broader stratification). The poverty line used for the unadjusted 1997 CSES results takes values of 1,923 riels per person per day in Phnom Penh, 1,398 in other urban, and 1,195 in rural.

almost 30 percentage points higher for round 1 than for round 2, while the poverty gap and poverty severity indexes are between four and six times higher. These troubling differences are also large relative to the variation across previous survey estimates of poverty in Cambodia, and would need to be investigated and fully discussed in a serious poverty profile. If the discrepancies between the two survey rounds are ignored, and the data are pooled, the resulting poverty estimates are fairly similar to the unadjusted 1997 estimates, showing a slight increase in all three poverty measures (table 7.7).

The pattern of poverty with respect to the age group of the household head is reported in table 7.8, based on round 2 of the Cambodia Socio-Economic Survey of 1999. It is apparent that poverty rates rise with age, reaching a maximum for the 36- to 40-year-old group of household heads, and then decline. A similar pattern was reported in the 1997 poverty profile. Once again, the definition of headship and its economic interpretation may confound the results, so a more detailed examination would be needed before any interventions might be designed on the basis of these age patterns. For example, the household head need not be the major economic contributor to the household; respondents may simply have nominated the oldest or most senior member. Thus, the relatively low poverty rate for people living in households whose head is age 61 years and above may reflect the wealth accumulation that this elderly head has achieved, or it could be that there is a younger generation within the household whose economic success is sufficient to allow them to support their elders within the same household. As a general rule, it is wise not to put too much

Table 7.8 Distribution of Poverty by Age and Gender of Household Head in Cambodia, 1999

	Headcount index (P_0)		Poverty gap index (P_1)		Poverty severity index (P_2), × 100		Share of total population (percent)
	Index (percent)	Contribution to total (percent)	Index (percent)	Contribution to total (percent)	Index	Contribution to total (percent)	
	35.9	100.0	6.5	100.0	2.0	100.0	100.0
Age of head							
18–30 years	36.7	10.7	5.6	9.1	1.4	7.5	10.5
31–35 years	35.4	10.9	5.4	9.2	1.6	8.8	11.1
36–40 years	43.6	21.2	8.0	21.6	2.7	23.3	17.5
41–45 years	40.3	15.7	7.3	15.8	2.2	15.3	14.0
46–50 years	36.5	14.4	7.7	16.9	2.4	16.9	14.2
51–60 years	28.3	15.8	5.3	16.3	1.7	16.8	20.0
61 and above	32.0	11.3	5.6	11.1	1.8	11.3	12.7
Male	36.4	84.4	6.6	84.2	2.1	85.1	83.3
Female	33.6	15.7	6.1	15.8	1.8	14.9	16.7

Source: Gibson 1999, based on round 2 of the CSES of 1999.

emphasis on breakdowns by household head, given the problems involved in its definition. Reflecting this, the United States Census no longer even asks who the head of the household is; it has also become less socially acceptable to identify a "head" of household in the United States.

Note that the poverty level is lower among female-headed households in Cambodia. This is not unusual in Southeast Asia. Often a finer breakdown is more helpful—for instance, households headed by widows, by married women with an absent husband (who may send remittances home), and so on.

There are two reasons why widow-headed households, and households where there has been a dissolution (that is, separation or divorce), could be at greater risk of poverty. The loss of an economically active household member, as would occur with the death of a husband in war, for example, is likely to cause a large income shock that could push a household into poverty. The second factor, and the one that links marital status with household size, is that households headed by widows tend to be smaller than average, which will constrain the effective living standards of their members if there are economies of scale in household consumption.

In Cambodia, the headcount poverty rate in 1999 increased smoothly with household size to a maximum rate for households with eight members (figure 7.2). In the round 1 data, the highest headcount poverty rate was for households with nine members. A relationship like that shown in figure 7.2 needs to be treated with caution, because it does not control for economies of scale in household consumption: large households may have lower expenditures (per capita), not because their members are poor but because they do not need to spend as much per person to reach the

Figure 7.2 Poverty by Household Size, Cambodia, 1999

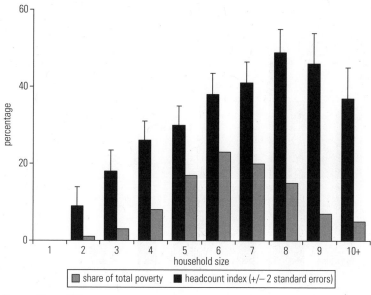

Source: Gibson 1999.

same standard of living. However, there is some evidence that such economies of size are relatively unimportant for Cambodian households, in which case the pattern shown by figure 7.2 may be a useful basis for identifying the poor.

Previous poverty profiles showed that poverty rates were relatively high among those whose household heads either had no schooling or had only primary schooling. Poverty rates then fall with the attainment of lower secondary education, fall farther with upper secondary, and are almost zero if the household head is a university graduate. But those whose household heads had a technical or vocational or other form of education had a higher poverty rate than those with primary schooling (at least in the 1997 poverty profile), for reasons that are not entirely clear. This is a good example of a case where the poverty profile raises questions that require further examination.

According to the survey estimates, there was little difference in 1999 in poverty rates between those whose household heads has no schooling and those whose heads has some primary education (figure 7.3). Although the survey estimate of the headcount poverty rate is slightly higher for the primary schooled group, the estimates for both groups are surrounded by wide and overlapping confidence intervals. One possible explanation for this somewhat surprising result is that primary education is of very low quality, so it adds little to one's earning ability. The finding is in line with evidence from a number of other countries that suggests that a secondary education is required to truly pull someone out of poverty.

Figure 7.3 Poverty by Education Level of Household Head, Cambodia, 1999

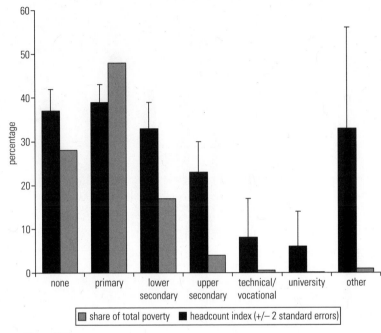

Source: Gibson 1999.

Poverty Mapping

It is still unusual for living standards surveys to sample more than 10,000 households because of the high cost of administering long and complex questionnaires. A corollary is that poverty rates based on these surveys can only be disaggregated reliably to the level of a handful of broad regions. For example, the Cambodian Socio-Economic Survey of 1999 allowed one to estimate poverty for Phnom Penh, other urban areas, and rural areas, but not reliably for every district in the country.

Yet we are often interested in a more detailed poverty map that would show poverty rates for relatively small geographic units, because even within a given region there are typically wide divergences in standards of living, and hence poverty. Relatively detailed poverty maps can, in principle, improve the targeting of interventions. In designing poverty alleviation projects and allocating subsidies, resources will be used more effectively if the neediest groups can be better targeted, which both reduces the leakage of transfer payments to nonpoor persons and reduces the risk that poor persons will be missed by a program. Poverty maps can also help governments articulate their policy objectives. Basing allocation decisions on observed geographic poverty data rather than on subjective rankings of regions increases the transparency of government decision making and thus can help limit the influence of special interests in allocation decisions. There is a role for well-defined poverty maps in lending credibility to government and donor decision making.

But detailed poverty maps cannot be generated from survey data alone. The problem is that if one tries to use the survey data to measure poverty in each district, those estimates would be based on just a few observations, and so would be too imprecise to be useful. To illustrate this, suppose that we wish to measure the headcount poverty rate (P_0), and that our survey data give an estimated poverty rate of $\hat{P}_0 = 0.30$ with a standard deviation of $s = 0.40$. We are interested in knowing how accurate our estimated poverty rate really is. If we were to redo the survey on a new sample, our estimated poverty rate would not be quite the same, simply because of sampling error.

For reasonably large samples (above about 30 or so), we may invoke the central limit theorem to argue that the estimate of the poverty rate is approximately normally distributed, with mean μ and variance σ^2/N, where N is the sample size, so $\hat{P}_0 \sim N(\mu, \sigma^2/N)$ Using estimated values for the mean and variance, we may create confidence intervals: there is a 95 percent probability that the true poverty rate is in the interval (0.289, 0.311) if the sample size is 5,000; but if we only have 30 observations—from a single cluster of households, for instance—then the 95 percent confidence interval for the poverty rate would be (0.157, 0.443). At this level of detail, the estimate of the poverty rate is too imprecise to be of any real value.

One solution is to increase the size of the sample of households surveyed. This is the approach taken by Vietnam, which has 64 provinces and cities, each of which wants its own measure of poverty (and other indicators of welfare, such as per capita expenditure)—both to evaluate the performance of provincial governments, and to help determine the size of subsidies paid by the central to the provincial authorities. The Vietnam Living Standards Survey of 1992/93 sampled 4,800 households, but the Vietnam Household Living Standards Survey of 2006 interviewed 9,189 households.

An alternative solution is to *combine the survey data with census data to create more detailed poverty maps*. Household surveys generate rich data, from which one may estimate such measures as expenditure, income, and poverty, but they cover relatively few households. Conversely, census data (and sometimes large household sample surveys) are available for all households (or very large samples of households) and can provide reliable estimates at highly disaggregated levels such as small municipalities, towns, and villages. But censuses do not contain the income or consumption information necessary to yield reliable indicators of the level and distribution of welfare such as poverty rates or inequality measures.

The basic idea is to use the detailed survey data to construct a "model" of consumption expenditure (or any other household- or individual-level indicators of well-being) as a function of variables that are common to both the household survey and the census. For example, a simple model might take the form

$$\ln(y_i) = \mathbf{X}'_i \mathbf{b} + e_i,$$

(7.3)

where y_i is expenditure per capita (or some other welfare measure) for the ith household, and the matrix $\mathbf{X}_i$ includes variables common both to the survey and to the census, such as household size, the educational level of the household head, the proportion of the household consisting of prime-age adults, and sometimes information about the quality of housing.

The second step uses the estimates from equation 7.3, along with census data on the X_i variables, to get predicted values of y_i for every household in the country. These predicted values can then be used to measure poverty at a much more disaggregated level. This whole process is often referred to as small-area estimation (or "micro-level estimation").

We now need to ask how accurate these disaggregated measures are. Elbers, Lanjouw, and Lanjouw (2003) distinguish three types of error:

- *Model error*. Model error occurs because the model in equation (7.3) is not known exactly; the coefficients are estimated ($\hat{\mathbf{b}}$) and are subject to error. The importance of this source of error depends on how tightly model (7.3) fits the data.

- *Computation error*. Typically quite small, computation error is due to the need (in many cases) to use simulation techniques in the estimation process.

- *Idiosyncratic error*. This is the error that arises because we do not observe, in the census, all the characteristics of the household that are relevant when measuring welfare. This source of error becomes more important as we try to measure welfare for smaller and smaller target populations (for example, a village or ward rather than a region or country).

Elbers, Lanjouw, and Lanjouw (2003) illustrate both the uses and limits of small-area estimation using data from Ecuador. The 1994 Encuesta sobre las Condiciones de Vida[1] obtained 4,391 usable responses from households, which allowed a reasonably accurate measurement of poverty rates at the level of eight regions, but was clearly inadequate for measuring poverty at the level of each of the country's thousand parishes (*parroquias*). However, the 1990 census counted about 2 million households, and collected information on a range of demographic variables such as household size, age, education, occupation, housing quality, language, and location.

Elbers, Lanjouw, and Lanjouw (2003) fit models similar to (7.3) separately for each of the eight regions, using data from the 1994 Encuesta; they also allowed for correlation within the clusters of primary sampling units, a refinement explained more fully in their paper. They then drew groups of 100 households randomly from

Table 7.9 Mean and Standard Error of Headcount Poverty Rate for Different Sample Sizes, Rural Costa Province, Ecuador, 1994

	Number of households			
	100	1,000	15,000	100,000
Estimated headcount poverty rate ($\hat{P}_0$)	0.46	0.50	0.51	0.51
Estimated standard error	0.067	0.039	0.024	0.024

Source: Elbers, Lanjouw, and Lanjouw 2003.

the 1990 census data for the rural Costa region, and grouped these into units of 1,000 households, 15,000 households, and 100,000 households. The results of this experiment are shown in table 7.9, which displays the estimated headcount poverty rate, and standard error of this measure, for the different sizes of units. At the level of 100 households, the standard error of the estimate of the headcount poverty rate is 0.067. This is a large number; roughly, it implies that with 95 percent probability, the true poverty rate is in the interval 0.33 to 0.59, which is too high a level of imprecision for the results to be very useful. However, the precision at $N = 15,000$ is essentially the same as at $N = 100,000$, so this technique does—in Ecuador at least—allow one to measure poverty fairly reliably at the level of a medium-size town.

The gain in precision from wedding survey to census data is illustrated in table 7.10, which is based on Table II in Elbers, Lanjouw, and Lanjouw (2003). For each of the eight regions of Ecuador, column (2) shows the standard error of the estimated poverty rate, based directly on the survey data, along with the population in each region (column (3)). Elbers, Lanjouw, and Lanjouw then use small-area estimation, following the steps outlined above, to measure poverty at the parish level (or at the level of zones, in the urban provinces of Quito and Guayaquil). These are a hundred times less populous (see column (5)) than the regions, yet have roughly the same standard errors. In other words, small-area estimation allowed for a hundred times more disaggregation for a given level of reliability than the use of survey data alone would permit.

How useful is this result? Elbers, Lanjouw, and Lanjouw (2003) caution that even at the parish level in Ecuador, poverty targeting would be highly imperfect because only 15 percent of rural inequality is due to differences *between* parishes; the remaining 85 percent of rural inequality is due to inequality within parishes. Even at the local level, living standards in Ecuador are heterogeneous; thus, interventions designed to ameliorate poverty by targeting poorer parishes will

• Help many nonpoor (the more affluent residents of poor parishes)

• Leave out many poor (the poor residents in rich parishes).

Thus, even a sophisticated poverty mapping has serious limitations as a practical guide to geographic targeting.

Table 7.10 Standard Errors of Estimates of Headcount Poverty Rates, for Survey Data and for Small-Area Estimation, Ecuador, 1994

Area	Sample data only (regions)		Combined data (parishes, zones)/Small-area estimation	
	Standard error of estimate (2)	Population (thousands) (3)	Standard error of estimate, median (4)	Population median (thousands) (5)
Rural Sierra	0.027	2,509	0.038	3.3
Rural Costa	0.042	1,985	0.046	4.6
Rural Oriente	0.054	298	0.043	1.2
Urban Sierra	0.026	1,139	0.026	10.0
Urban Costa	0.030	1,895	0.031	11.0
Urban Oriente	0.050	55	0.027	8.0
Quito	0.033	1,193	0.048	5.8
Guayaquil	0.027	1,718	0.039	6.5

Source: Elbers, Lanjouw, and Lanjouw 2003.

For a recent application to Vietnam, see Minot and Baulch (2002); discussions of the methodology may be found in Hentschel et al. (2000); Elbers, Lanjouw, and Lanjouw (2000); and Alderman et al. (2000).

Automating Poverty Profiles: The ADePT 2.0 Program

The creation of poverty profiles requires some computer programming proficiency, and can be time consuming. In an effort to make the process easier and quicker, the World Bank has developed a package within Stata that makes it simpler to generate a number of standard tables and graphs. The package is programmed as an *.ado file, and may be installed by first opening Stata and then typing, in the command line, net install adept, replace from(http://siteresources.world bank.org/INT POVRES/Resources). To use the package one needs a computer that is working with Microsoft Windows, has Microsoft Excel, and is using version 9.2 or higher of Stata.

After the program has been installed, it suffices to type adept within Stata to invoke the program, which then prompts the user for, at a minimum, information on the welfare indicator of interest (for example, expenditure per capita), household ID, a binary variable that measures the urban or rural location of the household, the size of the household, and the poverty line. It allows, but does not require, the user to provide information on a number of other variables, including region and sampling weights; and it will also handle data from multiple years. The program then generates a series of tables (that it puts into an Excel file) and graphs (which are put into *.emf image files).

It took the authors less than half an hour, using ADePT, to generate 10 tables and two graphs using basic data from the Vietnam Household Living Standards Survey of 2006. To illustrate the sort of output that the program generates, two examples are provided here. Table 7.11 (which corresponds to table 3.2a in ADePT) provides three measures of inequality, both for Vietnam overall and separately for urban and rural areas, based on real expenditure per capita. It then separates inequality into that part that is due to differences between groups, and that occurring within groups. Although it depends somewhat on the measure used, about a fifth of inequality is attributable to the urban-rural divide; most inequality is within these broad areas, with more inequality within the urban than the rural areas. Figure 7.4 also provides information on the distribution of expenditure per capita for the country at large, and for urban and rural areas. The vertical lines in the figure represent the means of the respective distributions.

While the ADePT 2.0 program offers convenience, it is most useful at providing a first draft of a poverty profile. Ultimately, it is desirable to recheck all the numbers using one's own Stata commands—they may not always agree with the ADePT version—but this becomes much easier once ADePT has helped clarify what breakdowns of the data are likely to be useful.

Table 7.11 Decomposition of Inequality (in Expenditure per Capita) by Urban and Rural Areas, in Vietnam, 2006

Component of inequality	Theil's L index GE(0)	Theil's T index GE(1)	GE(2)
Overall inequality			
2006	24.7	27.9	45.0
Urban	23.2	25.2	37.2
Rural	17.3	18.8	26.7
Within-group inequality			
2006	18.8	21.4	37.8
Between-group inequality			
2006	5.9	6.5	7.2
Between-group inequality as a percentage of overall inequality			
2006	24.0	23.2	16.1

Source: Table generated by ADePT 2.0 program, using data from the Vietnam Household Living Standards Survey of 2006.

Note: See chapter 6 for an explanation of GE(0), GE(1), and GE(2), the generalized entropy components of inequality.

Figure 7.4 Distribution of Real Expenditure per Capita, Vietnam, 2006

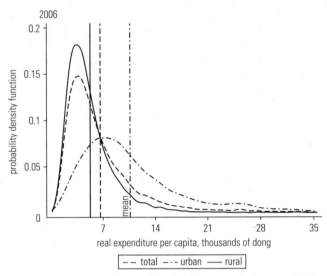

Source: Authors, based on Vietnam Household Living Standards Survey, 2006.

Review Questions

5. In table 7.6, the single largest contributor to the reduction in poverty in Indonesia between 1984 and 1987 was:

   ○ A. The reduction in poverty among farmers.
   ○ B. Workers leaving agricultural employment and moving to the cities.
   ○ C. Lower rates of urban poverty.
   ○ D. Slower population growth.

6. According to figure 7.2, in Cambodia in 1999,

   ○ A. The headcount poverty rate was highest for six-person households.
   ○ B. Eight-person households contributed the most to overall poverty.
   ○ C. Poverty among three-person households was significantly lower than among four-person households. .
   ○ D. We are about 95% confident that the headcount poverty rate for two-person households is between 4% and 17%.

7. The steps taken in poverty mapping include all of the following *except*:

   ○ A. Build a model of the determinants of consumption, based on household survey data.
   ○ B. Use the household survey data to compute poverty rates for small areas within the country.
   ○ C. Use predicted consumption to estimate poverty rates in small areas.
   ○ D. Apply a model based on survey data to census data, and predict consumption for every household.

8. The ADePT 2.0 program is designed to:
○ A. Work as a stand-along program to generate standard tables and graphs quickly and easily.
○ B. Work within Stata to generate standard tables and graphs quickly and easily.
○ C. Work well to generate measures of poverty, provided that sample weights are not used.
○ D. Work well at generating specialized measures of inequality.

Note

1. This is a living standards measurement survey; see http://go.worldbank.org/MSCLPQKKY0 for further details.

References

Alderman, Harold, Jere Behrman, Victor Lavy, and Rekha Menon. 2000. "Child Nutrition, Child Health, and School Enrollment: A Longitudinal Analysis." CARESS Working Paper 97–21, University of Pennsylvania Center for Analytic Research and Economics in the Social Sciences.

Deaton, Angus. 2001. "Computing Prices and Poverty Rates in India, 1999–2000." Working Paper, Research Program in Development Studies, Princeton University.

Elbers, Chris, J. O. Lanjouw, and Peter Lanjouw. 2000. "Welfare in Villages and Towns: Micro-Measurement of Poverty and Inequality." Tinbergen Institute Working Paper No. 2000-029/2. Revised version: 2002. "Micro-Level Estimation of Welfare." Policy Research Working Paper No. 2911, World Bank, Washington, DC.

———. 2003. "Micro-Level Estimation of Poverty and Inequality." *Econometrica* 71 (1): 355–64.

Gibson, John. 1999. "A Poverty Profile of Cambodia, 1999." Report to the World Bank and the Ministry of Planning, Phnom Penh.

Hentschel, Jesko, Jean Olson Lanjouw, Peter Lanjouw, and Javier Poggi. 2000. "Combining Census and Survey Data to Trace the Spatial Dimensions of Poverty: A Case Study of Ecuador." *The World Bank Economic Review* 14 (1): 147–66.

Huppi, Monika, and Martin Ravallion. 1991. "The Sectoral Structure of Poverty during an Adjustment Period: Evidence for Indonesia in the Mid-1980s." *World Development* 19 (12): 1653–78.

Knowles, James C. 1998. "An Updated Poverty Profile for Cambodia – 1997: Technical Report." Ministry of Planning, Phnom Penh.

Malawi National Economic Council. 2000. "Profile of Poverty in Malawi, 1998: Poverty Analysis of the Malawi Integrated Household Survey, 1997–98." Lilongwe.

Minot, Nicholas, and Bob Baulch. 2002. "The Spatial Distribution of Poverty in Vietnam and the Potential for Targeting." Policy Research Working Paper No. 2829, World Bank, Washington, DC.

Ravallion, Martin, and Monika Huppi. 1991. "Measuring Changes in Poverty: A Methodological Case Study of Indonesia during an Adjustment Period." *World Bank Economic Review* 5 (1): 57–82.

Vietnam General Statistics Office. *Vietnam Household Living Standards Survey 2006.* Hanoi.

World Bank. 1992. *Poverty Reduction Handbook.* Washington, DC: World Bank.

———. 1996. *Ecuador Poverty Report.* World Bank Country Study. Washington, DC: World Bank.

Chapter 8

Understanding the Determinants of Poverty

Summary

A poverty profile describes the pattern of poverty, but is not principally concerned with explaining the causes of poverty. Yet, a satisfactory explanation of why some people are poor is essential if we are to be able to tackle the roots of poverty.

Among the key causes, or at least correlates, of poverty are

- *Region-level characteristics*, which include vulnerability to flooding or typhoons, remoteness, quality of governance, and property rights and their enforcement

- *Community-level characteristics,* which include the availability of infrastructure (roads, water, electricity) and services (health, education), proximity to markets, and social relationships

- *Household and individual characteristics,* among the most important of which are

  - *Demographic,* such as household size, age structure, dependency ratio, gender of head

  - *Economic,* such as employment status, hours worked, property owned

  - *Social,* such as health and nutritional status, education, shelter.

Regression analysis is commonly undertaken to identify the effects of each of these characteristics on income (or expenditure) per capita. Attention is needed to choose the independent variables carefully, to be sure that they are indeed exogenous. A number of more exotic techniques are now available for this purpose, including classification and regression tree (CART) models and multiple-adaptive regression splines (MARS models).

Regression techniques are good at identifying the immediate, proximate causes of poverty, but are less successful at finding the deep causes; they can show that a lack of education causes poverty, but cannot so easily explain why some people lack education.

Learning Objectives

After completing the chapter on *Understanding the Determinants of Poverty*, you should be able to

1. Identify the main immediate ("proximate") causes of poverty.

2. Classify the main causes of poverty by characteristics related to the country or region, the community, and the household and individual.

3. Explain how regression techniques may be used to identify the proximate causes of poverty and their relative importance.

4. Explain why researchers generally prefer to use regressions to explain income (or expenditure) per capita rather than whether an individual is poor.

5. Evaluate the assertion that the weakest part of poverty analysis is the understanding of poverty's fundamental causes, and that this represents a "missing middle" that makes it difficult to define a successful antipoverty strategy.

Introduction: What Causes Poverty?

A poverty profile describes the pattern of poverty, but is not principally concerned with explaining its causes. Yet, a satisfactory explanation of why some people are poor is essential if we are to be able to tackle the roots of poverty. This chapter addresses the question of what causes poverty.

Poverty may be due to national, sector-specific, community, household, or individual characteristics. This chapter summarizes some of the characteristics of the poor by region, community, household, and individual characteristics and then discusses how regression techniques can be used to determine the factors "causing" poverty.

Two cautions are in order. First, it can be difficult to separate causation from correlation. For instance, we know that poor people tend to have low levels of education; but are they poor because they have little education, or do they have little education because they are poor? A statistical association alone is not enough to establish causality, and additional information is likely to be required.

Second, most of the "causes" of poverty that we identify in this chapter are immediate (or "proximate") causes, but not necessarily "deep" causes. For instance, suppose that we can demonstrate that low levels of education do indeed increase the risk of poverty. This is interesting, but now begs the question of why some people have low levels of education in the first place: Were the school fees too high? Was there no school nearby? Was the quality of the education abysmal? Were their parents unsupportive, or even hostile to education? Was there a concern that an educated woman could not find a husband?

The weakest part of poverty analysis—what Howard White and David Booth (2003) call the "missing middle"—is developing a clear understanding of the fundamental causes of poverty in a way that leads naturally to an effective strategy to combat poverty. Because there is no reason to believe that the root causes of poverty are the same everywhere, country-specific analysis is essential.

Region-Level Characteristics

At the regional (or countrywide) level, numerous characteristics might be associated with poverty. The relationship of these characteristics with poverty is country specific. In general, however, poverty is high in areas characterized by geographical isolation, a low resource base, low rainfall, and other inhospitable climatic conditions. For example, many argue that economic development in Bangladesh is severely retarded because of its susceptibility to annual floods; and Nghe An province in north-central Vietnam is poor in part because it is regularly hit by typhoons, which destroy a significant part of the accumulated stock of capital. In many parts of the world the remoteness of rural areas—which lowers the prices farmers get for their goods and raises the prices they pay for purchases because of high transport costs— is responsible for generating food insecurity among the poor. Inadequate public services, weak communications and infrastructure, as well as underdeveloped markets, are dominant features of life in rural Cambodia, as in many other parts of the world, and clearly contribute to poverty.

Other important regional and national characteristics that affect poverty include good governance; a sound environmental policy; economic, political, and market stability; mass participation; global and regional security; intellectual expression; and a fair, functional, and effective judiciary. Region-level market reforms can boost growth and help poor people, but they can also be a source of dislocation. The effects of market reforms are complex, deeply linked to institutions and to political and social structures. The experience of transition, especially in countries of the former Soviet Union, shows that market reforms in the absence of effective domestic institutions can fail to deliver growth and poverty reduction, at least initially.

Inequality is also relevant to the analysis of poverty; its measurement is the subject of chapter 6. Gender, ethnic, and racial inequality are both dimensions of—and

147

causes—of poverty. Social, economic, and ethnic divisions in regions are often sources of weak or failed development. In the extreme, vicious cycles of social division and failed development erupt into internal conflict (within or across regions), as in the Balkans and Liberia, with devastating consequences for people.

Community-Level Characteristics

As with regional characteristics, a variety of community-level characteristics may be associated with poverty for households in that community. At the community level, infrastructure is a major determinant of poverty. Indicators of infrastructure development often used in econometric exercises include proximity to paved roads, availability of electricity, proximity to large markets, availability of schools and medical clinics in the area, and distance to local administrative centers. Other indicators of community-level characteristics include average human resource development, access to employment, social mobility and representation, and land distribution.

Recently, there has been more emphasis on the importance of social networks and institutions, and "social capital," which includes, for instance, the level of mutual trust in the community (Putnam 1995). In addition to removing social barriers, effective efforts to reduce poverty require complementary initiatives to build up and extend the social institutions of the poor. Social institutions refer to the kinship systems, local organizations, and networks of the poor and can be thought of as different dimensions of social capital. Research on the roles of different types of social networks in poor communities confirms their importance. An analysis of poor villages in north India, for example, shows that social groups play an important role in protecting the basic needs of poor people and in reducing risk (Kozel and Parker 2000). A study of agricultural traders in Madagascar shows that social relationships are central; close relationships with other traders help lower transactions costs, while longstanding ties to creditors are vital sources of security and insurance (Fafchamps and Minten 1998).

How does social capital affect development? The narrowest view holds social capital to be the social skills of an individual—one's propensity for cooperative behavior, conflict resolution, tolerance, and the like. A more expansive "meso" view associates social capital with families and local community associations and the underlying norms (trust, reciprocity) that facilitate coordination and cooperation for mutual benefit. A "macro" view of social capital focuses on the social and political environment that shapes social structures and enables norms to develop. This environment includes formalized institutional relationships and structures, such as government, the political regime, the rule of law, the court system, and civil and political liberties. Institutions have an important effect on the rate and pattern of economic development.

As the World Bank (2000, 129) writes, "An integrating view of social capital recognizes that micro, meso, and macro institutions coexist and have the potential to complement one another. Macro institutions can provide an enabling environment in which micro institutions develop and flourish. In turn, local associations help sustain regional and national institutions by giving them a measure of stability and legitimacy—and by holding them accountable for their actions." Social capital is clearly a complicated characteristic and often researchers find it difficult to identify appropriate variables that measure social capital quantitatively.

Household and Individual-Level Characteristics

Some important household and individual characteristics would include the age structure of household members, education, gender of the household head, and the extent of participation in the labor force. In recent times, other components under this category have included domestic violence prevention and gender-based antidiscrimination policies. The following discussion organizes these characteristics into groups and discusses them in greater detail. These groups are demographic, economic, and social characteristics.

Demographic Characteristics

Indicators of household size and structure are important in that they show a possible correlation between the level of poverty and household composition. Household composition—the size of the household and characteristics of its members (such as age)—is often quite different for poor and nonpoor households. The Cambodia Socio-Economic Survey (CSES) of 1993–94 shows that the poor tend to live in larger households, with an average family size of 6.6 persons in the poorest quintile compared with 4.9 in the richest quintile (Gibson 1999). Similar patterns are found in most countries, although the effect is attenuated if welfare is measured on a per adult equivalent rather than a per capita basis. The poor also tend to live in younger households, with the bottom quintile having twice as many children under age 15 per family as the top quintile, and slightly fewer elderly people over age 60. Better-off households also tend to be headed by people who are somewhat older.

The dependency ratio is the ratio of the number of family members not in the labor force (whether young or old) to those in the labor force in the household. This ratio allows one to measure the burden weighing on members of the labor force within the household. One might expect that a high dependency ratio will be associated with greater poverty.

It is widely believed that the *gender of the household head* significantly influences household poverty, and more specifically, that households headed by women are poorer than those headed by men. This might be expected to be of particular importance in Cambodia. Because of male casualties in past wars, women are often the heads of households. Women play an important role in the labor force, both in the financial management of the household and in the labor market, but appear to face a large degree of discrimination. They are severely affected by both monetary and nonmonetary poverty; for example, they have low levels of literacy, are paid lower wages, and have less access to land or equal employment. Thus, many observers are surprised to learn that poverty rates are *not* higher among female-headed than male-headed households in Cambodia. Likewise, female-headed households in neighboring Vietnam are no more likely to be in poverty than their male-headed counterparts.

Economic Characteristics

Apart from income or consumption—which are typically used to define whether a household is poor—there are a number of other economic characteristics that correlate with poverty, most notably household employment and the property and other assets owned by the household.

There are several indicators for determining *household employment*. Within this array of indicators, economists focus on whether individuals are employed, how many hours they work, whether they hold multiple jobs, and how often they change employment.

The *property of a household* includes its tangible goods (land, cultivated areas, livestock, agricultural equipment, machinery, buildings, household appliances, and other durable goods) and its financial assets (liquid assets, savings, and other financial assets). These indicators are of interest because they represent the household's inventory of wealth and therefore affect its income flow. Furthermore, certain households, especially in rural areas, can be poor in income, but wealthy when their property is taken into consideration. Despite its importance, property is difficult to value in practice in any reliable way. First, one encounters the problem of underdeclaration. Second, it is very difficult to measure certain elements of property, such as livestock. Finally, the depreciation of assets may be difficult to determine for at least two reasons: (a) the life span of any given asset is variable, and (b) the acquisition of these assets occurs at different moments in each household. Therefore, property is more difficult to use than certain other elements in the characterization of poverty.

Social Characteristics

Aside from the demographic and economic indicators, several social indicators are correlated with poverty and household living standards. The most widely used are measures of health, education, and shelter.

Four types of indicators are normally used to characterize *health* in analyzing a household's living standards. These indicators include

- Nutritional status, for example, anthropometric indicators such as weight for age, height for age, and weight for height

- Disease status, for example, infant and juvenile mortality and morbidity rates as related to certain diseases such as malaria, respiratory infections, diarrhea, and sometimes poliomyelitis

- Availability of health care services such as primary health care centers, maternity facilities, hospitals and pharmacies, basic health care workers, nurses, midwives, doctors and traditional healers; and medical service such as vaccinations and access to medicines and medical information

- The use of these services by poor and nonpoor households.

Three types of indicators are normally used to characterize *education* in an analysis of household living standards. These include the level of education achieved by household members (basic literacy, years of education completed); the availability of educational services, such as proximity to primary and secondary schools; and the use of these services by the members of poor and nonpoor households. For this last item, commonly used measures include children's registration in school, the dropout rate of children by age and gender and reasons for dropping out, the percentage of children who are older than the normal age for their level of education, and average spending on education per child registered.

Literacy and schooling are important indicators of the quality of life in their own right, as well as being key determinants of poor people's ability to take advantage of income-earning opportunities. Based on CSES data, Cambodia by 1993–94 had achieved a self-reported basic literacy rate of 67 percent among adults (older than age 15), implying a high degree of literacy among the poor. However, the literacy gap remained quite large, with literacy ranging from just over half of adults (58 percent) among the poorest quintile of the population to 77 percent among the richest quintile. Much larger differentials appear in the distribution of schooling attainment: adults in the poorest quintile averaged 3.1 years of schooling, compared with 5.3 years among the richest quintile. Men averaged 5.1 years of education, compared with 3.2 years for women.

Shelter refers to the overall framework of personal life of the household. It is evaluated, by poor and nonpoor household groups, according to three components (some of which overlap with the indicators mentioned above): housing, services, and the environment. Housing indicators include the type of building (size and type of materials), the means through which one has access to housing (renting or ownership), and household equipment. The service indicators focus on the availability and the use of drinking water, communications services, electricity, and other energy sources. Finally, the environmental indicators concern the level of sanitation, the degree of isolation (availability of roads and paths that are usable at all times, length of time and availability of transportation to get to work), and the degree of personal safety.

> ***Example:*** It is generally established that poor households live in more precarious, less sanitary environments, which contribute to the poorer health and lower productivity of household members. To illustrate, the data from the CSES of 1993–94 show that water and sanitation are especially important influences on health and nutritional status. The CSES showed that only 4 percent of the poorest quintile had access to piped water, while more than 17 percent of the richest quintile had the same. Similar differences are apparent in access to sanitation. Just 9 percent of the poor had access to a toilet in the home, while around half of the richest quintile did.
>
> Another indicator of housing standards is access to electricity. Here again, access of the poor lagged far behind. Access to electricity from a generator or line connection rose sharply with income, from a mere 1 percent among people in the bottom quintile to 37 percent of Cambodians in the richest quintile. Other indicators of household wealth include ownership of transportation. Access to bicycles is quite evenly distributed, with at least one-half of households owning a bicycle in every quintile, even the poorest. However, access to cars, jeeps, or motorbikes is very rare among the poor and rises sharply with income.

A summary of the main influences on poverty is provided in table 8.1.

Analyzing the Determinants of Poverty: Regression Techniques

Tabulated or graphical information on the characteristics of the poor is immensely helpful in painting a profile of poverty. However, it is not always enough when one wants to tease out the relative contributions of different influences on poverty. For example, tabulated data from the Vietnam Living Standards Survey of 1998 showed per capita expenditure to be significantly higher in female-headed households than in households headed by a man. However, after controlling for other influences—where the household lived, the size of the household, and so on—the effect proved to be statistically insignificant.

By far, the most widespread technique used to identify the contributions of different variables to poverty is regression analysis, a subject treated in some detail in chapter 14. Here we simply summarize the essentials of regression, to allow this chapter to be self-contained.

Table 8.1 Main Determinants of Poverty

Regional characteristics	Isolation or remoteness, including less infrastructure and poorer access to markets and services
	Resource base, including land availability and quality
	Weather (for example, whether typhoons or droughts are common) and environmental conditions (for example, frequency of earthquakes)
	Regional governance and management
	Inequality
Community characteristics	Infrastructure (for example, piped water, access to a tarred road)
	Land distribution
	Access to public goods and services (for example, proximity of schools, clinics)
	Social structure and social capital
Household characteristics	Size of household
	Dependency ratio (that is, unemployed old and young relative to working-age adults)
	Gender of head, or of household adults on average
	Assets (typically including land, tools, and other means of production; housing; jewelry)
	Employment and income structure (that is, proportion of adults employed; type of work—wage labor or self-employment; remittances inflows)
	Health and education of household members on average
Individual characteristics	Age
	Education
	Employment status
	Health status
	Ethnicity

Source: Created by the authors.

There are two main types of analysis:

- Attempts to explain the level of expenditure (or income) per capita—the dependent variable—as a function of a variety of variables (the "independent" or "explanatory" variables). The independent variables are typically of the type discussed above in Household and Individual-Level Characteristics.

- Attempts to explain whether a household is poor, using a logit or probit regression. In this case the independent variables are as above, but the dependent variable is binary, usually taking a value of 1 if the family is poor and 0 otherwise.

We now consider each of these in somewhat more detail.

A regression estimate shows how closely each independent variable is related to the dependent variable (for example, consumption per capita), holding all other influences constant. There is scope for a wide variety of regressions; for instance, the dependent variable could measure child nutrition, or morbidity, or schooling, or other measures of capabilities; the regressions could be used to examine the determinants of employment or labor income; or regressions could be used to estimate agricultural production functions (which relate production to information on type of crops grown per area, harvest, inputs into agricultural production, and input and output prices). For an accessible discussion and many examples, in the context of Vietnam, see *Health and Wealth in Vietnam* (Haughton et al. 1999).

A typical multiple regression equation, as applied to poverty analysis, would look something like this:

$$\log\left(\frac{y_i}{z}\right)=\alpha_0+\alpha_1 X_i^1+\alpha_2 X_i^2+\cdots+\alpha_n X_i^n, \tag{8.1}$$

where z is the poverty line, y_i is per capita income or consumption, the X_i^j are the "explanatory" variables, and the α_j are the coefficients that are to be estimated. Note that y_i/z is in log form, which is a common way of allowing for the log normality of the variable. Because we are interested in the determinants of individual poverty, but typically have information at the level of the household, it is standard (but in this context, not universal) to estimate the regression using weights that reflect the size of the household. The "regress" command in Stata is flexible and allows the use of weights.

The independent (right-hand side) variables may be continuous variables, such as the age of the individual. But often we want to represent a categorical variable—the gender of the person, or the region in which he or she lives. In this case we need to create a "dummy" variable; for instance, the variable might be set to 1 if the person is a man and 0 for a woman. If there are, say, 10 regions in a country, each region would need to have its own dummy variable, but one of the regions needs to be left out of the regression, to serve as the point of reference.

Often we believe that the determinants of poverty differ from one area to the next, which would mean that there are differences in "structure." In this case we could estimate separate regressions, for instance, for each region in a country. Sometimes it is sufficient to specify the regression equation in a way that is flexible enough to allow for such differences, by allowing interactive effects. For example, one could create a variable that multiplies educational level by age, instead of estimating separate regressions for individuals in different age groups.

The fit of the equation is typically measured using $\bar{R}^2$ ("adjusted R squared"), which will vary between 0 (no fit) and 1 (perfect fit). There is no hard and fast rule for determining whether an equation fits well, although with household survey data, one is often pleased to get an $\bar{R}^2$ of 0.5 or more.

We also need to know how much confidence to place in the accuracy of the coefficients as guides to the truth; this is commonly done by reporting t-statistics, which are obtained by dividing a coefficient by its standard error. The rule of thumb is that if the t-statistic is, in absolute terms, less than 2, the coefficient is not statistically significantly different from zero (at about the 95 percent confidence level); in other words, we cannot be sure that we have picked up an effect, and it is possible that the coefficient just reflects noise in the data. Many researchers prefer to report p-values, which give the confidence level directly; a p-value of, say, 0.03 indicates that we are

Table 8.2 Determinants of Household Spending Levels in Côte d'Ivoire, about 1993

	Urban		Rural	
	Coefficient	t-statistic	Coefficient	t-statistic
Dependent variable: ln(expenditure/capita)				
Educational level of most educated male				
Elementary	0.38	5.3	0.04	0.6
Junior secondary	0.62	8.6	0.08	0.9
Senior secondary	0.80	9.6	0.05	0.4
University	0.93	9.4		
Educational level of most educated female				
Elementary	0.11	1.7	0.07	1.0
Junior secondary	0.24	3.1	0.27	2.2
Senior secondary	0.34	4.1		
University	0.52	4.1		
Value of selected household assets				
Home	0.06	5.3		
Business assets	0.04	3.3	0.16	4.9
Savings	0.08	4.7		
Hectares of agriculture land				
Cocoa trees			0.17	4.3
Coffee trees			0.04	1.3
Distance to nearest paved road			−0.04	−2.9
Distance to nearest market			−0.09	−3.3
Unskilled wage			0.37	6.4

Source: Adapted from Grosh and Munoz (1996, 169), based on Glewwe (1990).

97 percent confident that the coefficient is not 0. So we hope to find low p-values (and we usually do when working with large data sets). Arbitrarily, it is standard to consider a coefficient to be statistically significant if the p-value is less than 0.05, but this rule is not graven in stone.

Table 8.2 shows typical regression output from an example based on data from Côte d'Ivoire. Here, the dependent variable is the log of per capita household expenditure. Separate regressions were estimated for households in urban and in rural areas, on the thinking that the determinants of poverty might be quite different in these two areas.

The results of the urban equation show that education is an important determinant of expenditure per capita. The coefficients for most of the educational variables are statistically significant and quite large; having an elementary education boosts income by approximately 38 percent relative to someone with no education; this comes from the coefficient of 0.38, and the fact that the dependent variable is in log form.[1]

However, in rural areas education does not appear to explain expenditure per capita levels very well, a not uncommon finding. Conversely, the infrastructure variables have substantial predictive power: households located in villages that are nearer to both paved roads and public markets are better off, as are households living in areas with higher wage levels. The results raise further questions about the quality of education in rural areas (or its applicability in rural areas), and the importance of rural infrastructure in helping families grow out of poverty, which could be addressed in putting together a poverty reduction strategy.

It is vital to choose the independent variables carefully, and to be sure that they are truly exogenous. For instance, in the example above, one could have included income as an independent variable, along with education, assets, and the like. But that does not advance us much, because income is in turn determined by such variables as educational levels and household assets. In our drive to find the underlying causes of poverty, we need to dig deep to find variables that are indeed predetermined. A good start is to work with the variables identified in table 8.1.

When multiple cross-sectional surveys are available, the same regression can be repeated for different years to see how the association of certain correlates with income or consumption varies over time. Variations over time will be reflected in changes in coefficients or parameters. The results of repeated cross-section regressions can also be used to decompose variations in poverty by changes in household characteristics, and changes in the returns to (or impact of) these characteristics (for example, Baulch et al. 2004; van de Walle and Gunewardena 2001; Wodon 2000).

Some researchers prefer to use, on the left-hand side, a binary variable that is set equal to 1 if the household is poor, and to 0 otherwise. Some of the information is lost by doing this, and the resulting logit or probit regression is relatively sensitive to specification errors, which is why this is rarely the preferred approach. However, such an analysis is likely to be useful when designing targeted interventions (for example, educational vouchers for poor households) because it allows one to assess the predictive power of various explanatory variables used for means testing. It is also possible to undertake a multiple logit analysis, where the dependent variable could be in one of several categories, for instance, expenditure quintiles. For further details see chapter 14.

Recent research has explored more exotic forms of analysis, including nonparametric regression, classification and regression trees (CART models), and multiple-adaptive regression splines (MARS models). The goal of all such efforts is to unearth a parsimonious number of determinants of poverty, and quantify their effects, even when those effects are highly nonlinear.

Review Questions

1. By the "missing middle," White and Booth mean those households that are too affluent to be counted as poor, but too poor to be considered comfortably off.

   o True
   o False

2. Region-level characteristics that are expected to influence poverty include all of the following *except*

- ○ A. Geographic isolation.
- ○ B. Insufficient rainfall.
- ○ C. Low educational levels of households.
- ○ D. An ineffective judiciary.

3. Which of the following is *not* generally considered to be a component of social capital?

- ○ A. An individual's social skills.
- ○ B. An individual's level of education.
- ○ C. The level of mutual trust in a society.
- ○ D. The extent of the rule of law in a society.

4. The dependency ratio measures the proportion of young and old to working-age individuals in a household.

- ○ True
- ○ False

5. *Shelter* includes:

- ○ A. The type of building in which one lives.
- ○ B. Whether a household has piped drinking water.
- ○ C. The sanitation level of housing.
- ○ D. All of the above.

An analyst estimates the following regression equation, based on household survey data:

Ln(expenditure/capita)

$$= 2.1 + 0.3 \text{ (has elementary education)} - 0.03 \text{ (distance to nearest paved road)}$$
$$t = 5.7 \quad t = 4.1 \quad\quad\quad\quad\quad\quad t = -1.5$$

The value of R^2 is 0.37. Expenditure per capita is measured in thousands of dollars per year. The following three questions refer to this equation:

6. Are the signs of the coefficients plausible?

- ○ Yes
- ○ No

7. Are all the coefficients significantly different from zero with at least 95% probability?

- ○ Yes
- ○ No

> 8. Achieving elementary education will raise expenditure per capita by $300 per year.
>
> o True
> o False

Note

1. Strictly speaking, in this case it boosts income by $e^{0.38} - 1 = 0.462 = 46.2\%$. For small changes it is common to ignore this refinement.

References

Baulch, Bob, Truong Thi Kim Chuyen, Dominique Haughton, and Jonathan Haughton. 2004. "Ethnic Minority Development in Vietnam: A Socio-Economic Perspective." In *Economic Growth, Poverty and Household Welfare in Vietnam*, ed. Paul Glewwe, Nisha Agrawal, and David Dollar. Washington, DC: World Bank.

Fafchamps, Marcel, and Bart Minten. 1998. "Relationships and Traders in Madagascar." MSSD Discussion Paper No. 24, International Food Policy Research Institute, Washington, DC.

Gibson, John. 1999. "A Poverty Profile of Cambodia, 1999." Report to the World Bank and the Ministry of Planning, Phnom Penh.

Glewwe, Paul. "1990. Investigating the Determinants of Household Welfare in Côte d'Ivoire in 1985." Living Standards Measurement Study Working Paper No. 29, World Bank, Washington, DC.

Grosh, Margaret E., and Juan Muñoz. 1996. "A Manual for Planning and Implementing the Living Standards Measurement Study Surveys." LSMS Working Paper Series No. 126, World Bank, Washington, DC.

Haughton, Dominique, Jonathan Haughton, Sarah Bales, Truong Thi Kim Chuyen, and Nguyen Nguyet Nga. 1999. *Health and Wealth in Vietnam: An Analysis of Household Living Standards*. Singapore: Institute of Southeast Asian Studies.

Kozel, Valerie, and Barbara Parker. 2000. "Integrated Approaches to Poverty Assessment in India." In *Integrating Quantitative and Qualitative Research in Development Projects*, ed. Michael Bamberger. Washington, DC: World Bank.

Putnam, Robert D. 1995. "Bowling Alone: America's Declining Social Capital." *Journal of Democracy* 6 (1): 65–78.

Smith, Stephen C. 2005. *Ending Global Poverty: A Guide to What Works*. New York: Palgrave Macmillan.

van de Walle, Dominique, and Dileni Gunewardena. 2001. "Sources of Ethnic Inequality in Vietnam." *Journal of Development Economics* 65 (1): 177–207.

Vietnam General Statistics Office. 2000. *Viet Nam Living Standards Survey 1997–1998*. Statistical Publishing House, Hanoi.

White, Howard, and Richard Booth. 2003. "Using Development Goals to Design Country Strategies." In *Targeting Development: Critical Perspectives on the Millennium Development Goals*, eds. Richard Black and Howard White. London and New York: Routledge Studies in Development.

Wodon, Quentin T. 2000. "Poverty and Policy in Latin America and the Caribbean." Technical Paper No. 467, World Bank, Washington, DC.

World Bank. 2000. *World Development Report 2000/2001: Attacking Poverty*. Washington, DC: World Bank.

Chapter 9

Poverty Reduction Policies

Summary

Given a description and analysis of poverty, what policies may be invoked to reduce poverty?

There is a very strong link between economic growth and poverty reduction; Dollar and Kraay (2002) found, based on a study of 418 "episodes" worldwide that a 1 percent increase in per capita income is associated with a 1 percent increase in the incomes of the poor. The relationship is robust and has not changed over time. Although a number of policy variables, as measured by economic openness, the rule of law, and fiscal discipline, appear to boost economic growth, they do not have a discernible independent effect on the incomes of the poor.

The World Bank classifies its antipoverty activities into three groups:

- *Fostering opportunity*—through well-functioning and internationally open markets, and investments in infrastructure and education.

- *Facilitating empowerment*, which amounts to including people in the decision-making process. This requires government accountability, strong media, local organizational capacity, and mechanisms for participation in making decisions.

- *Addressing income security*, which tackles the problem of vulnerability. This calls for insurance programs, disaster relief procedures, and a solid public health infrastructure.

The chapter concludes with a brief sketch of poverty reduction policies in Tanzania.

Learning Objectives

After completing the chapter on *Poverty Reduction Policies*, you should be able to

1. Explain the methodology used by Dollar and Kraay to reach the conclusion that growth is good for the poor.

2. Evaluate the role of other influences—including government spending, openness to trade, democracy, fiscal discipline, and the rule of law—on the growth of incomes, and of the incomes of the poor.

3. Describe what is meant by "pro-poor growth."

4. For each of the three groups of antipoverty activities identified by the World Bank, that is,

   • promoting opportunity,

   • facilitating empowerment, and

   • enhancing income security,

   justify the importance of each broad activity and identify specific policies within each of these activities that are likely to work to reduce poverty.

Introduction

Previous chapters have discussed the concept of poverty and well-being, the various indicators used to measure poverty, the idea of poverty profiles, and the factors that determine poverty. In this chapter, we address a more difficult question: What policies might one pursue in an effort to reduce, or at least alleviate, poverty?

Is Growth Good for the Poor?

Few economists doubt that economic growth is necessary for the long-term reduction of poverty. But how close is the link between the two? If the incomes of the poor rise closely in line with incomes overall, the key to poverty reduction is rapid economic growth; however, if the relationship is weak, other policies, such as targeted subsidies, are likely to be important and the concept of "pro-poor growth" has more relevance.

David Dollar and Aart Kraay have addressed the problem directly, in a paper entitled "Growth is Good for the Poor" (Dollar and Kraay 2002). They gathered information on the per capita incomes of the poor (defined as those in the bottom quintile of the income distribution) and on overall per capita income. The data come from 137 countries over the period 1950–99. Dollar and Kraay were able to piece together 418 "episodes"—periods with an interval of at least five years during which it was possible to measure changes in the income of the poor and of the country overall.

They first regressed the log of per capita income of the poor (ln(poor)) on overall per capita income (ln(inc)) and got

$$\ln(\text{poor}) = 1.07 \ln(\text{inc}) -1.77. \quad R^2 = 0.88. \tag{9.1}$$

This relationship and the underlying data are reproduced in figure 9.1 (top panel). Two points are worth noting: First, the relatively high value of R^2 means that 88 percent of the variation in the log of per capita income of the poor is associated with changes in the log of per capita income overall. Second, the coefficient on the ln(inc) term is 1.07, which means that when average incomes are 10 percent higher, the incomes of the poor can be expected to be about 10.7 percent higher. This coefficient is close to 1, so perhaps it would be wiser to conclude that the incomes of the poor tend to rise and fall in line with incomes in the country as a whole.

As an alternative, Dollar and Kraay regressed the change in ln(poor) on the change in ln(inc), where these changes are typically measured (at an annualized rate) over intervals of at least five years. In this case they found (see figure 9.1, bottom panel)

$$\Delta\ln(\text{poor}) = 1.19 \, \Delta\ln(\text{inc}) - 0.007. \quad R^2 = 0.49. \tag{9.2}$$

The fit is weaker in this equation, with only about half of the variation in the change in the log of incomes of the poorest quintile being associated with changes in the log of overall income. The elasticity (1.19) is still close to unity. A reasonable interpretation of these results is that while the association between average income and the income of the poor is very strong over the long term, there is considerably more variation in the medium term; this raises the possibility that other influences on the income of the poor may be important, especially over a horizon of several years.

To test the robustness of their results, Dollar and Kraay estimated a number of variations on the original equation—adding dummy variables to account for different time periods, for countries that are growing and countries that are shrinking, for low- and high-growth countries, for poor countries and rich. They addressed the issues of measurement error (it washes out), omitted variable bias (the use of instruments gives similar results), and endogeneity (systems estimators also give similar results). They also included a number of measures of "policy," designed to capture the effects of economic openness, macroeconomic management, the size of government, the rule of law, and financial development. A sampling of these results is reproduced in table 9.1; the strongest conclusion is that the log of per capita income of the poor moves in synch with the log of per capita income in the country as a

Figure 9.1. Relating the Income of the Poor to Average Incomes

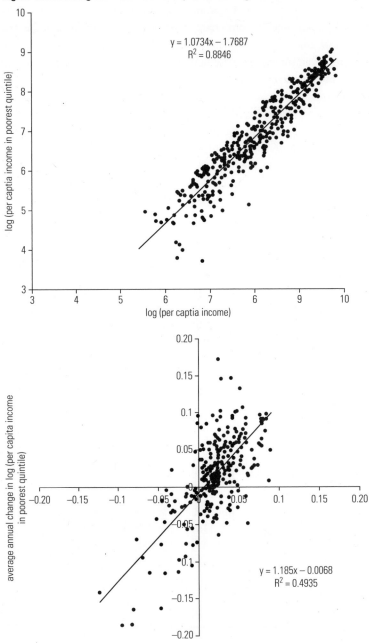

Source: Dollar and Kraay (2002, figure 1).

Note: The top panel graphs the log of per capita income of those in the poorest quintile (vertical axis) against average per capita income (horizontal axis); the bottom panel graphs the changes in these magnitudes.

Table 9.1 Growth Determinants and the Incomes of the Poor

Variable	Coefficient	Standard error
ln(per capita GDP)	1.020	0.128***
(exports + imports)/GDP	−0.067	0.208
government consumption/GDP	0.401	1.013
ln(1 + inflation)	−0.216	0.077***
commercial bank assets/total bank assets	0.264	0.282
rule of law	−0.011	0.071
Memo items		
Number of observations		137
p-value for hypothesis that first coefficient ≠ 1		0.876

Source: Dollar and Kraay 2002, table 5.

Note: Dependent variable is ln(per capita GDP) for those in the poorest quintile. The estimates shown here instrumented the ln(per capita GDP) variable, and included regional dummy variables (not shown here). Standard errors are corrected for heteroskedasticity.
*** denotes significantly different from 0 at the 1 percent level.

whole, and this conclusion holds whether a country is poor or rich, growing or shrinking, or whether one looks at earlier or more recent decades. However, with the exception of macroeconomic management (as measured by the inflation rate), none of the policy variables has any discernible additional effect.

Other researchers have also found that poverty trends tracked growth trends very closely in the 1980s and 1990s. According to Chen and Ravallion (2001), on average, growth in the consumption of the poorest fifth of the population tracked economic growth one-for-one over this period. In the vast majority of countries that they studied, growth led to rising consumption in the poorest fifth of the population, while economic decline led to falling consumption.

Dollar and Kraay conclude that their results imply that "policies that raise average incomes are likely to be central to successful poverty reduction strategies" (2002, 4). These might include improvements in education, health, infrastructure, and the like; but "existing cross-country evidence ... provides disappointingly little guidance as to what mix of growth-oriented policies might especially benefit the poorest in society" (Dollar and Kraay 2002, 27). This does not imply that growth is the only thing that matters for improving the position of the poor, but it does show how difficult it is to identify robust policies, other than those that enhance economic growth, that might make a large and sustainable difference to those at the bottom of the income distribution.

Pro-Poor Growth

If the incomes of the poor are closely tied to overall economic growth, how much room remains for a poverty reduction policy? Put another way, how much substance is there in calls for "pro-poor" growth?

In a controversial paper, Aart Kraay (2004, 1) argues that "in the medium run, most of the variation in changes in poverty is due to growth, suggesting that policies and institutions that promote broad-based growth should be central to pro-poor growth." He goes on to argue, "most of the remainder is due to poverty-reducing patterns of growth in relative incomes," but "cross-country evidence provides little guidance on policies and institutions that promote these other sources of pro-poor growth." In other words, we do not know enough about what drives pro-poor growth—roughly, growth accompanied by a reduction in inequality— to be in a position to design viable pro-poor policies.

The important qualifier here is "in the medium run," because the evidence shows that in the short run, meaning over a period of five years or so, changes in distribution can overwhelm the effects of income growth on poverty rates. To see this, it is helpful to decompose the change in poverty rates into a component resulting from growth, and a component resulting from changes in distribution.

Suppose that we have information on poverty rates, as shown by one of the Foster-Greer-Thorbecke measures, for a country at two points in time ($P_{\alpha,t=0}$ and $P_{\alpha,t=1}$), based on data that are reliable enough to allow for a viable comparison between the two. We would like to determine the extent to which the change in poverty is due to a rise in mean expenditure (for a given distribution), and the extent to which the change is due to a change in the distribution of expenditure (for a given mean level of expenditure). Datt and Ravallion (1991) propose the following decomposition (see Ravallion 1992, 54):

$$P_{\alpha,t=1} - P_{\alpha,t=0} = \text{growth component} + \text{redistribution component} + \text{residual}$$
$$= (P^{*}_{\alpha,t=1} - P_{\alpha,t=0}) + (P^{**}_{\alpha,t=1} - P_{\alpha,t=0}) + \text{residual}$$

Here, $P^{*}_{\alpha,t=1}$ is an estimate of poverty in the second period that is found by grossing up the first-period expenditure of every individual in the survey by β (where β is the average growth rate of expenditure between the two periods) and then recomputing the poverty rate; it measures the change in poverty that would have occurred if there were no change in the distribution of expenditure. The redistribution component, $P^{**}_{\alpha,t=1}$, is measured by reducing second-period expenditure by its average growth rate; by comparing this with $P_{\alpha,t=0}$—which now has the same mean—we can isolate the effect of changes in the distribution of expenditure. In practice there will also be a residual, which is typically quite small.

Table 9.2 presents information on headcount poverty rates in the mid- and late 1990s, and again early in the new millennium, for a selection of countries. It decomposes the changes in the poverty rates into the growth component, the distribution component, and a residual. In some cases these pull in the same direction: the poverty rate in Moldova fell from 51 percent in 1998 to 29 percent by 2003; this 22 percentage point drop was largely the result of growing incomes, but income distribution became

Table 9.2 Growth and Distribution Effects of Poverty

Country	Starting survey year	End survey year	Headcount index (P_0) in starting year	Headcount index (P_0) in end year	Gini in starting year	Gini in end year	Decomposition of change in headcount index (P_0)		
							Growth component	Distribution component	Residual
Brazil	1998	2004	22.7	19.8	0.598	0.570	0.9	-3.7	0.0
China, rural	1996	2001	72.5	71.0	0.336	0.363	-2.2	0.4	0.2
China, urban	1996	2001	9.7	6.5	0.291	0.333	-6.9	6.0	-2.3
Jordan	1997	2002/03	7.4	7.5	0.364	0.389	-3.3	4.6	-1.2
Madagascar	1993	2001	46.3	61.0	0.461	0.475	13.6	3.3	-2.1
Moldova	1998	2003	51.2	29.1	0.391	0.351	-17.8	-1.8	-2.5
Nigeria	1996/97	2003	77.9	71.0	0.520	0.436	-3.6	-2.3	-1.0
Pakistan	1998/99	2002	13.6	17.8	0.330	0.306	7.7	-2.9	-0.3
Peru	1996	2002	28.4	32.1	0.462	0.547	-5.7	9.4	0.0
Ukraine	1996	2003	16.4	5.0	0.351	0.281	-3.9	-8.4	0.9

Source: Tables D.2 and D.4 in World Bank (2006).

more equal over the same period, which helped lower poverty even more rapidly. Madagascar had a less happy experience: between 1993 and 2001, incomes fell and income distribution worsened. These combined to raise the poverty rate from 46 percent to 61 percent.

Sometimes growth and distribution tug in opposite directions. Between 1996 and 2002, the poverty rate actually increased in Peru, despite some growth in incomes. This increase was due to a sharp worsening in the income distribution. The poverty rate also rose in Pakistan at about the same time, but in this case incomes fell, and the rise in poverty would have been worse but for an improvement in the distribution of income.

The central conclusion is that even if the growth effects dominate in the medium term, distributional considerations play a non-negligible role.

Ravallion (2007) makes this case more strongly, arguing that inequality is bad for the poor. First, he argues that economic development does not inevitably require a period of rising inequality; then he finds that when countries are more unequal, overall growth translates less successfully into higher incomes for the poor; and he suggests that more unequal countries may often grow less rapidly in the first place. These are important arguments and merit some further explanation.

Using data from 290 pairs of surveys in 80 countries over the period 1980-2000, Ravallion graphs the percentage change in the Gini coefficient between one survey and the next against the percentage change in real per capita income (or expenditure) over the same interval. He estimates the coefficient of correlation to be 0.13, and finds that it is not statistically significantly different from zero. In other words, there is no robust correlation between economic growth and changes in inequality, and, on average, economic growth tends to be distributionally neutral. These results also imply that rising inequality is not inevitable as countries grow and develop, a conclusion that is somewhat at odds with the finding by Simon Kuznets that (at least for the United States and the United Kingdom) inequality first worsens and then improves in the course of economic development.

Now define the *elasticity of poverty reduction* (ε) as the percentage change in the poverty measure divided by the percentage change in per capita income (or expenditure). For instance, if per capita income rises by 10 percent and, as a result, the headcount poverty rate falls from 20 percent to 19 percent (that is, by 5 percent), then $\varepsilon = -0.5$. We expect ε to be a negative number and typically find that it lies in the range of $[-3.5, -0.5]$.

Again using survey results from multiple countries over the period 1980–2000, Ravallion finds that, in practice, the elasticity of poverty reduction is smaller (absolutely) in countries in which income is distributed more unequally. More specifically, he found that when the Gini coefficient of inequality is very low, the elasticity of poverty reduction is about –4, but when the Gini coefficient rises to 0.6 (which represents very considerable inequality), the elasticity of poverty reduction is close to zero. The relationship is statistically significant, if not watertight. The finding is important, because it means that "poverty responds more slowly to growth in high inequality countries" (Ravallion 2007, 14). This suggests that countries may need to strive to keep inequality low if economic growth is to translate effectively into improvements in the position of the poorest.

There is also some evidence that countries that are more unequal grow more slowly. To the extent that this is true, then poor people in highly unequal countries "face a double handicap" (Ravallion 2007, 19): not only is national income expected to increase less rapidly, but when it does rise, the reduction in poverty will be slower. However, it would be unwise to push the argument too far; China and Vietnam have grown rapidly over the past two decades, in part because they allowed for greater inequality and the associated increase in incentives to work, invest, and take risks.

The *World Development Report 1990* (World Bank 1990) focused on tackling poverty and proposed a two-part strategy that would (a) encourage labor-intensive growth (essentially by removing antilabor biases in public policy), and (b) invest in the human capital of the poor, especially in education and health. These remain important, but in the influential *World Development Report 2000/2001: Attacking Poverty* (World Bank 2000), the World Bank broadened the analysis, separating its antipoverty—as distinct from pro-growth—activities into three groups: promoting opportunity, facilitating empowerment, and enhancing (income) security. We now consider each of these in some detail.

Opportunity

We argued in chapter 8 that, at the level of individual households, a lack of material opportunities is a direct cause of poverty. As Lustig and Stern (2000) put it, "poor people consistently emphasize the centrality of material opportunities: jobs, credit, roads, electricity, and markets for their produce, as well as schools, clean water, sanitation services, and health care."

The human, physical, natural, financial, and social assets that poor people possess—or have access to—affect their prospects for escaping poverty because these assets can enable poor people to take advantage of opportunities. For example, a study of irrigation in Vietnam (van de Walle 2000a) found that there are complementarities between education and gains from irrigation, and more specifically that households with higher education levels received higher returns to irrigation.

It is widely, if not universally, believed that well-functioning markets are helpful in generating sustainable growth and expanding opportunity for the poor. This is because poor people in most countries rely on formal and informal markets to sell their labor and products, to finance their investments, and to insure against risks. Case studies of Chile, China, Ghana, Uganda, and Vietnam show that agricultural reforms have helped raise producer prices for small farmers by eliminating marketing boards, changing real exchange rates through broader economic reforms, lowering tariffs, and eliminating quotas (for an example, see Haughton and Kinh [2003]).

The World Bank argues that robust economic growth is at the heart of generating opportunity. Growth, in turn, requires investment, both private and public. Private investment is seen as effective in creating jobs and labor income, and in turn is helped by a sound fiscal and monetary policy, stable investment rules, and a sound financial system. Encouragement to microenterprises—for instance, through microcredit or simplified tax and licensing procedures—and to small and medium enterprises is likely to be helpful.

However, private investment must also be complemented by public investment in expanding infrastructure and communications, and also in education and training. Many developing countries face the challenge of increasing the quality, rather than merely the quantity, of their educational systems. Getting infrastructure and knowledge to poor and remote areas can be a particular challenge because the costs are high relative to the number of beneficiaries, and there are often linguistic and other barriers that have to be tackled.

Economic growth is also likely to be enhanced by opening up to international markets, especially for countries with the infrastructure and institutions to stimulate a strong supply response (for example, call centers in Ghana, coffee farmers and garment factories in Vietnam). Therefore, the market opening needs to be well designed with special attention to bottlenecks.

Even with economic growth, measures may be needed to ensure that poor people can expand their assets. These measures might include scholarships for children from poor families; free health care for the poor; or land reform, including land redistribution (as in parts of Brazil) or titling (as in Vietnam since about 1990). In some countries, special efforts may be needed to address socially based inequality, such as underschooling of girls relative to boys, or the limited independence of women resulting from lack of access to productive means, or ethnic inequalities in access to public services. Ethnic inequalities can easily erupt into violence; civil war inevitably sets back economic development for a generation (Haughton 1998).

Empowerment

The premise underlying an emphasis on empowerment is that a lack of representation in the policy-making process, resulting from social and institutional barriers, has impeded poor people's access to market opportunities and to public sector services.[1] It follows that empowerment—defined succinctly as including people who were previously excluded in the decision making process—should help. Unfortunately, there is very little empirical evidence, to date, on how well empowerment policies along the lines discussed below contribute to reducing poverty.

Broadly, empowerment refers to being able to make informed decisions and choices effectively. But there is some disagreement about the true content of empowerment. Mahatma Gandhi emphasized self-reliance; Paolo Freire (2000) stressed the need for conscientization, for helping the poor to learn about and perceive "social, political and economic contradictions" and then to stir to act against "the oppressive elements of society." E.F. Schumacher, author of *Small is Beautiful* (1973), argues that empowerment follows when one makes up deficiencies in education, organization, and discipline. The World Bank finesses these differences by defining empowerment as "the expansion of assets and capabilities of poor people to participate in, negotiate with, influence, control, and hold accountable institutions that affect their lives" (World Bank 2002, vi). The Bank sees the four major elements of empowerment as (a) access to information, (b) inclusion and participation, (c) accountability, and (d) local organizational capacity.

State institutions must be responsive and *accountable* to poor people. In nearly every country the public sector often pursues activities that are biased against poor people, and poor people have trouble getting prompt, efficient service from the public administration. Accountability is helped when there is good *access to information.*

> ***Example:*** The Public Expenditure Tracking Survey conducted in 1996 in Uganda found that only 22 percent of the central government funds intended to support locally run schools were reaching their intended destination. By 1999–2000, after the government made the budgetary transfers public via the media and required schools to share financial information, 80–90 percent of the funds began to reach the schools for which they were intended.

Amartya Sen (1999) sees poverty as consisting of a "deprivation of capabilities," so that the poor have inadequate resources (financial, informational, and so on) to participate fully in society; in short, they are socially excluded. It follows that *inclusion*, which encompasses economic and political participation, is inherently part of the solution to poverty. The process of including the poor is likely to require the development of their social capital, the "features of social organization, such as networks, norms, and social trust that facilitate coordination and cooperation for mutual benefit" (Putnam 1995, 67). Social capital takes time to build, but contributes to stronger *local organizational capacity.*

Good social institutions—kinship, community organizations, and informal networks—can play an important role in poverty reduction. For example, many development programs succeed because they mobilize local groups of project beneficiaries in program design and implementation. However, when social institutions are weak, fissures such as ethnic cleavages can explode into open conflict; most of the world's 20 poorest countries have experienced civil war within the past generation.

Some social norms and practices help generate and perpetuate poverty. Discrimination on the basis of gender, ethnicity, race, religion, or social status can lead to social exclusion and create barriers to upward mobility, constraining people's ability to participate in economic opportunities and to benefit from and contribute to economic growth. For example, one cross-country study indicates that countries that invest in girls' education have higher rates of economic growth (Klasen and Woolard 1999).

It is difficult to empower the poor if decision making is concentrated in a far-away capital city; hence, the conclusion that a major component of empowering the poor is the need to decentralize power, particularly through delegating it to subnational levels of government, and privatizing some activities (for example, grain marketing). Decentralization is not, however, a panacea (see Bardhan and Mookherjee [2006]); when decentralization is done badly, power may be captured by local elites, who may be even less concerned about the poor than the central government. In India, for instance, the state of Kerala has used its powers to spread development widely, while in the state of Bihar local decision making has not been particularly beneficial to the poor.

Empowerment is difficult to measure. The UNDP's Gender Empowerment Measure (GEM) includes indicators such as male and female shares of parliamentary seats, managerial positions, and earned income, but also has serious limitations in that it does not include information on the informal sector, or on such items as the right to vote. By design, the GEM focuses on gender empowerment, and not specifically on empowerment of the poor.

To empower poor people, policies needed to facilitate active collaboration among the poor and other groups in society include strengthening the participation of poor people in political processes and local decision making; making changes in governance that make public administration, legal institutions, and public services delivery more efficient and accountable to all citizens; and removing the social barriers that result from distinctions of gender, ethnicity, race, and social status. Worthy as this sounds, it is not at all obvious how to achieve such changes, but some policies that have been suggested include the following:

- To improve *access to information*, encourage the development of the media. For instance, Besley and Burgess (2002) show that there is a robust link between media development and government responsiveness in India; states with higher newspaper circulation also undertake more extensive relief efforts in the wake of natural disasters.

- To increase *participation and inclusion*, it helps to institutionalize transparent, democratic, and participatory mechanisms for making decisions and monitoring implementation. In this context, it may also be useful to provide legal assistance to poor people who usually have limited access to the legal system.

- *Accountability* is increased by strengthening the mechanisms used to monitor the performance of public administrations and by providing access to budgetary information and participatory mechanisms. There are many possible ways to do this:

    - Publication of complete and timely budgetary information. Until recently, Vietnam did not publish such information, for instance, so it was impossible to hold the government to account for how it spent its money.

    - Institutional and Governance Reviews, which use surveys and other quantitative measures to analyze the functioning of public institutions.

    - Citizen Report Cards, which allow citizens to express their opinions on the performance and quality of government services.

    - World Bank Corruption Surveys, which are designed to extract information on corruption from households, the private sector, and public officials. Based on such a survey, for instance, Albania requested an anticorruption program to undermine patronage in judicial and civil service appointments (Orhun 2004, 7).

    - Public Expenditure Tracking Surveys, which have helped ensure that budgeted funds get to their intended recipients in places such as Ghana and Uganda.

    - Private Enterprise Surveys of the Business Environment, and Investor Roadmaps. These indicate the problems and costs faced by entrepreneurs.

    - Participatory Poverty Assessments. Using focus groups, in-depth interviews, and other measures, Participatory Poverty Assessments complement survey data to help build a more detailed picture of the nature and roots of poverty; they have been influential in Vietnam, for instance.

- To increase *local organizational capacity*, it helps to do the following:

    - Promote decentralization and community development to enhance the control that poor people and their communities have over the services to which they are entitled. Decentralization needs to be combined with effective participation and monitoring mechanisms.

    - Promote gender equality by promoting women's representation in decision making and providing special assistance for women's productive activities.

    - Tackle social structures and institutions that are obstacles to the upward mobility of poor people by fostering debate over exclusionary practices and supporting the participation of the socially excluded in political processes.

    - Support poor people's social capital by assisting networks of poor people to engage with market and nonmarket institutions to strengthen their influence over policy.

Income Security

Poor people are exposed to a wide array of risks that make them vulnerable to income shocks and losses of well-being. Reducing poor people's vulnerability to ill health, economic shocks, natural disasters, and violence enhances well-being on its own and encourages investment in human capital and in higher-risk, higher-return activities as well. Although the issue of vulnerability is treated in more detail in chapter 12, a few more comments are in order here.

Households and communities respond to their risk exposures through diversification of assets and sources of income, and through various types of self-insurance and networks of mutual insurance mechanisms. For instance, some family members may travel to cities to seek work, sending remittances home; if they cannot find work they return home. Or farmers may store grain from one season to the next, in case crops fail. In a number of countries, such as Mali, some very poor rural women wear large gold ornaments—in effect carrying their savings, which could be sold if necessary to tide the household over during a bad year.

Mechanisms such as these help to reduce risks or soften the impact of negative events, but the effect may be limited. To counter the incentive and information problems that exclude poor people from many market-based insurance mechanisms, the state has, in principle, a special role in providing or regulating insurance and setting up safety nets. Health, environmental, labor market, and macroeconomic policies can all reduce and mitigate risk.

Large adverse shocks—economic crises and natural disasters—cause poor people to suffer not only in the short run. Such shocks undercut the ability of the poor to move out of poverty in the long run as well, by depleting their human and physical assets, which depletion may be irreversible. So it is crucial to prevent economic crises and be prepared to react quickly to natural disasters, as well as to protect poor people when these events occur.

National programs to manage economywide shocks and effective mechanisms to reduce the risks faced by poor people, as well as to help them cope with adverse shocks when they occur, are useful. Appropriate measures might include the following:

- Formulating programs to help poor people manage risk. Micro-insurance programs, public works programs, and food transfer programs may be mixed with other mechanisms to deliver effective risk management.

- Developing national programs to prevent and respond to macro shocks—financial or natural.

- Supporting minority rights and providing the institutional basis for peaceful conflict resolution, to help prevent civil conflict and mobilize more resource into productive activities.

- Tackling health problems, including widespread illnesses such as malaria and tuberculosis, as well as moderately common but serious conditions such as HIV/AIDS.

The World Bank (2000, 40) argues for a modular approach, "with different schemes to cover different types of risk and different groups of the population," and where "the tools include health insurance, old age assistance and pensions, unemployment insurance, workfare programs, social funds, microfinance programs, and cash transfers." These safety nets should not only support immediate consumption needs, but also "protect the accumulation of human, physical, and social assets by poor people."

There is no simple, universal blueprint for implementing this strategy for poverty alleviation and reduction. Each country needs to prepare its own mix of policies, reflecting national priorities and local realities. But there are examples of approaches that work, particularly at the level of individual projects, as the optimistic assessment by Smith (2005) illustrates.

An Example: Tanzania

Any good poverty reduction plan begins with an analysis that identifies the nature and evolution of poverty, a profile of poor people, and the factors that contribute to poverty. Building on an accurate understanding of poverty, the strategy for poverty reduction has to prioritize the poverty reduction goals and take into account complementarities and compatibilities of various policy tools. Then specific implementation modules, including resource allocation and monitoring mechanisms, need to be designed. By way of an illustration, we finish this chapter with a brief sketch of Tanzania's program for tackling poverty.

In the years following independence, the government of Tanzania focused on three development problems: ignorance, disease, and poverty. National efforts to tackle these problems were initially channeled through centrally directed, medium-term and long-term development plans; despite high levels of foreign aid, these efforts were a complete failure, and poverty was higher in 1990 than at the time of independence.

In June 2005, Tanzania issued its "National Strategy for Growth and Reduction of Poverty 2005–2010," known more commonly by its Swahili acronym MKUKUTA. The strategy is divided into three main clusters: growth and the reduction of income poverty, improvement in the quality of life and social well-being, and governance and accountability. The broad outcomes that are hoped for within each cluster are shown in table 9.3, along with the associated goals. As stated here many of the goals are rather general, although some do, in fact, have specific targets. An elaborate monitoring

Table 9.3 Summary of Tanzania's National Strategy for Growth and Reduction of Poverty (MKUKUTA)

Cluster 1: Growth and reduction of income poverty

Broad outcomes   Achieve and sustain broad-based and equitable growth

Goal 1	Ensure sound economic management
Goal 2	Promote sustainable and broad-based growth
Goal 3	Improve food availability and accessibility at the household level
Goals 4 and 5	Reduce income poverty, both for men and women, and in urban and rural areas
Goal 6	Provide reliable and affordable energy to consumers

Cluster 2: Improvement of quality of life and social well-being

Broad outcomes   Improve quality of life and social well-being, with particular focus on the poorest and most vulnerable groups; and reduce inequalities (for example, education, survival, health) across geographic, income, age, gender, and other groups

Goal 1	Equitable access to quality primary and secondary education; universal literacy among men and women; expansion of higher, technical, and vocational education
Goal 2	Improved survival, health, and well-being of all children and women, especially for vulnerable groups
Goal 3	Increased access to clean, affordable, and safe water; sanitation; decent shelter; and a safe and sustainable environment
Goal 4	Adequate social protection and provision of basic needs and services for the vulnerable and needy
Goal 5	Effective systems to ensure universal access to quality and affordable public services

Cluster 3: Governance and accountability

Broad outcomes   Good governance and the rule of law; accountability of leaders and public servants; democracy, and political and social tolerance; peace, political stability, national unity, and social cohesion deepened

Goal 1	Structures and systems of governance as well as the rule of law to be democratic, participatory, representative, accountable, and inclusive
Goal 2	Equitable allocation of public resources with corruption effectively addressed
Goal 3	Effective public service framework in place to provide foundation for service delivery improvements and poverty reduction
Goal 4	Rights of the poor and vulnerable groups are protected and promoted in the justice system
Goal 5	Reduction of political and social exclusion and intolerance
Goal 6	Improve personal and material security, reduce crime, and eliminate sexual abuse and domestic violence
Goal 7	Natural cultural identities to be enhanced and promoted

Sources: Tanzania 2005, 2007.

component is built into the process: the annual implementation report for 2006/2007 was produced by the Ministry of Planning, Economy, and Empowerment "in collaboration with a wide range of stakeholders, including government ministries, departments, and agencies, local government authorities, research and academic institutions, as well as non-state actors" (IMF 2007, 1) but was hampered by a lack of timely data and the fact that it was not integrated with the domestic budget and accountability systems (IMF 2007).

At the heart of the strategy is a strong emphasis on sustaining economic growth, which MKUKUTA states should be in the range of 6–8 percent annually. In this respect, Tanzania has seen a remarkable turnaround. In contrast to the anemic rates of economic growth in the 1990s, the real increase in GDP has exceeded 6 percent annually in every year since 2001, as figure 9.2 shows. This has been achieved in the context of sound macroeconomic management, including fairly modest rates of inflation, and adequate fiscal discipline. However, the growth has been geographically uneven, and most private credit goes to "a small number of enterprises with solid collateral in key urban areas" (Tanzania 2007, 9). Although Tanzania achieves food self-sufficiency in most years—it exported food in 2006–07—almost all agriculture is dependent on rainfall, and some regions and districts have experienced seasonal food shortages in the months before the harvest.

The second cluster in the MKUKUTA strategy aims to improve the quality of, and access to, health and education. There has been recent improvement in this goal: the net primary enrollment rate rose from 89 percent in 2003 to 97 percent

Figure 9.2 Real GDP Growth, Tanzania, 1993–2007 (in Constant Prices)

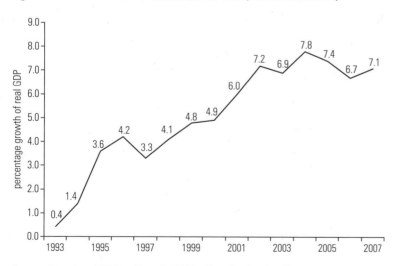

Sources: Data since 1998 from Tanzania (2008, 15); earlier data from Tanzania (2007, 4).

in 2007, and is on target to reach the goal of 99 percent by 2010. However, the quality of primary schools remains poor, with a pupil-to-teacher ratio of 53:1; fewer than three teachers in four have relevant qualifications; and there is, on average, only one textbook for every three pupils. And although half of all pupils at the start of primary education are girls, this proportion falls to a third at the level of higher education. All of these indicators are improving markedly, but the MKUKUTA goal of one textbook per pupil by 2010 is unlikely to be achieved. There have been some improvements in health, with the under-five mortality rate dropping from 147 per 1,000 in 1999 to 112 per 1,000 in 2004–05, although by world standards this is still a very high rate.

The third cluster in the MKUKUTA strategy—governance and accountability—deals with many of the issues considered under the "empowerment" label above. As part of the monitoring efforts, two national surveys undertaken in 2007 asked respondents for their opinions on the efficiency of public services, and the extent of actual or perceived corruption. It is too soon to be able to judge the trends in these areas because this is the first time that such surveys have been undertaken in Tanzania, but they indicate that improvement is needed: over a third of respondents said that there is "a lot" of corruption in the police, in the legal system, and in the health services. In Dar es Salaam, over half of those who came into contact with the police (one person in five) said they paid a bribe. These findings point to the potential value of a solid structure for monitoring performance; the statement of goals and objectives is not enough, and will achieve little unless there is follow through, which, in turn, is usually helped by the availability of good data and sound analysis—the very subjects of this book.

Review Questions

1. In reaching their conclusion that "growth is good for the poor," Dollar and Kraay (2002)

- A. Regress national poverty rates on income.
- B. Regress the log of the income of the poorest quintile on the log of total income.
- C. Regress the change in the poverty rate on the growth in income.
- D. Regress the income share of the poorest quintile on the log of income.

2. Changes in P_0 can be decomposed into all of the following *except*:

- A. A redistribution component reflecting a change in the Gini coefficient over time.
- B. A growth component reflecting change in P_0 for a given Gini.
- C. A between component, reflecting change in the rich/poor gap over time.
- D. A residual.

3. There is strong empirical evidence that empowerment policies contribute to reducing poverty.

- ○ True
- ○ False

4. Accountability has been improved by all of the following *except*:

- ○ A. Public Expenditure Tracking Surveys.
- ○ B. Citizen Report Cards.
- ○ C. Poverty Reduction Strategy Papers.
- ○ D. Institutional and Governance Reviews.

5. According to the discussion in the text, which is *not* true about Tanzania's efforts at poverty reduction?

- ○ A. GDP growth was above 6 percent per year from 2001 through 2007.
- ○ B. They include attention to governance and accountability.
- ○ C. They favor low-income provinces.
- ○ D. Sustaining growth is at the heart of the poverty reduction strategy.

Note

1. The material in this section relies heavily on Orhun (2004).

References

Bardhan, Pranab, and Dilip Mookherjee. 2006. "Decentralization, Corruption and Government Accountability: An Overview." In *International Handbook on the Economics of Corruption*, ed. Susan Rose-Ackerman. Cheltenham, UK: Edward Elgar.

Besley, Timothy, and Robin Burgess. 2002. "The Political Economy of Government Responsiveness: Theory and Evidence from India." *Quarterly Journal of Economics* 117 (4): 1415–51.

Chen, Shaohua, and Martin Ravallion. 2001. "How Did the World's Poorest Fare in the 1990s?" *Review of Income and Wealth* 47 (3): 283–300.

Datt, Gaurav, and Martin Ravallion. 1991. "Growth and Redistribution Components of Changes in Poverty Measures: A Decomposition with Applications to Brazil and India in the 1980s." Living Standards Measurement Study Working Paper No. 83, World Bank, Washington, DC.

Dollar, David, and Aart Kraay. 2002. "Growth is Good for the Poor." Development Research Group, World Bank, Washington, DC.

Freire, Paulo. 2000. *Pedagogy of the Oppressed*. 30th Anniversary Edition. New York: Continuum International Publishing Group Inc.

Haughton, Jonathan. 1998. "The Reconstruction of War-Torn Economies." Working paper, Harvard Institute for International Development, Cambridge, MA.

Haughton, Jonathan, and Hoang Van Kinh. 2003. "The Effect of Devaluation on Household Welfare in Vietnam." Suffolk University, Boston, MA.

IMF (International Monetary Fund). 2007. "United Republic of Tanzania: Poverty Reduction Strategy Paper – Annual Implementation Report – Joint Staff Advisory Note." IMF, Washington, DC.

Klasen, Stephan, and Ingrid Woolard. 1999. "Levels, Trends and Consistency of Employment and Unemployment Figures in South Africa." *Development Southern Africa* 16 (1): 3–35.

Kraay, Aart. 2004. "When Is Growth Pro-Poor? Cross-Country Evidence." Working Paper No. 04/47, International Monetary Fund, Washington, DC.

Lustig, Nora, and Nicholas Stern. 2000. "Broadening the Agenda for Poverty Reduction: Opportunity, Empowerment, Security." *Finance & Development* 37 (4).

Orhun, Zehnep. 2004. "Empowerment." Draft, World Bank Institute, World Bank, Washington, DC.

Putnam, Robert. 1995. "Bowling Alone: America's Declining Social Capital." *Journal of Democracy* 6 (1): 65–78.

Ravallion, Martin. 1992. "Poverty Comparisons: A Guide to Concepts and Methods." LSMS Working Paper No. 88, World Bank, Washington, DC.

———. 2007. "Inequality *Is* Bad for the Poor." In *Inequality and Poverty Re-Examined,* ed. Stephen Jenkins and John Micklewright. Oxford, UK: Oxford University Press.

Schumacher, Ernst Friedrich. 1973. *Small Is Beautiful: Economics as if People Mattered.* New York: Harper Perennial.

Sen, Amartya. 1999. "The Possibility of Social Choice." *American Economic Review* 89 (3): 349–78.

Smith, Stephen C. 2005. *Ending Global Poverty: A Guide to What Works.* New York: Palgrave Macmillan.

Tanzania. 2005. "National Strategy for Growth and Reduction of Poverty." Vice President's Office, Dar es Salaam. http://www.povertymonitoring.go.tz/.

———. 2007. "Poverty and Human Development Report 2007." Dar es Salaam. http://www.povertymonitoring.go.tz/.

———. 2008. Hali ya Uchumi wa Taifa Katika Mwaka 2007. Dar es Salaam.

UNDP (United Nations Development Programme. various years. *Human Development Report.* [For information on the Gender Empowerment Measure.]

van de Walle, Dominique. 2003. "Are Returns to Investment Lower for the Poor? Human and Physical Capital Interactions in Rural Vietnam." *Review of Development Economics* 7 (4): 636–53.

World Bank. 1990. *World Development Report 1990: Poverty.* Washington, DC: World Bank.

———. 2000. *World Development Report 2000/2001: Attacking Poverty.* Washington, DC: World Bank.

———. 2002. "Empowerment and Poverty Reduction: A Sourcebook." PREM, World Bank, Washington, DC.

———. 2006. *Annual Review of Development Effectiveness 2006: Getting Results.* Independent Evaluation Group. Washington, DC: World Bank.

Chapter 10

International Poverty Comparisons

Summary

The central target of the Millennium Development Goals (MDGs) is to halve, between 1990 and 2015, the proportion of people in developing countries whose income is less than $1/day. To measure progress toward this goal it is necessary to compare poverty rates across countries.

The World Bank measures world poverty by (a) establishing a dollar-valued poverty line (now $1.25 per person per day in 2005 dollars), (b) converting it to local currencies using purchasing power parity (PPP) exchange rates, (c) using local consumer price indexes to determine the local-currency poverty line for any given year, (d) estimating Lorenz curves from household survey data, (e) thereby inferring local poverty rates and levels, and (f) aggregating the results by region and worldwide. The World Bank reports that the $1.25/day poverty rate fell from 52 percent of the population of developing countries in 1981 to 25 percent by 2005, with the biggest decline occurring in East Asia (from 78 percent to 17 percent) and almost no reduction in Sub-Saharan Africa.

This approach has been criticized for using a poverty rate that is not rooted in theory; for being overly sensitive to measurements of PPP exchange rates; for not using poor-person price indexes to inflate poverty lines locally; and for not adequately recognizing the uncertainties in poverty measurement in India and China, where half of the population of the developing world lives. An alternative approach would be to compute poverty levels and rates based on basic needs, for each country (as set out in chapter 3), but this approach has its own methodological problems, and is time and labor intensive.

Household survey data understate income (and expenditure). When reconciling the results with national accounts it is tempting, but often misleading, to gross up the income of every household by the same proportion to achieve consistency with the measure of national income. Over the long run, economic growth powers poverty reduction, but in the short run the link is weaker.

Learning Objectives

After completing the chapter on *International Poverty Comparisons*, you should be able to

1. Describe the main target of the Millennium Development Goals.

2. Justify the need to make international comparisons of poverty.

3. Identify those parts of the world where poverty has fallen most quickly, and least quickly, since 1981, according to the World Bank.

4. Summarize the methodology used by the World Bank to compute world poverty rates, and explain

   • the role played by the initial choice of poverty line,

   • the need to use purchasing power parity (PPP) exchange rates,

   • the use of domestic consumer price indexes to adjust local currency poverty lines to the survey year, and

   • how the poverty rate and level is measured using a Lorenz curve and poverty line.

5. Explain and evaluate the main elements of the criticisms of the World Bank approach to measuring world poverty.

6. Explain how world poverty could be measured using a cost of basic needs approach.

7. Summarize the challenges involved in reconciling household survey data (where income and expenditure are typically undervalued) with national accounts data.

8. Recognize that while economic growth drives poverty reduction in the long run, this need not be the case in the short run.

Introduction

The first target of the MDGs is to halve, between 1990 and 2015, the proportion of people in the developing world living on less than $1/ day.[1] This naturally leads to a simple question: Are we on track to meet this goal? But to answer this question we need to be able to compare poverty rates across countries.

The World Bank and other donor and lender agencies have limited resources. Many are interested in channeling these scarce resources to countries where poverty is especially high. But to do this one again needs to be able to compare poverty rates across countries.

The approach taken by the World Bank (see, for example, Chen and Ravallion 2004, 2008) measures world poverty based on a modest amount of information from over 600 household surveys, coupled with data on purchasing power parity (PPP) exchange rates and domestic consumer price indexes. We first set out this approach, and then address two main issues: First, how should survey data be reconciled with national accounts? The difficulty here is that when one adds up consumption based on household budget survey (HBS) data, the result is typically smaller than one would expect based on national income data. Second, would it be preferable instead to use a cost of basic needs approach to measure poverty rates in each country—an approach that would avoid the use of PPP exchange rates but require more detailed examination of survey data?

Overview of Poverty Analysis

To recapitulate briefly, the key steps in the measurement of poverty are to specify a minimal socially acceptable level of income or consumption (the poverty line), implement a representative survey in which the corresponding income or consumption concept is measured, and choose and calculate a specific poverty measure. The most common implementation of these steps is to have a fixed, monetary, consumption-based threshold for poverty, with data coming from a household survey, and poverty measured as the percentage of individuals with per capita consumption below the poverty line (the headcount measure).

Even at this broad level, notice the subtle restrictions that have already emerged; we are defining poverty in absolute and not relative terms; we tend not to focus on nonmonetary measures of well-being, such as health; poverty is a concept that applies to individuals but is measured from household data; and in practice, we nearly always use the headcount measure, even though this is just one of many possible measures.

Chapter 2 discussed the need to identify the preferred indicator of welfare according to which the poverty line will be specified. For economists, the choice of indicator typically boils down to income versus consumption. There tends to be a preference for measuring poverty using consumption, especially for developing countries in which participation in the formal labor market (and the associated income paper trail) is generally limited. First, it is consumption that appears in utility functions. Second, consumption corresponds more closely to "permanent income." Third, the conceptual advantage of consumption over income is strengthened by data considerations. The measurement of income suffers from

183

deliberate understatement, measurement error, and omission of key components (for example, capital gains on infrequently marketed assets).

However, consumption also poses difficult measurement issues, especially bearing in mind that it requires data on both quantities and prices. There is relatively good experience worldwide with measurement of nondurable consumption. But we should also be including the service flow from all durable goods, and only some household surveys attempt to do this. With a perfect rental market in durable goods, this would be easy: consumption service flow would correspond to the market or shadow rent on the durable good, which in turn would equal depreciation plus opportunity cost. But durable goods markets exist for few goods and can be thin even when they do exist. We are therefore forced to make essentially arbitrary assumptions about depreciation, and the opportunity cost, of durable goods used by the poor; in particular, the standard procedure of using market interest rates as a measure of opportunity cost may make little sense for the poor, who have constrained access to capital markets.

Review Questions

> 1. International comparisons of poverty are needed for all of the following reasons except
>
> - A. To judge whether the World Bank is effective in its goal of achieving a world free of poverty.
> - B. To identify where in the world the poorest people live.
> - C. To determine each country's contribution to the International Monetary Fund.
> - D. To measure progress toward the attainment of the Millennium Development Goals.

> 2. Which of the following is not part of the normal process of determining the poverty rate in a country?
>
> - A. It is necessary to impute the rental value of a household's durable goods when measuring expenditure.
> - B. A poverty line needs to be determined.
> - C. Census data are required to determine the proportion of people who are poor.
> - D. It is assumed that members of a household have the same level of welfare.

International Poverty Comparisons

World Bank researchers Shaohua Chen and Martin Ravallion (2008) have recently undertaken a massive revision of their earlier estimates of developing world poverty. These new results are summarized in table 10.1; after commenting on the results, we discuss in more detail the underlying methodology used.

Table 10.1 Headcount Indexes: Percentage of Population in Developing Countries Living below $1.25/Day

Region	1981	1984	1987	1990	1993	1996	1999	2002	2005
East Asia and Pacific	77.7	65.5	54.2	54.7	50.8	36.0	35.5	27.6	16.8
China	*84.0*	*69.4*	*54.0*	*60.2*	*53.7*	*36.4*	*35.6*	*28.4*	*15.9*
Europe and Central Asia	1.7	1.3	1.1	2.0	4.6	4.6	5.1	4.6	3.7
Latin America and the Caribbean	11.5	13.4	12.6	9.8	9.1	10.8	10.8	11.0	8.4
Middle East and North Africa	7.9	6.1	5.7	4.3	4.1	4.1	4.2	3.6	3.6
South Asia	59.4	55.6	54.2	51.7	46.9	47.1	44.1	43.8	40.3
India	*59.8*	*55.5*	*53.6*	*51.3*	*49.4*	*46.6*	*44.8*	*43.9*	*41.6*
Sub-Saharan Africa	53.7	56.2	54.8	57.9	57.1	58.7	58.2	55.1	51.2
All developing countries	**51.8**	**46.6**	**41.8**	**41.6**	**39.1**	**34.4**	**33.7**	**30.6**	**25.2**
Memo items									
LDC poverty rate at $1.00 a day	41.4	34.4	29.8	29.5	27.0	23.1	22.8	20.3	16.1
LDC poverty rate at $2.00 a day	69.2	67.4	64.2	63.2	61.5	58.2	57.1	53.3	47.0
LDC poverty rate at $2.50 a day	74.6	73.7	71.6	70.4	69.2	67.2	65.9	62.4	56.6

Source: Chen and Ravallion 2008, table 7. Also available on the World Bank's PovcalNet.

Note: LDC = Less-developed country. $1.25 refers to prices in 2005, converted to local currency equivalents using purchasing power parity exchange rates.

The most important finding is that the proportion of people in less-developed countries living on less than US$1.25 a day (in 2005 prices) more than halved between 1981 and 2005, falling from 52 percent to 25 percent. The absolute number of poor people also fell during this time, from 1.9 billion in 1981 to 1.4 billion by 2005, with three-fifths of this reduction occurring since 1999.

Of particular note are the rapid reduction in the poverty rate in East Asia between 1981 and 2005, largely a result of the drop in poverty in China (from 84 percent to 16 percent); the rise in poverty in Europe and Central Asia (mainly in the states of the former Soviet Union) in the 1990s; and the high and relatively steady poverty rates in Sub-Saharan Africa.

The reduction in the headcount poverty rate is robust to the choice of poverty line; if a $1/day line is used, the headcount poverty rate fell from 41 percent in 1981 to 16 percent in 2005; if the line is set at $2.50 per person per day, poverty fell from 75 percent in 1981 to 57 percent in 2005. However, the choice of poverty line matters when examining the absolute number of those in poverty: using the low poverty line of $1/day, there were 1.5 billion (extremely) poor people in 1981 and 0.9 billion in 2005, but if the bar is set at $2.50/day, there were 2.7 billion poor in 1981 and 3.1 billion in 2005, representing 48 percent of total world population, and 57 percent of the population of less-developed countries, at this latter date.

Estimating Poverty in the Developing World

To compare (absolute) poverty across countries, it is first necessary to establish a poverty line. Chen and Ravallion (2008) argue that an appropriate standard is US$1.25 per person per day, in 2005 prices. They base this on the mean of the poverty lines in the poorest 15 countries in their sample.[2] The *mean* level of consumption per person in these countries was US$1.40 per day in 2005; once consumption per person rises above about US$2.00 per day, the poverty line itself begins to rise, as we saw in chapter 3. It appears that the poverty line is robust to the choice of the set of poor countries used to compute it.

Before these recent revisions, the World Bank used a "dollar a day" poverty line. It was actually based on the purchasing power of US$1.08 per person per day in 1993, and in their earlier work Chen and Ravallion (2001, 2004) argued that this line was representative of the poverty lines used in very poor countries at that time.

A major practical problem arises in the conversion of local poverty lines, which are denominated in local currencies, into US dollars, and vice versa. The problem arises because the official (or market) exchange rate is a poor guide to measuring the relative costs of living in different countries: a dollar in Boston (USA) buys less than 43 rupees in India, even when the exchange rate is 43 rupees per U.S. dollar (as was the case in mid-2008). Someone living on $500 per month in the United States would be poor; in India they would be comfortably off.

So why do exchange rates not reflect the relative purchasing powers of different currencies? The answer is that tradable goods (for example, TVs, basmati rice) have similar prices everywhere—allowing for transport costs, of course. This is not true of nontradable goods. For instance, a simple haircut in Hanoi (Vietnam) costs $0.33, while in Boston (USA) it costs $12. Despite this price differential, it does not make sense for people to fly from Boston to Hanoi to get a haircut. The standard solution to the exchange rate problem is to recompute incomes, for different countries, in a common set of international prices. First done on a large scale by the UN-sponsored International Comparison Project, this is the basis for PPP cross-country comparisons of per capita GDP.

To see how this works, suppose that we want to compare two countries, the "USA" (which uses dollars and has a million people) and "India" (which uses rupees and has 2 million people). For simplicity, suppose that these economies only produce wheat and education, with the latter only involving the cost of teachers. Assume that the USA has 1,000 teachers, each paid $30,000 annually; and produces 40,000 tons of wheat annually at $250/ton. As table 10.2 shows, total GDP will then be $40 million, for a GDP per capita of $40 per year.

Assume further that the exchange rate is 46 rupees per dollar. Wheat is a tradable good, so roughly should cost the same everywhere. Thus, in India a ton of wheat will cost 11,500 rupees. And let us suppose that teachers in India are paid 36,800 rupees annually (equivalent to $800 annually when converted at the exchange rate). No doubt, many Indian teachers would like to move to the USA to earn a higher salary, but visa restrictions do not permit this; thus, the salary differential persists. As may be seen from table 10.2, total GDP will be 174.8 million rupees, or 87.4 rupees per capita.

Table 10.2 Computing GDP per Capita in Purchasing Power Parity (PPP) Terms

	USA		India	
	Price ($)	Quantity	Price (Rs)	Quantity
Teachers	30,000	1,000	36,800	1,000
Wheat	250	40,000	11,500	12,000
GDP	$40 million		Rs 174.8 million	
			= $3.8 million at 46 Rs/$	
Population	1,000,000		2,000,000	
GDP/capita	$40		Rs 87.4	
			= $1.90 at 46 Re/$	
GDP/capita, U.S. prices	$40		$16.50	
GDP/capita, Indian prices	Rs 496.8		Rs 87.4	

Source: Author's compilation.

Using the exchange rate, Indian GDP is just $1.90 per capita, or 4.8 percent of the U.S. level. Yet, it is clear that this does not do justice to the volume of goods and services produced in India, and thus understates India's real GDP relative to that of the USA.

One solution would be to value GDP in both countries using U.S. prices. This gives a GDP per capita of $16.50 for India, or 41.3 percent of the U.S. level of $40. Alternatively, one might value GDP in both countries using Indian prices. This gives a GDP per capita of 496.8 rupees for the USA; now the Indian level is 17.6 percent of the U.S. level. In short,

	GDP per capita		
	In USA	In India	India/USA (%)
Using exchange rate, in $	40.00	1.90	4.8
Using U.S. prices ($)	40.00	16.50	41.3
Using Indian prices (rupees)	496.8	87.4	17.6

So, although it is clear that using exchange rates to compare GDP per capita is not generally appropriate, we are left with the difficult issue of what common set of prices to use instead. There is no entirely satisfactory answer to this question.

Note the numbers in our example also allow us to compute the PPP exchange rate. If U.S. prices are used, India's GDP of Rs 87.4/capita is worth $16.50, which implies a PPP exchange rate of Rs 5.3/$. Alternatively, if Indian prices are used, the US GDP of $40.00 is worth Rs 496.80, which implies a PPP exchange rate of Rs 12.4/$. Both of these are very different from the official (or market) exchange rate of Rs 43/$.

Review Questions

3. According to the World Bank, the "$1/day" poverty rate approximately halved between 1980 and 2001, and most of the reduction was due to rapid reductions in poverty in China and India.

   o True
   o False
   o Uncertain

> **4. A U.S. dollar buys fewer goods and services in the United States than a dollar's worth of dong buys in Vietnam because**
>
> - A. Inflation is higher in the United States.
> - B. Nontradable services are cheaper in Vietnam, but the dong-dollar exchange rate is mainly based on the prices of tradable goods.
> - C. Living standards are rising more slowly in Vietnam.
> - D. Vietnam deliberately keeps the dong cheap.

> **5. In the example set out in table 10.2, suppose that the exchange rate were Rs 50/$ instead of Rs 46/$. Then the value of Indian GDP/capita, using U.S. prices, would be**
>
> - A. $1.90.
> - B. $1.75.
> - C. $16.50.
> - D. $2.07.

Until about 2000, World Bank estimates of poverty used estimates of the PPP exchange rates for 1993, based on work done by the International Comparison Project (ICP) run by the United Nations and the University of Pennsylvania (the Penn World Tables). Subsequent estimates augmented these exchange rates with PPP estimates undertaken by the World Bank's Development Data Group. These estimates all showed a strong "Penn effect"—the observed finding that market exchange rates systematically understate the incomes of less-developed countries.

A more ambitious round of PPP computations was undertaken in the 2005 round of the ICP: more countries were covered, including, for the first time, China, and the price comparisons were more extensive and accurate. The most striking result of these recent revisions is that the Penn effect is less pronounced than originally thought. In other words, official exchange rates do not understate less-developed country incomes by as much as had been believed. Some of the effects of the revision are dramatic: using the 2005 ICP data, China's GDP per capita was $4,091, while previous PPP estimates had put it at $6,750.

Given a dollar-denominated poverty line, such as $1.25 a day, and a PPP exchange rate, it is straightforward to compute the poverty line in local currency. Chen and Ravallion (2008) use local consumer price indexes to compute the poverty line in other years.

> **Example:** Suppose that the poverty line is $1.25 in 2005, and the PPP exchange rate in that year is 10 pesos/US$. This gives a poverty line of 12.50 pesos in 2005. We can now back into the peso value of the poverty line in 2003 and 2004 using the local consumer price index, as shown in the table at the top of p. 187.

The next step is to use household survey data, along with the poverty line, to determine the poverty rate. If, in a given year, there was no such survey, one could

	2003	2004	2005
Consumer price index	93.5	100.0	106.2
Poverty line in local prices (pesos)	11.01 (= 12.5 x 93.5/106.2)	11.77 (= 12.5 x 100.0/106.2)	12.5

interpolate a poverty rate for the intervening years.[3] Note that here, as always, such comparisons require that the surveys be designed so that they are comparable over time.

Given estimates of poverty rates for (almost) all countries for (almost) all years since 1981, one can trace the evolution of worldwide poverty over time, as well as its geographical distribution.

Further Methodological Considerations

Although the procedure outlined above is clean and relatively straightforward, there are a number of methodological problems of which one needs to be aware.

The first problem is that the computation of PPP exchange rates is based on comparing the costs, in different countries, of a basket of goods and services—teachers and grain in our simplified example—that reflects the average consumption patterns in a country. This is not generally appropriate when our concern is with comparing living standards *for the poor*.

Conceptually, the answer is not too difficult, as Deaton (2003b) emphasizes: to construct a PPP exchange rate that is appropriate for determining a poverty line, take a benchmark consumption basket of the poor in one country and price it directly in the other countries.

> **Example:** To illustrate, using our example, suppose that the poorest quarter of the population in "India" collectively uses the services of 100 teachers and 2,400 tons of grain. This is worth $3.6 million when valued directly in dollar prices and Rs 31.28 when valued directly in rupees, which gives a PPP exchange rate for the poor of Rs 8.7/$. In this case the "poor-PPP" exchange rate, at Rs 8.7/$, is closer to the market exchange rate (Rs 43/$) than is the "average" PPP exchange rate (Rs 5.3/$), and the use of the average PPP exchange rate—which is standard practice—would lead to the construction of a poverty line for India that is unduly low. To the extent that poor households consume relatively high amounts of tradable (relative to nontradable) goods, there would be a tendency for this procedure systematically to understate poverty lines in poor countries.

In practice, such computations are almost never done. They may not even be practical; it may be impossible to value the consumption basket of a poor Indonesian (cassava, rice, chili sauce, dried fish) in the United States (or other comparator country, such as India), where the diets of the poor are entirely different. There is also an urban bias in many of the PPP price baskets. A fuller discussion, including attention to related index number problems, is given in Alatas, Friedman, and Deaton (2004).

A second problem is that for a number of countries, PPP exchange rates are imputed, rather than estimated directly using micro-level price data. This is usually done by estimating a regression along the lines of

$$erPPP/er = a + b \times \text{literacy rate} + c \times \text{food consumption/capita} + \ldots$$

where erPPP is the PPP exchange rate, and er is the market exchange rate, for countries for which PPP computations have been made.[4] The estimated equation is then used to predict the PPP exchange rate for the remaining countries. Although some imputation may be unavoidable, we must recognize that it is a noisy and imperfect procedure.

The third problem is that measures of PPP exchange rates change over time. Indeed, an implication of the Penn effect is that as a country becomes richer, the gap between the PPP exchange rate and the market exchange rate narrows and eventually vanishes. Furthermore, PPP exchange rates can be affected by changes in a country's economic structure—for instance, if a country finds oil. Chen and Ravallion (2008) use just the 2005 version of PPP exchange rates to link currencies, even though they report poverty rates over a period of almost 25 years. An implication is that the degree of poverty reduction is likely to be overstated in (fast-) growing economies such as China.

One might be tempted to use the 1985 and 1993 versions of PPP exchange rates, rather than the 2005 version, for computations of the poverty rate in the earlier years. Unfortunately, the revisions to the earlier PPP exchange rates have been substantial, raising doubts about the viability of the earlier measures, at least for some countries.

In determining the poverty line within a country over time, the 2005 poverty line is adjusted using the local consumer price index (CPI). The problem here is that the CPI tracks a basket of goods consumed by the average consumer, and may not be a good guide to how the cost of living *for the poor* has evolved. In principle, it would be desirable to construct and use a "poor person's price index," but this is rarely done in practice.

The final problem is that the raw survey data may not be publicly available, so one is obliged to estimate the poverty rate based on tabulated data—for instance, data on expenditure per capita by quintile. The procedure that is typically used, and which also underpins the World Bank's interactive PovcalNet program,[5] is to fit a Lorenz curve to the data, apply the chosen poverty line, and read off the poverty rate. The procedure works relatively well, except at the tails of the distribution; but it is an approximation, so there is necessarily some loss of information in the process.

Review Questions

6. The use of PPP exchange rates to translate the $1/day standard into local currencies is noisy and imperfect because

- A. Some PPP exchange rates are imputed econometrically rather than computed directly.
- B. PPP exchange rates are not based on the consumption baskets of poor households.
- C. PPP exchange rates vary over time.
- D. All of the above.

7. Exercise

Use the World Bank's PovcalNet site to compute the poverty rates (P_0, P_1, and P_2) for Kenya for 2005 assuming (a) a poverty line of $1.25 per person per day; (b) a poverty line of $2.50 per person per day. (Note: You are on the right track if you find that the headcount poverty rate for the first of these poverty lines is 20 percent.)

Survey Data and National Accounts

Standard measures of poverty are constructed from household budget surveys (HBS). Thus, standard measures incorporate the HBS sampling frame and the HBS measure of consumption. The potential problems with this source have been long known but acquired new relevance with research on "pro-poor growth," which looks at the extent of poverty reduction arising from economic growth. There were some findings for the 1990s that poverty was not falling at the rate we would expect given economic growth, especially in India, yet there was no evidence of rising measured inequality; so where did the growth "go?"

A typical HBS is designed to be a representative sample (for example, via the most recent census). But even using a representative sample as a basis, the sample drawn from it can be systematically biased. There are actually two problems:

- *Nonresponse bias.* There is strong evidence that rich households are less likely to comply with HBS reporting.

- *Underreporting bias.* It is a general rule that richer households, when they do respond to a survey, are more likely to understate their true income (or expenditure).

These effects probably reflect a desire to conceal income or consumption, as well as the opportunity cost of time spent responding to a survey.

The first result is that upper-income households are underrepresented in the HBS, so the headcount measure of poverty is potentially overstated.

But this is not the end of the story. The macroeconomic national accounts will "see" the transactions of upper-income households in their expenditures, so they are reflected in key aggregates (national income or private consumption or both). There is a universal tendency for "average" national accounts consumption to be higher than "average" consumption as measured by grossing up the figures from the HBS. Furthermore, this gap is not simply an invariant level effect—it is systematically related to the level of development and the growth rate. As a rule of thumb, national accounts consumption exceeds HBS consumption and the divergence increases as per capita GDP rises. Deaton (2003b) reports that HBS consumption averages 86 percent of national accounts consumption, and grows about half as rapidly.

One solution to the underreporting problem is to adjust the HBS figures upward. Suppose that national consumption, based on extrapolation from HBS data, is $80 million, but national accounts indicate consumption of $90 million. Then one could adjust the HBS data by scaling consumption upward, that is, multiplying everyone's reported consumption by 1.125 (= 90/80). This would, of course, reduce the measured poverty rate.

The net effect of underreporting plus rescaling is unclear, as the example in table 10.3 shows. Suppose a society has 12 individuals, with incomes as shown in the first row of the table, and a poverty line of 130. The true headcount poverty rate is 33.3 percent. If a rich individual does not respond, the observed poverty rate rises to 36.4 percent. But if an effort is made to scale all incomes upward, the observed poverty rate would be 18.2 percent, which represents an overadjustment because one is adjusting all income categories for underreporting when the problem is confined to high-income individuals. Underreporting can have a similar effect, as the bottom panel in table 10.3 shows, in that it would raise the observed poverty rate; however, rescaling runs the risk of understating poverty, again because the problem of underreporting is not found equally in all income groups, but is generally believed to be a greater problem for high-income individuals.

Why HBS and National Accounts Totals Differ

Part of the difference in consumption measured by the HBS and by national accounts reflects different concepts of consumption. National accounts, but typically not HBSs, measure the imputed rent on housing, imputed financial intermediation (the savings-lending interest rate gap), and consumption by nonprofits. The HBS does provide a better stock-flow link than the national accounts (which do not measure changes in stocks at all), so in principle, the HBS allows "sustainable" consumption out of financial income to be separated from consumption resulting from drawing down assets. However, the practical usefulness of this feature is limited by the fact that households may not report the relevant data correctly. Furthermore, neither source properly measures consumption of publicly provided goods (such as schooling), access to which plausibly varies with income.

Table 10.3 Illustrating the Effects of Response Bias and Underreporting

	Individual number												Headcount index P_0 (percent)
	1	2	3	4	5	6	7	8	9	10	11	12	
Response bias													
True income/capita	80	100	110	121	140	220	270	310	400	490	620	750	33.3
Observed income/capita with response bias	80	100	110	121	140	220	270	310	400	490	620	Not reported	36.4
Scaled income/capita to adjust for response bias	101	126	139	153	177	278	341	391	505	618	783	—	18.2
Underreporting													
True income/capita	80	100	110	121	140	220	270	310	400	490	620	750	33.3
Observed income/capita with underreporting	80	100	108	121	125	220	250	300	400	450	560	600	36.4
Scaled income/capita to adjust for underreporting	87	109	118	132	136	240	272	327	436	490	610	654	25.0

Source: Author's illustration.

Note: To rescale for response bias, divide the sum across individuals of true income per capita by the sum across individuals of observed income per capita, then multiply by the observed income per capita for each individual. A similar adjustment is made to rescale for underreported income. The poverty line is 130.

Review Questions

8. Survey data suffer from nonresponse bias and underreporting bias, typically leading to

- A. An overstatement of the headcount poverty rate and an understatement of the degree of inequality.
- B. An overstatement of the headcount poverty rate and an overstatement of the degree of inequality.
- C. An understatement of the headcount poverty rate and an understatement of the degree of inequality.
- D. An understatement of the headcount poverty rate and an overstatement of the degree of inequality.

> 9. Rescaling household survey data on expenditure to ensure that it is consistent with national accounts data is only appropriate when trying to measure poverty if the proportion by which expenditure is underreported is the same across all expenditure groups.
>
> ○ True
> ○ False
> ○ Uncertain

Overall, though, the consumption of items missed by the HBS is correlated with wealth, both in cross-section and over time. The growth process reinforces the gap because the national accounts register the increase in market-based consumption as an economy grows—not all of which represents true economic growth. Similarly, growth shifts activities from the informal to the formal sector. However, and we will return to this point later, it is precisely because the national accounts tend to better reflect the process of wealth accumulation that the HBS measure could still be a "truer" measure of consumption *for the poor*.

Debate 1: Is World Poverty Falling?

The current debate about poverty trends is centered on the appropriate measure of consumption. Bhalla (2002) argues that the national accounts measure is more accurate. Thus, he measures the distribution of consumption from the HBS, but adjusts the level upward to correspond to the national accounts. This method results in a much lower level of measured poverty in India, because the divergence between the two sources is severe in India; and the method predicts much more optimistic trends in poverty reduction than standard projections. In fact, it implies that the world has already met, or will soon meet, the MDGs for poverty.

This debate has been conducted in most detail for India, which, because of its size, matters significantly for global poverty monitoring. However, the issues are germane for other countries as well.

Critics have focused on the fact that Bhalla uses the HBS to get the distribution of consumption but the national accounts to get the mean. He is thus assuming a very specific type of measurement error in the HBS—that all of it is in the mean, and none is in the variance. Conversely, there is an assumption that the national accounts have less measurement error in the mean than does the HBS. It is highly unlikely that the measurement errors take exactly this form. In reality, both sources have errors in both mean and variance.

Consider in particular the national accounts estimate of consumption. The fundamental macroeconomic identity gives

$$GDP \equiv C + I + G + X - IM, \tag{10.1}$$

where C is consumption spending, I is investment, G is government spending on goods and services, X is exports, and IM is imports.

In most cases, consumption spending is estimated as a residual, obtained from estimated final production (that is, GDP) less net exports, investment, and government consumption (for which relatively good data exist). For a poor country, the production estimate begins as physical volume (for example, projected crop yields multiplied by estimated crop area), and is then converted to values. This is coupled with a fixed coefficient assumption for the rest of the production sector (for example, the allocation of goods to intermediate versus final usage). Notice the multiple entry points for error.

The information on distribution may also be suspect. Practitioners of the national accounts method often use the published income or consumption quintiles (as opposed to the unit-level survey data), which may disguise severe problems in the underlying data. Of course, in this respect it is unfair to blame researchers for their use of quintile data, because the unit-level data are often not publicly available.

In any event, the direction of errors induced by the acknowledged flaws in the HBS is not clear. Even if the underrepresentation of upper incomes causes the HBS to underestimate mean and variance, the "true" distribution may not have a greater mass below the poverty line than the estimated one. However, the national accounts consumption adjustment, being a pure scale adjustment, clearly reduces the headcount measure.

This seemingly technical debate about data sources has been conducted against the background of an increased orientation in international development policy toward achieving results, and specifically an expectation that the cumulative official resource flows to developing countries and the associated initiatives (such as Poverty Reduction Strategy Papers and the Highly Indebted Poor Countries initiative) should by now have led to an appreciable reduction in poverty. However, countries that have been considered success stories in their pursuit of these new development frameworks (Uganda, for instance) have displayed disappointing rates of poverty reduction relative to per capita GDP growth.

Increased research attention has therefore been directed to the issue of "pro-poor growth," namely, the extent to which those at the lower end of the income distribution benefit from the growth process. It is the antithesis of this approach to simply ascribe the mean rate of consumption growth to the entire distribution, which assumes that the benefits of growth across the income distribution are neutral. A fuller discussion of the decomposition of poverty changes into growth and distribution components is given in chapter 11, along with some recent examples that show that, in the short run at least, changes in distribution have an appreciable effect on the extent to which economic growth translates into lower poverty rates.

The assumption that national accounts data represent a simple grossing up of household budget survey data is a problem for the consumption categories where the two measures do not overlap and where consumption patterns differ systematically across the income distribution. Nevertheless, these arguments cut both ways; if we acknowledge that the HBS data do seem to miss some aspects of growth, whether it is safe to use them to study pro-poor growth can be questioned. All our information about income distribution comes from the HBS, meaning that we know very little about the distribution of national accounts consumption, yet it is this distribution that may drive public perceptions of the equality of the growth process.

Finally, as with many seemingly tempestuous disputes in economics, some of the apparent differences between different schools of thought weaken in the face of pragmatism. For instance, Karshenas (2004) advocates a hybrid approach to measuring poverty in which HBS and national accounts are combined, in recognition of potential errors in both. Similarly, while World Bank researchers have doggedly defended their reliance on survey data, they use national accounts consumption growth data to extrapolate their poverty counts between survey years and to generate forecasts of poverty reduction.

Debate 2: Is World Poverty Really Falling?

The World Bank's estimates of the fall in poverty since the early 1980s have been criticized by Sanjay Reddy and his coauthors (Pogge and Reddy 2003; Reddy and Minoiu 2006; Reddy, Visaria, and Asali 2006), and while few of the points they raise are new, they have argued them with considerable vigor. To recap, the methodology used by the World Bank (Chen and Ravallion 2004, 2008)

- Picks a poverty line (now $1.25 per person per day in 2005 prices)

- Uses PPP exchange rates to translate this into poverty lines in domestic currencies in 2005

- Uses domestic consumer price indexes to find the poverty line, in domestic currencies, for years other than 2005

- Applies the poverty line to expenditure distribution data that have been collected by 675 household surveys in 116 developing countries; where possible, original survey data are used, but often the computations are based on fitting Lorenz curves to published tabulated data from the surveys, to establish the number and proportion of people who are poor

- Establishes poverty rates and levels for three-year intervals, using interpolation for those cases where household surveys were undertaken on "off" years

- Aggregates the numbers for individual countries to provide poverty rates and levels by broad region and worldwide.

Each of these steps may be criticized, and the debate is summarized below. Ravallion offers a spirited defense of the World Bank's approach, arguing that Reddy and his coauthors overstate the possible weaknesses of the Bank's methodology, and have "sidestepped the problem" of setting up an international poverty line that reflects constant purchasing power over commodities (Ravallion 2008).

Review Questions

> 10. Bhalla adjusts household survey data on expenditures upward to ensure consistency with national accounts figures, and argues that the result is that the world is already close to meeting, or may even have met, the Millennium Development Goals for poverty reduction.

- ○ True
- ○ False
- ○ Uncertain

> 11. Which of the following steps is not part of the World Bank's methodology for computing the $1/day world poverty rate?

- ○ A. Pick a poverty line that allows households to buy enough food and other basic needs.
- ○ B. Use an average PPP exchange rate to translate the poverty line into domestic currency terms.
- ○ C. Use a domestic consumer price index to find the appropriate poverty line, in domestic currency, for the years in which household surveys were undertaken.
- ○ D. Measure the number of poor in a country by determining, based on fitting Lorenz curves, how many fall below the poverty line.

Choice of Poverty Line

Pogge and Reddy (2003) argue that the original "$1/day" poverty line—in effect, $1.08 per person per day in 1993 prices—is too low. They claim that this level is arbitrary and is not properly rooted in a "capabilities" (or basic needs) approach to measuring poverty, and they suggest that one could hardly survive on such a small amount in the United States; by implication, if this poverty line is appropriately translated into other currencies, it would be difficult to survive at such a low poverty line in those currencies, too. The revision of the poverty line to US$1.25 in 2005 prices would not alter this criticism.

A more recent article by Reddy, Visaria, and Asali (2006) no longer makes the case that the $1/day poverty line is too low. They compare poverty lines for Nicaragua, Tanzania, and Vietnam generated using a cost of basic needs approach (as outlined in chapter 3), with poverty lines based on the $1/day and $2/day standards. The results are displayed in table 10.4, and show that for Nicaragua and Tanzania the cost of basic needs approach actually gives a lower poverty line than the $1/day approach; however,

Table 10.4 Poverty Lines Using $1/Day and $2/Day and Basic Needs Measures

Poverty line	Nicaragua, 1998 (cordobas)	Tanzania, 2000/01 (shillings)	Vietnam, 1993 (dong)	Vietnam, 1998 (dong)
$1/day	4,017	147,614	629,341	953,794
$2/day	8,034	295,227	1,258,682	1,907,588
Cost of basic needs	3,018	80,365	1,160,363	1,758,581

Source: Reddy, Visalia, and Asali 2006.

for Vietnam the cost of basic needs poverty line is close to the $2/day poverty line. The conclusion is clear: the $1/day or $2/day standard provides a poor approximation to the (relatively theoretically satisfactory) cost of basic needs approach, but does not necessarily systematically underestimate it.

Use of PPP Exchange Rates

There are two further distinct issues. The first involves the stability of PPP exchange rates over time, and the appropriateness of using an "average" PPP exchange rate. Pogge and Reddy (2003) note that when a new set of PPP exchange rates was published for 1993, superseding those of 1985, they led to considerable changes in measured poverty rates (using the $1/day poverty line); a similarly large set of revisions occurred when the 2005 PPP exchange rates were introduced. Thus, international comparisons of poverty are not robust to the measures of PPP exchange rates, many of which are, in any case, imputed using regression techniques rather than being based on direct price observations. Deaton (2003b) suggests that a pragmatic response is to avoid revising the PPP exchange rates too often; but eventually revisions become inevitable, and the problem re-emerges, and we know (theoretically from the Balassa-Samuelson effect, empirically from the Penn effect)[6] that PPP exchange rates vary systematically over time, showing a faster appreciation in countries with more rapid economic growth.

The second problem is that the World Bank uses a PPP exchange rate that is applied to a broad basket of goods and services, and not necessarily the basket of goods and services that is relevant for poor households. Pogge and Reddy (2003) suggest that poverty (measured using the $1/day standard) is understated as a result, on the grounds that the poor mainly consume tradable goods, so the use of a PPP exchange rate overadjusts for price differentials. However, this is by no means self-evident, and merits further study.

Use of Consumer Price Indexes to Adjust the Poverty Lines over Time

Ideally, one would use a price index that reflects the costs faced by poor consumers, not by the average consumer, to adjust poverty lines over time, but this is rarely done.

Sometimes it is possible to adjust the poverty line using an index of food prices, but this, of course, ignores the evolution of the prices of nonfood items, which constitute about a third of total expenditures for someone at the poverty line. The problems involved in finding appropriate price indexes are serious, as our discussion of the studies of poverty in Indonesia following the financial crisis of 1997 makes clear (see chapter 11).

Applying the Poverty Line to Household Survey Data

About half of all the people in the developing world live in China and India alone. It follows that the evolution of world poverty will depend heavily on the course of poverty in these two countries. Unfortunately, the data on poverty for these two countries have some serious problems. The surveys done in China in the 1980s were of questionable quality; and until recently there was no direct measure of China's PPP exchange rate. A change in the survey methodology used in the "thick" round of the Indian National Sample Survey in 1999–2000 appeared to imply that poverty in India had fallen but little in the 1990s, which was hardly plausible given the rapid economic growth experienced during that decade. A number of efforts have been made to adjust the 1999–2000 numbers to make them more comparable with previous survey data (there is an extended discussion of this in chapter 16) but there remains considerable uncertainty about the true extent of poverty reduction in India during the period in question. Reddy and Minoiu (2006) present the results of a sensitivity analysis showing that it is just possible that the world poverty rate (using the $1/day level) did not fall in the 1990s, and it is more possible that the number of people in poverty did not fall during that decade. The real message here is that measures of world poverty are not yet robust enough to be used to make strong statements about progress in reducing poverty.

Pogge and Reddy (2003) argue that the World Bank approach to measuring world poverty is too flawed to be useful. Instead, they would ask every country to measure poverty using a cost of basic needs approach—they refer to it as measuring a "set of elementary capabilities," but it comes to the same thing—based on the expenditure required to provide enough calories to live on, plus a reasonable nonfood component. This is an attractive, if not particularly new, idea. Why, then, has this approach not been used? The answer is that it is costly and has its own methodological problems.

The World Bank's $1/day approach—now US$1.25 a day—makes parsimonious use of survey data; all that is really needed are the average expenditure level and a breakdown by, for instance, expenditure per capita quintiles, along with PPP exchange rates and consumer price indexes. A good researcher could input the data for hundreds of surveys into PovcalNet and come up with estimates of world poverty and its evolution in a matter of a few weeks. However, to implement a cost of basic needs approach, researchers have to work with the underlying survey data, which is relatively tedious (and requires that the data be available, which is by no means always the case).

Over time, it is likely that most countries will have in-house analysts who can measure poverty using the cost of basic needs approach, following a consistent set of guidelines. But perfect comparability will never be achieved: surveys will ask different questions and in different ways; they will differ in sample size and design; they will use different techniques to measure food and other prices; they will use different methods to inflate prices over time. And one still has to address the issues of whether survey data need to be adjusted to be compatible with national accounts; whether one should use adult-equivalence methods; and how precisely to determine an appropriate level of nonfood (or even food) spending.

Perhaps these problems are no different from those faced by statisticians who compile national accounts data, even though they all follow the same UN guidelines. A similar effort might be worthwhile for poverty measurement—the compilation of a set of formal guidelines for measuring poverty using the cost of basic needs method.

Review Questions

> 12. Which of the following is not a criticism that Reddy and his co-authors have levied at the World Bank's approach to measuring world poverty?
>
> o A. Measured PPP exchange rates vary over time.
> o B. The $2/day standard is too low.
> o C. The data on poverty reduction on India are subject to considerable uncertainty.
> o D. The use of a consumer price index does not necessarily reflect the evolution of prices of the goods and services consumed by the poor.

> 13. The World Bank's approach to measuring world poverty requires less information from individual household surveys than would be required if one were to apply a cost of basic needs approach.
>
> o True
> o False
> o Uncertain

Conclusion

We conclude by mentioning some current directions of research on the link between macroeconomic and poverty outcomes. It is now well documented that the elasticity of poverty with respect to growth varies over time and space, prompting investigation of what set of initial conditions makes this elasticity bigger. Furthermore, it is increasingly recognized that while growth remains central to poverty reduction—as the discussion of the Dollar and Kraay results in chapter 9 made clear—it is not the only way to reduce poverty; particularly in the short and medium term, inequality also matters.

There are certain policies with modest immediate growth effects but strong poverty impacts, or in the terminology above, policies that lead to a high elasticity of poverty reduction with respect to growth. Prime examples are reforms to security of land tenure, microcredit, and the expansion of basic education. A strict focus on a growth-poverty link might overlook such policies.

Poverty analysts are also looking at methods to improve the measurement of consumption, with the objective of balancing the gain from better source data with the loss of comparability to previous data.

Notes

1. Information on the overall MDGs and progress toward them can be found at http://www.developmentgoals.org/.
2. The countries are Malawi, Mali, Ethiopia, Sierra Leone, Niger, Uganda, The Gambia, Rwanda, Guinea-Bissau, Tanzania, Tajikistan, Mozambique, Chad, Nepal, and Ghana (Chen and Ravallion 2008, 11).
3. For years in which there are no household surveys, Chen and Ravallion adjust the household survey data on consumption from other years by linking this information to the evolution of consumption in the national accounts; they then recompute the poverty rate using the consumption data thus interpolated.
4. Chen and Ravallion (2008) used PPP exchange rates for 98 of the 116 countries in their sample, and used PPPs based on regression models for Algeria, Costa Rica, the Dominican Republic, El Salvador, Guatemala, Guyana, Haiti, Honduras, Jamaica, Nicaragua, Panama, Papua New Guinea, St. Lucia, Suriname, Timor-Leste, Trinidad and Tobago, Turkmenistan, and Uzbekistan.
5. Available on the Web at http://go.worldbank.org/NT2A1XUWP0.
6. See http://en.wikipedia.org/wiki/Balassa-Samuelson_effect.

References

Alatas, Vivi, Jed Friedman, and Angus Deaton. 2004. "Purchasing Power Parity Exchange Rates from Household Survey Data: India and Indonesia." Working paper, Research Program in Development Studies, Princeton University.

Bhalla, Surjit. 2002. "Imagine There Is No Country: Poverty, Inequality, and Growth in the Era of Globalization." Institute for International Economics, Washington, DC.

Carey, Kevin. 2004. "Poverty Analysis for Macroeconomists." World Bank Institute, Washington, DC.

Chen, Shaohua, and Martin Ravallion. 2001. "How Did the World's Poorest Fare in the 1990s?" *Review of Income and Wealth* 47 (3): 283–300.

———. 2004. "How Have the World's Poorest Fared Since the Early 1980s?" Development Economics Working Paper No. 3341, World Bank, Washington, DC.

———. 2008. "The Developing World Is Poorer Than We Thought, But No Less Successful in the Fight against Poverty." Policy Research Working Paper No. 4703, World Bank, Washington, DC.

Deaton, Angus. 2003a. "How to Monitor Poverty for the Millennium Development Goals." *Journal of Human Development* 4 (3): 353–78.

———. 2003b. "Measuring Poverty in a Growing World (or Measuring Growth in a Poor World)." NBER Working Paper No. 9822, National Bureau of Economic Research, Cambridge, MA.

Karshenas, Massoud. 2004. "Global Poverty Estimates and the Millennium Goals: Towards a Unified Framework." International Labour Organisation Employment Strategy Papers, 2004/5, ILO, Geneva.

Pogge, Thomas, and Sanjay Reddy. 2003. "Unknown: The Extent, Distribution, and Trend of Global Income Poverty." Columbia University, NY.

Ravallion, Martin. Forthcoming. "How *Not* to Count the Poor? A Reply to Reddy and Pogge." In *Debates on the Measurement of Poverty*, ed. Sudhir Anand, Paul Segal, and Joseph Stiglitz. Oxford, UK: Oxford University Press.

Reddy, Sanjay, and Carnelia Minoiu. 2006. "Has World Poverty Really Fallen?" Columbia University, NY.

Reddy, Sanjay, Sujata Visaria, and Muhammad Asali. 2006. "Inter-Country Comparisons of Poverty Based on a Capability Approach: An Empirical Exercise." Working Paper No. 27, International Poverty Centre, UNDP, Brasilia.

Chapter 11

The Analysis of Poverty over Time

Summary

It is often necessary to measure how poverty changes over time, if only to monitor and evaluate the effects of specific shocks, policies, or projects on poverty.

Changes in poverty rates are typically based on comparisons of cross-sectional data. In some cases, however, it is possible to collect panel data for which the same household (or person) is surveyed at two or more points in time.

Panel surveys have some important advantages. Only with panel data can one measure who moves in to and out of poverty over time. The persistently poor and the chronically poor (who are poor on average, but occasionally escape poverty for a while) need help to raise their income or consumption levels; the transient poor, who sometimes outnumber the chronically poor, may have a greater need for help with smoothing their consumption profiles. The substantial movement of people in to and out of poverty can be captured in the form of a transition matrix.

Panel data allow a more accurate measurement of whether poverty has changed over time, because paired tests become possible. They also have econometric advantages, often allowing one to avoid bias due to unobservable factors and to avoid the problems of endogenous program placement and selective migration in evaluating the impact of government programs.

Panel surveys have drawbacks, too. They are subject to attrition bias, as respondents gradually drop out of the panel; they may become less representative over time of the population they are supposed to reflect; and they require considerable managerial skills and expense. Nor is there any entirely satisfactory way to track households as they divide and re-form over time.

The chapter ends with a case study that summarizes the methods, and associated controversies, used to measure the extent to which poverty rose in Indonesia in the aftermath of the Asian financial crisis of 1997–98. The example touches on many of the issues that arise in measuring poverty, with or without panel data. Depending on the assumptions used, poverty rose by anywhere between 24 and 81 percent between 1997 and 1998.

Learning Objectives

After completing the chapter on *The Analysis of Poverty over Time*, you should be able to

1. Explain the value of measuring the evolution of poverty over time ("poverty dynamics").

2. Describe the main sources of data on poverty dynamics, including panel data, repeated cross-sectional data, and data from rotating panels.

3. Distinguish between panel data based on repeated surveying of households, dwellings, and individuals.

4. Itemize the advantages of panel surveys, and explain how panel data can give more precise estimates of changes in poverty over time (compared with data from cross-sections).

5. Summarize the drawbacks of panel surveys, including attrition bias, decreased representativeness, and high managerial demands.

6. Distinguish between the chronically poor, the persistently poor, and the transient poor, and explain the practical importance of these distinctions.

7. Explain how to construct a transition matrix.

8. Assess the extent to which poverty in Indonesia rose after the Asian financial crisis in 1997–98, and evaluate the choices made by different research teams in making such measurements.

Introduction: Sources of Information on Poverty over Time

A single cross-sectional survey can provide a snapshot of poverty at one point in time.[1] Helpful as this is, it does not allow one to track the evolution of a household's poverty status over time. Information on the "dynamics of poverty" is needed for a number of purposes, including the following:

- Distinguishing households that are poor occasionally from those that are poor all the time. This is of practical importance, because the types of intervention relevant for dealing with persistent and transient poverty are likely to be different.

- Monitoring and evaluating the effect of a specific shock, policy, or project on poverty—for instance, the degree to which a microcredit scheme might help the poor. This issue is treated in more detail in Chapter 13.

- Tracking the evolution of poverty over time, which would presumably also allow one to adjust the way in which poverty alleviation is targeted.

There are three main ways to measure what happens to poverty over time: appropriate questions in a single cross-section survey, repeated cross-sectional surveys, and panel data. Let us consider each in turn.

Questions in a Single Cross-Sectional Survey

In this case, we have information on a sample of households or individuals at a single point in time. In addition to asking for information about current living standards, one could include some questions about living standards in the past, such as "is your income higher now than it was a year ago?" or "by how much has your income changed since last year?"

This is the least satisfactory way to get a measure of how poverty or living standards have evolved, because few people can remember their situation a year before with any degree of accuracy. On the other hand, if a country is hit by a shock such as a drought, and one wants to get an idea of what segments of society were hardest hit, but there is no pre-crisis survey information, then this is the only approach that will yield any worthwhile information.

An interesting variant on this theme is the effort by Krishna et al. (2004) to elicit changes in poverty over long periods of time. In a study of 316 households in 20 villages in western Kenya, Anirudh Krishna and his team asked villagers to identify who among them was poor 25 years previously, and who was poor at the time of the study. Based on group meetings, corroborated by individual interviews, they found that one household in five had escaped poverty over this period, while another one in five had fallen into poverty. This research tapped local knowledge about the economic circumstances of one's neighbors; Vietnam uses a similar approach when it expects villagers to identify who among them should be eligible for educational and other subsidies.

Repeated Cross-Sectional Surveys

The most common way that poverty is tracked is by using the results from two or more household surveys over time. To allow for comparisons over time, the questions need to be comparable in each wave of the survey. Examples of such surveys include the following:

- The annual national labor force survey in Indonesia (SAKERNAS)

- The Malaysian household income surveys

- The U.S. census long form (based on a longer questionnaire sent to a sample of households in the context of the decennial census)

- The Cambodia socioeconomic surveys (discussed in chapter 2 and table 2.2.)

The list is substantial. As discussed in chapter 9, Dollar and Kraay (2002) found 418 "episodes" from 137 countries over four decades for which poverty could be compared over an interval of at least five years; each such episode could only be measured by comparing results from two household surveys. Chen and Ravallion (2008, 13) use information from 675 surveys for 116 countries for their estimates of the evolution of poverty in less-developed countries between 1981 and 2005.

Panel Data

When a survey is repeated, and we have multiple observations for the same person (or household, or firm, or community), then we have **panel data.** There are a number of different ways to design a panel. Among the most common—

Use a sample of households. Here the sampling unit is the household, and subsequent rounds of the survey return to the same households each time. This is probably the commonest form of panel, but is not without problems (see below). Some effort has to be made to locate households that have moved.

> *Example 1:* The 1993 Vietnam Living Standards Survey (VLSS) interviewed 4,800 households. Many of these households were interviewed again in 1998. More specifically, 96 households were deliberately omitted from the original sample, and a further 399 dropped out ("attrited"), leaving 4,305 households in the panel. In passing one might note that an additional 1,694 households were added in 1998 to bring the total number surveyed to 5,999.

> *Example 2:* The Institute for Crop Research in the Semi-Arid Tropics (ICRISAT), based in Hyderabad, surveyed a total of 240 households annually from 1975 to 1985 in six villages in southwestern India. This is an unusual case of a panel of households sustained for more than two rounds of surveying.

Use a sample of dwellings. In this case the sampling unit is the dwelling unit (house, apartment, boat, yurt, and so on). In practice, the subsequent analysis tends to focus on a panel of households that were surveyed in both rounds.

Example: The Peru Living Standards Survey was first undertaken in 1985–86. In 1990, interviewers returned to the 1,280 dwellings in the Lima area that had been included in the initial survey. This yielded a total of 1,052 interviews, including 745 cases where the same household was interviewed in both rounds of the survey.

Use a sample of individuals. Given that households change shape and size over time, it is frequently more satisfactory to sample individuals. The biggest problem in practice is keeping track of individuals over time, an expensive process.

Example: The Michigan Panel Survey on Income Dynamics (PSID) began surveying about 4,800 individuals in 1968 and has continued to survey them regularly since then.

Constructing a panel from repeated cross-sections. If there are repeated cross-sections that sample the same set of communities (for example, villages, districts, city wards), then one could aggregate the data to the community level. In this case, the observational unit is the community, and there is information on the community over time. For an example, see Pitt, Rosenzweig, and Gibbons (1993).

Some surveys use a *rotating panel.* For round 1, a sample of households is chosen; in round two, a fraction (usually about half) of the original households are resurveyed, and a new set of households added to the sample; in round three the new households are resurveyed and the remaining original households replaced by another set of households; and so on.

Example: The first living standards survey in Côte d'Ivoire was undertaken in 1985 using a sample of 1,600 households. In 1986, about 800 of these households were resurveyed, and 800 new households added to give a total second-round sample of 1,600.

Review Questions

1. In comparing poverty rates from household surveys undertaken in two different years it is important to do all of the following *except:*

   - A. Adjust the poverty line to take into account price inflation between the two years.
   - B. Adapt the sample weights to ensure that the sample size is comparable between the two years.
   - C. Correct for major differences in the sampling frame.
   - D. Ensure that the definitions of consumption (or income) remain substantially unchanged over time.

2. It is possible to measure the evolution of poverty over time using repeated cross-section survey data.

- ○ True
- ○ False

Advantages of Panel Surveys

Panel data are more expensive to collect than repeated cross-sectional data, and so are worth gathering only if there are some compensating advantages. There are a number of arguments in favor of collecting panel data; for a more detailed treatment, see Glewwe and Jacoby (2000).

Only panel data allow one to measure transitions over time—that is, gross changes. For instance, suppose we want to know how many people moved out of poverty between 1993 and 1998, and how many moved into poverty over the same period. Repeated cross-sectional data only allow us to compute the net effects (that is, the old and new poverty rates), while the panel data show the gross movements.

In this context, a common issue that is addressed with panel data is whether a household's poverty is transient or persistent; we discuss this issue in more detail below. And if we want to know who is most likely to move in to or out of poverty over time, then panel data are helpful; this issue is also discussed further in chapter 12 under the heading of "vulnerability."

With panel data there is less reliance on retrospective reporting. For instance, to compute true income, we need (in principle) data on the household's assets both at the time of the survey, and a year before. Given the tricks of memory ("people telescope the past"), the data for a year ago are unreliable. But if the household were surveyed a year earlier, then reasonably reliable information on those assets exists.

> *Example:* Vijverberg and Haughton (2004) constructed a panel of *household enterprises* using data from the VLSS of 1993 and 1998. To get an accurate idea of how enterprise performance evolved, it was essential to have first-hand information, drawn from both surveys, and not to rely on retrospective reporting based merely on questions in the 1998 survey.

Panel data allow one to compare changes in the means of variables (such as expenditure per capita) more precisely, because one can use a paired t-test rather than the less powerful unpaired t-test. This may be an advantage if there was relatively little change between one survey and the next—the Côte D'Ivoire LSMS surveys come to mind—and so the greatest possible precision is needed when comparing the results of one round to those of the next.

Example: Suppose that a survey of 10 individuals, undertaken in 2002, shows that they have the levels of consumption per capita given in the first column of consumption numbers in table 11.1. The mean level of consumption per capita is 3,750. Now suppose that a second survey, undertaken in 2004, shows the levels of consumption per capita given in the last column, with a mean level of 3,921. The question now is: was the increase in per capita consumption between the two periods statistically significant?

If the data come from a panel, so that each row represents two observations from the same person—that is, individual 1 had consumption of 2,000 in 2002 and of 2,131 in 2004, and so on—then we can use a paired t-test. This gives a t-statistic that is 5.393, which indicates a highly statistically significant difference. The p-value for a one-tailed test is 0.00022, which implies that there is a 99.978 percent probability that consumption per capita was higher in 2004 than in 2002.

If the data come from two independent samples, then the t-statistic is 0.181, so the difference is clearly not statistically significant. This is confirmed by the p-value for a one-tailed test, which is 0.429.

In short, in this example the panel data were able to confirm a change in consumption per capita, but the repeated cross-section data were not.[2] Deaton (1997, 21) notes that if one rotates half of a panel, then the standard error will be no more than 30 percent higher than the standard error based on a complete panel. The implication is that rotating panels can provide much of the gain in precision that is so useful.

Table 11.1 Hypothetical Data on Consumption per Capita for 10 Individuals

Individual no.	Consumption per capita	
	2002	2004
1	2,000	2,131
2	2,600	2,736
3	8,750	8,916
4	1,825	1,978
5	4,355	4,426
6	5,680	5,992
7	2,830	2,888
8	3,010	3,202
9	2,560	2,935
10	3,890	4,008
	Mean: 3,750	**Mean: 3,921**

Source: Data constructed by the authors.

209

Measurement error is a problem in all survey data. However, if reporting errors are similar for a given household, then the *change* in consumption or income from a panel will be relatively accurate (Deaton 1997, 21), but there can be no presumption that this is always the case. Even the greater precision of panel data is unlikely to help much if there is little or no growth in consumption between the two surveys—for instance, in a stagnant economy, or if the surveys are too close in time.

In principle, the collection of panel data allows one to reduce the costs of interviewing and sampling. Because one is revisiting the same households, no expense is incurred in developing a sample of households. And with data from prior rounds in hand (such as the age of household members), fewer questions are needed in subsequent rounds. In practice, the savings in time and expense are minimal.

With panel data one may control for unobserved characteristics (heterogeneity). This is an econometric issue of some importance.

For instance, we know that some farmers are better managers than others, but we cannot identify which are good managers and which are not. Suppose that good managers use more fertilizers than bad managers. Then if we regress farm output on the amount of fertilizer inputs (and other variables), the estimated effect of fertilizer inputs will be overstated, because it is picking up both the true fertilizer effect, and the influence of the managerial skills with which it is correlated. On the other hand, suppose we have panel data, and so observe farmers' outputs at two points in time. Then a regression of the *change* in output on the *change* in fertilizer input will (by and large) give us an unbiased coefficient, because the unobserved factor (managerial expertise) will in effect drop out.[3] This issue is addressed more fully in chapter 14, which deals with econometric issues in some detail.

Panel data are useful in evaluating the impact of government programs, both because they mean we do not have to rely on retrospective reporting, but also because they allow us to avoid the effects—illustrated below—of endogenous program placement and selective migration. The implication is that it is helpful to have baseline survey data before undertaking a program, and then to revisit these households (or individuals) once the program has been put into place.

To illustrate, consider the following assignment. You have been asked to evaluate the impact of a government program that is designed to help sick children by providing additional funds to rural health clinics. You decide to undertake a survey of households, chosen randomly throughout the country. To your surprise, you find that the sickest children are those in villages that received subsidies. It appears that the government program is doing just the opposite of what it was designed to do.

Of course, this conclusion is almost certainly wrong. The difficulty is that there is *endogenous program placement*: the government probably targeted its subsidies to the areas where the sickest children were to be found in the first place. The solution is to survey a panel of households both before and after the program, and then to ask whether the improvement was larger for households with access to the new program than for households without such access.

A repeated cross-section would not necessarily provide a satisfactory evaluation of the effectiveness of the program, because of the problem of *selective migration*. Suppose we have information on the incidence of sickness in a village before and after the program that provides subsidies to local clinics. If the improved clinics induce households to move to the favored villages to get better health care for, say, a sick child, then the reported incidence of sickness in the subsidized villages could actually rise over time. Again, the solution is to use a panel, which would exclude the migration effects.

Drawbacks of Panel Surveys

Given the significant advantages of panel data, it is perhaps surprising that panels are not used more often. The reason is that there are some significant drawbacks, of which the most important are problems related to attrition, representativeness, and managerial requirements.

Over time, a panel of households (or individuals) becomes smaller and smaller, creating potential attrition bias. Some households dissolve, as their members die. Others migrate. Some may refuse to answer the second time around. This attrition is serious because it is generally nonrandom, and so the panel becomes less representative over time. The households that die are older; the migrants are probably more vigorous and more affluent; and those who refuse to answer are likely to be atypical in one way or another.

> *Example:* The 1993 VLSS sampled 4,800 households; efforts were made to interview 4,704 of these households in 1998, but only 4,305 responses were actually obtained. This represents a total attrition of 8.5 percent, equivalent to 1.8 percent per year. By the standards of most panels, this actually represents a relatively low rate of attrition.

> *Example:* The Michigan PSID found that 12–15 percent of those initially interviewed dropped out after the first round. But then the panel "settled down," and 61.6 percent of the initial sample were still in the panel 14 years later, representing an annualized attrition rate of 3.4 percent, or 2.4 percent if the first year is excluded.

To attenuate the attrition problem, the ideal approach is to track down the migrants. This is often done by collecting information from neighbors, former employers, and schools. The VLSS98 survey tracked down households that had moved to another address within the same commune, but not those that moved away from the commune.

The best panels match households (or individuals, or firms, or dwellings) based on IDs. That is, a household surveyed in 1993 would be given the same ID as the same household in 1998 (or at least an ID that can be matched exactly). The Indonesian Family Life survey uses identical IDs over time; the VLSS uses different IDs, but they can be matched easily.

Sometimes matching is more difficult. For example, Vijverberg and Haughton (2004) wanted to create a panel of nonfarm household enterprises using data from the VLSS93 and VLSS98. For each enterprise in each survey information was included on the age of the enterprise, the entrepreneur, and the line of activity, but no ID was included. Thus, to determine whether an enterprise in 1998 was the same as one that had been surveyed in 1993, the matching had to be based on these characteristics. The process is fundamentally unreliable; for instance, households reported some enterprises in 1998 that were younger than the apparently same enterprise had been in 1993.

> **Example:** Skoufias, Suryahadi, and Sumarto (1999) created a panel based on the 100-village survey in Indonesia, undertaken in 1997 and 1998. To do this, they had to match households based on names and birth dates, because the households had not been assigned ID numbers.

Over time, a panel becomes less representative of the population at large. Even if there were no attrition, a panel would become, over time, less and less representative of the population it is supposed to reflect. This is, because the panel, by construction, does not add new households, and so newly formed households are excluded, and households that split up—for instance, due to a divorce—are imperfectly followed.

The VLSS of 1998 addressed this problem of representativeness by adding new households to the original panel, including recently formed households; the latter were then given a relatively high weight, to compensate for the fact that they were underrepresented in the panel part of the sample. The main justification for rotating panels is to ensure the continued representativeness of the survey.

The construction of a viable panel requires considerable managerial capacity, and can be costly. The costs arise in tracking down migrant households, and possibly in the need for a longer initial questionnaire. Managerial skills are also needed to store the initial information reliably and to maintain the confidentiality of the data.

Other Issues in Panel and Repeated Cross-Sectional Data

A number of other issues need to be borne in mind when comparing poverty rates over time, with or even without panel data.

Comparability in questionnaire. When the goal is to measure change over time, it is important to ensure that the questions are the same, and that the length of the recall period is also the same. This does leave an awkward problem: What is the researcher to do if the question asked in the first round was a bad one? The question could be improved, but only at the cost of less comparability over time.

Timing of fieldwork. Ideally, one would interview any given household at the same time of the year. This is because some variables, such as school enrollments, or farm cash income, vary seasonally. A farmer interviewed in August may remember the value of the recent harvest quite clearly; interviewed in March, the memory may have faded.

Defining the household. Consider figure 11.1. At the time of the first survey, a couple is living together with a child. Five years later, when the survey is repeated, the husband has divorced and remarried, and they have a new child; the former wife is now living alone with the original child. Which of the two new households is the true heir to the original one?

There is no single correct answer to this, but it does introduce a significant element of judgment into the construction of panels that are based on households. To ensure consistency, a clear protocol for dealing with such cases needs to be articulated before undertaking the second and subsequent rounds of a panel survey.

Deflating. Over time, prices change. This means that monetary measures, such as income or expenditure, have to be deflated to make comparisons over time. This can be difficult, especially when prices change rapidly, as is likely in a crisis. The fundamental conclusions about what happened to poverty in Indonesia over 1997–99 hinge on which price deflator it is appropriate to use; this issue is discussed in more detail in the final section of this chapter.

Figure 11.1 Defining the Household

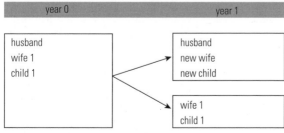

Source: Authors' creation.

Chronic versus Transient Poverty

Some households are persistently poor, while others move in to and out of poverty from year to year (the "transient poor"). One of the most valuable applications of panel data is to identify who falls into each of these categories.

It is common to distinguish four categories of people:

- The **chronically poor** are those whose average consumption per capita over time ($\bar{c}$) is at or below the poverty line (z). Clearly one of the priorities in such cases is to help raise average consumption levels above the poverty line.

- The **persistently poor** are those, among the chronically poor, who never emerge from poverty, not even for a year or two. In this respect, they may be distinguished from those chronically poor who have an occasional good year when they escape from poverty for a while.

- The **transient poor** are those who are poor from time to time, but who are not poor on average. With better smoothing of their consumption stream they could, in principle, avoid all spells of poverty.[4]

- The **never poor**, who do not even drop into poverty occasionally (at least in the time frame under study).

These distinctions are important for a number of reasons. First, moving into and out of poverty looks less serious than remaining stuck in poverty. Someone who is poor now, but can reasonably expect to be out of poverty next year, is in a better position that someone who is equivalently poor now, and is likely to remain there in the future.

Second, the policies needed to address the various types of poverty may differ. The transient poor are more likely to need short-term relief, through insurance or income stabilization schemes—as the discussion on vulnerability in chapter 12 makes clear. On the other hand, the chronically poor are more likely to need more education, skills, and assets, and to become less isolated from the rest of the economy.

A corollary is that the existence of transient poverty makes poverty targeting harder, if we only have information at a single point in time. If I know you are poor, but I don't know if you are chronically or temporarily poor, I may deliver the wrong type of support. Or if the goal is to provide budget support only to the chronically poor, the presence of a large number of transient poor will undermine the effort at targeting.

Panel data are essential to measure these different types of poverty. Jalan and Ravallion (1998) use data from four large provinces in China for each year from 1985 to 1990 to measure the extent of persistent, chronic, and transient poverty. The survey was not designed as a panel—the same households were surveyed over time for administrative convenience—but the households can be matched and a panel created. They use an expenditure-based poverty line; the measure of expenditure includes an imputation for the costs of housing and consumer durables.

A sample of their results is shown in table 11.2, and cover the relatively wealthy province of Guangdong, the poor province of Guizhou, and the provinces of Guangxi and Yunnan. What is striking from their results is the modest amount of persistent poverty, and the large extent of transient poverty, particularly in the less poor provinces.

The first four columns of numbers refer to the headcount measure of poverty. The final column measures the percentage of all poverty that is transient, using Jalan and Ravallion's preferred measure of poverty, which is P_2 (the squared poverty gap measure); by this measure, about half of all the poverty, at any given moment in time, is accounted for by the transient poor, with particularly high proportions of transient poor in the more affluent provinces.

An important implication of Jalan and Ravallion's results is that subsidies that are designed to erase chronic poverty will be wasteful if they are based on the currently observed level of poverty for any given household. With perfect targeting of the chronically poor only, chronic poverty could have been eliminated during the 1985–90 period in all four provinces at the cost of 6.9 yuan (Y) per capita per year (in 1985 prices), which represents 1.9 percent of mean consumption across all provinces. With uniform transfers—that is, transfers that go to everyone, and are large enough to eliminate chronic poverty—the cost would be Y 25.1 per capita per year, or almost four times as much. Targeting transfers based on current consumption would cost almost as much as the uniform transfers. Full details are shown in table 11.3, taken from Jalan and Ravallion (1998).

Table 11.2 Chronic, Persistent, and Transient Poverty, China, 1985–90

	Chronically poor		Transient poor (and not chronically poor) $\bar{c} > z, c_t \leq z$	Never poor $c_t > z, \forall t$	Percentage of poverty (measured by P_2) that is transient
	Persistently poor $c_t \leq z, \forall t$	Not persistently poor $\bar{c} \leq z, c_t > z$ for some t			
Total sample	6.2	14.4	33.4	46.0	49
Guangdong	0.4	1.0	18.3	80.3	84
Guangxi	7.1	16.1	37.4	39.4	49
Guizhou	11.9	21.2	40.2	26.7	43
Yunnan	4.9	18.0	35.6	41.5	57

Source: Jalan and Ravallion 1998.

Note: c_t is the consumption by a person in time t, z is the poverty line, and $\bar{c}$ is mean consumption of the person over the time period under study.

Table 11.3 Cost of Poverty Elimination in China, 1985–90

	Perfect targeting	Uniform transfer	Targeting on the basis of current consumption	
			1985	1990
All four provinces	6.94	25.07	24.88	22.96
	(100)	(361)	(358)	(331)
Guangdong	0.33	0.88	0.72	0.83
	(100)	(267)	(218)	(251)
Guangxi	6.30	24.00	18.89	18.05
	(100)	(379)	(300)	(286)
Guizhou	14.35	46.23	44.44	36.96
	(100)	(322)	(310)	(257)
Yunnan	7.62	26.20	22.21	23.88
	(100)	(344)	(292)	(314)

Source: Jalan and Ravallion 1998, table 4.

Note: The table shows the expenditure per capita in yuan in 1985 prices needed to fill exactly the poverty gaps (in terms of the six-year mean consumption) under alternative assumptions about the information available to the policy maker. Figures in parentheses are percentages of the total budget required to eliminate chronic poverty under perfect targeting.

Transition Matrix

Another way to show the effects of the movement of people in to and out of poverty over time is by means of a transition matrix. This can be done in a number of ways.

Table 11.4 is based on panel data from Vietnam for 1993 and 1998, and shows how many households from any given quintile (defined by expenditure per capita) in 1993 are still in the same quintile in 1998, and how many have moved into each other quintile. The table, from Haughton et al. (2001), shows a high degree of mobility: of the 856 households in the middle quintile in 1993, only 234 were in the same quintile in 1998; 339 had moved up and 283 had moved down in the expenditure distribution. Haughton et al. (2001) refer to households that jumped at least two quintiles as *shooting stars* (the shaded cells in the northeast of table 11.4) and those that fell at least two quintiles as *sinking stones*. Households that were in one of the bottom three quintiles in 1993 and also in one of the bottom two quintiles in 1998 may be considered to be persistently poor and are shown in the block of shaded cells in the top left-hand corner of table 11.4. Other types of transition matrix are also possible. Table 12.1 (in chapter 12, on vulnerability) shows poor and nonpoor groups in each year, demonstrating how many people moved in to and out of poverty between the two survey years.

Review Questions

3. Which of the following is never used in panel microdata (that is, data collected at the "micro" level of individual agents or firms):

- ○ A. A sample of households surveyed at more than one point in time.
- ○ B. A sample of individuals followed and surveyed year after year.
- ○ C. A sample of countries over time.
- ○ D. A sample of dwellings surveyed in two different years.

4. A household is surveyed in year 0 and consists of a couple with two children. Two years later, when the panel is surveyed again, the eldest child has married and moved away. It is not possible to make comparisons of household income or expenditure over time in this case.

- ○ True
- ○ False

5. A *chronically poor* household is defined as a household that

- ○ A. Is in poverty in every year covered by the panel survey.
- ○ B. Is poor for at least one of the years covered by the panel survey.
- ○ C. Is expected to be poor next year.
- ○ D. Has an average level of consumption (or income) per capita that is below the poverty line.

6. In the context of poverty dynamics, a transition matrix

- ○ A. Tabulates poverty status in the base year against poverty status in the subsequent survey year.
- ○ B. Shows the time that it takes households in each quintile to exit from poverty.
- ○ C. Shows the number of people who move from one sector of the economy to another between the survey years.
- ○ D. Measures what has happened to the proportion of households in poverty in countries of the former Soviet Union and Eastern Europe.

7. Which of the following is *not* a strength of panel data (relative to data from repeated cross-sections)?

- ○ A. Panel data remain representative of the population as a whole.
- ○ B. Panel data increase the precision with which one can measure changes in poverty over time (for a given sample size).
- ○ C. Only panel data allow one to measure expenditure (or income) transitions over time.
- ○ D. Panel data are helpful in measuring the impact of government programs.

8. Panel data suffer from attrition bias, which occurs because

- ○ A. Over time, the panel does not reflect some parts of the population (such as newly formed couples).
- ○ B. Some households decline to answer the survey the second time around.
- ○ C. Cluster sampling becomes increasingly difficult over time.
- ○ D. Durable assets wear out over time.

Table 11.4 Quintile Transition Matrix for Households, 1993–98

| | Number of households, by expenditure/capita quintile, 1998 | | | | | |
	Poor	Poor-middle	Middle	Mid-upper	Upper	Total
Quintile 1993						
Poor	**384**	216	*127*	*54*	*9*	790
Poor-mid	193	**264**	223	*120*	*32*	832
Middle	*100*	183	**234**	254	*85*	856
Mid-upper	*38*	*127*	217	**301**	205	888
Upper	*12*	*35*	*100*	209	550	·906
Total	727	825	901	938	881	4,272

Sources: Vietnam Living Standards Surveys of 1993 and 1998.

Case Study: The Asian Financial Crisis and Poverty in Indonesia

In this final section of the chapter, we provide an extended discussion of a simple question: By how much did the Asian financial crisis of 1997–98 reduce poverty in Indonesia? The case study touches on many of the practical issues that emerge when using panel data.

After the devaluation of the Thai baht in July 1997, investors and bankers began to change their perceptions of the economic prospects of other countries in Southeast and East Asia. Indonesia was hard hit, as capital flight and a sharp drop in foreign direct investment created an exchange rate crisis. The rupiah fell from Rp 2,400 per U.S. dollar prior to the crisis to Rp 4,800 per dollar by December 1997; it collapsed to Rp 15,000 per dollar in January 1998, recovering by the end of the year to just under Rp 7,000 per dollar.

As the rupiah fell, interest rates rose rapidly; many borrowers were unable to maintain loan payments, triggering a banking crisis. And the lack of credit meant that many businesses were starved of working capital and were forced to contract. The problem was compounded by a severe drought, related to El Niño, which hit the country in 1997. Where gross domestic product (GDP) rose by 7 percent annually before the crisis, it fell by 13.2 percent in 1998 and rose by a mere 0.2 percent in 1999.

The government responded by launching a Social Safety Net (SSN) program, which provided a rice price subsidy for the poor, more scholarships for children from poor families, a Health Card providing free basic health services for the poor, and a public works program.

How much did poverty rise following the onset of the crisis? One way to answer this is to focus on current consumption expenditure deficit (CCED) poverty, looking at the households whose current expenditure levels fall below some predefined poverty line. A fuller answer would consider other dimensions of poverty, a point to which we return below.

It is difficult even to compute "conventional" poverty rates for the periods before, during, and after the crisis. The problems are technical ones, mainly related to how to choose the appropriate price indexes during a period of rapid inflation, when food prices were rising particularly quickly.

Consider the poverty rates shown in table 11.5, reported in table 1 of Said and Widyanti (2001). All of these numbers are based on National Socio-Economic Surveys (*Susenas*), including full surveys in February 1996 and February 1999, and *Mini-Susenas* surveys in December 1998 and August 1999. The *Susenas* surveys sample around 200,000 households every February, and collect core data annually; three large modules, including one on expenditure and income, are used on a rotating basis. The *Mini-Susenas* surveys sampled about 10,000 households and were designed to collect data in a more timely manner than the full surveys.

The Indonesian Statistics Office (BPS) figures use the official methodology for computing the poverty line, as revised substantially in 2000. The steps taken are as follows (see appendix 2 of Said and Widyanti 2001):

1. Identify those households whose nominal expenditures fall in the second and third deciles (the "initial reference population").

2. Identify the "national bundle" of 52 commodities that represent the most important expenditures of these households, along with their share in total expenditure.

3. Construct the price of this "national bundle" in each province, using data on unit costs from the initial reference population, and express these regional price deflators as a proportion of the price level in Jakarta.

4. Deflate total expenditures using the provincial deflators, to arrive at "real expenditure."

5. Use the distribution of real expenditure to identify the "new reference population" whose spending is in the second and third deciles. Use the consumption

Table 11.5 The Headcount Poverty Rate (P_0), S&W and BPS Methods

(based on expenditure)

	Urban (%)		Rural (%)		All Indonesia (%)	
	S&W	BPS	S&W	BPS	S&W	BPS
Feb 1996	12.1	13.6	17.8	19.9	15.7	17.7
Dec 1998	18.7	21.9	31.4	25.7	26.4	24.2
Feb 1999	18.9	19.4	25.4	26.0	22.9	23.4
Aug 1999	13.1	15.0	22.6	20.0	18.8	18.0

Sources: Said and Widyanti 2001; Suryahadi et al. 2000.

Note: S&W = Said and Widyanti approach; BPS = Indonesian Statistics Office (official) approach.

pattern of this group to compute the amount of calories consumed and the cost of these calories.

6. Scale up this cost of calories to determine the annual cost of 2,100 Calories per person per day. This is the food poverty line.

7. Add the cost of nonfood items. The BPS approach is to add the cost of 27 commodities (26 in rural areas), based on the results of the 1995 Survey of the Basic Needs Commodity Basket that covered 5,000 households in all 27 provinces.

Said and Widyanti follow steps 1–6, but take a different approach to estimating the cost of nonfood items. Following Ravallion and Bidani (1994) they estimate a relationship between food spending and total spending that takes the following form:

$$S_{ij} = \alpha + \beta_1 \ln\left(\frac{y_{ij}}{z_j^f}\right) + \beta_2 \left[\ln\left(\frac{y_{ij}}{z_j^f}\right)\right]^2 + \sum \phi_j D_{ij} + \text{residual} \qquad (11.1)$$

where S_{ij} is the share of total expenditure (y_{ij}) devoted to food, z_j^f is the food poverty line, and the D_{ij} are dummy variables for provinces and urban and rural areas. The value of the intercept estimates the average food share of households that can just afford the reference bundle of food. The total poverty line for region j is then given by $Z_j = z_j^f + (1 - \alpha - \phi_j)z_j^f$. This takes, as nonfood spending, the amount of expenditure on nonfood that a household is expected to make if it were just able to afford to buy enough food, and so is a relatively conservative (that is, low) number.

Whether one looks at the Said and Widyanti measure, or the BPS measure, the figures in table 11.5 paint a clear picture:

- The proportion of people in poverty rose by about half between February 1996 and December 1998, stabilizing thereafter and falling sharply in the first half of 1999 most, but not all, of the way back to their pre-crisis levels.

- Poverty rose in 1996–98 both in urban and rural areas; the BPS measures a larger rise in urban poverty, while Said and Widyanti find a much larger increase in rural than urban poverty.

Even if the measures of poverty shown here are sound, they do not really measure the effect of the financial crisis (or El Niño). To measure this effect, it would be necessary first to determine what the poverty rates would have been if the crisis had not occurred at all.

The fact that the poverty rate rose and fell so sharply suggests that it is worthwhile to distinguish between transient and persistent poverty. This is possible between December 1998 and August 1999 because the *Mini-Susenas* surveys constitute a panel. An example of this comes from table 7 in Said and Widyanti (2001), partly reproduced in table 11.6.

Table 11.6 Poverty Transition Matrix, December 1998–August 1999

(percentage of population)

		August 1999		
		Not poor	Poor	Total
December 1998	Not poor	67.8	6.2	74.0
	Poor	13.9	12.1	26.0
	Total	81.8	18.3	100.0

Source: Said and Widyanti 2001, table 7.

Note: Poverty headcount rates shown here vary slightly from those in table 11.5 because of sample attrition; about 80 percent of households surveyed in December 1998 were matched in August 1999.

According to table 11.6, almost a third of the population was poor at some point between December 1998 and August 1999. Only one person in eight was poor both in December 1998 and August 1999 ("persistently poor"), while one person in five was poor at the time of one of the surveys but not both ("transitory poor").

Controversies

The measurement of poverty in Indonesia is controversial. First, there is much debate about the appropriate techniques that should be used to arrive at a headcount measure of poverty. And second, a strong case can be made for measuring other dimensions of poverty.

The Problem of Technique: Poverty Rates at a Point in Time. Pradhan et al. (2000) point out that estimates of poverty rates are highly sensitive to the method used to calculate them. As noted above, one typically

- Measures the cost of buying a diet that provides 2,100 Calories per person per day (the food poverty line)

- Adds nonfood expenses.

However, the diet of the rich is more expensive (per calorie) than the diet of the poor. This raises the question of what reference population to use when computing the cost of calories that are used in estimating the money value of the food poverty line.

Pradhan et al. (2000) find that the choice of reference population is important in Indonesia. A researcher that chooses a wealthier reference population will compute a higher cost of calories, and so will put a higher money value on the poverty line, which in turn will lead to a higher poverty rate. Conversely, by choosing a poor group as the reference population, the estimated poverty rate will turn out to be lower. This introduces a considerable degree of arbitrariness into the determination of poverty rates.

To solve this problem Pradhan et al. (2000) propose an *iterative procedure*. First choose the cost of food for a reference population and then proceed to compute the poverty line. Now take, as the reference group, those households close to this poverty line. Recompute the poverty rate. Repeat the procedure until the poverty line stabilizes. It is to be hoped that this algorithm will converge, but it appears to do so in practice.

Using the iterative method, and applying an Engel curve procedure to compute nonfood expenditures (as done by Said and Widyanti 2001), Pradhan et al. (2000) find a headcount poverty rate of 27.1 percent on the basis of the February 1999 *Susenas*. This is somewhat higher than the official BPS figure of 23.6 percent. The numbers summarized in table 11.7 (from Pradhan et al. 2000, table 3) also show that the iterative method finds a wide difference in poverty rates between urban and rural areas, in contrast to the modest gap reported by the official BPS numbers.

The Problem of Deflation: Poverty Rates over Time. To compare poverty rates over time, it is necessary to deflate the poverty lines to account for inflation. If prices rise modestly, and especially if all prices rise at about the same rate, then deflating poverty lines is relatively straightforward and the results are typically satisfactory.

In the Indonesian case, however, the price of food in the consumer price index (CPI) rose by 160 percent between February 1996 and February 1999, while the rise in the price of the nonfood components of the CPI was just 81 percent. Not only was there high overall inflation, but also a massive change in *relative* prices over this

Table 11.7 Alternative Measures of Poverty in Indonesia

	Reference population (Rp/month)		Poverty line (Rp/month)	Poverty incidence (%)
	Lower limit	Upper limit		
Iterative method				
Urban	72,392	108,588	90,490	16.3
Rural	64,947	97,421	81,184	34.1
Ratio	1.11	1.11	1.11	overall: 27.1
BPS method				
Urban	80,000	100,000	93,869	20.0
Rural	60,000	80,000	73,8998	25.9
Ratio	1.33	1.25	1.27	overall: 23.6

Source: Pradhan et al. 2000, table 3.

Note: BPS = Indonesian Statistics Office (official) approach.

period. The relative increase in the price of food was due in large measure to the substantial real devaluation of the rupiah, making food imports (and hence food in general) relatively more expensive.

One could use the CPI to deflate the February 1999 poverty lines to get poverty lines in the prices of February 1996. But this would not be satisfactory, because food makes up just 40 percent of the CPI basket; it therefore understates the inflation faced by poor households, who devote far more than 40 percent of their expenditures to food. Suryahadi et al. (2000) experiment with three different methods of deflating. Given prices of food and nonfood—

1. Deflate each household's consumption using their actual share of food in consumption expenditures

2. Deflate each household's consumption using the share of food in the poverty basket

3. Deflate the *food* poverty line using the food price index and compute the nonfood allowance using the Engel curve methodology

For each method, they first used prices from the CPI; and then unit values as reported by households (that is, actual spending on an item divided by the

Table 11.8 Poverty Rates Computed Using Different Food Shares and Prices, February 1996 and February 1999

	Base case 1996	1999 using CPI	1999 using unit values
Working forward: start with poverty rate in February 1996			
Method 1: actual share of food in consumption, at poverty line	9.8	15.3	16.9
Method 2: share of food in the poverty basket	9.8	16.3	17.9
Method 3: deflate to get poverty line + recomputed nonfood share	9.8	20.3	22.4
	1996 using CPI	1996 using unit values	Base case 1999
Working backward: start with poverty rate in February 1999			
Method 1: actual share of food in consumption, at poverty line	20.0	18.3	27.2
Method 2: share of food in the poverty basket	17.6	15.7	27.2

Source: Suryahadi et al. 2000, tables 4 and 6.

Note: For definitions of the methods, see text. Base cases used iterative method; see discussion of Pradhan et al. (2000) results, above.

quantity bought). The results are summarized in table 11.8 (from table 4 in Suryahadi et al. 2000):

In the upper panel, an iterative method was used to compute the poverty rate in February 1996. The three methods were used to compute poverty rates for February 1999. They range from 15.3 to 22.4 percent—all of them purporting to measure the same thing. If method 3 is excluded—and it tends to deflate the poverty line by almost as much as the change in food prices, which is excessive—then the measures of the headcount index of poverty varied from 15.3 to 17.9 percent in 1999, up about 70 percent from the level of 9.75 percent that was computed (using the iterative method) for February 1996.

In the lower panel, an iterative method was used to compute the poverty rate in February 1999, and methods 1 and 2 were used to deflate to get the rates in February 1996. Although both approaches yield similar trends, they give strikingly different overall poverty rates, which is not particularly satisfactory.

All of the discussion above is based on the use of *Susenas* data. Indonesia is unusual in that there is a second set of high-quality survey data that provide information on living standards. The Indonesia Family Life Survey (IFLS) is "an ongoing longitudinal survey of individuals, households, families, and communities in Indonesia" (Frankenberg, Thomas, and Beegle 1999, 1). Households and individuals were interviewed in 1993–94 for IFLS1, in late 1997 for IFLS2, and a 25 percent subset of the same individuals and households about a year later for IFLS2+. The survey covers half of the country's provinces, including the most populous ones. The interviewers made a lot of effort to track down households for the IFLS2+, with the result that 98.5 percent of the households interviewed for IFLS2 were also interviewed for IFLS2+, a very low attrition rate.

In common with other researchers, Frankenberg, Thomas, and Beegle (1999) wrestled with the problem of how to deflate expenditures (or, equivalently, poverty lines) between the two surveys. They first used the CPI figures; they then noted that the CPI numbers are based on *urban* prices, and rural prices appear to have risen more quickly than urban ones between 1997 and 1998; and finally they inflated all CPI numbers by about 15 percent, on the grounds that the official CPI showed lower inflation that the prices collected in the course of the survey. Not surprisingly, this led to different poverty rates, as table 11.9 shows.

It is disturbing that the data are not accurate enough for us to determine whether the headcount poverty rate rose by about a quarter, or about four-fifths, between 1997 and 1998.

To finish this section, we reproduce in table 11.10 the main features of a useful table from Suryahadi et al. (2000), which summarizes the poverty rates that have been estimated using different methods, and by different researchers. Despite the real differences in estimates, a clear picture emerges: Poverty continued to fall until

Table 11.9 Poverty Rates Using Different Assumptions about Deflation, 1997 and 1998

	1997	1998	Change	Increase (%)
Using BPS inflation rates				
Urban	9.2	12.0	2.8	30
Rural	12.4	15.2	2.8	23
Overall	11.0	13.8	2.8	24
Using BPS inflation rates + 5% in rural areas				
Urban	9.2	12.0	2.8	30
Rural	12.4	16.2	3.8	31
Overall	11.0	14.3	3.3	30
Using BPS inflation rates adjusted upward				
Urban (prices 14% higher)	9.2	15.8	6.6	71
Rural (prices 16% higher)	12.4	23.0	10.6	85
Overall	11.0	19.9	8.9	81

Source: Frankenberg, Thomas, and Beegle 1999, table 2.2. Based on IFLS2 and IFLS2+.

Note: BPS = Indonesian Statistics Office.

mid- or late 1997. It then rose rapidly, peaking in early 1999, after which it fell again rapidly. By mid-1999 the poverty rate was back to the level of early 1996, but still somewhat above the historically low levels of mid-1997.

Frankenberg, Thomas, and Beegle (1999) go well beyond a discussion of poverty rates to examine other social changes that occurred in Indonesia between 1997 and 1998. Among their notable findings:

- Wages fell sharply, but hours worked and participation rates rose.

- Younger men, and women in most age groups, were more likely to get a job than lose a job between 1997 and 1998; men age 35 and older were more likely to lose a job than get one.

- Children ages 13–19 were less likely to be in school in 1998 than in 1997; the change was particularly marked for children from poor households, and in urban areas. The effect was smaller for children ages 7–12, although non-negligible in the case of poor households.

- Households reported less sickness in 1998 than 1997; fewer used the public health facilities, while more (especially better-off) households turned to private providers. Contraceptive use rates barely changed.

- Public health facilities experienced greater difficulty getting supplies, but immunization rates were maintained.

- The nutritional status of children did not worsen; the Body Mass Index fell slightly for adults, but the incidence of iron deficiency fell.

Table 11.10 Estimates of Poverty Rates in Indonesia, 1996–99

Date	Author, database	Method, price series for inflation of poverty line	Actual estimate	"Best guess" consistent series of P_0	
				Iterative initial point	BPS initial point
February 1996	SMERU, Susenas	Base case	9.75	9.75	11.34
	BPS, Susenas	Base case	11.34	9.75	11.34
February 1997	Gardiner, Susenas Core	Food share of bottom 30%	9.36	7.64	8.89
May 1997	SMERU, 100 villages	Method II, CPI	7.53	7.53	8.78
Aug.–Oct. 1997	Rand & LD, IFLS 2+	Normalization	11.00	6.57	7.64
February 1998	Gardiner, Susenas Core	Food share of bottom 30%	14.82	13.10	15.24
August 1998	SMERU, 100 villages	Method II, CPI	16.07	16.07	18.69
Sept.–Dec. 1998	Rand & LD, IFLS 2+	Own estimate inflation rate (15 points over DPI)	19.90	17.35	20.18
December 1998	SMERU, Mini Susenas	Method II, CPI	12.33	12.33	14.34
	BPS, Mini Susenas	February 1996 bundle	16.64	14.31	16.64
May 1999	SMERU, 100 villages	Method II, CPI	11.29	11.29	13.13
August 1999	SMERU, Mini Susenas	Method II, CPI	9.79	9.79	11.39
	BPS, Mini Susenas	February 1996 bundle	11.72	10.08	11.72

Source: Suryahadi et al. 2000, table 7.

Note: All figures are adjusted between the last two columns using the ratio of 11.34 to 9.75.

Review Questions

9. Here is some information about poverty in Indonesia.

Poverty Transition Matrix, December 1998–August 1999

(percentage of population)

		August 1999		
		Not poor	Poor	Total
December 1998	Not poor	67.8	6.2	74.0
	Poor	13.9	12.1	26.0
	Total	81.8	18.3	100.0

Source: Said and Widyanti 2001, table 7.

Note: Poverty headcount rates shown here vary slightly from those in table 11.5 because of sample attrition; about 80 percent of households surveyed in December 1998 were matched in August 1999.

According to these data,

- o A. 26.0 percent of the population were persistently poor.
- o B. 32.2 percent of the population were chronically poor.
- o C. Poverty rose in Indonesia between 1998 and 1999.
- o D. Indonesia rebounded rapidly from the 1997 financial crisis and poverty fell.

10. One of the biggest problems in determining the extent to which poverty fell in Indonesia after 1997 is that of deflating expenditures correctly; depending on the method used, headcount poverty rates rose by either 24 percent or 81 percent.

- o True
- o False

Some of these changes are not just correlates of poverty; they may be thought of as actually reflecting poverty itself. Most of these measures changed less dramatically than did the headcount poverty rate, implying that households drew on a variety of coping mechanisms to soften the blow of the economic crisis of 1997–99.

Notes

1. Kathleen Beegle contributed substantially to an earlier version of this section.
2. Let X_1 be income from the first sample and X_2 be income from the second sample. Then the variance of the difference between these is $\text{var}(X_1 - X_2) = \text{var}(X_1) + \text{var}(X_2) - 2 \text{ cov}(X_1 X_2)$. If the samples are independent, then $\text{cov}(X_1 X_2) = 0$; but if the data come from a panel, then it is likely that X_1 and X_2 are highly positively correlated. This reduces $\text{var}(X_1 - X_2)$ and so makes the test for a difference between X_1 and X_2 more powerful.
3. This will be true only if the unobserved factors do not change over time, and influence output linearly.

4. Some researchers count as transient poor anyone who is observed to be in poverty in some years but not in others, regardless of whether their average consumption level is above or below the poverty line. The choice of appropriate definition depends on the purpose of the underlying analysis.

References

Chen, Shaohua, and Martin Ravallion. 2008. "The Developing World Is Poorer Than We Thought, But No Less Successful in the Fight against Poverty." Policy Research Working Paper 4703, World Bank, Washington, DC.

Deaton, Angus. 1997. *The Analysis of Household Surveys: A Microeconometric Approach to Development Policy*. Baltimore: Johns Hopkins University Press.

Dollar, David, and Aart Kraay. 2002. "Growth Is Good for the Poor." Development Research Group, World Bank, Washington, DC.

Frankenberg, Elizabeth, Duncan Thomas, and Kathleen Beegle. 1999. "The Real Costs of Indonesia's Economic Crisis: Preliminary Findings from the Indonesia Family Life Surveys." RAND, Santa Monica, CA, July.

Glewwe, Paul, and Hanan Jacoby. 2000. "Recommendations for Collecting Panel Data as a Part of LSMS Surveys." In *Designing Household Survey Questionnaires*, ed. Margaret Grosh and Paul Glewwe. Washington, DC: World Bank.

Haughton, Dominique, Jonathan Haughton, Le Thi Thanh Loan, and Nguyen Phong. 2001. "Shooting Stars and Sinking Stones." In *Living Standards During an Economic Boom: The Case of Vietnam*, ed. Dominique Haughton, Jonathan Haughton, and Nguyen Phong. Hanoi: Statistical Publishing House.

Jalan, Jyotsna, and Martin Ravallion. 1998. "Transient Poverty in Postreform Rural China." *Journal of Comparative Economics* 26: 338–57.

Krishna, Anirudh, Patti Kristjanson, Maren Radeny, and Wilson Nindo. 2004. "Escaping Poverty and Becoming Poor in 20 Kenyan Villages." *Journal of Human Development* 5 (2): 211–26.

Pitt, Mark, Mark Rosenzweig, and Donna Gibbons. 1993. "The Determinants and Consequences of the Placement of Government Programs in Indonesia." *World Bank Economic Review* 7: 319–48.

Pradhan, Menno, Asep Suryahadi, Sudarno Sumarto, and Lant Pritchett. 2000. "Measurements of Poverty in Indonesia: 1996, 1999 and Beyond." Social Monitoring and Early Response Unit (SMERU), Jakarta.

Ravallion, Martin, and Benu Bidani. 1994. "How Robust Is a Poverty Profile?" *The World Bank Economic Review* 8 (1): 75–102.

Said, Ali, and Wenefrida D. Widyanti. 2001. "The Impact of Economic Crisis on Poverty and Inequality in Indonesia." Presented at Symposium on Poverty Analysis and Data Initiative (PADI), Manila, Philippines, April 30–May 3.

Skoufias, Emmanuel, Asep Suryahadi, and Sudarno Sumarto. 1999. "The Indonesian Crisis and Its Impacts on Household Welfare, Poverty Transitions, and Inequality: Evidence from

Matched Households in 100 Village Survey." Social Monitoring and Early Response Unit (SMERU), Jakarta.

Suryahadi, Asep, Sudarno Sumarto, Yusuf Suharso, and Lant Pritchett. 2000. "The Evolution of Poverty during the Crisis in Indonesia, 1996 to 1999 (Using Full Susenas Sample)." Social Monitoring and Early Response Unit (SMERU), Jakarta.

Vietnam, General Statistical Office. 2000. *Vietnam Living Standards Survey 1997–1998.* Hanoi: Statistical Publishing House.

Vietnam, State Planning Committee and General Statistical Office. 1994. *Vietnam Living Standards Survey 1992–1993.* Hanoi.

Vijverberg, Wim, and Jonathan Haughton. 2004. "Household Enterprises in Vietnam: Survival, Growth and Living Standards." In *Economic Growth, Poverty and Household Welfare in Vietnam,* ed. Paul Glewwe, Nisha Agrawal, and David Dollar. Washington, DC: World Bank.

Chapter 12

Vulnerability to Poverty

Summary

Between one year and the next, many people move into or out of poverty. Thus measures of who is poor now are imperfect guides to who will be poor next year, yet it is the latter that is relevant for public policies that aim to reduce poverty.

The solution is to identify those who are *vulnerable to poverty*—that is, who have a significant probability of being poor next year. People are highly vulnerable if they have more than an even chance of being poor in the next period, and moderately vulnerable if they are more likely than the typical person to be poor next year.

Vulnerability can only be quantified by making some simplifying assumptions. With an estimation of expected consumption per capita ($E(c_{t+1})$), its variance (σ^2), and the poverty line (z), and assuming that consumption per capita (or its log) is normally distributed, it is straightforward to estimate the probability that a household will be poor (v_{ht}) and so to determine whether the household may be considered to be vulnerable or not. Vulnerability to poverty is due to either low expected consumption or high variability in consumption.

A measure of $E(c_{t+1})$ is typically found by estimating a regression model of c_t and using it to predict c_{t+1}. The variance is best estimated using longitudinal or panel data; however, because such data are rare, variance is often inferred from cross-sectional variation instead. Unfortunately, this misses the effects of unusual economy-wide shocks such as the Asian financial crisis of 1997.

Studies of vulnerability typically find that the proportion of people who are vulnerable to poverty substantially exceeds the proportion who are currently poor. One implication is that this makes targeting more difficult.

The World bank is encouraging the development and use of Risk and Vulnerability Assessments, which aim to understand the sources of risk, identify the most vulnerable, and design instruments to increase social protection. This is an area of active research.

Learning Objectives

After completing the module on *Vulnerability to Poverty*, you should be able to

1. Explain why measures of current poverty are inadequate as guides to antipoverty policy.

2. Define *vulnerability to poverty*.

3. Explain how the measurement of vulnerability to poverty requires measures of

   • Shocks to welfare

   • The socially defined minimum level of well-being

   • The propensity to suffer a significant shock of being poor.

4. Describe how to measure vulnerability to poverty (v_{ht}), given measures of expected consumption ($E(c_{t+1})$), its variance (σ^2), the poverty line (z), and a normality assumption.

5. Outline the steps required to measure vulnerability to poverty, given data from a cross-sectional household survey.

6. Summarize the methodological issues related to the practical measurement of vulnerability to poverty and how they might be resolved.

7. Itemize the main sources of risk faced by households.

8. Describe the nature, purpose, and principal contents of Risk and Vulnerability Assessments.

Introduction: Why Measure Vulnerability?

The study of poverty focuses on those who are currently poor (or were poor in the past). This is because poverty can be measured only ex post. Such an approach has its merits: for instance, by using actual data one may measure the effects of past public interventions on the extent of poverty; and it allows us to identify whose poverty needs to be alleviated.

But governments and policy makers are typically more interested in the effects that their measures will have in the future. For this it would be valuable to be able to identify those who are expected to be poor ex ante (that is, in the future). Such households are considered to be *vulnerable to poverty*. As Chaudhuri, Jalan, and Suryahadi (2002, 2) put it, "for thinking about appropriate forward-looking anti-poverty interventions (. . . that aim to prevent or reduce future poverty . . .), the crucial need then is . . . an assessment of households' vulnerability to poverty."

A household is vulnerable to poverty if it is likely to be poor in the future. Dercon (2001, 1) defines vulnerability as "ex ante poverty." Since vulnerability is a forward-looking concept, it measures "exposure to poverty rather than the poverty outcome itself" (Dercon 2001, 27).

Information on who is poor today serves as a good guide to those who will be poor next year only if people are persistently poor. Table 12.1 illustrates this point using data from Vietnam, and shows a transition matrix based on a panel of 4,281 households that were surveyed both in 1993 and 1998. The headcount poverty rate was 56 percent in 1993 and fell to 34 percent in 1998. Almost half of those who were identified as poor in 1998 were not poor in 1998; and more than a tenth of those who were not poor in 1993 were found to be poor in 1998, despite the rapid economic growth of about 8 percent annually that occurred between these two years.

The evidence is not confined to Vietnam. Table 12.2 summarizes some results from a survey by Baulch and Hoddinott (2000), based on six sets of panel data,

Table 12.1 Transition Matrix for Poverty, Vietnam, 1993 and 1998

	Poor in 1998	Not poor in 1998	Poverty rate in 1993
Poor in 1993	0.287	0.274	0.561
Not poor in 1993	0.048	0.391	
Poverty rate in 1998	0.335		

Source: Glewwe, Gragnolati, and Zaman 2002.

Note: Based on Vietnam Living Standards Surveys (VLSS) 1993 and 1998. Size of panel: 4,281 households.

Table 12.2 Changes in Poverty from Panel Surveys in Selected Countries

Country	Period	Headcount (%)		
		Always poor	Sometimes poor	Never poor
Zimbabwe	1992/93–1995/96	11	60	30
Pakistan	1986–91	3	55	42
South Africa	1993–98	23	32	46
Russian Federation	1992–93	13	30	57
Ethiopia	1994–97	25	30	45
Côte d'Ivoire	1987–88	25	22	53

Source: Pritchett, Shryahadi, and Sumarto 2000, based on Baulch and Hoddinott (2000).

Note: The definitions of poverty line vary from country to country, so the poverty rates are not comparable across countries. Totals may not add to 100 due to rounding.

which show that the fraction of people who were "always poor"—that is, poor in both periods, and so persistently poor—is generally quite modest; on the other hand, a large fraction of the population in most of the countries covered were poor in one or other of the years, but not in both years ("stochastically poor").

The message here is that the identification of those who are poor now is an inadequate indicator of those who are expected to be poor in the future. This is why a good measure of vulnerability to poverty is needed.

Review Question

1. The difference between poverty and vulnerability is that
○ A. Vulnerability is poverty ex post.   ○ B. More people are poor than are vulnerable.   ○ C. Poverty measures whether one fell below the poverty line in the past while vulnerability measures the probability of falling below the poverty line in the future.   ○ D. Vulnerability measures those who are "sometimes poor" while poverty measures those who are "always poor."

Vulnerability to Poverty Defined

An attractive definition of vulnerability to poverty is "the propensity to suffer a significant welfare shock, bringing the household below a socially defined minimum level" (Kühl 2003, 4, citing Alwang, Siegel, and Jorgensen 2001).[1] While this definition captures the spirit of what we mean by vulnerability to poverty, it needs to be made more precise if we are actually to measure vulnerability. Three points require clarification.

First, what is meant by a "welfare shock"? The measure of welfare most commonly used by economists in this context is consumption per capita (or per adult equivalent), although other measures such as income could be used instead. In their study of vulnerability in Mali, Christiaensen and Boisvert (2000) use a measure of malnutrition as their indicator of welfare.

So a welfare "shock" is commonly measured as a change in consumption per capita. The shock could be negative or positive, although we typically are concerned with shocks in the more traditional sense of harmful events. By focusing on consumption rather than income or assets, we are implicitly allowing for household coping mechanisms to operate. For instance, consider a village that is hit by drought every few years. Households, anticipating periods of drought, store grain in good years to tide them over the bad years. If we use income as our measure of welfare, we would overstate household well-being in good years and understate it in drought years; by using consumption as the indicator of welfare, we are allowing for household response.

Second, what "socially defined minimum level" of welfare is appropriate? Here, we typically use a poverty line, which is subject to all the caveats set out in chapter 3, where we discuss how best to pick a suitable poverty line. Studies of vulnerability to poverty generally use an absolute poverty line.

Third, how might one measure the "propensity to suffer a significant ... shock" of being poor? A good practical way to measure vulnerability is as the probability of being poor

- In the next year (Chaudhuri, Jalan, and Suryahadi 2002), or

- At some point over the next few years (Pritchett, Shryahadi, and Sumarto 2000).

But how high does this probability of being poor need to be for us to consider the person (or household) as being vulnerable? If I have a 1 percent probability of being poor next year, am I vulnerable? Or 10 percent? Or 50 percent?

Review Question

> 2. A good definition of vulnerability is "the fact of having suffered a significant welfare shock, bringing the household below a socially defined minimum level."
>
> ○ True
> ○ False
> ○ Uncertain

The choice of line separating those who are vulnerable to poverty from those who are not is arbitrary, but researchers typically use one of two thresholds:

- A probability of being poor of 50 percent. In this case, a household has at least an even chance of being poor next year. Such households are sometimes referred to as "highly vulnerable."

- A probability of being poor of P_0 (where P_0 is the headcount poverty rate). It can be shown that under plausible assumptions the average vulnerability to poverty—that is, the average probability of being poor—is equal to the head-count poverty rate. If your probability of being poor is higher than this—for example, 20 percent, when the poverty rate is 12 percent—then you might be considered vulnerable by this measure. In effect, this means that you are more likely than the typical household to be poor in the next period. Households whose probability of being poor is higher than P_0 but lower than 50 percent are sometimes put into the category of "low vulnerability."

Households whose probability of being poor is below P_0 are sometimes referred to as "not vulnerable," but this label should not be taken literally, because there is some probability that they may indeed find themselves in poverty in the next year (or over the next few years).

The probability of being poor rises as the time horizon lengthens; someone with a 50 percent probability of being poor next year may have a 75 percent probability of being poor in at least one of the next two years and an 87.5 percent probability of being poor in at least one of the next three years.[2]

More formally, in the one-period case, let $c_{h,t}$ be the per capita consumption level of household h in time t and z be the poverty line. Then a household is poor if

$$c_{h,t} \le z. \tag{12.1}$$

Now define the vulnerability of household h in time t as $v_{h,t}$ giving the probability that the household will find itself poor in time $t + 1$. This may be written as

$$v_{h,t} = \Pr(c_{h,t+1} \le z). \tag{12.2}$$

The practical problem here is that $c_{h,t+1}$ is not directly observable, because it represents our expectation of the household's per capita consumption level in the next period. We now consider techniques for actually quantifying $v_{h,t+1}$.

Review Question

3. Which of the following statements about vulnerability is not true?
○ A. The measurement of vulnerability requires one to estimate a household's consumption in the future.
○ B. The "highly vulnerable" are those with at least a 50:50 chance of being poor in the future.
○ C. Households that are "not vulnerable" may nonetheless fall into poverty at some point.
○ D. As the time horizon into the future gets longer, vulnerability decreases.

Quantifying Vulnerability to Poverty

At first sight, the task of measuring vulnerability to poverty seems daunting. In principle, we would need to know the following information for every household:

- What resources they can draw on in the next year, including assets such as land as well as their educational endowments and their skills and experience

- What risks they face—such as drought, higher prices for food, family illness, and so on; the probability of each set of risks ("states of the world"); and the effect of each set of risks on their resources

- Their ability to handle each set of risks—for instance, by eating into stocks of corn, or drawing on family support networks, or borrowing money, or working harder.

It is clearly impossible to collect all the information needed for such an analysis, and it may be equally hard to model all the possible behavioral responses by households.

The solution, as in all modeling, is to simplify enough to make the problem tractable. In the simplest case, three pieces of information and one additional assumption are enough to allow us to measure a household's vulnerability to poverty. The required pieces of information are as follows:

- The household's expected level of consumption per capita in the next period, given by $E(c_{t+1})$

- The variance of the household's expected level of consumption per capita in the next period, σ^2

- The poverty line, z.

To this we add the assumption that the expected level of consumption follows a known distribution such as the normal (Gaussian) distribution. Then we may proceed as set out in this example:

> **Example:** Suppose what we expect the per capita consumption of a household to be 50 next year. This is only an estimate, and we believe that the standard deviation of this estimate is 12 (that is, the variance is 144). The poverty line is 40. What is the probability that this household will be poor next year?
>
> Assuming that the shocks to per capita consumption are normally distributed, then the probability that this household will be poor next year (that is, its vulnerability) is 0.202.[3] In other words, given the expected consumption per capita and its associate variance, there is a 20.2 percent probability that this household will in fact find itself below the poverty line. This is illustrated by the shaded area in figure 12.1.

Figure 12.1 Illustrating the Probability of Poverty for a Household

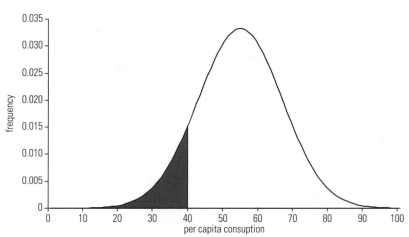

Source: Authors.

Note: Poverty line is 40, Expected income per capita is 50; standard deviation of expected income is 12.

Now consider another household, with expected per capita consumption of 45 and estimated standard deviation of 6. This household also has a 20.2 percent probability of finding itself in poverty next year—that is, its vulnerability is also 0.202.

Review Question

> 4. A household has expected per capita consumption of 95 and the variance of this consumption is 36. The poverty line is 100. Then the probability that the household will be poor next year is:
>
>   o A. 0.555
>   o B. 0.798
>   o C. 0.445
>   o D. 0.202

This illustrates an important point: households may be vulnerable even if they have high expected consumption, provided that the variance in consumption is sufficiently large. Or put another way, vulnerability to poverty may be due to low consumption, or to high variability in consumption. In figure 12.2, households have vulnerability greater than 0.202 if they are anywhere below the vulnerability line.

This example is helpful, but does not explain how to measure $E(c_{t+1})$ or σ^2 in practice. Let us take each piece in turn.

Measuring Expected Consumption and Its Variance

Although we do not know what a household's level of consumption will be next year, it may be possible to arrive at a reasonable estimate by first building a model

Figure 12.2 Identifying Vulnerable Households

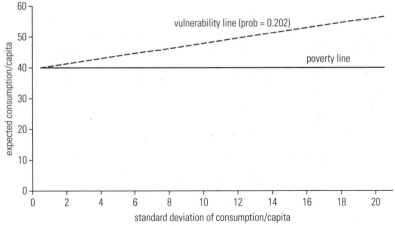

Source: Based on authors' calculations.

of the determinants of consumption and then using the model to predict next year's consumption.

Formally, we have

$$c_{h,t} = c(X_h, \beta_t, \alpha_h, e_{ht}) \tag{12.3}$$

where

X_h is a vector of observable household characteristics such as the age and education level of the household head, the number of household members, and so on

β_t is a set of economy-wide parameters that pick up the effects of nationwide shocks, such as a financial crisis or a political revolution

α_h captures any unobserved time-invariant household effects, such as the abilities of household members, for instance

e_{ht} is an error term that measures "idiosyncratic" factors, meaning the sort of shocks that might buffet one household but not another. The variance of this error could vary substantially from one household to the next.

If we could estimate this relationship, including the variance of expected consumption, then we could measure vulnerability as

$$v_{h,t} = \Pr\left(c_{h,t+1} = c(X_h, \beta_{t+1}, \alpha_h, e_{h,t+1}) < z \mid X_h, \beta_t, \alpha_h, e_{ht}\right). \tag{12.4}$$

With data from a single cross-section it is possible to estimate a simplified version of equation (12.4), as is done by Chaudhuri, Jalan, and Suryahadi (2002). Using Indonesian data for 1998–99, they estimate a model of household consumption of the form

$$\ln c_h = X_h \cdot b + e_h, \tag{12.5}$$

where

$$e_h \sim N(0, X_h \theta). \tag{12.6}$$

Practically, this involves

• Regressing the log of per capita consumption on a set of independent variables, to get the estimated coefficients in equation (12.5)

• Squaring the residuals from this estimated equation and regressing them on the same independent variables, to get the coefficient $\hat{\theta}$ and hence the estimated variance from $X_h\hat{\theta}$ to arrive at a measure of the idiosyncratic variance for each household.

Then, on the assumption that the independent variables (household size, education of household head, and so on) do not change from one year to the next, one can generate a value of expected log consumption (as predicted by equation (12.5)) and the standard deviation of the log of consumption (from equation (12.6)) and hence construct a measure of vulnerability to poverty for each household. Using Indonesian data for 1998–99, Chaudhuri, Jalan, and Suryahadi (2002) estimated

$$\hat{v}_h = \Pr(\ln c_h < \ln z \mid X_h) = \Phi\left(\frac{\ln z - X_h a}{\sqrt{X_h \hat{\theta}}}\right).$$ (12.7)

where Φ is the cumulative density function of the standard normal distribution. They then sorted households into three categories:

- The highly vulnerable, for whom $\hat{v}_h > 0.5$

- The "relatively vulnerable," for whom $0.22 < \hat{v}_h < 0.5$, where 0.22 is the headcount poverty rate

- Those who are "not vulnerable."

Their key results are set out in table 12.3.

Perhaps the most important point to note in table 12.3 is that although 22 percent of those surveyed by the Mini-SUSENAS survey in Indonesia in 1998–99 were poor, fully 45 percent were considered to be vulnerable, of which 8 percent were highly vulnerable to poverty and the other 37 percent somewhat vulnerable. In other words, vulnerability (as defined here) is more widespread than poverty. This finding accords with the results of participatory poverty assessments, which typically show that a substantial part of the population is seriously and legitimately concerned about falling into poverty, even if they are not currently poor. It also makes the targeting of (future) poverty more difficult, since more people have significant potential for falling into poverty.

In this example, the poor constitute 22 percent of the population, but more than 60 percent of those who are highly vulnerable. Or, to put the same point slightly differently, a poor person is almost six times as likely to be vulnerable to poverty as someone who is not currently poor. At first sight, this suggests that poverty predicts vulnerability quite well.

Table 12.3 Poverty and Vulnerability in Indonesia, 1998–99

	Criterion	Proportion of total population		
		Poor	Nonpoor	Poor and nonpoor
High vulnerability	$\hat{v}_h \geq 0.50$	0.05	0.03	0.08
Low vulnerability	$0.22 < \hat{v}_h \leq 0.50$	0.12	0.25	0.37
Not vulnerable	$\hat{v}_h < 0.50$	0.05	0.50	0.55
All groups		0.22	0.78	1.00

Source: Dercon 2001, 35, based on Chaudhuri, Jalan, and Suryahadi (2002).

But more than half of the vulnerable population is *not* currently poor. This is why it is not sufficient to use current poverty status as a proxy for whether someone will be poor in the next period.

It might seem surprising that a significant number of poor households are considered to be "not vulnerable." Yet this is indeed what table 12.3 is telling us. The point is that these particular households may be currently poor, but they are considered to have a relatively low (but not zero) probability of being poor in the next time period. Presumably, they have good consumption prospects, but are down on their luck for now—perhaps their crops failed, or someone lost his or her job, but they will recover in the near future.

Review Question

> 5. Chaudhuri, Jalan, and Suryahadi (2002) measure vulnerability in Indonesia by
>
> ○ A. Using historical data to determine the probability that a household was poor, and then projecting these probabilities into the future.
> ○ B. Sorting households into three categories: "highly vulnerable," "vulnerable," and "not vulnerable."
> ○ C. Estimating consumption and its variance using cross-section data, and using the predicted values, along with a standard normal cumulative density function, to work out the probability of poverty (and hence the vulnerability) for each household.
> ○ D. Using panel data to estimate average consumption and its variance for each household, and then comparing the values to a standard normal cumulative density function to work out the probability of poverty (and hence the vulnerability) for each household.

Methodological Issues

The measurement of vulnerability to poverty is inherently more problematic than the measurement of poverty itself, because of the challenges involved in arriving at adequate predictions of the future. The approach outlined above draws on that followed by Chaudhuri, Jalan, and Suryahadi (2002) but can, or perhaps should, be refined in a number of ways. These refinements may sound technical, but they are important:

Measurement Error. It is generally accepted that there is substantial error in the measurement of consumption—a point that was discussed in chapter 2. A consequence of this measurement error is that we are almost certainly overstating the extent to which households move into and out of poverty. It also implies that the estimates of the variance of the idiosyncratic shocks that affect households (that is, the estimate of σ^2) are overstated. Pritchett, Shryahadi, and Sumarto (2000) argue that between a third and half of the variance is due to measurement error, and in their work they adjust it downward by 30 percent.

In passing, one might note that a major "shock" to a household's consumption per capita is the arrival of a new baby. Kamanou and Morduch (2002) claim that demographic changes of this type in the Côte d'Ivoire account for a quarter of all variation in consumption per capita. Yet it is not at all clear that one should interpret the arrival of a new family member as a reduction in household welfare.

Measurement of σ^2. Chaudhuri, Jalan, and Suryahadi (2002) measured the variance of future consumption by looking at the structure of errors in the consumption equation. However, this equation was estimated with cross-section data, which allows us to measure variation across space but not over time. Ideally we would like to measure the variation of a household's income over time. In principle, this requires data from longitudinal studies, which follow individuals (or households) over an extended period of time; in practice, such data are almost nonexistent in less-developed countries, and even if they were, one would have to assume that there was no change in economic structure, so that the historic record of consumption variability is an adequate guide to its future variability.

In a number of cases, panel data are available, allowing one to compare the consumption of households at two (or occasionally more) points in time. This is helpful, especially in validating the results of using cross-section-based measures of σ^2 (see Chaudhuri, Jalan, and Suryahadi 2002 for an example in the context of Indonesia), but it is not a panacea. Pritchett, Shryahadi, and Sumarto (2000) use Indonesian panel data to compute the variance of *changes* in consumption per capita, but their measure is still largely based on cross-sectional variation.

The main problem is that unless one has information for many years, it is likely to be difficult or impossible to pick up the effects of rare but important shocks, such as the Asian financial crisis of 1997/98. One approach is to include questions, in household surveys, that directly ask households about the shocks that they have faced; Dercon (2001) and others have had some success with this technique in surveys in Ethiopia. Another approach is to trace the effects of rare events through simulations; for example, Haughton and Kinh (2004) have taken such an approach to quantifying the effects on poverty and income distribution of a major devaluation of the Vietnamese dong.

The Normality Assumption. It is typically assumed that the log of consumption is normally distributed. However, this may not be the case, and some authors (Kamanou and Morduch 2002; Kühl 2003) have based their estimates of vulnerability to poverty on the actually observed distribution of the errors of the consumption equation, using bootstrapping.

Estimation Procedures. For the purposes of this chapter, we have assumed that regression estimates can be based on using ordinary least squares (OLS). It turns out that this may not be consistent, and more elaborate procedures may be called for; for an example, see the use of Amemiya's three-step feasible generalized least squares estimator by Chaudhuri, Jalan, and Suryahadi (2002).

Review Question

6. Which of the following is not generally a problem faced by researchers when measuring vulnerability?
o A. The welfare measure (for example, expenditure per capita, or its log) may not be normally distributed, leading to mismeasurement of the expected probability of being in poverty. o B. Measurement error leads one to overstate vulnerability. o C. In the absence of panel or longitudinal data, the variance of expenditure cannot be estimated fully satisfactorily. o D. The level of expenditure reported by households is understated, which leads to an underestimate of vulnerability.

Sources of Vulnerability

Vulnerability to poverty has been measured in only a handful of studies, and Dercon (2001) makes a strong case for further attention to the quantification of vulnerability. This conclusion is based on the idea that a clear sense of the causes of vulnerability to poverty is needed if one is to craft successful policies to combat it.

However, Alwang, Siegel, and Jorgensen (2001) argue that while the economic approach to vulnerability has been relatively successful at measurement, it has been far less successful at modeling the causes of vulnerability. In their words,

> [W]ithout producing a structural model that includes specific shocks, it will be impossible to understand how household vulnerability to such shocks is affected by ownership of and the access to assets, prices, etc. Panel data sets rarely have the richness of detail or the sample size to estimate structural models of how, for instance, realization of a bad outcome (e.g., illness of a key worker) will affect well-being. (p. 32)

The attempt to understand the causes of vulnerability to poverty is not futile. Dercon (2001) proposes a framework for analysis that is helpful in this context, and is reproduced here (in modified form) in table 12.4. The basic idea is that households have assets, such as land, labor, and physical, human, and social capital. They deploy these assets to generate income. And the income in turn is used to generate well-being, mainly through consumption.

At each point in the process there are risks. Assets may be degraded if there is war, or uncertain land tenure, or a theft. Income may be reduced if there is a drought or output prices fall. The ability to consume may be reduced if the cost of food rises or food is rationed.

An implication of this analysis is that policies to reduce vulnerability to poverty need to operate in two ways: first, they need to try to raise the average level of well-being, much as any antipoverty program would try to do. And, second, they need to focus on reducing risk and its consequences, essentially through insurance mechanisms.

Table 12.4 A Framework for Analyzing Vulnerability to Poverty

Assets	Incomes	Well-being/capabilities

• Human capital, labor
• Physical/financial capital
• Common and public goods
• Social capital
	• Returns to activities and assets
	• Returns from asset disposal
	• Savings, credit, investment
	• Transfers and remittances
		• Ability to obtain
		  • Consumption
		  • Nutrition
		  • Health
		  • Education

Examples of risk (a)	**Examples of risk (b)**	**Examples of risk (c)**
• Loss of skills due to ill health or unemployment • Land tenure insecurity • Asset damage due to climate, war, disaster • Uncertain access to common and public goods • Loss of value of financial assets	• Output falls due to climatic shocks, disease, conflict • Output prices rise • Reduced returns on financial assets • Uncertain cash flow during production • Weak contract enforcement, wages not paid • Imperfect information about opportunities	• Price risk in food markets • Food availability/rationing • Uncertain quality of public provision in health and education • Imperfect information on how to achieve good health, nutrition

Source: Based on Dercon (2001, 17).

Review Question

> 7. An agricultural household is likely to become more vulnerable to poverty (as typically measured) for all of the following reasons, except—

    ○ A. The frequency of typhoons (hurricanes) increases.
    ○ B. The head of the household falls ill.
    ○ C. A brother who lived nearby moves to the city.
    ○ D. A new son is born in the household.

This is the starting point for the growing interest in Social Risk Management, which is an approach to ensuring social protection. The World Bank is encouraging the use of Risk and Vulnerability Assessments (RVAs), which are "diagnostic tools" designed to

• Understand the sources of vulnerability to poverty, and most notably—

    • What are the most prevalent and severe shocks?

    • Which groups are at the highest risk of falling into poverty as a result of these shocks (which is the point at which vulnerability needs to be measured)?

• Catalog the public interventions aimed at managing social risks

• Identify the "policy gap," by which is meant the menu of interventions that could be used to reduce risk or exposure to risk (Holzmann, Sherburne-Benz, and Tesliuc 2003).

Underlying RVAs is a widespread belief that the poor are the ones most subject to shocks (perhaps) and they have the fewest mechanisms for dealing with such shocks (probable). This makes them understandably risk averse, and so they may be less prone to innovate; it may also force them to pull their children out of school prematurely. Either way, this represents lower investment, so they are more likely to remain trapped in poverty. In short, addressing risk is not only desirable in its own right, but it may also help a country grow economically.

Risk and Vulnerability Assessments devote considerable attention to ways in which the vulnerable can reduce risk (for instance, by migrating or building flood dikes), mitigate risk (for instance, by diversifying sources of income or building up savings), and cope with shocks (for instance, by selling assets or borrowing). Table 12.5, drawn

Table 12.5 Mechanisms for Managing Risk

	Informal Mechanisms		Formal Mechanisms	
	Individual and household	Group-based	Market-based	Publicly provided
Reducing risk	• preventive health practices • migration • more secure income sources	• collective action for infrastructure, dikes, terraces • common property resource management		• sound macroeconomic policies • environmental policy • education and training policy • public health policy • infrastructure • labor market policies
Mitigating risk Diversification	• crops and plots • income source • investment in physical and human capital	• occupational associations • rotating credit associations	• savings accounts in financial institutions • microfinance	• agricultural extension • liberalized trade • protection of property rights
Insurance	• marriage and extended family • sharecropping • buffer stocks	• investment in social capital	• old age annuities • accident, disability and other insurance	• pension systems • mandatory insurance for unemployment, illness, disability
Coping with shocks	• sale of assets • borrowing from moneylenders • child labor • reduced food consumption • seasonal/temporary migration	• transfers from mutual support networks	• sale of financial assets • loans from financial institutions	• social assistance • workfare • subsidies • social funds • cash transfers

Source: World Bank 2000, 141 (slightly modified).

from the World Bank's *World Development Report 2000/2001*, summarizes some of the most important mechanisms for reducing, mitigating and coping with risk.

Lessons from Studies of Vulnerability to Poverty

A number of clear findings emerge from the literature on vulnerability to poverty. The first is that vulnerability to poverty is measurable, albeit imperfectly. It is also harder to measure than is poverty. But if the intention is to design measures to prevent poverty in the future, as opposed to alleviating the suffering of the current poor, then there is no escaping the need to measure vulnerability.

As typically defined, vulnerability to poverty is more widespread than poverty itself. A wide swathe of society risks poverty at some point of time; put another way, in most societies, only a relatively modest portion of society may be considered as economically secure.

Although the poor are likely to be vulnerable, a focus on poverty can be misleading and lead one to overlook the economic precariousness of many households. Pritchett, Shryahadi, and Sumarto (2000), using the "mini-Susenas" data for Indonesia for 1998–99, find that while urban poverty is just 8 percent, fully 30 percent of urban residents are vulnerable to poverty. This suggests that it is important not to overlook urban areas when trying to tackle poverty in the future.

Part of the solution to vulnerability is the traditional one of antipoverty measures: raise consumption. But the other part focuses on social protection. Just as the measurement of poverty is justified in part by the need to keep poverty reduction on the agenda, the measurement of vulnerability is justified in part by the need not to forget the importance of social protection.

Some groups in society may be vulnerable in other ways than to poverty—for example, children may be vulnerable to sexual abuse or forced labor. This is a somewhat different issue from that tackled in a handbook on poverty analysis; the social protection unit of the World Bank has produced some interesting papers on this and related issues, which may be found at www.worldbank.org/sp.

Review Question

8. Which of the following conclusions does not follow from a discussion of the conventional measurement of vulnerability?

- A. Vulnerability cannot be measured as easily as poverty.
- B. Vulnerability is more widespread than poverty.
- C. The main solution to poverty is raising consumption per capita; any reduction in vulnerability also requires attention to social protection.
- D. Vulnerability is more widespread in urban than in rural areas.

Notes

1. This is not the only possible definition of vulnerability, or even vulnerability to poverty; it is an outcomes-based definition that has the advantage of being measurable (see below in the text). Alwang, Siegel, and Jorgensen (2001) discuss a number of other definitions of vulnerability in more detail.

2. These calculations assume that the probability of being poor does not change over time. The probability of being poor in at least one year over a time interval x is 1 minus the probability of not being poor in any of these x years. Someone with a 50 percent probability of being poor in any given year has a 12.5 percent probability (that is, one in eight chance) of not being poor in any of the next three years, and so has an 87.5 percent probability of being poor in at least one of the three years.

3. In Microsoft Excel, one can find this probability by typing=normdist (40,50,12,1).

References

Alwang, Jeffrey, Paul Siegel, and Steen Jorgensen. 2001. "Vulnerability: A View from Different Disciplines." Social Protection Discussion Paper No. 0115, Social Protection Unit, Human Development Network, World Bank, Washington, DC.

Baulch, Bob, and John Hoddinott. 2000. "Economic Mobility and Poverty Dynamics in Developing Countries." *Journal of Development Economics* Special issue: 1–24.

Chaudhuri, Shubham, Jyotsna Jalan, and Asep Suryahadi. 2002. "Assessing Household Vulnerability to Poverty from Cross-sectional Data: a Methodology and Estimates for Indonesia." Discussion Paper Series No. 0102-52, Department of Economics, Columbia University, New York.

Christiaensen, L. J., and R. N. Boisvert. 2000. "On Measuring Household Food Vulnerability: Case Evidence from Northern Mali." Working Paper 2000–05, Department of Applied Economics, Cornell University, Ithaca, New York.

Dercon, Stefan. 2001. "Assessing Vulnerability to Poverty." Paper prepared for the UK Department for International Development. Department of Economics, Oxford University.

Glewwe, Paul, Michele Gragnolati, and Hassan Zaman. 2002. "Who Gained from Vietnam's Boom in the 1990s?" *Economic Development and Cultural Change* 50 (4): 773–92.

Haughton, Jonathan, and Hoang Van Kinh. 2004. "Does Devaluation Worsen Income Distribution? Evidence from Vietnam." Suffolk University, Boston, Massachusetts.

Holzmann, Robert, Lynne Sherburne-Benz, and Emil Tesliuc. 2003. *Social Risk Management: The World Bank's Approach to Social Protection in a Globalizing World.* Washington, DC: World Bank.

Kamanou, Gisele, and Jonathan Morduch. 2002. "Measuring Vulnerability to Poverty." Discussion Paper No. 2002/58, WIDER, United Nations University.

Kühl, Jesper J. 2003. "Household Poverty and Vulnerability—A Bootstrap Approach." Nordic Conference in Development Economics 2, Copenhagen, Denmark, June 23–24.

Pritchett, Lant, Asep Shryahadi, and Sudarno Sumarto. 2000. "Quantifying Vulnerability to Poverty: A Proposed Measure, Applied to Indonesia." Social Monitoring and Early Response Unit, Jakarta.

World Bank. 2000. *World Development Report 2000/2001: Attacking Poverty.* Washington, DC: World Bank.

Chapter 13

Poverty Monitoring and Evaluation

Summary

A poverty monitoring and evaluation system is required to determine whether a country's overall poverty reduction strategy, and its main components, are effective.

The first step in poverty monitoring is to define the goals of the strategy. Operationally, this requires the identification of measurable indicators and the establishment of realistic targets that can help policy makers set priorities.

Final indicators measure the *outcomes* of poverty reduction policies and the *impact* on dimensions of well-being. Intermediate indicators measure the *inputs* into a program and the *outputs* of the program. A good indicator is unambiguous, relevant, reliable, and sensitive to changes, and may be tracked cheaply and frequently. It can also be disaggregated, for instance by geographic area or gender.

Impact evaluation seeks to measure the changes in well-being that can be attributed to a particular project or policy (an "intervention"); the results can help inform decisions about whether the intervention should be expanded or eliminated. The central challenge of impact assessment is constructing a plausible counterfactual.

Several evaluation designs are used in impact evaluation, depending in part on the data that are available. Among the most important are experimental design (randomization); and quasi-experimental designs, including matching comparisons (typically using propensity scores), double differences, instrumental variables ("statistical control"), and reflexive comparisons. Both experimental and quasi-experimental methods try to tackle the problem of sample bias that bedevils impact analysis.

It is difficult to measure the impact of economy-wide shocks, although attempts have been made by measuring deviations from trends, building computable general equilibrium and other simulation models, applying panel data, and asking households to assess how much they have been affected. While no method of impact evaluation is perfect, such evaluations have had an important influence on policy decisions.

Learning Objectives

After completing the chapter on *Poverty Monitoring and Evaluation*, you should be able to

1. Describe the function of a monitoring and evaluation system and explain why it is useful.

2. Summarize the three steps in poverty monitoring.

3. Distinguish between the different categories of poverty indicators, and list the characteristics of a good indicator.

4. Explain why it is necessary to be able to disaggregate indicators.

5. Describe the purposes of impact evaluation.

6. Explain why impact evaluation requires the construction of a counterfactual and why this is difficult to do.

7. Summarize the steps required in an experimental design, and assess the applicability of this method of impact evaluation.

8. For each of the main types of quasi-experimental design—matching comparisons, double differences, instrumental variables, and reflexive comparisons—summarize the steps needed to apply them, and the data requirements, and evaluate their applicability and usefulness.

9. Summarize the principal methods that have been used to measure the impact of economy-wide shocks, and critically assess the value of each method.

Introduction

A country has developed a poverty reduction strategy and put in place several specific measures to combat poverty, including a food-for-work program, supplemental nutrition packages for mothers and infants, free school textbooks in poor villages, and accelerated construction of rural roads.

Two questions naturally arise:

- Is the overall strategy effective?

- How large is the impact of each of the main components of the strategy?

The answers to these questions require monitoring and evaluation.

A poverty monitoring system tracks key indicators of poverty over time and space. The resulting data can then be used to evaluate the program. *Process evaluation* examines how the programs operate, and focuses on problems of service delivery. *Cost-benefit analysis* and *cost-effectiveness analysis* weigh program costs against the benefits they deliver. They in turn require thorough *impact evaluations*, which quantify the effects of programs on individuals and households.

This chapter summarizes the elements required for a good monitoring system and introduces the techniques of impact evaluation at the micro level and at the level of the whole economy. Prennushi, Rubio, and Subbarao (2000) provide an excellent introduction to monitoring and evaluation, Baker (2000) has compiled a useful handbook on impact evaluation, Ravallion's witty and accessible introduction (1999) to some of the finer points of impact evaluation is well worth reading, and Haughton and Haughton (forthcoming) provide a somewhat more formal treatment. A growing number of impact evaluations are now available on the Web and can serve as templates for new evaluations; for a useful list, see www.worldbank.org/poverty (and follow the links for Impact Evaluation and then Selected Evaluations).

Poverty Monitoring

The first challenge in monitoring progress toward poverty reduction is to

- Identify the *goals* that the strategy is designed to achieve, such as "eradicate hunger" or "halve poverty within a decade."

- Select the key *indicators* that measure progress toward the goals, such as the proportion of individuals consuming less than 2,100 Calories per day, or the proportion of households living on less than a dollar a day.

- Set *targets*, which quantify the level of the indicators that are to be achieved by a given date—for instance, halve the number of households living on less than a dollar a day by the year 2015.

The Millennium Development Goals consist of a set of goals, indicators, and targets that the countries of the world have agreed to pursue. They are summarized in table 13.1 and give a good sense of the nature and scope of goals, indicators, and targets that individual countries may want to achieve.

Table 13.1 Millennium Development Goals, Indicators, and Targets

Goals and targets	Indicators
Goal 1: Eradicate extreme poverty and hunger	
Target 1 — Halve, between 1990 and 2015, the proportion of people whose income is less than $1 a day	1. Proportion of population below $1 a day 2. Poverty gap ratio (incidence x depth of poverty) 3. Share of poorest quintile in national consumption
Target 2 — Halve, between 1990 and 2015, the proportion of people who suffer from hunger	4. Prevalence of underweight children (under 5 years of age) 5. Proportion of population below minimum level of dietary energy consumption
Goal 2: Achieve universal primary education	
Target 3 — Ensure that, by 2015, children everywhere, boys and girls, will be able to complete a full course of primary schooling	6. Net enrollment ratio in primary education 7. Proportion of pupils starting grade 1 who reach grade 5 8. Literacy rate for 15- to 24- year-olds
Goal 3: Promote gender equality and empower women	
Target 4 — Eliminate gender disparity in primary and secondary education, preferably by 2005 and to all levels of education no later than 2015	9. Ratio of girls to boys in primary, secondary and tertiary education 10. Ratio of literate females to makes of 15- to 24-year-olds 11. Share of women in wage employment in the nonagricultural sector 12. Proportion of seats held by women in national parliament
Goal 4: Reduce child mortality	
Target 5 — Reduce by two-thirds, between 1990 and 2015, the under-5 mortality rate	13. Under-5 mortality rate 14. Infant mortality rate 15. Proportion of 1 year olds immunized against measles
Goal 5: Improve maternal health	
Target 6 — Reduce by three-quarters, between 1990 and 2015, the maternal mortality ratio	16. Maternal mortality ratio 17. Proportion of births attended by skilled health personnel

Goal 6: Combat HIV/AIDS, malaria, and other diseases

Target 7   Have halted by 2015, and begun to reverse, the spread of HIV/AIDS

Target 8   Have halted by 2015, and begun to reverse, the incidence of malaria and other major diseases

Goal 7: Ensure environmental sustainability

Target 9   Integrate the principles of sustainable development into country policies and programs and reverse the loss of environmental resources

Target 10   Halve, by 2015, the proportion of people without sustainable access to safe drinking water

Target 11   By 2020, to have achieved a significant improvement in the lives of at least 100 million slum dwellers

18. HIV prevalence among 15- to 24-year-old pregnant women
19. Contraceptive prevalence rate
20. Number of children orphaned by HIV/AIDS
21. Prevalence and death rates associated with malaria.
22. Proportion of population in malaria risk areas using effective malaria prevention and treatment measures
23. Prevalence and death rates associated with tuberculosis
24. Proportion off TB cases detected and cured under DOTS (Directly observed treatment short course)

25. Change in land area covered by forest
26. Land area protected to maintain biological diversity
27. GDP per unit of energy use (as proxy for energy efficiency)
28. Carbon dioxide emissions (per capita)
29. Proportion of population with sustainable access to an improved water source
30. Proportion of people with access to improved sanitation
31. Proportion of people with access to secure tenure

Source: Based on Prennushi, Rubio, and Subbarao (2000, 109).

253

Selecting Indicators

It is helpful to classify indicators into two groups:

- *Final indicators* measure the *outcomes* of poverty reduction policies (for example, increased school attendance rates) and the *impact* on dimensions of well-being (for example, higher literacy rates).

- *Intermediate indicators* measure the *inputs* into a program (for example, spending on health care) and the *outputs* of the program (for example, clinics built, doctors hired).

Viewed in this way, a poverty monitoring system encompasses both implementation monitoring as well as performance (or results-based) monitoring. Intermediate indicators typically change more quickly than final indicators, respond more rapidly to public interventions, and can be measured more easily and in a more timely fashion.

A good indicator has several qualities, including the following:

- It is a direct unambiguous measure of progress and is easy to understand.

- It is relevant to the objectives, which in the current context concern poverty reduction.

- It varies across areas, groups, and time.

- It is sensitive to changes in policies, programs, and "shocks."

- It is reliable and hard to manipulate.

- It can be tracked frequently and cheaply.

It is essential to be able to disaggregate the indicators in ways that are useful—for instance, by geography (urban vs. rural, by administrative region, by geoclimatic zone), by gender, by socially defined group (ethnic, linguistic, religious), and by income or expenditure level. The disaggregation is central to the political economy of poverty reduction, but it is also highly sensitive. For instance, Malaysia does not make its household survey data available for public use, in part because of concerns about what the data might reveal about the evolution of the ethnic breakdown of poverty and income.

Setting Targets

There are two reasons to set concrete targets for poverty reduction: (1) it forces decision makers to clarify their priorities and adjust the allocation of resources in consequence; and (2) it strengthens accountability.

The standard advice is to set a small number of targets in clear and unambiguous terms. The targets need to be consistent with other national goals, and to be achievable, given the country's overall level of economic development and its implementation capacity. They also need to be realistic about the resources that will be available.

One of the challenges in setting up a good poverty monitoring system is collating the data and channeling it to policy makers and the public in a timely and coherent manner. The relevant data will come from many sources, including administrative information on public spending or the number of teachers, project information, household survey data, and so on. Thus the development of a poverty monitoring system requires attention to the statistical system as a whole. Some countries have established poverty monitoring units, sometimes attached to the prime minister's office, to manage the flow of data related to poverty reduction.

Prennushi, Rubio, and Subbarao (2000) make the case that poverty monitoring systems in most less-developed countries need to pay more attention to speeding up the flow of actual expenditure data, because expenditure tracking is often quite slow. They argue for greater use of cost accounting so, for instance, one can more easily determine the cost of educating a child or serving a hospital outpatient. They call for improving the accuracy of data on actual spending, if necessary through the use of expenditure tracking surveys. In an often-cited example, such a survey found that in 1991–95 in Uganda, only 30 percent of the nonsalary funds intended for public schools actually reached the schools; the remaining funds were siphoned off by district administrations. Additionally, Prennushi, Rubio, and Subbarao hope to see a speedier analysis of household survey data, which are sometimes out of date by the time they are published. In this context, simple and rapid surveys based on Core Welfare Indicator Questionnaires (CWIQ) may have a role to play, although as discussed in chapter 2, such methods cannot generate accurate proxies for income or expenditure.[1]

Review Questions

1. Which of the following is *not* one of the three main tasks in poverty monitoring?

   o A. Set targets.
   o B. Identify goals.
   o C. Select key indicators.
   o D. Measure the impact of policies.

2. A key Millennium Development Goal is to halve, between 1990 and 2015, the number of people living on less than a dollar a day.

   o True
   o False

> 3. A good indicator includes all of the following *except*:
>
> ○ A. It can be adjusted to accommodate varying political needs.
> ○ B. It can be tracked frequently and cheaply.
> ○ C. It is sensitive to shocks.
> ○ D. It is an unambiguous measure of progress.

Impact Evaluation: Micro Projects

Suppose that a nongovernmental organization or government sets up a microcredit project or builds an irrigation canal.[2] How does one

- Forecast the impact of projects such as these on poverty reduction or other development objectives?

- Find out if the policy or program is cost-effective?

- Improve the design of programs and interventions?

To answer these questions an *impact evaluation* is required. Generally, an impact evaluation seeks to measure the changes in well-being that can be attributed to a particular project or policy (an "intervention"). The results of an impact evaluation can show which interventions have been effective, and thus inform decisions on whether they should be eliminated, modified, or expanded, as well as what priority they should be accorded.

Impact evaluations are expensive and can be technically complex. It thus makes sense to undertake one only if the policy or program is of strategic importance, or is innovative, and the information from the evaluation is likely to fill gaps in current knowledge. It is also important to master the institutional details of the program or project that is being analyzed before proceeding with the statistical analysis. And the validity of the quantitative part of the evaluation is only as good as the quality of the data that can be brought to bear on the issue.

Not every manager welcomes an impact evaluation, particularly if the results are expected to show a project in a poor light. Ravallion (2008) suggests that, as a consequence, too few evaluations are undertaken, and those that are done are biased toward programs that work well or programs that produce quick, measurable benefits. Such biases in turn weaken the potential usefulness of impact evaluations in general. He also suggests that there is underinvestment in research on the extent to which impact evaluations may be generalized—their external validity—and that all too often evaluators fit their favored techniques to convenient problems, rather than starting with a problem and asking how to measure its impact.

The Challenge of the Counterfactual

To evaluate the impact of an intervention, we need to compare the actual outcome with our evaluation of what would have happened in the absence of the intervention (the *counterfactual*). The central challenge of impact assessment is constructing a plausible counterfactual.

The challenge is a difficult one. Consider the case of a program that provides additional food—for example maize or milk powder—to poor mothers with infants. Now suppose that the data show that the mothers and infants covered by the program are less well nourished than those who are not covered. Are we to conclude that the project is a failure?

Perhaps; but then again, it is likely that the project targeted poor mothers with malnourished infants, so it is not surprising that households with underweight children are getting additional food. The problem here is one of estimating how malnourished the mothers and infants covered by the program would have been in the absence of the program, in other words, establishing an appropriate counterfactual. A number of methods ("evaluation designs") have been developed to address questions of this sort, and we now examine these one by one.

Experimental Design

Widely regarded as the best approach to measuring the impact of an intervention, the idea behind experimental design, also known as randomization, is as follows:

(1) Before the intervention begins, identify those who are eligible to benefit from it.

(2) Then randomly select those who will benefit (the *treatment group*) and deny the benefit to the others (who will serve as the *control group*).

(3) After the intervention, measure the appropriate outcome variables (for example, degree of malnutrition, poverty gaps).[3]

The difference in the mean values of the outcome variables between the control and treatment groups can be attributed to the effects of the intervention, give or take some sampling error.

In practice, researchers more commonly gather information on income, individual and household characteristics (X), and village and community characteristics (V), for the individuals that do, and do not, participate in the scheme. Then they estimate

$$Y_{ij} = X_{ij}\beta_y + V_j\gamma_y + C_{ij}\delta + \varepsilon_{ij}^y, \qquad (13.1)$$

where C_{ij} is a dummy variable that is equal to 1 if the individual i in village j participates in the scheme, and 0 otherwise. In this case, the individual, household, and community characteristics control for other differences, and it is reasonable to expect that estimated coefficient δ would measure the impact of the intervention.

In the context of poverty interventions, it is rarely possible to use randomization, although the study by Glewwe, Kremer, and Moulin (2000) of the effects of textbooks on learning in Kenya was able to do so by randomly selecting which schools would receive textbooks. In this case, there was no evidence that the provision of additional textbooks raised average test scores or reduced dropout rates.

Another good example is the study by Angrist et al. (2002) of school vouchers in Colombia. In 1991, the government of Colombia established the PACES (Programa de Ampliacion de Cobertura de la Educacion Secundaria, or Program for the Expansion of Educational Coverage) program, which provided vouchers (that is, scholarships) to students who had applied to and been accepted into private secondary schools. The vouchers were awarded based on a lottery; this provided the randomization that allowed the authors to compare the outcomes for applicants who received vouchers with the outcomes for those who did not. Among the more interesting findings are the following:

- Voucher winners were 15–16 percentage points more likely to be in private school when they were surveyed in 1998.

- The program had a positive and significant effect on the number of years of schooling completed. Those who received vouchers in 1995 in the capital (Bogotá) had completed 0.12–0.16 more years than those who did not.

- Repetition rates fell significantly as a result of the project. In the 1995 Bogotá sample, the probability of repetition was reduced by 5–6 percentage points for lottery winners.

The most serious problem with randomized experiments is that the withholding of treatment may be unethical. For instance, if we are trying to determine the effects of providing vitamin A supplementation, which helps prevent blindness, it is likely to be unethical to withhold this inexpensive treatment from significant numbers of young children. It also may be politically difficult to provide a treatment to one group and not to another. In some cases—if a program is applied universally, for instance—there may be no control group. True random assignment is often difficult in practice. And people may respond to a program, by moving into or out of a treatment area, for instance, thereby contaminating the results. Randomization may be subject to unobserved heterogeneity bias that affects the outcomes of treatment.

So, in practice, randomization can either produce inconsistent results or cannot be implemented, in which case most impact assessments have to rely on quasi-experimental methods.

Quasi-Experimental Methods

If households are not assigned randomly to an intervention—such as food stamps, vaccinations, or irrigation water—then those who benefit are unlikely to be typical of the eligible population. There are two reasons for this. First, there may be nonrandom program placement, of which the researcher may or may not be aware; for instance, an antipoverty program may be more likely to be set up in poor villages. This is the problem of *unobserved area heterogeneity*. Second, there may be self-selection into program participation; for instance, more dynamic individuals may be the first to sign up, or program benefits may flow to those who are politically well connected, or sick people may move to villages that have been equipped with clinics. Such effects are often hard to detect, and give rise to the problem of *unobserved individual and household heterogeneity*.

The presence of these unobservables immediately creates the problem of *selection bias*. The basic idea behind quasi-experimental designs is to construct statistical models of selection—matching, double differences, instrumental variables, reflexive comparisons—that permit one to compare program participants and nonparticipants (the *comparison* group) holding the selection processes constant.

To see why these problems arise, suppose we are interested in determining whether a microcredit scheme, initiated in time period 0, raises the income of individual i in time period 1. An appealing approach would be to collect data on the outcome indicator (income, given by Y_{i1}), and on individual and household characteristics (X_{i1}), for a sample of individuals that do, and do not, participate in the scheme. Then we could estimate an impact equation of the form—

$$Y_{i1} = X_{i1}\beta + P_{i1}\delta + \varepsilon_{i1}^{Y}, \qquad (13.2)$$

where P_{i1} is a dummy variable that is set equal to 1 if the individual i participates in the scheme and to 0 otherwise. At first sight, it would appear that the value of the estimated coefficient δ would measure the impact of the microcredit scheme on income.

Unfortunately, this is unlikely to be the case, because program participation is often related to the other individual, household, and village variables, some of which may not be observable. For instance, those who borrow money may be better educated, or younger, or live in villages with a loan office, or be more motivated. With enough information it may be possible to control for many of these variables, including education and age, but it is never possible to control for all the relevant effects. For example, the degree of individual motivation is unobservable; but a more motivated individual is more likely to participate in the program (a higher P_{i1}) and to benefit more from it (a higher p_{i1}^{Y}). This creates a correlation between P_{i1} and ε_{i1}^{Y} and so leads to a biased estimate of δ. As a practical matter, unobservables are always present in such circumstances, and thus this selection bias (which may also be thought of as a form of omitted variable bias) is present as well.

The path to a solution requires us to envisage a separate program *participation equation* of the form—

$$P_{ij} = Z_{i1}\gamma + \varepsilon_{i1}^{P}. \tag{13.3}$$

where the Z variables may be the same as the X variables, or include additional variables.[4] If one can identify a set of variables that affect only participation, equation (13.3), and not the household outcome, equation (13.2)—generally a difficult task—then it may be possible to arrive at a satisfactory estimate of δ, the impact of program participation on the outcome of interest. Many quasi-experimental evaluations have been informative; they can often be done fairly quickly and cheaply, and do not necessarily require the collection of data before the project begins. We now consider some specific solutions in more detail.

Review Questions

4. The central challenge of impact assessment is constructing a plausible counterfactual.

  o True
  o False

5. Ideally, with randomization,

  o A. We randomly pick a sample of treated and nontreated individuals.
  o B. We randomly assign the treatment to individuals.
  o C. We randomly select those who have been treated and compare them with a nontreated group.
  o D. All of the above.

6. Selection bias may result from all of the following *except*:

  o A. Nonrandom program placement.
  o B. Unobserved area heterogeneity.
  o C. Unobserved household heterogeneity
  o D. Random assignment.

Solution 1. Matching Comparisons. This approach is widely used and is often feasible even if experimental design is not possible. To undertake matching, one needs survey data for a substantial number of nonparticipants as well as for the participants. The basic idea is to match each participant with a similar nonparticipant (or a small "comparison group") and then to compare the outcomes between them.

Given survey information, the most common procedure starts by pooling the two samples (that is, the participants and nonparticipants, or in the jargon of matching, the treatment and comparison groups) and estimating a logit model of program participation as a function of all the variables that might influence participation—equation (13.3). Ironically, one does not want the equation to fit too well, because that would make it difficult to identify nonparticipants who are otherwise similar to participants.

The next step is to generate the *propensity score*, which is the predicted probability of participation, given the observed characteristics Z. Some of the individuals in the comparison group may have propensity scores that are far outside the range of the treatment group—they are said to have a "lack of common support"—and these cases may need to be dropped and the logit model reestimated.

Next, for each person in the treatment group, find the member of the comparison group with the closest propensity score (the "nearest neighbor"), or a small group of, say, five nearest neighbors. Compute the difference between the outcome indicator of the person in the treatment group and the mean of the outcome indicators for the nearest neighbors. The mean of these differences, over all the members of the treatment group, gives a measure of the overall impact of the program.

When the correlates of participation in the project are observable, this approach works well, but it is not satisfactory if unobservable differences are important—for instance, if those who sign up for microcredit are the more dynamic individuals. The procedure fails in this case because the differences between the treatment and comparison groups cannot be entirely attributed to whether or not they participated in the program; some, or even most, of the difference may be due to (possibly unobserved) differences in the inherent characteristics of individuals in the two groups.

Box 13.1 Case Study: Workfare and Water in Argentina

The Trabajar II program in Argentina was introduced in 1997 in response to a sharp rise in unemployment. The program provided low-wage work on community projects, and was intended to raise the incomes of the poor.

To analyze the impact of this "workfare" program, Jalan and Ravallion (1999) used the results of the 1997 *Encuesta de Desarrollo Social* (Social Development Survey), coupled with a similar survey of participants in the Trabajar program, to estimate a logit model of program participation. They used variables such as gender, schooling, housing, and subjective perceptions of welfare, and used the data to derive propensity scores for participants and nonparticipants (after taking care to limit the sample of nonparticipants to those with "common support").

The key findings were that the program raised incomes by about half of the gross wages paid out and that four-fifths of the participating workers came from the poorest quintile of the population.

The 1997 *Encuesta*, which surveyed 40,000 urban households, has also been used to assess the impact of Argentina's efforts to privatize the provision of water. By comparing data from the *Encuesta* with earlier data from the census, and comparing municipalities where the water supply was, and was not, privatized, Galiani, Gertler, and Schargrodsky (2002) found that privatization increased access to water by 11.6 percent. Using data on child deaths, and applying propensity score matching to municipalities (rather than households), they also found that the privatization of water supply reduced child mortality by 6.7 percent on average, and by 24 percent in poor municipalities.

Solution 2. Double Differences. Also known as the difference-in-difference method, this approach requires information both from a baseline survey before the intervention occurs and a follow-up survey after the program is operating. Both surveys should be comparable in the questions used and the survey methods applied, and they must be administered both to participants and nonparticipants.

In the simplest version, compute the difference between the outcome variable after (Y_{i1}) and before (Y_{i0}) the intervention, both for the treatment and comparison samples. The difference between these two gives an estimate of the impact of the program.

> *Example:* Suppose that the literacy rate rose from 25 percent to 35 percent for the treatment sample, between the beginning and end of an adult literacy project, and that the literacy rate rose from 28 percent to 34 percent over the same period for the comparison group. Then the project may be considered to have raised the literacy rate, for those treated, by 4 percentage points. The logic is that one might have expected literacy to rise by 6 percentage points for everyone, judging by the experience of the comparison group; however, for the treatment group, it rose by 10 percentage points, of which 4 percentage points may thus be attributable to the project.

The double difference method may be refined in a number of ways. By using propensity score matching with data from the baseline survey, one can ensure that the comparison group is similar to the treatment group. And one could use a differenced form of the regression in equation (13.2) to get a better estimate of the impact of the project (see Ravallion 1999, 23–24, for details).

Done right, this is a relatively satisfactory approach, but it will give biased results if there is selective attrition of the treatment group—for example, if some of the treatment group cannot be resurveyed a second time, or if those who drop out are not a random sample of the treatment group (for instance, if they are older or richer than their peers in the treatment group). The double difference method is also relatively expensive to implement, as it requires at least two rounds of survey data.

Solution 3. Instrumental Variables. Sometimes referred to as the *statistical control* method, the idea behind this widely used method is to identify variables that affect participation in the program, but not the outcomes of interest—that is, that enter into equation (13.3) but not equation (13.2). The estimates of equation (13.3) are used to predict participation, and this *predicted* participation is then used in equation (13.2). By using predicted, rather than actual, participation in equation (13.1), one removes (in principle) the biases that would otherwise contaminate the estimates of the impact coefficient δ.[5]

To see why this works, consider the case of a dynamic individual who, we assume, might be more likely to participate (so $\varepsilon_{i1}^{P} > 0$) and to perform well (so $\varepsilon_{i1}^{Y} > 0$). As a result, ε_{i1}^{Y} and P_{il} would be correlated and the estimate of δ (the impact effect) biased. But by using $\hat{P}_{il}$ instead of P_{il}, the forces that influence ε_{i1}^{Y} and P_{il} now only affect ε_{i1}^{Y}, but not $\hat{P}_{il}$, so the correlation disappears along with the bias. This, however, is true only if there are influences on P_{il} that do not influence Y_{il}. The idea is to create variation in $\hat{P}_{il}$ so that we have some people in the sample who, even if they have the same X_{il}, may have different P_{il}; in effect, we now have a source of variation in Y_{il} that is attributable to the program.

The major practical problem is finding appropriate instruments that influence program participation but not the outcome of the program once one is enrolled. However, it is sometimes possible. A recent study of the effect of famine relief in Ethiopia was able to use past climatic variation as one such instrument (Yamano, Alderman, and Christiaensen 2003); and interventions that are undertaken randomly in some villages but not others clearly provide a suitable instrument, because living in a given village determines whether you will covered by the intervention, but now how much you will profit from it. Pitt and Khandker (1998) used the exogenous program eligibility condition as an instrument to identify the impact of microcredit on household welfare (see box 13.2).

The instrumental variables method is helpful if there is measurement error. Suppose that, because of measurement errors, observed program participation is more variable than true participation; this will lead to an underestimation of the impact of the program ("attenuation bias"), essentially because the noise of

13

Box 13.2   Case Study: Microfinance and the Poor in Bangladesh

Microfinance, or the provision of small loans to the poor, is often touted as an important tool for reducing poverty. A widely admired model is the Grameen Bank in Bangladesh, brainchild of Mohammed Yunus, which provides small loans to poor people, mainly women. The Bank also runs related education programs. The Bangladesh Rural Advancement Committee and the Bangladesh Rural Development Board run similar operations.

Does microfinance work? More specifically, does it alleviate poverty? Benefit women? Is it cost-effective? Sustainable?

These questions have been addressed using information collected in three postharvest surveys undertaken in Bangladesh in 1991 and 1992, covering 1,798 households in 87 villages. The villages were chosen from 24 subdistricts where microcredit programs had been implemented for at least three years before the survey and from five subdistricts where they had not been implemented. The programs target households who own less than half an acre of land, but not all of the targeted households borrow.

One may divide up the surveyed households as shown here:

Surveyed Households

	Villages with a program in place	Villages without a program
Nontarget households (own more than half an acre of land)	A	B
Target/eligible households that ...		
Do not or cannot participate	C	E
Participate	D	

One possibility would be to compare the impact of the program for households D with that of households C. The results are shown in the box table below:

Mean of Individual and Household Outcomes by Program Participation

Outcome	Program households (D)	Eligible nonprogram households (C)	Noneligible households (A ∪ B ∪ E)	All households
Boys' school enrollment rate (age 5–25)	45.4	33.3	52.8	43.9
Girls' school enrollment rate (age 5–25)	43.7	35.8	49.2	41.5

Box 13.2 continued

Outcome	Program households (D)	Eligible nonprogram households (C)	Noneligible households (A ∪ B ∪ E)	All households
Current contraceptive use rate (currently married women, 14–50)	41.9	35.9	35.6	36.9
Household weekly per capita consumption (taka)	86.4	78.2	124.8	95.7

Source: Khandker 2000.

The problem with this comparison is that there is likely to be selection bias; it appears, for instance, that those who are eligible for microfinance but do not participate say that they are concerned about their ability to repay, suggesting that they are more risk averse, or perhaps less motivated, than borrowers. If landowning is exogenous, then one could compare the outcomes of households C and D on the one hand with households E on the other. This assumes, however, that program and nonprogram villages are the same. An even better approach would be to use a double difference, by comparing $Y_{(C \cup D)} - Y_A$ with $Y_E - Y_B$, where Y is the impact of interest (consumption or income per capita, school enrollment rates, and the like).

Morduch (1998) used a similar approach and found that the microfinance programs appeared to improve the outcomes of interest. However, on further examination, he found that the programs were seriously mistargeted, with 20–30 percent of the borrowers owning more than the half-acre maximum. When these borrowers were excluded, the microfinance programs had essentially no discernible effects, except perhaps for lowering the variance of consumption and income for participants. On the other hand, it is possible that the comparison households may not have lacked access to microfinance, in which case Morduch's conclusion would be unsurprising. A serious problem with Morduch's simple difference-in-difference analysis is that program participation is exogenous or randomly given.

Because of sample selection bias that is inherently present with such nonrandom distribution of borrowers and nonborrowers, Pitt and Khandker (1998) used an instrumental variable method to estimate the program effect. The instrument is based on the exogenous land-based eligibility conditions. They found that program participation matters a lot when sample selection bias is corrected. However, the results are sensitive to the assumption of the land-based exogenous eligibility condition.

A follow-up panel survey was undertaken in 1998–99 to measure the effects of microfinance. Khandker (2005) estimated a number of regressions, using both instrumental variables and fixed effects (at the level of villages and households). A selection of results for

Box 13.2 continued

female participants is shown in the box table below; each row represents a different dependent variable, and each column a different estimation technique. Although the magnitudes of the impacts vary with the technique used, the overall results are more positive for borrowing by women than for men. That is, impacts are sensitive to controlling for household-specific unobservables.

Based on these and other findings, Khandker (2005) concludes that microcredit can reduce poverty in a cost-effective way, and benefits do flow to women. While a subsidy is required to develop the initial institutions, this subsidy dependence can be reduced over time (Khandker 1998).

Khandker also found that the ultrapoor do not join microcredit programs. A similar conclusion was reached by Patten and Rosengard (1991) in their evaluation of the microlending activities of Bank Rakyat Indonesia (BRI) in the 1980s; however BRI, unlike the Grameen Bank, did not require a subsidy for its microcredit.

Impact of Women's Borrowing from Grameen Bank on Individual and Household Outcomes

Outcome	Naïve model	Instrumental variables (IV) method	Village-level fixed effects & IV method[c]	Household-level fixed-effects model
Boys' school enrollment rate (age 5–25)	0.062[a] (4.461)	0.131 (4.022)	0.103 (2.364)	0.013 (2.587)
Girls' school enrollment rate (age 5–25)	0.019[a] (1.412)	0.085 (2.289)	0.013 (0.334)	0.016 (3.405)
Current contraceptive use rate (currently married women, age 14–50)	0.026[a] (1.942)	0.095 (2.580)	−0.091 (−2.011)	−0.001 (−0.260)
Household weekly per capita consumption (taka)	0.004[b] (1.765)	0.037 (2.174)	0.043 (4.249)	0.010 (2.697)

Source: Khandker 2000.

Note: Figures in parentheses are t-statistics. Household-level fixed effects estimates are preliminary.

a. probit

b. OLS.

c. Results in column 3 are considered to be the best.

measurement error is getting in the way of isolating the effects of program participation. However, the predicted value of program intervention ($\hat{P}_{i1}$) is less likely to reflect measurement error and can reduce the effects of attenuation bias.

Solution 4. Reflexive Comparisons. In this approach, one first undertakes a baseline survey of the treatment group before the intervention, with a follow-up survey afterward. The impact of the intervention is measured by comparing the before-and-after data; in effect, the baseline provides the comparison group.

Such comparisons are rarely satisfactory. The problem in this case is that we really want a "with" and "without" comparison, not a "before" and "after." Put another way, in the reflexive comparison method, there is no proper counterfactual against which the outcomes of the project may be compared. There is also a problem if attrition occurs, so that some of those surveyed before the project drop out in some systematic way. On the other hand, this may be the only option in trying to determine the impact of full-coverage interventions, such as universal vaccinations, where there is no possibility of a comparison or control group.

Review Questions

7. Which of the following is *not* a step in propensity score matching?

- A. Compare each treated case with its nearest untreated neighbor.
- B. Find the average difference between treated and matched comparators.
- C. Compute the change in the gap between treated and comparators at two points in time.
- D. Estimate a participation equation using logit or probit.

8. A potable water project raised connections in a project area from 16 percent to 28 percent. The number of connections in a comparator area rose from 14 percent to 25 percent during the same period. Using double differences, the impact of the project on connections was,

- A. 12 percent.
- B. 3 percent.
- C. 1 percent.
- D. 5 percent.

9. Reflexive comparisons are especially useful in assessing impact because they compare the "after" results with the "before" results.

- True
- False

Qualitative Methods

Some evaluations rely largely on qualitative information, from focus groups, unstructured interviews, survey data on perceptions, and a variety of other sources. Such information complements, but does not supplant, the more quantitative impact evaluations, because qualitative methods are based on subjective evaluations, do not generate a control or comparison group, and lack statistical robustness.

Impact Evaluation: Macro Projects

It is much harder to evaluate the impact of an economy-wide shock (for example, a devaluation) or macroeconomic policy change (for example, increase in the money supply) than a project or program change, because the universal nature of the change makes it impossible to construct an appropriate counterfactual. Recognizing that the analysis will always be less than perfect, economists and others have nonetheless used the following methods to try to measure the effect of macro shocks:

Time-Series Data Analysis: Before and After

A time series is a set of data on a variable over time (for example, gross domestic product [GDP] for each of the past 20 years). One could compare the situation of households, using survey data, before and after the shock (that is, in time $t-1$ and time t). This is frequently done, but is quite imperfect because, as in reflexive comparisons, it does not establish an appropriate counterfactual. It implicitly assumes that if there had been no shock, the level of the variables in time $t-1$ would have persisted into time t.

Time-Series Data Analysis: Deviations from Trend

An improvement over the simple before-and-after comparison is to begin by constructing a counterfactual, usually by predicting what would have happened in the absence of the crisis by projecting past trends into the future. The impact of the crisis is then calculated as the difference between the actual outcome after the crisis, and the predicted one based on the past trend. This is the approach taken by Kakwani (2000) in estimating the effects of the Asian financial crisis of 1997 on poverty and other indicators in Korea and Thailand.

The first difficulty with this method is arriving at a robust counterfactual; for instance, how far back in time should one go when developing an equation that is used for the projections. Second, it is much harder to establish a counterfactual for an individual household than for the economy as a whole. And, third, this method does not control for the unobserved components of a household's response to a shock.

Computable General Equilibrium and Simulation Models

A computable general equilibrium (CGE) model of an economy is a set of equations that aims to quantify the main interrelationships among households, firms, and government in an economy. CGE models range from just a few to many hundreds of equations. In principle, they may be used to simulate the effects of poverty reduction interventions. Unfortunately, CGE models are technically difficult to build, are typically highly aggregated (which makes it difficult to identify the effects of policies on income distribution and poverty with much precision), require considerable data to construct the underlying social accounting matrix, and produce results that are sensitive to the assumptions made about the parameters. They have been used, however, with some success to evaluate the economic and distributional effects of such interventions as programs to reduce HIV/AIDS, food subsidies, and trade policies. The International Food Policy Research Institute (IFPRI) has developed a standard CGE model that has been applied to a number of problems in developing countries (Loefgren, Harris, and Robinson 2001).

Household Panel Impact Analysis

If we have panel data on households—that is, data on households from both before and after the shock—then we can compare the situation of each household before and after the shock. By including household fixed effects in our estimating equation (that is, a separate dummy variable for each household), we can largely eliminate the effects of "time-invariant household and area-specific heterogeneity" (that is, the special or unique features of households, many of which are unobservable, such as whether the head is an alcoholic, or sick, or entrepreneurially inclined).

Again, the main difficulty here is that a before-and-after comparison does not establish an adequate counterfactual. For instance, if the income of a household in the Philippines fell between 1996 and 1998, how do we know that it was due to the 1997 financial crisis? It might have been caused by some other event—a family member falls ill, the village suffers from drought, and so on. No survey is ever complete enough to capture every conceivable relevant explanatory variable.

Self-Rated Retrospective Evaluation

Another possibility is to ask the household to assess how much it has been affected by the crisis—as was done, for instance, in the Annual Poverty Indicators Survey in the Philippines in 1998.

By definition, self-rated evaluations are subjective, which makes it difficult to assess whether the reported effects are indeed due to the shocks. In Vietnam, households reported higher levels of illness in 1998 than in 1993, despite being much better off in 1998. This result, which is not uncommon, is hardly plausible, unless one supposes that the definition of "illness" changes over time or with affluence. Whatever the reason, it makes the subjective evaluations untrustworthy.

A variant on this theme is to ask households whether they were hit by a shock. We then compare the situation of households that reported being affected with that of households that did not report being hit by the shock. Because self-reported shocks are highly endogenous—any household that has had a spell of bad luck is likely to report being hit by a shock—researchers often use the shock reported by a cluster (for example, the village or the city ward) as an instrumental variable to help resolve this endogeneity.

Even with this latter adjustment, we are left with the problem of unobserved community-level heterogeneity—for instance, for reasons that may not be apparent, some communities or clusters may report a shock more than others, even if objectively the shock hit all areas equally.

Three final points about impact evaluation are worth mentioning. First, no method of impact evaluation is perfect; the method used will depend on the problem, as well as on the resources and time available. Second, impact evaluation is more difficult with economy-wide policy interventions and crises than with micropolicies. And third, program evaluation is important; it serves as a tool for learning whether and how programs matter, and it has had an important effect on public policy in a number of cases (for some interesting examples, see Bamberger 2005). The usefulness of impact evaluation often requires the creation of adequate feedback mechanisms, however, so that policy makers take the lessons of impact evaluation to heart. The World Bank earmarks about 1 percent of project funds for monitoring and evaluation.

Review Questions

10. Real GDP rose by 3 percent in 2005, 2 percent in 2006, 4 percent in 2007, and fell 1 percent in 2008, apparently due to a financial crisis. Which of the following is the most plausible measure of the impact of the crisis on economic growth?

   - A. It lowered GDP growth by 6 percentage points.
   - B. It lowered GDP growth by 1 percentage point.
   - C. It lowered GDP growth by 7 percentage points.
   - D. It lowered GDP growth by 4 percentage points.

Notes

1. The eight-page questionnaire may be found at http://www4.worldbank.org/afr/stats/pdf/ cwiq2000.pdf.
2. Much of this section draws on lecture notes prepared by Shahid Khandker (2000).
3. Sometimes the results of a baseline survey are available, which can add precision to the results, particularly in ensuring that the treatment and control groups are indeed comparable.
4. Equation (13.2) as shown here is linear, but other forms, including logit and probit specifications, are typically used in practice.
5. A variant on this approach is to put the errors from equation (13.2), along with the actual participation rate, into equation (13.1) before estimating it.

References

Angrist, Joshua, Eric Bettinger, Erik Bloom, Elizabeth King, and Michael Kremer. 2002. "Vouchers for Private Schooling in Colombia: Evidence from a Randomized Natural Experiment." *American Economic Review* 92 (5): 1535–58.

Baker, Judy 2000. *Evaluating the Impact of Development Projects on Poverty: A Handbook for Practitioners.* Washington, DC: World Bank.

Bamberger, Michael. 2005. "Influential Evaluations." Presentation to the Monitoring and Evaluation Thematic Group, April 26, World Bank, Washington, DC.

Galiani, Sebastian, Paul Gertler, and Ernesto Schargrodsky. 2002. "Water for Life: The Impact of the Privatization of Water Services on Child Mortality." Universidad de San Andres, Buenos Aires.

Glewwe, Paul, Michael Kremer, and Sylvie Moulin. 2000. "Textbooks and Test Scores: Evidence from a Prospective Evaluation in Kenya." University of Minnesota.

Haughton, Dominique, and Jonathan Haughton. Forthcoming. "Impact Evaluation." In *Statistical Techniques for the Analysis of Living Standards Survey Data.* Boston: Springer.

Jalan, Jyotsna, and Martin Ravallion. 1999. "Income Gains to the Poor from Workfare: Estimates for Argentina's Trabajar Program." Policy Research Working Paper No. 2149, World Bank, Washington, DC.

Kakwani, Nanak. 2000. "Impact of Economic Crisis on Poverty and Inequality in Korea, Thailand and the Philippines." Presentation at the 2000 World Bank Institute and Philippine Institute of Development Studies Training Workshop on "The Impact of the East Asian Crisis: Poverty Analysis Using Panel Data." Manila.

Khandker, Shahidur R. 1998. *Fighting Poverty with Microcredit: Experience in Bangladesh.* New York: Oxford University Press.

———. 2000. "Program Impact Evaluation." PowerPoint presentation, World Bank, Washington, DC.

———. 2005. "Microfinance and Poverty: Evidence Using Panel Data from Bangladesh." *World Bank Economic Review* 19: 263–86.

Loefgren, H., R. L. Harris, and S. Robinson. 2001. "A Standard Computable General Equilibrium Model in GAMS." TMD Discussion Paper No. 75, International Food Policy Research Institute, Washington, DC.

Morduch, Jonathan. 1998. "Does Microfinance Really Help the Poor? New Evidence from Flagship Programs in Bangladesh." Unpublished, Harvard University.

Patten, R. H., and J. K. Rosengard. 1991. *Progress with Profits: The Development of Rural Banking in Indonesia.* San Francisco, CA: ICS Press.

Prennushi, Giovanna, Gloria Rubio, and Kalanidhi Subbarao. 2000. "Monitoring and Evaluation." In *Sourcebook for Poverty Reduction Strategies.* Washington, DC: World Bank.

Pitt, Mark, and Shahidur R. Khandker. 1998. "The Impact of Group-Based Credit Programs on Poor Households: Does the Gender of Participants Matter?" *Journal of Political Economy* 106 (5): 958–96.

Ravallion, Martin. 1999. "The Mystery of the Vanishing Benefits: Ms Speedy Analyst's Introduction to Evaluation." Policy Research Working Paper No. 2153, World Bank, Washington, DC.

———. 2008. "Evaluation in the Practice of Development." Policy Research Working Paper No. 4547, Development Research Group, World Bank, Washington, DC.

Yamano, Takashi, Harold Alderman, and Luc Christiaensen. 2003. "Child Growth, Shocks and Food Aid in Rural Ethiopia." World Bank Policy Research Working Paper No. 3128, World Bank, Washington, DC.

Chapter 14

Using Regression

Summary

Regression is a useful technique for summarizing data and is widely used to test hypotheses and to quantify the influence of independent variables on a dependent variable. This chapter first reviews the vocabulary used in regression analysis, and then uses an example to introduce the key notions of goodness of fit and statistical significance (of the coefficient estimates).

Much of the chapter is taken up with a review of the main problems that arise in regression analysis: there may be errors in the measurement of the variables, some relevant variables may be omitted or unobservable, "dependent" and "independent" variables may in fact be determined simultaneously, the sample on which the estimation is based may be biased, independent variables may be correlated ("multicolinearity"), the error term may not have a constant variance, and outliers may have a strong influence on the results.

The chapter suggests solutions to these issues, including the use of more and better data, fixed effects (if panel data are available), instrumental variables, and randomized experiments.

Logistic regression has a binary dependent variable and is often used to explain why some people are poor and others are not. The chapter explains how to interpret the results of logistic regression.

14

Learning Objectives

After completing this chapter on *Regression*, you should be able to

1. Explain how regression may be used to summarize data, and why it is useful for testing hypotheses and quantifying the effects of independent on dependent variables.

2. Define the essential terms used in regression, including coefficient, slope, error, residual, y hat, p-value, R^2, and ordinary least squares (OLS).

3. Evaluate an estimated regression equation based on its fit and the signs and magnitudes of the coefficients.

4. Assess the confidence we have in a coefficient estimate, based on the t-statistic or p-value.

5. Describe and explain the main problems that arise in regression analysis, including

   • Measurement error

   • Omitted variable bias

   • Simultaneity bias

   • Sample selectivity bias

   • Multicolinearity

   • Heteroskedasticity

   • Outliers

6. Summarize the most important solutions to the problems that arise in regression, including using more or better data, fixed effects, instrumental variables, and randomized experiments.

7. Explain how to interpret the results of a logistic regression, and determine when such an approach to regression is useful.

Introduction

At its most basic, regression is a technique for summarizing and describing data patterns. For instance, figure 14.1 graphs food consumption per capita (on the vertical axis) against expenditure per capita (on the horizontal axis) for 9,122 Vietnamese households in 2006. The axes show spending in thousands of Vietnamese dong (VND) per year; VND 1 million is equivalent to about US$65. The data points are so numerous and dense that it is difficult to get a good feel for the essential underlying relationships.

Figure 14.1 Scatter Plot and Regression Lines for Food Consumption per Capita against Total Expenditure per Capita, Vietnam, 2006

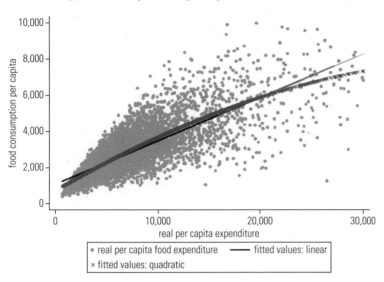

Source: Vietnam Household Living Standards Survey 2006.

One solution is to estimate a regression line—for instance using the `regress` command in Stata—that summarizes the information. There are actually two regression lines shown in figure 14.1—a straight line (the continuous line) and a quadratic (the curve of x's). Both of these lines capture the essential feature of the numbers, which is that food expenditure rises when total spending rises. The straight line estimated here (using Stata) may be written as follows:

(food spending per capita) = 1,078 + 0.24 (total spending per capita).

This shows that just under a quarter of any additional spending is devoted to food; in economic jargon, the marginal propensity to spend on food is 0.24. The quadratic curve shown in figure 14.1 may be written as follows[1]:

(food spending per capita) = 725 + 0.33 (total spending per capita)
$$- 0.0038 \text{ (spending/capita)}^2.$$

It follows from this equation that, as total spending rises, food spending rises but less quickly—an example of Engel's Law at work. For someone who is very poor, almost a third of incremental spending goes to food, but as per capita spending levels rise, the squared term becomes increasingly important and moderates the extent to which extra spending is devoted to food.

But regression is used for much more than just summarizing voluminous data. It is widely used to test theories and hypotheses; indeed, it is the workhorse of much of

275

social science. The use of regression for statistical inference is more difficult than its use for description, but an appreciation of the issues involved is essential both to assess the work of others and to do good research oneself. In what follows, we outline the essential features of regression, interpret a useful equation, list and discuss the most important problems that arise when using regression, consider solutions to these problems, and explain how to use and interpret logistic regression. There is an enormous literature on regression: Anderson, Sweeney, and Williams (2008) provide a basic treatment; Wooldridge (2008) gives a comprehensive introductory treatment of econometrics; and Greene (2007) is the essential reference for academic researchers and advanced graduate students.

The Vocabulary of Regression Analysis

Suppose that we are interested in explaining why some households have higher levels of consumption per capita than others. This is the dependent variable, conventionally labeled y. For each of the N households, we have a different value of y_i, $i = 1, \ldots, N$.

On the basis of theory, or prior practice, we have some variables that we believe "explain" differences across households in consumption per capita—for instance, the educational attainment of adult household members or whether a household lives in an urban area. These are the independent variables, sometimes referred to as the covariates, and usually are denoted by $X_1, X_2, \ldots, X_k$, if there are k variables.

We may write the true linear relationship between the independent and dependent variables, for the case with two covariates, as follows

$$y_i = \beta_0 + \beta_1 X_{1i} + \beta_2 X_{2i} + \varepsilon_i. \tag{14.1}$$

Here β_0 is the intercept (or constant term), and the β_j are the coefficients (or slopes) of the X variables. We have information on the y and X variables, and have to estimate the β coefficients, which typically is done using statistical software such as Stata, SPSS, or SAS. In practice, the independent variables never "explain" the dependent variable exactly; this is why equation (14.1) includes a random error ε_i, which picks up measurement error as well as the effects of unobservable (and unobserved) influences.

By the nature of its construction, we cannot measure ε_i directly. But for the purposes of statistical inference, we need to know how the random errors are distributed. Ideally, we would like the error terms ε_i to be identically and independently distributed following a normal distribution with mean 0 and constant variance σ^2. In practice, this may not always be reasonable, in which case we may need to adapt the model in equation (14.1), as explained below.

Although the true ε_i errors cannot be observed directly, we can estimate them. First estimate the coefficients in equation (14.1); by convention, these estimated values are typically written as $\hat{\beta}_j$. Now apply these coefficient estimates to the independent variables to get the predicted values of y, which are usually written as $\hat{y}$ ("y hat"), as follows:

$$\hat{y}_i \equiv \hat{\beta}_0 + \hat{\beta}_1 X_{1i} + \hat{\beta}_2 X_{i2}. \qquad (14.2)$$

Now we may compute the *residual*, defined as $e_i \equiv y_i - \hat{y}_i$, which is the difference between the actual value of y and the value as predicted by the model that we are using. If equation (14.1) fits well, these residuals will be very small relative to y.

The most common method for estimating linear regression equations such as that in equation (14.1) is ordinary least squares (OLS). It essentially picks estimates of the coefficients (that is, the $\hat{\beta}_j$ values) that minimize the sum, over all the observations, of the squared residuals. This is not the only possible method of estimation, but it is so standard that it is the default in all statistical packages.

In the linear case shown here, the coefficient estimates are relatively easy to interpret. Take $\hat{\beta}_1$ for example; it measures the effect that a one-unit increase in X_1 will have on y, holding all other effects constant (or, put differently, "controlling for the effects of other covariates").

This is an important point. The tables in a poverty profile can suggest links between variables such as education and the incidence of poverty, but they do not quantify strengths of such links. Nor do they control for the effects of other variables. For instance, in Cambodia, female-headed households are less likely to be in poverty than male-headed households. However, if female-headed households tend to be in the cities, then the higher income levels of these households may not be a result of the fact that they are headed by a woman, but rather because they are urban. One of the most powerful features of regression analysis is that it allows one to separate out effects of this nature—in this case, to control for the urban effect and measure the importance of female-headedness separately from any confounding influences.

Examining a Regression Example

We are now ready to look in more detail at an actual example of a regression estimate. Based on information from the Cambodian Socio-Economic Survey (SESC) undertaken in 1993–94, Prescott and Pradhan (1997, 55) estimate the following regression:

Ln(Consumption/capita) = 7.17 − 0.64 dependency ratio
215   −17.9
+ 0.15 femaleness + 0.86 Phnom Penh
3.97   45.7

+ 0.23 Other urban + 0.06 Average years of education of adults,
11.6   21.1

where $R^2 = 0.47$.

Let us now interpret this equation:

- **The value of R^2 is 0.47.** This measures the goodness of fit of the equation and lies between 0 (no fit) and 1 (a perfect fit). Although one cannot say that a value of 0.47 is good or bad, it is certainly in line with what one would expect from a cross-section regression of this nature. It may often be interpreted as saying that 47 percent of the variation in the log of consumption per capita is "explained" by the independent (that is, right-hand side) variables, although here as always one must be cautious about inferring causality rather than mere correlation.

- **The coefficients (that is, –0.64, +0.15, and so on) have the expected signs.** For instance, more years of education are associated with higher consumption per capita. In this particular case, a household in which the adult members have, on average, one more year of education than an otherwise identical household, will have 6 percent higher consumption per capita. This is because an extra year of education is associated with an increase in ln(consumption/capita) of 0.06, or about 6 percent.

- **Consumption per capita is expressed in log terms.** This is common. The untransformed measure of consumption per capita is highly skewed to the right (that is, the distribution has a long upper tail), which probably means that the errors in this regression are not normally distributed. A log transformation usually solves this problem. The broader question here is how to make the appropriate choice of functional form for the equation.

- **The numbers under the coefficients are t-statistics.** The t-statistic is computed as the estimated coefficient divided by its standard error. The rule of thumb is that if the t-statistic is greater (in absolute value) than about 2, then we are roughly 95 percent confident that the coefficient is statistically significantly different from zero—that is, we have not picked up a statistical effect by mistake. Most software packages automatically generate the p-value, which is one minus the degree of statistical significance of the coefficient. Thus, a p-value of 0.02 means that there is a 98 percent probability that the coefficient is different from zero. Low p-values, typically under 0.05 or 0.1, give us confidence in the estimates of the coefficients.

- **The Phnom Penh variable is binary.** This variable is set equal to 1 if the household is in Phnom Penh, and to 0 otherwise. This is also true of the "other urban" variable. The "rural" category has been left out (deliberately) and serves as the reference category. Thus we may say, in the above equation, that consumption per capita in other urban areas is about 23 percent higher than in rural areas.

- *The dependency ratio.* This ratio measures the number of young plus old household members to prime-age household members. When the dependency ratio is high, we expect consumption per capita to be low, and indeed this is what the regression shows.

- *The "femaleness" measure.* This measures the percentage of working-age household members (15–60 years old) who are women. This is probably a better measure than the gender of the head of household, because it is not always clear what is meant by "head" of household. The U.S. census no longer uses the term at all. The regression here shows that more-female households have *higher* levels of consumption per capita in Cambodia, holding other variables constant.

Problems in Regression Analysis

It is not too difficult to gather data and estimate regression equations. That may be the easy part, because there are plenty of pitfalls in the analysis of regression, and dealing with these problems requires some practice and experience. In this section, we outline the most important problems; some ways to deal with these problems are set out briefly in the subsequent section.

Measurement Error

No variable is measured with complete precision, and many socioeconomic variables, including income and expenditure variables, are quite imprecise. In some cases, even a variable that should be easy to quantify, such as a respondent's age, may not be correct; in many surveys, too many people report their age as, say, 70 or 75, and too few report their age as 71 or 74.

Let S be the true measure of a variable, but assume that we only observe S*. Thus

$$
\underset{\text{observed}}{S^*} = \underset{\text{true value}}{S} + \underset{\text{random error}}{w.}
$$

The effects of measurement error depend on whether it appears in the dependent or in the independent variables.

Case 1. Measurement Error in Y. Suppose that we have the true equation

$$Y = a + bX + \varepsilon$$

but all we observe is Y*, so

$$Y^* = a + bX + (\varepsilon + w).$$

In this case, the estimate of the coefficient b will not be biased, but the overall fit of the equation will be poorer, because the error term is larger and hence noisier.

Case 2. Measurement Error in X. Again suppose that the true equation is

$$Y = a + bX + \varepsilon$$

but what we observe is now

$$Y = a + bX^* + (\varepsilon - bw).$$

This time we have a noisy measure of the true X, and the estimate of b will be biased toward 0, because the dependence of Y on X is masked. Formally,

$$E(\hat{b}) = b\,\frac{\sigma_x^2}{\sigma_x^2 + \sigma_w^2},$$

where σ^2 represents the true variance of the variable in question. As the error w becomes more variable, the estimated value of b (that is, $E(\hat{b})$) tends to zero. This problem can easily arise. For instance, if we have

$$\text{health} = a + b\,\text{schooling} + \varepsilon$$

and if there is error in measuring the schooling variable, then the effect of schooling on health will be understated.

Omitted Variable Bias

Suppose we leave a right-hand side ("independent") variable out of the equation that we estimate—perhaps because it is unobserved, or unavailable, or just overlooked. Then the estimated coefficients on the remaining variables generally will be wrong if the included variables are correlated with the omitted variables.

To see this, suppose the correct model is

$$
\begin{array}{lllll}
H_C & = a + & bS_M & + cA_M & + \varepsilon \\
\text{Child's} & & \text{Mother's} & \text{Mother's} & \\
\text{health} & & \text{schooling} & \text{ability} &
\end{array}
$$

In this case, the health of the child depends in part on the mother's ability, but this is a variable that we cannot observe. So when we regress H_C on S_M, we have, in effect, a compound error term $c.A_M + \varepsilon$. In this case, it can be shown that

$$E(\hat{b}) = b + c\sigma_{S,A}$$

where the last item is the covariance between schooling and (unobserved) ability. If higher ability leads to more schooling (as is likely, so $\sigma_{SA} > 0$), and if higher ability leads to better health (so $c > 0$), then the estimated value of b (that is, $\hat{b}$) will be too high. In effect, the estimated value $\hat{b}$ is picking up ability as well as schooling effects, and in doing so, it overstates the contribution of schooling to child health.

The problem of omitted variables is widespread. We are rarely able to specify a model so completely that nothing important has been overlooked. And several personal characteristics—ability, drive, motivation, flexibility—defy reliable quantification. If bright, motivated farmers are more likely to use fertilizer and to use it well, then the measured effect of fertilizer use on output is likely to be overstated, because it is confounded with relevant unobservables. If clever, driven individuals are more likely to get a good education, then the measured effect of education on earnings will surely be overstated, because it reflects, in part, the contribution that should properly be attributed to personal traits rather than to education per se.

Simultaneity Bias

Many applied research problems come up against the problem of simultaneity bias. Although common, this can be a difficult problem to solve. We may illustrate it as follows: Suppose

$$\text{Child health} = a + b \text{ Nutrients} + \varepsilon.$$

Our goal is to explain child health, and we believe, quite reasonably, that better-fed children will be healthier. But the problem here is that the child's health may determine how much the household feeds her or him. For instance, parents might feed a sick child more, in the hope that he or she will get better faster that way. But then we would see a negative relationship, whereby more nutrients could be associated—in the regression analysis—with poorer child health.

Formally, if there is simultaneity present, the estimate of the coefficient will generally be wrong. In our example, if parents provide better feeding to sick children, then the estimate will be too low. One solution is to include lots of predetermined variables in the estimated equation so that in the presence of simultaneity, its effect will be attenuated.

Sample Selectivity Bias

Frequently, observations are available only for a subset of the sample that interests us. For instance, we might want to measure the spending of the very poor, but we have information only for people with a home. In this case, our sample would omit the homeless, and our results are likely to underestimate the true extent of poverty. Or again, we might want to know how much people would be willing to pay for piped water, but we have information only about willingness-to-pay for households that currently have piped water—hardly a representative sample of the population at large. In both of these cases, the problem is that our data may not come from a random sample of the relevant population, and so our regression estimates risk being biased.

Again, an illustration from Behrman and Oliver (2000) is helpful. Consider the common situation in which we are interested in determining the extent to which additional schooling leads to higher wages. The immediate problem is that we observe wages only for those who are skilled, dynamic, or educated enough to receive a wage (rather than work on a farm or in self-employment). This means that wage earners are not a random sample of the population.

The result is that we may have a situation as illustrated in figure 14.2. As shown, each dot represents one person, and the estimated line linking wages to schooling is too flat compared with the true relation. Thus, our estimate is biased.

The most common solution to the sample selection problem is to use Heckman's two-step procedure.

- First, estimate a probit model to determine who earns a wage. This is similar to a logistic model (see the section, "Logistic Regression"), in which the dependent variable is binary (1 if the person earns a wage, 0 otherwise).

- Second, estimate the wage equation—that is, wage as a function of schooling, experience, location, and so on—in which one includes an additional term (the inverse Mills ratio; also sometimes referred to as Heckman's λ) that is derived from the residuals of the probit model. Most statistical packages have commands that do this quite easily.

Figure 14.2 A Hypothetical Example of the Link between Schooling and Wages

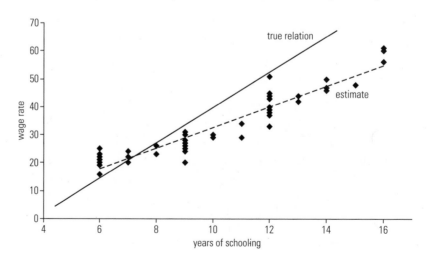

Source: Authors' creation.

Note: The true relation here is relatively steep; the estimated line is based only on individuals who work for a wage.

For this procedure to work, the initial probit model needs to include at least some variables that do not appear in the wage equation, so that the wage effect may be identified. This is not always easy, because the variables that affect what wage you get are also likely to influence whether you work for a wage or not.

Multicolinearity

One of the most common problems in regression analysis is that the right-hand variables may be correlated with one another. In this case, we have multicolinearity, and the problem is that the estimated coefficients can be quite imprecise and inaccurate, even though the equation itself may fit well.

To see how this might occur, suppose that we are interested in modeling the determinants of the number of years of schooling that girls get (y). We believe that a girl will tend to get more schooling if her mother has more education (ME), or her father has more education (FE), or she lives in an urban area (URB). A simple regression model would then look like this:

$$y_i = \beta_0 + \beta_1 ME_i + \beta_2 FE_i + \beta_3 URB_i + \varepsilon_i.$$

Many studies have found that the education of the mother has a strong influence on whether a girl goes to school. However, it is typically the case that educated people tend to marry each other (assortative mating); thus, a high level of ME will be associated with a high level of FE. The problem is that this makes it particularly difficult to disentangle the effect of ME on y from the effect of FE on y. If our only interest is in the value of β_3 then this may not be troublesome, but frequently, we cannot get out of the dilemma so easily. And because ME and FE really do affect y, the fit of the equation is likely to be good.

When an equation fits well but the coefficients are not statistically significant, it is appropriate to suspect that multicolinearity is at work. It is a good idea to look at the simple correlation coefficients among the various independent variables; if any of these are (absolutely) greater than about 0.5, then multicolinearity is likely to be a problem.

In the extreme case in which $ME_i = \gamma.FE_i$ exactly, we are unable to measure either β_1 or β_2 correctly. Substituting in for ME_i gives the following:

$$y_i = \beta_0 + \beta_1(\gamma FE_i) + \beta_2 FE_i + \beta_3 URB_i + \varepsilon_i$$
$$= \beta_0 + (\beta_1\gamma + \beta_2) FE_i + \beta_3 URB_i + \varepsilon_i.$$

In this regression, we have left out ME, but the coefficient on the FE variable is no longer correct. In other words, dropping a variable that is collinear with other variables does not solve the problem. Indeed there is no easy solution to multicolinearity; the best hope is more, or perhaps more accurate, data, but finding such data is easier said than done.

Heteroskedasticity

When working with cross-sectional data—the numbers that come from household surveys—one frequently encounters heteroskedasticity. This is the term used when the error in the regression model, ε_i, does not have a constant variance. The situation is illustrated in figure 14.3; the true relation here is

$$y = 2 + 0.8\,X,$$

but it is clear from panel A that the relationship fits well at low values of X—the observations are close to the line—but is more imprecise at higher values of X.

Heteroskedasticity does not bias the estimates of the coefficients, so even if it is present, the estimates of the slopes will be correct. However, it reduces the efficiency with which the standard errors of the coefficients (and hence the t-statistics and p-values) are estimated. Sometimes the problem can be solved with a simple transformation: the picture illustrated in figure 14.3, panel B, shows the same relationship except that the dependent variable is now the natural log of y, $\ln(y)$, rather than y. In this case, there is no visible evidence of heteroskedasticity, and we can proceed satisfactorily with testing hypotheses and creating confidence intervals.

Outliers

One last problem is worth noting, which is that of outliers. Quite frequently, a small number of observations take on values that are far outside the range of what one would expect. Figure 14.4, panel A, shows a hypothetical data set with a clean-looking estimated regression line. Panel B shows the same data, except that in the case of one observation the value of the y variable is 80.2 rather than 8.02. This is an outlier, and it had a major effect on the fit and form of the estimated equation.

Figure 14.3 Heteroskedasticity Illustrated

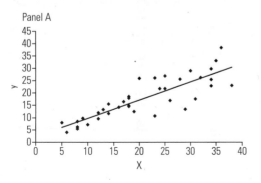
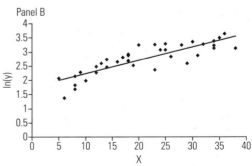

Source: Authors' creation.

Figure 14.4 Outliers Illustrated

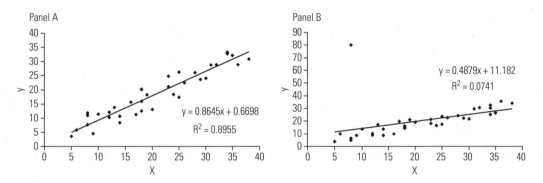

Source: Authors' creation.

In this case, it is quite likely that the data point was entered incorrectly and is simply wrong. The process of data cleaning is largely one of tracking down errors (and missing values) in the original data set. The situation is more problematic if it appears that the outlier does not represent an error. Some researchers remove outliers, or apply more robust estimation methods that reduce the influence of outliers on the regression results. However, it is difficult to justify the exclusion of data observations just because they happen to be inconvenient; after all, they convey information, and indeed may be more informative than most of the other observations.

Solving Estimation Problems

As a general rule, it is not easy to solve the estimation problems outlined above. However, here are some possibilities:

Get more, or better, data. This is typically expensive or difficult, but is occasionally possible. More data are useful in dealing with multicolinearity; better data are essential if measurement error is a problem.

Use fixed effects. Consider the following problem: We would like to estimate the determinants of rice production (Q), and believe that output will be influenced by fertilizer use (F), and the inherent ability of the farmer. Thus,

$$\text{rice output} = a + b \text{ fertilizer input} + c \text{ ability} + \varepsilon. \qquad (14.3)$$

The problem is that ability is unobserved, so we end up estimating

$$\text{rice output} = d + e \text{ fertilizer input} + w. \qquad (14.4)$$

285

In this case the coefficient on fertilizer input will be overstated if the level of fertilizer used is positively related to one's ability, as is plausible. The coefficient would be picking up the effects of both fertilizer use and ability, but attributing these effects to fertilizer use alone.

But now suppose that we have two observations per individual—for example, from panel data—so that we have equation (14.3) at two points in time. Using subscripts to denote the two time periods (0 and 1), we may difference equation (14.3) to get

$$Q_1 - Q_0 = b(F_1 - F_0) + (\varepsilon_1 - \varepsilon_0) \qquad (14.5)$$

which will now give us an unbiased estimate of the return to fertilizer inputs. The "ability" term has been dropped, assuming that ability does not change over time. More generally, we could include *fixed effects*, so that we are in effect estimating

$$Q_{ti} = a_i + bF_{ti} + \varepsilon_i, \qquad (14.6)$$

where t refers to the year and i to the household. Here, each household has a separate constant term (the a_i), which controls for such factors as differences in ability or other unobserved differences as dynamism, health, or the like.

Use instrumental variables. The idea here is to estimate equation (14.4) but, instead of using fertilizer input, use an estimated value of fertilizer input that is purged of any contamination by the ability variable. Typically there are three steps: (1) estimate a preliminary equation where fertilizer input is the dependent variable, and the independent variables constitute of a set of variables that are not correlated with any of the other variables in the production equation; (2), use this first equation to generate a set of predicted ("purged") values for fertilizer input; and (3), estimate the production equation itself using these purged values as instruments for fertilizer input, rather than the actual values. Most statistical packages have straightforward commands for this estimation.

It is important that at least some of the variables in the preliminary equation do not appear in the main equation of interest, yet are closely correlated with the variable of interest (here, fertilizer input). It is often hard to find good instruments, which is the main weakness of this approach.

Experiments. Glewwe et al. (2000) wanted to know whether the use of flip charts affected education achievement. They were able to arrange for charts to be given to some schools in Kenya and to compare these schools with a control sample. It is not always easy, however, to design or implement experiments of this nature. An effort to give gifts of $100 to some, but not all, of the households surveyed in the Vietnam Living Standards Survey of 1998 to measure the pure income effect on consumption was not considered appropriate by the Vietnamese authorities; it was seen as invidious. These are examples of efforts to measure the impact of projects, a topic that was addressed in more detail in chapter 13.

Logistic Regression

Often, the research issue of interest is whether a household is poor or not, owns a car, has another child, or works in industry. These cases all have a point in common: the dependent variable is binary, taking on values of 1 if the event is true, or 0 otherwise.

Mechanically, one can apply OLS to this situation. But the result is not satisfactory, since the predicted values of the equation might, in some cases, be higher than 1 or lower than 0, which makes little sense. This is illustrated in figure 14.5 for some hypothetical data. The horizontal axis shows household income per capita, and each dot is set equal to 1 if the household owns a motorbike, or 0 if it does not own a motorbike. Our interest is in fitting a curve to these observations. The OLS line is shown as the dashed line in figure 14.5; for income above 30, it predicts that the probability of owning a motorbike is greater than 1. The thick line in figure 14.5 is based on a logistic regression, which is of the form

$$y = \frac{1}{1 + e^{X\beta}},$$

and calls for some further explanation.

The easiest way to approach this is to look in more detail at a real example, which comes from Haughton and Haughton (1999). Table 14.1 gives the results of

Figure 14.5 Logistic Regression Compared with OLS

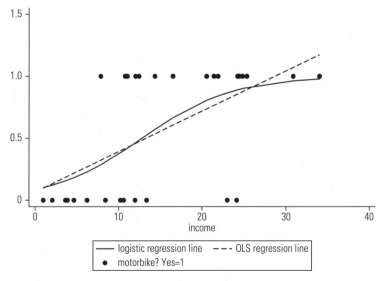

Source: Authors' creation.

a logistic model of migration to urban areas in Vietnam, using data from the Vietnam Living Standards Survey of 1993. At first sight, the output looks similar to that of a standard regression, and indeed the p-values can be interpreted in the same way: variables with small p-values are significant, and it is unlikely that their true coefficients are zero. The difference lies in the interpretation of the coefficients, as the following discussion will show.

Define the odds of migrating as follows:

$$Odds(\text{migrating}) = \frac{p(\text{migrating})}{p(\text{not migrating})}$$

The key point is that in a logistic regression, when an independent variable increases by 1 (for instance, the age of the migrant, AGE), and all other variables are held constant, the estimated odds of migrating change by the exponential of the value of the coefficient. In this example, for AGE, we have $e^{0.438} = 1.5496$. This means that one more year of age multiplies the estimated odds of migrating by 1.5496. Since *P(migrating) = 1–P(not migrating)*, we have

$$p(\text{migrating}) = \frac{Odds(\text{migrating})}{Odds(\text{migrating}) + 1}.$$

For instance, consider a person whose estimated probability of migrating is 0.03 (3 percent). An otherwise identical person who is one year older would then have

$$Odds(\text{migrating}) = 1.5496 \times (0.03/0.97) \approx 0.0479.$$

So, for this second person, the estimated probability of migrating is

$$p(\text{migrating}) \approx 0.0479/1.0479 \approx 0.0457.$$

Thus, one more year of age, holding all other variables constant, raises an estimated probability of migrating of 3 percent to about 4.57 percent.

The most important variable in the migration model is the one that measures the differential between the log of expenditure per capita now and the log of expenditure per capita that the person would have experienced had he or she not migrated. The coefficient of 2.368 means that, when the ratio of current expenditure per capita to expenditure per capita at place of birth is multiplied by e (= 2.72, a large change), and all other variables are held constant, an estimated probability of migrating of 3 percent would rise to 24.8 percent.

The coefficients for the regional dummy variables can be interpreted as follows. Consider a person residing in one of the reference regions (here the Red River Delta, North Central Coast, Central Highlands, or Mekong Delta) with an estimated probability of migrating of 7 percent. An otherwise similar person residing in the Northern Uplands would have an estimated probability of migrating of 11.6 percent.

Table 14.1 Logistic Model of Rural-Urban Migration, Vietnam, 1993

	Coefficients	P–values	Estimated probability of migrating when independent variable changes by one unit and initial probability is (percent):		
			3.0	7.0	11.0
Dependent variable					
Does person migrate from rural to urban area? (Y=1)					
Independent variables:					
Age of person (years)	0.438	0.000	4.6	10.4	16.1
Years of education	0.117	0.000	3.4	7.8	12.2
Δ ln(expenditure per capita)	2.368	0.000	24.8	44.5	56.9
Male household head (Y=1)	−1.498	0.000	0.7	1.6	2.7
Size of household	0.105	0.000	3.3	7.7	12.1
Married (Y=1)	1.700	0.000	14.5	29.2	40.4
Divorced (Y=1)	1.618	0.000	13.5	27.5	38.4
Separated (Y=1)	1.176	0.026	9.1	19.6	28.6
Widowed (Y=1)	1.146	0.000	8.9	19.1	28.0
Regional effects					
Northern Uplands	0.558	0.000	5.1	11.6	17.7
Central Coast	0.905	0.000	7.1	15.7	23.4
Southeast	1.404	0.000	11.2	23.5	33.5

Source: Based on data from Vietnam Living Standards Survey 1992–93.

Note: Based on 10,954 observations. Pseudo R^2 = 0.34. Effect for expenditure per capita variable in last three columns assumes a 2.72-fold rise in ratio of expenditure per capita at current residence to estimated expenditure per capita if person had stayed at place of birth. Omitted regions are Red River Delta, North Central Coast, Central Highlands, and Mekong Delta. Nonmigrants include those who were born in a rural area and are still living in the location where they were born.

Table 14.1 also gives a value for the pseudo-R^2, which can be interpreted in roughly the same way as the nonadjusted R^2 for standard regression. As in the case of standard regression, one must guard against overfitting, which is the addition of too many independent variables in the hope of getting a "better" model. Adding more variables will always increase the pseudo-R^2, but sometimes by minute amounts. The problem is that a model with too many variables might not fit well on other similar data sets.

The use of logistic regression is not always appropriate. For instance, suppose we are trying to model the determinants of poverty. Based on a poverty line and expenditure per capita data, we have classified every households as either poor (1) or not poor (0). We certainly could apply logistic regression to this variable, but such a model is unlikely to be efficient, because it is throwing away information. We not only know whether a household is poor (the binary variable used in the logistic regression), but also have information on consumption per capita, so we know how poor the household is. This is more informative, and it might well be more useful to estimate a model of the determinants of expenditure.

Review Questions

1. You have estimated an equation using ordinary least squares regression. To determine whether the equation fits the data well, the most useful statistic is:

   o A. The t-statistic.
   o B. The p-value.
   o C. R^2.
   o D. The standard error of the coefficient.

2. In logistic regression:

   o A. The dependent variable is binary.
   o B. A coefficient shows the effect of a unit change in the independent variable on the log of the odds ratio.
   o C. There is a loss of information relative to using a continuous variable on the left-hand side of the equation.
   o D. All the other answers are correct.

3. Measurement error

   o A. Always biases the coefficients toward zero.
   o B. Biases the coefficients toward zero if the independent variables are not measured correctly.
   o C. Biases the coefficients toward zero if the dependent variable is not measured correctly.
   o D. Is fortunately relatively rare when using micro data from household surveys.

4. An equation that seeks to explain whether a child attends school or not includes, as a right-hand variable, the schooling level of the child's mother, but not her ability. This is a case of

   o A. Attrition bias.
   o B. Simultaneity bias.
   o C. Sample selectivity bias.
   o D. Omitted variable bias.

5. In a regression model based on household data, fixed-effects estimation essentially amounts to including a separate intercept for each household, and requires panel data.

   o True
   o False

6. In a regression model of the form $y_i = \beta_0 + \beta_1 X_{1i} + \beta_2 X_{2i} + \varepsilon_i$, the covariates are

- ○ A. The ε_i.
- ○ B. The X_{ki}.
- ○ C. The β_k.
- ○ D. The y_i.

7. In a regression model of the form $y_i = \beta_0 + \beta_1 X_{1i} + \beta_2 X_{2i} + \varepsilon_i$, β_1 measures

- ○ A. The elasticity of output with respect to the input X_1.
- ○ B. The change in y_i that occurs when X_1 rises, holding other variables constant.
- ○ C. The value of y_i for each value of X_{1i}.
- ○ D. The correlation between y_i and X_1.

8. The main problem with multicolinearity is that

- ○ A. The equation will be a poor fit.
- ○ B. The estimated coefficients will be biased toward zero.
- ○ C. The error term will not be normally distributed.
- ○ D. The coefficients will be estimated imprecisely.

9. Which of the following is true about heteroskedasticity?

- ○ A. The variance of the error of the equation is not constant.
- ○ B. The coefficient estimates are unbiased.
- ○ C. Hypothesis testing is inefficient.
- ○ D. All the other answers are correct.

Note

1. The (spending/capita)^2 term is obtained by squaring spending per capita (which is in thousands of Vietnamese dong per year) and then dividing by 1,000.

References

Anderson, David R., Dennis J. Sweeney, and Thomas A. Williams. 2008. *Essentials of Statistics for Business and Economics*, 5th edition, South-Western College Pub/Cengage Learning.

Behrman, Jere, and Raylynn Oliver. 2000. "Basic Economic Models and Econometric Tools." In *Designing Household Survey Questionnaires for Developing Countries: Lessons from Ten Years of LSMS Experience*, ed. Margaret Grosh and Paul Glewwe. Washington, DC: World Bank.

Glewwe, Paul, Michael Kremer, Sylvie Moulin, and Eric Zitzewitz. 2000. "Flip Charts in Kenya." NBER Working Paper 8018, National Bureau of Economic Research, Cambridge, MA.

Greene, William H. 2007. *Econometric Analysis*, 6th edition. Upper Saddle River, NJ: Prentice Hall.

Haughton, Dominique, and Jonathan Haughton. 1999. "Statistical Techniques for the Analysis of Household Data." In *Health and Wealth in Vietnam*, ed. Dominique Haughton, Jonathan Haughton, Sarah Bales, Truong Thi Kim Chuyen, and Nguyen Nguyet Nga. Singapore: ISEAS Publications.

Prescott, Nicholas, and Menno Pradhan. 1997. "A Poverty Profile of Cambodia." Discussion Paper No. 373, World Bank, Washington, DC.

Wooldridge, Jeffrey. 2008. *Introductory Econometrics: A Modern Approach*, 4th edition. South-Western College Pub/Cengage Learning.

Chapter 15

The Effects of Taxation and Spending on Inequality and Poverty

Summary

The purpose of incidence analysis is to determine who bears the burden of taxes and who benefits from government spending. This is one of the elements needed in formulating tax and expenditure policy.

A tax is progressive if it takes a rising proportion of income (or expenditure) as one moves from poor to rich; a regressive tax represents a higher burden (relative to income or expenditure) on the poor than the rich. The progressivity of tax and spending may be seen visually using Lorenz and concentration curves, and summarized using the Kakwani measure or tax progressivity or the Reynolds-Smolensky measure of redistributive capacity.

To measure the incidence of a tax, first make assumptions about the true ("effective") incidence; then determine the effective tax rates. Combine these with household survey data to estimate the burden on each household and hence on groups. The discussion is illustrated with the case of the Peruvian value added tax (VAT).

To measure benefit incidence, begin by estimating the unit value of government subsidies (for example, to health or education). Then identify the beneficiaries, using household survey data, and combine this information with the unit values to get the benefit incidence. Examples discussed include education in Peru and health in Ghana.

There are a number of problematic aspects of incidence analysis. Most studies measure average incidence, but marginal incidence (for example who gains from more spending on health) is typically more useful. The pattern of tax incidence can look quite different depending on whether one uses income or expenditure to rank households. The valuation of the benefits of government spending is difficult, and the usual procedure (that is, use of the unit costs of services provided) is not entirely satisfactory. Even good information on incidence is rarely sufficient to generate policy implications and additional modeling usually is required.

Public expenditure analysis is useful only if the policy setting is right. Greater use of tax incidence analysis probably has more potential to inform policy.

Learning Objectives

After completing the chapter on *The Effects of Public Policy on Inequality and Poverty*, you should be able to

1. Explain the purpose of tax and expenditure incidence analysis.

2. Define what is meant by a *progressive* tax, a *proportional* tax, and a *regressive* tax.

3. Outline the steps required to measure the incidence of a tax.

4. Compute the Kakwani measure of tax progressivity and the Reynolds-Smolensky measure of redistributive capacity, given information on tax incidence.

5. Outline the steps required to measure the incidence of a government-provided good or service.

6. Assess the limits of tax and expenditure incidence analysis, with particular attention to the role of the following: average vs. marginal incidence; the use of income vs. expenditure to order households; the role of behavioral responses; the valuation of the benefits of government spending; the merits of partial vs. full incidence; and the proper role for further modeling.

7. Explain why public expenditure analysis is useful only if the policy setting is right.

Introduction

Governments raise tax revenue and spend it on such things as education, health, and pensions. But who benefits most from the spending? And who really bears the burden of the taxes? The answers to these questions are to be found in benefit and tax incidence analysis. This chapter sets out the steps required to undertake such analyses, evaluates the methodological choices that the researcher needs to make, and illustrates the discussion with some real examples.

It is useful to start by providing some context. Economists typically identify three main roles for government. First, governments have a role to play in ensuring economic efficiency, in part by setting and enforcing the rules of market interactions, and in part by acting to correct for market failures. The latter category includes efforts to check the power of monopolies, provide public goods such as defense and basic research, and tackle negative externalities such as air pollution. The second role of government is to maintain macroeconomic stability, for instance, by keeping inflation low and moderating the business cycle of boom and bust. Third, governments have a role to play in enhancing equity, although the extent to which they should do this is controversial.

Incidence analysis only measures the effects of government spending and revenues on the equity dimension. Such information is an essential input into informed decision making, but there is no reason to expect it to be the only determinant of the way spending and taxes are, or should be, structured.

Review Question

> 1. Incidence analysis measures who benefits or loses, and by how much, from government spending and taxes.
>
> o True
> o False
> o Uncertain

Presenting Incidence Results

The basic idea behind benefit or tax incidence is to determine how much each person gains from government spending or loses because of taxes paid. The distribution of these gains or losses can then be compared with a reference distribution—such as income or consumption per capita—to determine the degree of progressivity of the spending.

Suppose that we have successfully identified how much each person in our sample pays in, say, personal income tax (PIT). We now need to present the results in a clear and compelling way.

The simplest approach is to tabulate the results by quintile (or decile). This is illustrated in table 15.1 for some hypothetical numbers. Column (2) sets out the mean income of five groups of individuals, sorted from poorest to richest; the share of each in total income is shown in column (3).

Now suppose that the mean tax payments per person are those shown in column (4). In column (5), we compute the tax paid as a percentage of income. In this example, the proportion of income that goes to pay the tax rises as income rises, and so the tax is considered to be *progressive*. This may be seen in another way. The figures in column (6) show that the proportion of total tax paid by the poorest group (4 percent) is less than its share of total income (6 percent), and that this situation reverses as one moves to the higher-income individuals.

Table 15.1 Progressivity Illustrated

			Case 1: Progressive tax			Case 2: Proportional tax			Case 3: Regressive tax		
	Income	Percent of total	Tax paid	Percent of income	Percent of total	Tax paid	Percent of income	Percent of total	Tax paid	Percent of income	Percent of total
(1)	(2)	(3)	(4)	(5)	(6)	(7)	(8)	(9)	(10)	(11)	(12)
1	1,200	6.0	80	6.7	4.0	120	10.0	6.0	200	16.7	10.0
2	2,000	10.0	150	7.5	7.5	200	10.0	10.0	300	15.0	15.0
3	3,200	16.0	270	8.4	13.5	320	10.0	16.0	400	12.5	20.0
4	4,400	22.0	450	10.2	22.5	440	10.0	22.0	500	11.4	25.0
5	9,200	46.0	1,050	11.4	52.5	920	10.0	46.0	600	6.5	30.0
All	20,000	100.0	2,000	10.0	100.0	2,000	10.0	100.0	2,000	10.0	100.0

Source: Authors' creation.

Note: Data are hypothetical.

The case of a *proportional tax* is shown in columns (7)–(9). In this case, everyone pays the same proportion of their income in taxes. And in columns (10)–(12), we present an example of a *regressive* tax. In this example, although tax payments are higher in absolute terms for the rich than for the poor, the proportion of income paid to taxes actually falls as one moves from poorer to richer individuals.

The same information can be shown in the form of histograms; those in figure 15.1 are based on the three cases set out in table 15.1. It is easy to see at a glance that the first tax is progressive, the second proportional, and the third regressive. Sahn and Younger (1999) also make heavy use of graphs in their study of fiscal incidence in Africa.

There is some loss of information when data are aggregated into quintiles (or deciles) as done here. A solution is to graph the results in greater detail, as is done in figure 15.2 for the hypothetical income numbers underlying the summary statistics in columns (2) and (4) in table 15.1.

To construct figure 15.2, we first sorted all the individuals in the sample from poorest to richest, using income per capita as our welfare measure. Then we graphed the cumulative percentage of income on the vertical axis, against the cumulative percentage of individuals on the horizontal axis. This gives the Lorenz curve—the heavy curve in figure 15.2—which was discussed in more detail in chapter 6, "Inequality Measures." This serves as a point of reference, along with the diagonal representing the line of perfect equality.

We then added a *tax concentration curve*, which graphs the cumulative percentage of tax paid on the vertical axis. Note that the individuals are still sorted by income (and not by tax per capita). The concentration curve for the income tax shown in figure 15.2 is farther from the line of perfect equality than the Lorenz curve. In other words, tax payments are distributed more unequally than income, which means that the tax is progressive.

Figure 15.1 Histograms for Income Tax as a Percentage of Income, Three Cases

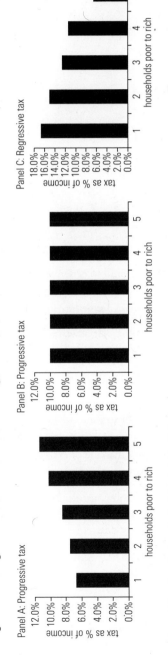

Panel A: Progressive tax

Panel B: Progressive tax

Panel C: Regressive tax

Source: Based on the hypothetical data in table 15.1.

Figure 15.2 Lorenz and Concentration Curves for PIT Example

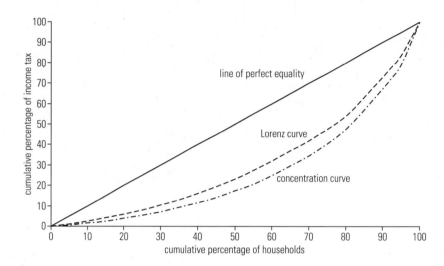

Source: Based on the hypothetical data in table 15.1.

It is sometimes helpful to generate a summary measure of the progressivity of a tax. There are two common approaches: (1) the ***Kakwani measure of tax progressivity*** and (2) ***Reynolds-Smolensky measure of the redistributive capacity of a tax***.

To compute the ***Kakwani measure of tax progressivity***, use the following steps:

- Compute the Gini coefficient for income (that is, A/(A+B), where A is the area between the Lorenz curve and the Line of Perfect Equality and B is the area under the Lorenz curve), G_y.

- Compute the concentration coefficient (or "quasi-Gini coefficient") from the tax concentration curve (that is, C/(C+D), where C is the area between the Concentration Curve and the Line of Perfect Equality, and D is the area under the Concentration Curve), C_T.

- Compute the Kakwani measure as $K = -[G_Y - C_T]$. Note that some authors define the term without the initial negative sign, so care is needed when making comparisons between one study and the next.

The measure will be positive for a progressive tax, zero for a tax that is proportional, and negative for a regressive tax. In our example, based on Case 1 in table 15.1, $G_Y = 0.387$, $C_T = 0.473$, so $K = 0.086 > 0$, therefore the tax is progressive. One may determine whether the result is statistically significant by bootstrapping to estimate the standard error of the estimate of K.

While the Kakwani measure indicates the progressivity of a tax, it does not serve as a good guide to the impact that a change in the tax would have on income distribution or poverty. For instance, a tax on salt may be highly regressive, but its abolition might do little to help the poor because the tax is so small.

The ***Reynolds-Smolensky measure of the redistributive capacity of a tax*** solves this problem. A popular version of this measure is given by the following:

$$RS2 = G_Y - G_{Y-T}$$

where G_Y is the Gini coefficient for pre-tax income and G_{Y-T} the Gini coefficient for post-tax income. In our example $RS2 = 0.387-0.378 = 0.0096 > 0$, which is—

• Positive, indicating a progressive tax, because the after-tax distribution of income (as measured by G_{Y-T}) is more equal than its pretax distribution (as measured by G_Y); and

• Relatively large, indicating that this tax has considerable redistributive potential. In other words, this tax is a good candidate for serious efforts to make the tax code more progressive.

The *redistributive capacity* of a tax depends both on its progressivity and on the tax rate. It can be shown that $RS2 \approx (t/(1-t))$ K, where t is the average tax rate relative to pretax income.[1] In our example, the tax rate averages 10 percent, so we have $(0.1/(1-0.1)) \times (0.086) \approx 0.0096$.

Review Questions

> **2. Household A has an income of 4,000 and pays tax of 300. Household B has an income of 20,000 and pays tax of 1,400. This tax is**

   ○ A. Proportional.
   ○ B. Progressive.
   ○ C. Regressive.
   ○ D. None of the above.

> **3. A concentration curve for a tax is computed by**

   ○ A. Sorting households by tax/capita and graphing the cumulative percentage of tax against the cumulative percentage of households.
   ○ B. Sorting households by expenditure per capita and graphing the cumulative percentage of tax against the cumulative percentage of households.
   ○ C. Sorting households by expenditure per capita and graphing the cumulative percentage of tax against the cumulative percentage of expenditure.
   ○ D. Sorting households by tax/capita and graphing the cumulative percentage of tax against the cumulative percentage of expenditure.

4. The Gini coefficient for gross income (G_Y) is 0.372; the concentration coefficient for a tax (C_T) is 0.407; the Gini coefficient for net income (G_{Y-T}) is 0.360. This tax is:

   o Progressive
   o Regressive

5. The Gini coefficient for gross income (G_Y) is 0.372; the concentration coefficient for a tax (C_T) is 0.407; the Gini coefficient for net income (G_{Y-T}) is 0.360. The Reynolds-Smolensky measure is:

   o A. 0.036 and reflects low redistributive capacity.
   o B. 0.012 and reflects high redistributive capacity.
   o C. 0.047 and reflects high redistributive capacity.
   o D. None of the above.

Tax Incidence

Any serious discussion of tax reform needs to include information about the redistributive effects of tax changes. Four steps are required:

1. For each tax, make appropriate assumptions about who bears the true burden of the tax.

2. Determine the tax rates.

3. Apply the information from 1 and 2 to household survey data to compute the tax burden on each household.

4. Present the results in an informative way.

None of these steps is trivial, so some further comments are in order.

The first challenge is in determining the *effective incidence* of each tax under consideration. This measures who truly bears the burden of a tax, and may be distinguished from the *statutory* (or *nominal*) *incidence*, which identifies who is legally responsible for paying the tax. To illustrate the distinction, consider the case of a 5 percent sales tax on the books. The store is obliged to collect the tax and remit it to the Treasury, but in practice, the seller effectively shifts the tax onto the buyer. In this case, the statutory incidence is on the seller, but the effective incidence is on the buyer.

In measuring tax incidence, the researcher is obliged to make assumptions about who bears the effective ("true") burden of each tax. Table 15.2 summarizes the incidence assumptions used in a recent study of tax incidence in Lebanon; these are fairly typical assumptions for tax incidence in a small open economy.

Table 15.2 Incidence Assumptions for Study of Tax Incidence in Lebanon, 2004

Tax	Incidence assumption
Wages and salaries	Borne by earners (because their take-home pay would rise if there were no tax).
Tax on personal companies and small businesses	Tax falls on owners/entrepreneurs.
Tax on corporate income (CIT)	Borne half by consumers (via higher prices) and half by owners. (Note: This is controversial, but is reasonable if capital is somewhat, but not completely, mobile internationally.)
Dividends tax	Borne by those who receive dividends.
Tax on interest	Burden falls on depositors; with mobile capital, banks are assumed to have limited ability to raise interest rates paid.
Built property tax	Borne by property owners. (Note: For land, this is the classical case examined by Henry George (1912).)
Property registration fees	Born by owners of real estate.
Inheritance tax	Borne by owner of assets.
Value added tax	Shifted onto consumers.
Fuel excise	Shifted onto consumers because of horizontal supply curve.
Tobacco excise	Shifted onto consumers because of horizontal supply curve.
Car taxes (including annual registration fees)	Shifted onto consumers.
Customs duties	Shifted onto consumers.
Other taxes (especially stamp duties)	Shifted onto consumers.

Source: Haughton 2004.

The second step is to compute the size of each tax. A good starting point is the statutory tax rates: for instance, a gasoline tax of $0.25/liter, a wage tax of 8 percent after the first $5,000, and so on. The major practical problem here lies in reconciling the statutory tax rates with actual collections. For instance, suppose there is a 10 percent tax on interest earnings, and total interest earnings, according to national accounts data, come to $2 billion. Then the tax on interest should raise $200 million annually. But now suppose, plausibly, that the interest tax yields just $140 million per year. Clearly the effective tax rate of 7 percent is lower than the statutory tax rate of 10 percent. The difference may be due to tax evasion, or measurement error, or delays in payment. A pragmatic solution in incidence analysis is to use the effective tax rate in one's calculations, so as not to overstate the true burden of this tax, but this is not entirely satisfactory, because it assumes everyone cheats (or misreports) equally.

The third step is to use the tax rates, and associated incidence assumptions, to calculate the burden of each tax on each household. For direct taxes—levied on income—one needs information on household income, broken down by source.

301

Example: Suppose a household gets $12,000 from wages, $800 for interest, and $2,500 from remittances, and assume there is a tax of 10 percent on interest and 8 percent on wages (after the first $5,000 annually). Then, under plausible assumptions about incidence, the direct tax burden on this household will be $640 (= 10% × $800 + 8% × ($12,000 − $5,000)).

For indirect taxes—levied on expenditure—one needs solid information on household spending patterns, with a substantial degree of detail.

Example: Suppose there is a VAT of 12 percent on all goods and services except food, and an additional tax of $0.25/liter on gasoline. Assume that the household spends $14,900 on purchases of goods and services, of which $600 goes to buy 1,000 liters of gasoline and $8,100 on food. Note that these are tax-inclusive numbers. Then, assuming that the incidence of these taxes falls on the consumer, the tax paid by this household will be $951.79.[2]

If the goal is to assess the incidence of the tax *system*, then it is necessary to have household survey data with relatively detailed information both on income and on expenditures. Some surveys collect good information on one, but not both, of these categories. In practice, tax incidence analysis requires access to the original survey data, and cannot be done satisfactorily with secondary data such as tables published in statistical abstracts, since the latter rarely show income and expenditure data together.

Case Study: VAT in Peru

Table 15.3 and figure 15.3 provide information on the incidence of the VAT in Peru in 2000. At that time, the tax rate was 18 percent, although the effective rate (on taxable items) was closer to 16 percent, and actual collections represented just 7.3 percent of household expenditure nationwide. The VAT is by far the most important single tax in Peru, generating more than two-fifths of tax revenue in 2000. When households are sorted by expenditure per capita, the VAT appears to be roughly proportional, or perhaps slightly regressive (the Kakwani measure of progressivity is −0.015), but the potential for making the tax system more progressive by lowering VAT rates is quite minimal, as reflected in the small magnitude of the Reynolds-Smolensky measure (RS2 = −0.00125). However, if the incidence of the tax is measured relative to income per capita instead of expenditure per capita, this tax appears to be highly regressive; we return to this point below.

The approach outlined above gives the incidence of existing taxes at a point in time. But often the analyst is interested in tracing the distributional effects of a *change* in taxes. Usually this is not difficult: for instance, if the wage tax is to be

Table 15.3 Incidence of Value Added Tax, Peru, 2000

Categories	Tax rates	Sorted by expenditure per capita			Sorted by inc./cap.
		Tax/Expend. (%)	Tax/Income (%)	Percent of VAT	Tax/Income (%)
Wide base of goods, 2003	*19.0%*				
Wide base of goods, 2000	18.0%				
Exports	0.0%				
Most services, some goods	Exempt				
All Peru (2000)		7.3	6.1	100.0	6.1
Decile 1 (poorest)		6.5	4.8	1.6	29.7
Decile 2		6.9	4.3	2.9	13.3
Decile 3		7.3	5.6	3.9	10.0
Decile 4		7.6	5.4	5.1	8.6
Decile 5		7.7	6.0	6.3	7.9
Decile 6		7.8	6.0	7.9	7.4
Decile 7		7.7	6.5	9.5	6.7
Decile 8		7.6	6.1	12.0	6.2
Decile 9		7.6	7.1	16.5	5.8
Revenue					
Tax revenue, 2000, million soles, net of refunds	9,550.6				
Tax revenue as percent of total tax revenue, 2000	41.5				
Actual tax revenue/estimated revenue	85%				
Decile 10 (richest)		6.7	6.1	34.2	4.3
Lima/Callao		6.9	n/a	41.8	5.7
Amazon (4 depts.)		7.8	n/a	13.6	6.8
Rest of Peru		7.5	n/a	44.6	6.4

Distributional effects, 2000	Expend per capita	Income per capita
Gini coefficient	0.470	0.535
Quasi-Gini coefficient, tax/capita	0.455	0.358
RS1 measure (>0 = progressive)	-0.00116	-0.01145
RS2 measure (>0 = progressive)	-0.00125	-0.01207
Kakwani measure (>0 = progressive)	-0.015	-0.176

Source: Based on ENNIV-2000. From Haughton (2005).

Note: RS1 is the Reynolds-Smolensky measure of disproportionality and RS2 is the Reynolds-Smolensky measures of redistributive capacity. VAT = value added tax.

Figure 15.3 Incidence of Value Added Tax, Peru, 2000

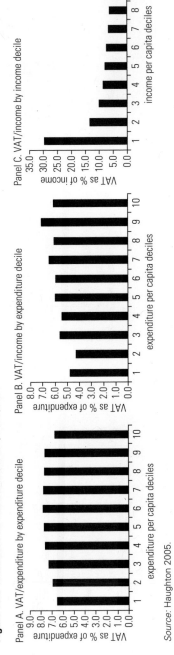

Source: Haughton 2005.

raised from 8 percent to 9 percent (on wages above $5,000), then one can simply compute the effective incidence, for each household, with the old and new rates. However, this assumes that there will be no behavioral response—such as a rise in tax evasion, or a shift to nonwage sources of income. In practice, it is useful to incorporate two types of reaction:

- A change in buying patterns. For example, the long-run own-price elasticity of demand for gasoline is about –0.3 in the United States. If tax rates were doubled, this would raise the retail price of gasoline by about 10 percent, which in turn would lead to a 3 percent fall in the quantity of gasoline purchased.

- A change in taxes declared. For example, Agha and Haughton (1996) estimate, based on data from member countries of the Organisation for Economic Co-operation and Development, that every percentage point increase in the VAT rate is associated with a 2.7 percent fall in compliance; they find that this implies that increases in the tax rate would boost revenue by 30 percent less than one would have expected if compliance were unaffected.

Benefit Incidence

The goal here is to work out how much each person gains from government spending, and compare the distribution of this spending with a point of reference such as the distribution of per capita consumption; Demery (2000) provides an excellent survey. Although some types of government spending—health, education, and social subsidies—can easily be attributed to beneficiary households, almost half of government spending cannot be so allocated. It is difficult, perhaps impossible, to determine who benefits most from spending on such items as the army, police, diplomatic service, judicial system, or pensions for public servants.

The first step in benefit incidence analysis is to estimate the value of unit subsidies: how much does the government subsidize each high school pupil, each visit to a rural health clinic, each recipient of school meals, and so on? This information is not to be found in household survey data, except perhaps for some direct social subsidies to households. It is important to base the measures of unit subsidies on actual rather than budgeted spending, and even then some digging may be required.

> *Example 1:* In a survey of the incidence of government spending on health in Africa, Castro-Leal et al. (2000) were obliged to use budgeted rather than actual spending in four of the six cases considered. The study of Ghana, undertaken in 1992, required a survey of hospitals to collect enough information to provide an adequate disaggregation of the unit costs of treating different types of patients (Demery 2000).

Example 2: A study of education in Uganda in the mid-1990s found that for every $1 allocated to primary education, just $0.37 reached the schools (Demery 2000, 4.).

The second step is to identify the coverage of the government services or subsidies and impute it to users. In this case, household survey data are needed to provide information on how many household members go to school and at what level, how many people visited a health clinic during the year, and so on.

There are two main problems at this stage—poor recall and rare events. Households tend to understate their use of government services, just as they understate income and consumption levels. For instance, in 1992 there were 73,800 in-patient visits in the Greater Accra area, but household survey data implied 8,500 visits, just 12 percent of the official figure (Demery 2000, 8). Furthermore, in any given year, few people are hospitalized or attend university. Thus, these events appear infrequently in survey data, and so inferences about the incidence of such spending are highly imprecise.

The third and final step is to aggregate and present the results in a useful way. To give a flavor of how this might be done, we next present a case study of education spending in Peru; in the annex to this chapter, we present a short case study of the incidence of health spending in Ghana.

Case Study: Education Spending in Peru

Approximately one-sixth of government spending in Peru goes to subsidize education. In 2000, based on information on actual budgetary spending, the recurrent subsidies were as follows:

- Prekindergarten 583 Peruvian soles (S/.) per child per year (US$180)

- Kindergarten and primary S/. 386 per pupil per year (US$120)

- Secondary S/. 624 per pupil per year (US$190)

- Tertiary S/. 2,506 per pupil per year (US$770)

These subsidies were imputed to households on the basis of data from the *2000 Encuesta Sobre El Nivel de Vida* (ENNIV), which surveyed 3,977 households nationwide and included information on which members of the household were enrolled in which level of education.

The essential results are shown in table 15.4 (Haughton 2005). Expressed as a percentage of household expenditure (or income), education spending appears to be highly progressive, in the sense that it represents a much larger *relative* subsidy to poor

Table 15.4 State Spending on Education, Peru, 2000

	Sorted by expenditure/capita			Sorted by income/capita
	Spending/ expend. (%)	Spending/ income (%)	Percent of spending	Spending/ income (%)
All Peru (2000)	3.6	3.0	100.0	3.0
By decile				
Decile 1 (poorest)	15.6	11.4	7.9	34.7
Decile 2	9.8	6.0	8.1	13.5
Decile 3	7.6	5.8	8.3	8.3
Decile 4	7.0	5.0	9.5	6.2
Decile 5	5.4	4.2	9.0	4.7
Decile 6	4.8	3.7	9.8	4.4
Decile 7	4.0	3.4	10.1	3.6
Decile 8	3.5	2.8	11.0	3.0
Decile 9	2.9	2.7	12.7	2.2
Decile 10 (richest)	1.3	1.2	13.7	1.0
By region				
Lima/Callao	2.2	1.8	27.2	1.8
Amazon (4 depts.)	4.5	3.9	15.7	3.9
Rest of Peru	4.8	4.0	57.1	4.0

Source: Based on ENNIV-2000. Haughton 2005.

than to rich households. In absolute terms, however, the share of all education spending going to those in the poorer deciles is substantially smaller than that going to households in the top deciles ("per capita regressive"). The situation is summarized in figure 15.4: the concentration curve for education spending shows much greater equality that overall expenditure per capita, but it is still below the line of perfect equality.

Further insight into the situation comes from figure 15.5, which examines the incidence of education spending overall (panels A and B) and by subsector. Spending on pre-K and primary education are clearly progressive, with poorer households receiving substantially more than richer ones; spending on secondary education is roughly proportional, and spending on higher education appears to be regressive.

A similar pattern is found in many countries (see van de Walle and Nead 1995), as table 15.5 shows.

Issues in Benefit Incidence Analysis

The techniques of tax and benefit incidence analysis should be included in the toolkit of all poverty analysts, but this analysis also has its limitations. In this section, we consider six issues that are still topics for debate.

Figure 15.4 The Incidence of Government Spending on Education, Peru, 2000

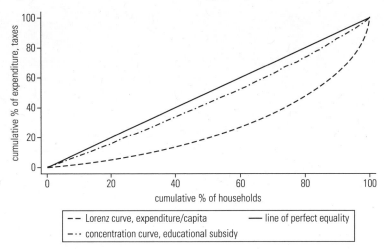

Source: Haughton 2005.

Note: Gini coefficient for expenditure per capita: 0.470. Concentration coefficient for educational subsidies: 0.102. Kakwani coefficient of progressivity: +0.369 (that is, "progressive").

Average or Marginal Incidence?

The approach set out above shows the average incidence of taxes or government spending. But policy analysis is usually more interested in marginal changes—who would gain from additional spending on education, for instance.

A problem arises because marginal and average incidence may vary substantially. Consider, for example, the case of a poor country such as Mali, where gross school enrollment rates are low—just 59 percent at the primary level. An analysis of the incidence of education spending would surely show that the bulk of the benefits accrue to richer households, because they are the ones whose children are most likely to attend school. But if Mali were to spend more on education, it is quite plausible that much of the marginal spending would expand access to schooling and disproportionately favor poor households. Stephen Younger (2003) believes that "early capture" of government benefits by the more affluent is widespread in Africa. The corollary is that marginal incidence—in this context at least—may be more progressive than average incidence.

The issue then becomes: how might one measure the marginal effects, especially on the benefit side? One solution is to use spatial variation. Lanjouw and Ravallion (1999) used data from Indian states, some of which are more affluent than others, to estimate the anticipated effects on the incidence of expanded spending on such items as education. A second solution is to estimate demand functions for publicly provided services, using information on such things as the time that people are

Figure 15.5 State Spending on Education by Level, Peru, 2000

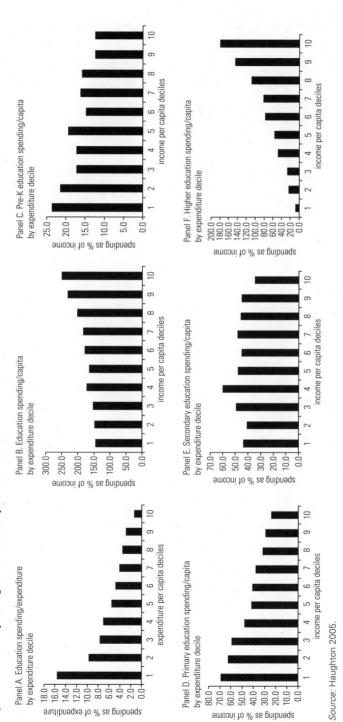

Panel A. Education spending/expenditure by expenditure decile

Panel B. Education spending/capita by expenditure decile

Panel C. Pre-K education spending/capita by expenditure decile

Panel D. Primary education spending/capita by expenditure decile

Panel E. Secondary education spending/capita by expenditure decile

Panel F. Higher education spending/capita by expenditure decile

Source: Haughton 2005.

Table 15.5 Benefit Incidence of Public Spending on Education in Selected African Countries

	Quintile shares of total spending								Total subsidy as share of household expenditure	
	Primary		Secondary		Tertiary		Total			
	Poorest	Richest	Poorest	Richest	Poorest	Richest	Poorest	Richest	Poorest	Richest
Côte d'Ivoire, 1995	19	14	7	37	12	71	13	35	12.5	4.6
Ghana, 1992	22	14	15	19	6	45	16	21	13.4	3.1
Guinea, 1994	11	21	4	39	1	65	5	44		
Kenya, 1992	22	15	7	30	2	44	17	21	27.8	1.9
Malawi, 1994	20	16	9	40	1	59	16	25	2.3	1.4
Madagascar, 1993	17	14	2	41	0	89	8	41	7.2	3.4
South Africa, 1994	19	28	11	39	6	47	14	35	42.1	5.1
Tanzania, 1993/94	20	19	8	34	0	100	14	37		
Uganda, 1992	19	18	4	49	66	47	13	32	4.3	1.5

Source: Castro-Leal et al. 1999, 64.

willing to wait in line for an appointment with a doctor, and to use these functions to infer the effects of expanded service provision.

A third solution is to appeal to time-series variation. For instance, van de Walle (2002) used information from a panel of Vietnamese households, surveyed in 1993 and 1998, to determine who gained from the increment in social transfer income during this period. Some of her results are reproduced in table 15.6; in this particular case, they actually show remarkably little difference in the allocation of social transfer income across quintiles between 1993 and 1998.

Income or Expenditure Progressivity?

Table 15.3 and figure 15.3 show something curious: when the Peruvian sample is sorted into deciles using expenditure per capita, the VAT appears approximately proportional, but when the sample is sorted by income per capita, then the VAT is highly regressive. Which conclusion is correct? This is not a mere academic point; it is at the heart of the debate about the role of the VAT in any tax system.

One can safely say that the use of income per capita overstates regressivity. This is because a significant fraction of those in the lowest income deciles are included only because they are temporarily poor—for example, due to a bad harvest, being laid off, studying at university—and their current income does not properly reflect their "permanent" income. We argued in chapter 2 that a household's expenditure may be a better proxy for permanent income, but this is true only if households can smooth their consumption streams to a substantial degree, something that not all households may be able to achieve. Based on longitudinal data in the United States,

Table 15.6 **Government Transfers to Households, Vietnam, 1993 and 1998**

Quintile	Share of 1993 transfers	Share of 1998 transfers	Share of total transfer increase, 1993–98
1	13.3	13.1	12.8
2	15.2	15.5	15.7
3	16.9	17.5	17.9
4	21.2	22.4	23.4
5	33.3	31.6	30.2
Total	100.0	100.0	100.0

Source: van de Walle 2002, 77.

Note: Covers social transfer income. Based on Vietnam Living Standards Survey 1993 and 1998.

Metcalf (1997) argues that using the expenditure (per capita) distribution may represent an overadjustment, and so understate regressivity somewhat.

One response is to report both sets of incidence curves, as we did in table 15.3, but this does not resolve the issue, which merits further attention.

How to Incorporate Behavior?

For the most part, the techniques set out in this chapter amount to an accounting exercise, and perhaps they would be better thought of as allowing one to measure "beneficiary incidence" (Demery 2000) than true benefit incidence.

The problem arises because government subsidies and taxes can lead to changes in behavior. For example, consider the case of a policy designed to maintain the consumption levels of individuals who are unemployed. The goal is laudable; instead of an income of $0, the unemployed person now receives, say, $100 from the state. But now suppose that the payments are so generous—as they were in Ireland in the early 1990s, for instance—that the individual would be worse off going back to work. So instead of working for $80, he or she continues to get $100 from the state. While the gross benefit received is $100, the net gain (over the alternative of working and assuming no disutility from working) is just $20.

Van de Walle (2000) demonstrated the importance of behavior in the context of Vietnam. Using data from a panel of 4,308 households surveyed in the course of the Vietnam Living Standards Surveys of 1993 and 1998, she estimated the effect on consumption (C) of government transfers (T), controlling for other effects (X) and allowing for a random error (ε). Using differences, she estimated

$$\Delta C_{it} = \alpha + \beta.\Delta T_{it} + \gamma.\Delta X_{it} \Delta \varepsilon_{it}$$

and found $\hat{\beta}(t = 4.3)$. This indicates that an additional $1 of transfers to households translated into an additional $0.45 in consumption, which is in line with findings from other studies. Presumably, households are responding to the transfers not only

311

by raising consumption, but also by working (and earning) less, or by saving more, or by receiving less in transfers from family members or elsewhere. There is nothing wrong with these responses, but if the goal is to raise household consumption levels, then they make the government's job harder, or at least more expensive.

How to Value Benefits

The simplest way to "value" the benefits to households of a government program is to determine who participates in the program, without necessarily putting a monetary value on the benefits. So if, for instance, 30 percent of primary school children come from households in the poorest quintile, then we might argue that 30 percent of the benefits of primary school spending go to that quintile.

The problem with the participation measure of benefits is that, in the absence of a monetary measure, it does not allow benefits from different programs to be aggregated. It also assumes that subsidies are the same for all participants, which implies, for instance, that a visit to an urban clinic costs the same to the government as a visit to a rural clinic. As a general proposition, this is implausible.

The most common way to value the benefits of a government program is to use the cost of provision ("unit costs"). Thus, if a rural primary school costs $100 per pupil per year to run, this cost is used to measure the benefit for each household that sends a child to such a school. But this is defensible only under a number of stringent conditions, of which the most important are as follows:

- The government must be efficient and honest. Otherwise some of the allocated spending, at least as measured at the central budgetary level, may be siphoned off before it gets to teachers and schools. The difficulty here is that the measured unit costs of provision are inflated.

- The recipient values the benefits, on average, at the cost of provision. For instance, suppose a patient goes to a government-supported clinic to see a doctor. The patient must be willing to pay $10 for the (free) visit, but the cost of provision is $16. In this example, the use of unit costs will overstate the magnitude, and hence incidence, of the program's benefits.

An alternative is to ask people to put a value on services they receive from the government. Contingent valuation surveys may be designed for this purpose, and although they may not always elicit completely reliable answers, in some cases they are the only way to value benefits. Such surveys are widely used in evaluating the benefits from public goods, such as policing; or clean air, for which there is no direct market price; or for qualitative improvements, such as shorter waiting times at clinics.

In some cases, it may be possible to estimate a demand curve for a publicly provided good—for instance, the demand for piped water in central Jakarta has been estimated based on information on the willingness of households to pay for water that is trucked into the city. Such techniques, which are widely used by environmental economists, then allow one to measure the willingness to pay for a good or service as the area under the demand curve.

It is sometimes possible to measure the impact of publicly provided goods and services by examining land prices. For instance, the value of property in neighborhoods with clean air will presumably be higher than the value of similar houses in a neighborhood where the air is polluted; by examining the price differential, one may infer the value that people put on clean air (the "hedonic price"), and hence measure the benefit of efforts to clean up the air.

Pieces or Whole?

Some practitioners of benefit and tax incidence argue that it is best to focus on one item at a time; or, in the words of Demery (2000, 52), to ask which expenditure items are most "efficient at transferring income to the poor?" This indeed can be very helpful; it shows, for instance, that in many countries a reduction in spending on higher education and a concomitant increase in spending on primary education would improve the progressivity of overall government spending.

Others prefer to think of the whole system of taxes and transfers as a package. For instance, Jenkins (1993) argues that the tax system should be designed to raise revenue efficiently, relegating concerns for distribution to the expenditure side.

At a minimum, it is important to look at the incidence of more than one tax or spending item. For instance, a higher VAT might be regressive (the partial incidence); but if the incremental proceeds were channeled into education spending, the net result might be progressive (the total incidence). Some of the most useful analyses of taxation impose the constraint that total tax revenue should not rise ("revenue neutrality") and then explore the distributional and efficiency implications of different mixes of taxes that might achieve this (for example, Haughton 2004, 2008).

Proximate vs. Deep Causes

Suppose that we find that only 30 percent of education spending in a country benefits girls—a common finding in benefit incidence. Can we draw lessons for public policy?

The problem here is that it is difficult to tease out the policy implications unless one has a theory that explains the finding. Does low enrollment of girls result because many parents do not want their daughters to get an education? Or because it is unsafe for girls to walk to school? Or because teachers ignore girls in the classroom? Or because girls marry young? In short, the benefit incidence measure only provides the starting point for the required analysis.

Realism is also in order. A tax system with a lower VAT and higher personal income tax might be more equitable than the current arrangements, but why is the current system, rather than a more equitable one, in place? There is an art to policy advising, and it is important to be mindful of what change is feasible, given the political economy considerations.

Conclusion

Demery (2003, 41), who has written lucidly and extensively on benefit incidence, cautions that "public expenditures can be effective in reducing poverty only when the policy setting is right." For example, it makes little sense to spend on agricultural extension if an overvalued exchange rate makes farming unprofitable. More generally, benefit incidence analysis only makes sense if spending decisions are "based on outcomes and impacts" rather than on continuing line items from one year to the next. And of course the analysis needs to rest on "a sound understanding [by the government] of the needs and preferences of the population at large," and not on the whims of a dictator or kleptocrat.

A strong case can be made that incidence analysis is more helpful on the tax than the spending side. Governments change taxes frequently, sometimes in minor increments, occasionally as major reforms. These changes have important incidence effects, yet decision makers in most less-developed countries are rarely provided with information on how tax changes affect poverty and income distribution. Once household survey data, with information on both income and expenditure, are available, this situation can be remedied easily.

Review Questions

6. A VAT is levied at 12 percent on all items except food. There is also a tax of $0.10/liter on gasoline. A household spends $15,200 per year on goods and services, including $7,800 on food. The household spends $1,000 to buy 1,100 liters of gasoline. The tax paid by this household is (to the nearest dollar):

  o A $1,824.
  o B $1,934.
  o C $997.
  o D $985.

7. To measure benefit incidence, which of the following steps is *not* required?

  o A. Get measures of unit subsidies.
  o B. Identify coverage of publicly provided goods and services and impute them to users.
  o C. Impute the taxes paid in order to finance the benefits.
  o D. Aggregate the incidence to generate measures of overall averages

> **8.** Early capture of the benefits of government spending implies that incremental spending by government is likely to be more progressive than average spending.
>
> - o True
> - o False

> **9.** Which of the following is *not* a significant problem in benefit incidence analysis:
>
> - o A. Survey data on educational attendance are unreliable.
> - o B. The choice of income vs. expenditure per capita in measuring the distribution of the benefits.
> - o C. Divergences between average and marginal benefits.
> - o D. Private valuations of government-provided services may differ from the cost of provision.

> **10.** Discussion question: Demery writes, "public expenditures can be effective in reducing poverty only when the policy setting is right."
>
> - o A. What does this mean?
> - o B. Give two more examples (preferably from your own experience).

Annex A. Case Study: Health Spending in Ghana

This case study reports the essential results of a study of the incidence of government spending on health in Ghana, and is largely drawn from Demery (2000) and Castro-Leal et al. (2000).

The first step in any benefit incidence study is to estimate the unit costs. Table 15.A1 shows some results based on a survey of hospitals and clinics in Ghana in 1992. Two points are worth noting: the unit subsidy for treating an inpatient is about 12 times that of an outpatient; and unit subsidies in the Accra area are three times as high as in regions outside the capital. Such disparities are not unusual, but clearly are needed for a credible benefit incidence analysis.

Table 15A.2 breaks down the users of health services by expenditure per capita quintile. This "imputation" exercise is based on data from the Ghana Living Standards Survey, in which households reported on their use of medical facilities. Better-off households are more likely to use public *and* private providers.

By combining the unit cost data with usage data, one arrives at the incidence of benefits, as summarized in table 15A.3. Health spending in Ghana may be characterized as "progressive, but not well targeted." It is progressive in the sense that the subsidies represent a higher proportion of the spending of poorer than of richer households; it is not well targeted in the sense that the rich receive substantially more in absolute subsidies than the poor (as shown in the final column of table 15A.3).

Table 15A.1 Government Unit Health Care Subsidies, Ghana, 1992 (million cedis)

	Hospitals		Primary facilities
	Inpatient	Outpatient	
E. Volta, Ashanti, W, regions	14.4	1.3	1.1
Greater Accra	49.6	1.0	6.5

Source: Demery 2000.

Table 15A.2 Health Service Visits, Percentage of Persons Reported Ill or Injured, Ghana, 1992

	Population quintiles (1 = poorest, 5 = richest)					All	Urban	Rural
	1	2	3	4	5			
Public providers	22.8	24.5	24.5	23.6	27.9	25.0	30.5	22.3
Hospital—in	0.7	0.9	0.6	1.0	1.1	0.9	1.0	0.8
Hospital—out	12.0	12.2	12.6	12.8	15.9	13.4	18.7	10.8
Clinics/health centers	10.1	11.4	11.4	9.8	10.9	10.8	10.9	10.6
Private providers	18.7	20.9	21.9	27.2	28.7	24.2	26.9	22.9
Modern	14.3	15.6	17.4	20.6	23.9	19.0	22.0	17.6
Traditional	4.4	5.5	4.5	6.6	4.8	5.2	4.9	5.3
Self/no treatment	58.5	54.5	53.6	49.1	43.3	50.8	42.6	54.8

Source: Demery 2000.

Table 15A.3 Incidence of Health Subsidies, Ghana, 1992

Population quintile (1 = poorest)	Health subsidy		Subsidy as share of	
	Total (million cedis)	Per capita (cedis)	Household expenditure per capita	Total subsidy
1	6,841	2,296	3.5	12
2	9,133	3,065	3.1	15
3	11,004	3,692	2.8	19
4	12,599	4,228	2.3	21
5	19,415	6,515	1.8	33
All	58,992	3,959	2.4	100

Source: Demery 2000, 34.

Table 15A.4 develops an interesting measure of the affordability of publicly provided health care, defined as household spending on fees and medications as a percentage of nonfood expenditures. For a poor household (the bottom expenditure quintile), the spending associated with one outpatient hospital visit represents 5.4 percent of annual spending. For someone in the top quintile, the proportion is 1 percent. The high private cost of accessing publicly supported health facilities is undoubtedly a significant deterrent to would-be users from poor households.

Table 15A.4 Affordability Ratios for Publicly Provided Health Care, Ghana, 1992

Population quintile (1 = poorest)	Household spending/visit (cedis)			Percent of nonfood expenditure		
	Hospitals		Clinics	Hospitals		Clinics
	Outpatient	Inpatient		Outpatient	Inpatient	
1	1,352	9,753	989	5.4	38.8	3.9
2	1,452	7,746	796	3.5	18.7	1.9
3	1,510	6,776	843	2.7	12.2	1.5
4	1,764	14,235	1,252	2.3	18.3	1.6
5	1,744	20,834	941	1.0	12.4	0.6
Ghana	1,606	13,750	957	2.2	18.6	1.3
Urban	1,916	11,598	1,167	2.2	18.6	1.0
Rural	1,355	14,919	856	2.5	27.7	1.6

Source: Demery 2000, 41. Based on Ghana Living Standards Survey 1992.

Note: Spending includes fees and medication costs only.

Notes

1. There is another definition of the Reynolds-Smolensky measure defined as $RS1 = G_Y - C_{Y-T}$, where the last term is the concentration coefficient (not Gini coefficient) of after-tax income. The distinction between RS1 and RS2 is that the former does not reorder the net-of-tax data while the latter does. Strictly speaking, it is RS1 that equals $(t.K/(1-t))$. The difference (RS1–RS2) is sometimes used as a measure of the horizontal inequity of a tax.

2. Of the $14,900 in spending, $8,100 goes to food, which is nontaxable, and $600 to buy gasoline. This leaves $6,200 of VAT-taxable spending. The tax on this is $0.12 \times (6,200/(1+0.12))$ = $664.29; by convention, the VAT rate is applied to the pre-VAT price. Gasoline is taxed in two ways. The excise tax of $0.25/liter yields $250 in revenue. But the remaining part of spending on gasoline (that is, $350) is subject to VAT, yielding $37.50. The sum of these taxes gives $664.29 + $250.00 + $37.50 = $951.79.

References

Agha, A., and J. Haughton. 1996. "Designing VAT Systems: How Many Rates and At What Levels?" *Review of Economics and Statistics* 78 (2): 303–08.

Castro-Leal, F., J. Dayton, L. Demery, and K. Mehra. 2000. "Public Spending on Health Care in Africa: Do the Poor Benefit?" *Bulletin of the World Health Organization* 78 (1): 66–74.

Demery, Lionel. 2000. *Benefit Incidence: A Practitioner's Guide.* Washington, DC: World Bank. [A very clear primer, with good examples.]

———. 2003. "Analyzing the Incidence of Public Spending." In *The Impact of Economic Policies on Poverty and Income Distribution*, ed. François Bourguignon and Luiz Pereira da Silva. New York: World Bank and Oxford University Press.

George, Henry. 1912. *Progress and Poverty: An Inquiry into the Cause of Industrial Depressions and of Increase of Want with Increase of Wealth: The Remedy.* Garden City, NY: Doubleday, Page & Co. (Originally published in 1879.)

Haughton, Jonathan. 2004. "An Assessment of the Tax System of Lebanon." Suffolk University, Boston, MA.

———. 2005. "An Assessment of Tax and Expenditure Incidence in Peru." Draft, Suffolk University, Boston, MA.

———. 2008. "Taxation in Vietnam: Who Pays What?" Unpublished. For World Bank, Hanoi.

Jenkins, Glenn. 1993. "Perspectives for Tax Policy Reform in Latin America in the 1990's." International Tax Program, Harvard University, Cambridge, MA.

Lanjouw, Peter, and Martin Ravallion. 1999. "Benefit Incidence, Public Spending Reforms, and the Timing of Program Capture." *World Bank Economic Review* 13 (2): 257–73.

Metcalf, Gilbert. 1997. "The National Sales Tax: Who Bears the Burden?" Cato Policy Analysis No. 289, Cato Institute, Washington, DC.

Sahn, David, and Stephen Younger. 1999. "Fiscal Incidence in Africa: Microeconomic Evidence." Cornell University. http://www.he.cornell.edu/cfnpp/images/wp91.pdf.

van de Walle, Dominique. 2002. "The Static and Dynamic Incidence of Vietnam's Public Safety Net." Policy Research Working Paper No. 2791, World Bank, Washington, DC.

van de Walle, Dominique, and Kimberly Nead. 1995. *Public Spending and the Poor: Theory and Evidence.* Baltimore, MD: Johns Hopkins University Press.

Younger, Stephen. 2003. "Benefits on the Margin: Observations on Marginal Benefit Incidence." *World Bank Economic Review* 17 (1): 89–106.

Chapter 16

Using Survey Data: Some Cautionary Tales

Summary

This chapter illustrates some of the major problems of data quality that every analyst has to confront. These problems are presented in the form of the following 11 "cautions":

1. Do the sampling right.

2. Use a consistent recall method.

3. Use a consistent recall period.

4. Remember that price indexes matter (a lot).

5. Use consistent questions.

6. Adjust for nonresponse bias (if possible).

7. Define expenditure consistently.

8. Value own-farm income properly.

9. Distinguish between values that are zero and those that are missing.

10. Use expenditure per capita, not expenditure per household.

11. Use weights when they are needed.

Be alert to extravagant claims of large jumps in poverty or inequality, and retain a healthy skepticism rather than cynicism. Above all, know your data.

Learning Objectives

After completing the chapter on *Using Survey Data: Some Cautionary Tales,* you should be able to

1. Illustrate what can happen if one uses partial or incomplete samples of data, and if there is nonresponse bias.

2. Explain why it is important to have a consistent method and period of data recall, and why the questions used must be consistent from survey to survey.

3. Show how price indexes are used to inflate poverty lines over time, and how such indexes can be constructed using unit value data.

4. Summarize the strengths and weaknesses four main price indexes—Laspeyres, Paasche, Fisher's Ideal, and Törnqvst—and explain how each is computed.

5. Illustrate the problems that can arise if own-farm income is incorrectly valued.

6. Explain why one cannot, as a general rule, substitute zeros for missing values.

7. Justify the use of expenditure per capita, rather than expenditure per household, in the measurement of poverty and inequality.

8. Explain why sampling weights must be used in almost all cases.

9. React with healthy skepticism to claims of large changes in poverty rates, and analyze the possible causes of such changes.

Introduction: Interpreting Survey Data

This is a chapter of cautionary tales. It provides a series of examples that illustrate how slippery the interpretation of survey data can be, and it draws heavily on examples that Shaohua Chen of the World Bank has compiled based on a decade and a half of working closely with datasets from more than a hundred countries.

The main theme of the chapter is that users of data must be alert to extravagant claims, such as large jumps in income or huge drops in inequality, because these claims rarely hold up to scrutiny. The antidote is to ask questions; before basing conclusions on survey data, it is essential to know enough about how the sample was chosen, how the questions were posed, and how the results were compiled. The examples in this chapter help us to ask the right questions.

Conversely, although we need to be skeptical, there is no reason to become completely cynical about survey data. Some data are unusable some of the time, but this does not imply that survey data are never informative. The examples in this chapter show how, with care, one can often draw useful conclusions from data that at first sight appear flawed, and how, with care, the quality of survey data can be improved.

Caution 1. Do the Sampling Right

The information in table 16.1 comes from household surveys undertaken in Malawi in 1997 and 2004. The numbers show remarkable progress—a 21 percent increase in mean income, an enormous reduction in inequality, and a sharp drop in the head-count poverty rate. And this occurred during a period when the Malawi's real gross domestic product (GDP) per capita actually fell by 1.3 percent per year.

Are these numbers too good to be true? The answer is yes! For some reason—perhaps due to missing information—more than 3,000 households were dropped from the 1997/98 sample when computing the statistics for that year; the reported sample is 6,586 households in 1997/98 and 11,280 in 2004–05. If the households were dropped randomly, then the results in table 16.1 may still be usable, but there is a suspicion that relatively high-income households were more likely to have been excluded. This would imply that the 1997/98 numbers understate income and over-state poverty, and that the improvement in incomes and poverty incidence shown in table 16.1 are overstated.

Quite apart from the sampling problem, it turns out that the questions used in the 2004–05 survey were more extensive than those used in the 1997/98 survey, so that the measures of expenditure cannot be directly compared between the two. An effort has been made to impute expenditure per capita for items that were not included in the 1997/98 questionnaire. To see how this works, suppose that only the latter question-naire asked households how much they spent on shoes; then, using the data from the 2004–05 survey, one could regress the value of spending on shoes against other household characteristics, such as total spending on food, the number of adult mem-bers, and so on. This estimated equation can then be applied to the data from the 1997/98 survey to generate the predicted ("imputed") value of spending on shoes. The process generates a poverty rate of 53.9 percent for 1997/98, which is more directly comparable to the 52.4 percent rate actually observed in 2004–05

Table 16.1 Income, Poverty, and Inequality in Malawi, 1997/98 and 2004

Survey year	Mean income per person per year, Malawian kwacha (prices of 1997/98)	Gini coefficient	Headcount poverty index (%)
1997/98	399.2	0.503	65.9
2004/2005	483.2	0.390	52.4

Sources: PovcalNet (at http://iresearch.worldbank.org/PovcalNet/doc/MWI.htm); Government of Malawi (2006).

(Government of Malawi 2006). Based on these adjusted numbers, one can conclude that the poverty rate barely fell between 1997/98 and 2004–05.

Caution 2. Use a Consistent Recall Method

A poverty monitoring survey undertaken in the southwest of China in 1995–96 yielded the following information:

- 1995 mean income per capita: 855 yuan

- 1996 mean income per capita: 993 yuan.

This represents a 16 percent increase in per capita income in one year. Even by Chinese standards, this is a rapid increase—too rapid to be plausible. The cumulative distribution curves for the two surveys are shown in figure 16.1.

Part of the explanation is due to the fact that the two surveys used different methods to collect information on income and expenditures. The 1995 survey used a one-time recall method, whereas the 1996 survey required households to keep daily diaries. It is well know that when the questions are more detailed, or when information is recorded in a more timely fashion, the amounts (spent or earned)

Figure 16.1 Cumulative Distribution Functions, Southwest China Poverty Monitoring Survey

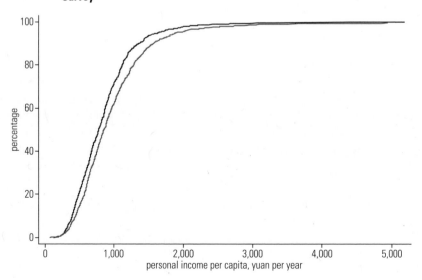

Source: Shaohua Chen, personal communication.

Note: Date for 1995 (upper line) and 1996 (lower line).

will be greater. Of course, this leaves us with a serious problem: there is no easy way to determine how much of the observed 16 percent rise in income was due to a real increase in income and how much to the change in survey procedures.

Caution 3. Use a Consistent Recall Period

Officially, the headcount poverty rate in India fell from 39 percent in 1987–88 to 36 percent in 1993–94 and then dropped dramatically to 26 percent in 1999–2000. The latter results were quickly criticized: was it really possible that poverty fell so rapidly after a period of only modest decline? The surprise was all the greater because an unofficial estimate of poverty, based on a "thin" (that is, smaller scale) survey undertaken in 1998, had shown a poverty rate of 39 percent.

It turns out that there was a technical problem with the results. Indian poverty rates are based on data from the National Sample Surveys (NSS), including the large and important 50th round of 1993–94 and 55th round of 1999–2000. Unfortunately, the expenditure modules of these two surveys are not strictly comparable, for three main reasons:

- The 1999–2000 survey distinguished 173 separate consumption items, which was somewhat fewer than the earlier survey. When there are fewer items, consumption tends to be understated.

- The 1999–2000 survey used a shorter recall period—7 rather than 30 days—for high-frequency consumption items (such as rice and lentils).[1] This would tend to increase measured consumption.

- The 1999–2000 survey used a longer recall period—a year instead of 30 days—for a number of low-frequency items, such as clothing.

The net effect of these changes on reported expenditure levels (relative to a situation in which the same questionnaire were used) is not clear a priori, and thus it is an empirical matter. However, in the case of some medium-frequency items, both surveys used the same questions and the same recall period. Deaton (2001) has found that spending on these items is a good predictor of poverty and has used this to impute the levels of spending on those items where the questionnaire was changed.

Deaton (2001) estimates that if there had been no change in the survey instrument, the official measure of poverty in 1999–2000 would have been 28 percent instead of the reported 26 percent. This represents a considerable degree of poverty reduction, but it is not as striking as the official numbers. And it is clear in retrospect that the results of the 1998 "thin" round of the National Sample Survey were incorrect (mainly because it collected data over a period of just half a year), as figure 16.2 (from Deaton 2002) shows.

Figure 16.2 Headcount Poverty Rates in India, 1970–2000

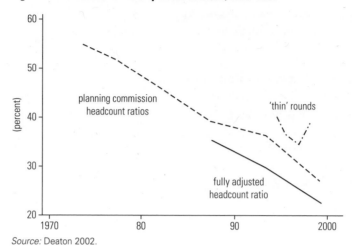

Source: Deaton 2002.

Note: The "thin" rounds refer to unofficial calculations based on small-scale household surveys, the central line shows the official results, and the lower line shows the calculations made by Deaton.

Caution 4. Remember That Price Indexes Matter (a lot)

There is another important lesson from the Indian experience with measuring poverty: it is essential to use the right price indexes.

Deaton (2001) shows that the official price indexes inflated the Indian poverty line too much between 1993–94 and 1999–2000, and this had the effect of understating the reduction in poverty. Moreover, the official price indexes overstate the price differential between rural and urban areas, greatly overstating urban poverty. Thus, poverty in India is lower than previously had been believed and is falling relatively quickly. This shows up in the "fully adjusted headcount ratio" in figure 16.2.

It is worth looking at Deaton's price calculations in more detail, because they both illustrate good practice and serve as templates for researchers who are trying to measure poverty. To recap, the problem to be tackled is adjusting a poverty line so that it reflects the same cost of living over time. In the Indian case, Deaton took as a given the national poverty line of Rp 115.70 per 30 days per person in 1987–88, but needed to find the equivalent poverty lines for 1993–94 and 1999–2000.

This is the challenge of constructing a price index. The Indian National Sample Surveys (NSS) collect information on the value of expenditures, and the associated quantities of purchases, for many items for each household. This allows one to compute unit values (that is, value divided by quantity), which are akin to prices. Not all of the items are well defined, however. For instance, in the 1999–2000 round of the Indian NSS, "other milk products" included both yogurt (inexpensive) and many sweets (expensive) and thus was not homogeneous enough to yield a unit value. In practice, Deaton (2001) was able to use items representing three-fifths of household expenditure in the construction of price indexes.

Given unit values (or prices), the next problem is aggregating them into a single price index. There are four common ways to do this (United Nations 2006), and the details are set out in box 16.1. Using data from the Indian NSS of 1993–94 and 1999–2000, Deaton constructed the price indexes that are set out in table 16.2. Panel A shows his estimates of price inflation between 1993–94 and 1999–2000 for rural and urban areas; he estimates that prices rose by about 4 percent less than shown by the official numbers. This implies a lower poverty line than the one used by the official measure, and hence a somewhat lower poverty rate.

Table 16.2, panel B, shows Deaton's estimates of the cost of living in urban, relative to rural, areas. He finds that the urban cost of living is about 15 percent higher, a differential that is less than half of the 37 to 39 percent reported by the official statistics.

The implications of these price adjustments for the measured (headcount) poverty rate in India, both for the 1987–88 to 1993–94 period and for the 1993–94 to 1999–2000 period, are shown in table 16.3. The rural poverty rate in 1987–88 is, essentially by construction, the same according to the official estimate and using Deaton's estimate, but Deaton's measure of urban poverty is far below the rate

Table 16.2 Price Indexes for Inflating Poverty Lines in India

| | Budget shares in index | | | | | | |
	1993–94	1999–2000	Laspeyres	Paasche	Fisher Ideal	Törnqvst	Official
Panel A. Prices in 1999–2000 relative to those in 1993–94							
Rural	65.5	59.6	156.4	152.5	154.5	154.5	159.1
Urban	57.8	50.3	162.0	155.7	158.8	157.7	161.4
Panel B. Prices in urban areas relative to those in rural areas							
1993–94	65.8	73.7	117.5	113.7	115.6	115.6	136.7
1999–2000	53.2	61.1	115.9	114.0	115.0	115.1	138.6

Source: Deaton 2001.

Table 16.3 Headcount Poverty Rates for India, Official and Adjusted

		1987–88	1993–94	1999–2000
Official	Rural	39.4	37.1	27.0
	Urban	39.1	33.2	23.5
Price-adjusted	Rural	39.0	32.9	21.6
	Urban	22.8	18.1	9.5
Price- and questionnaire-adjusted	Rural			25.3
	Urban			12.5

Source: Deaton 2001.

16

Box 16.1   Constructing Price Indexes

There are four popular methods for constructing prices indexes; the details are set out in this box.

1. The **Laspeyres "base-weighted" price index** combines prices by giving each price a weight equivalent to the share of the good in the initial expenditure "basket."

   Formally, let v_{it} be the value of spending on good i in time t, where we typically count $t = 0$ in the base period. And let p_{it} be the price (or, in this context, the unit value) of good i in time t, and q_{it} be the associated quantity. Then the Laspeyres price index is given by

   $$L_p = \sum_i \left(\frac{v_{i0}}{\sum_i v_{i0}} \right)\left(\frac{p_{it}}{p_{i0}} \right) = \frac{\sum_i p_{it} q_{i0}}{\sum_i p_{i0} q_{i0}}.$$

   This is probably the most widely used of all price indexes, because it is relatively straightforward to compute. Price data are needed for each period, and spending (or quantity) data are needed just for the base period, which makes it economical when computing regular measures of inflation, such as monthly data on a consumer price index. It generally overstates the "true" inflation in the cost of living, however, because it does not adjust for the fact that consumers substitute away from goods that become relatively expensive, and thus it retains an excessive weight on items that, over time, decline in relative importance.

2. The **Paasche "end-weighted" price index** combines prices by giving each price a weight equivalent to the share of the good in the end-of-period basket. Formally, it is given by

   $$P_p = \sum_i \left(\frac{v_{it}}{\sum_i v_{it}} \right)\left(\frac{p_{it}}{p_{i0}} \right) = \frac{\sum_i p_{it} q_{it}}{\sum_i p_{i0} q_{it}}.$$

   The Paasche index overcorrects for substitution effects, and so it generally is held to understate "true" inflation. It generally is not used to construct monthly or quarterly measures of consumer prices because of the expense of regularly updating the detailed information on the value of spending (or quantities bought).

3. **Fisher's ideal index** is the geometric mean of the Laspeyres and Paasche indexes, and so is given by

   $$F_p = \left(L_p \times P_p \right)^{1/2}$$

Box 16.1 **continued**

It can be shown that if households have quadratic utility functions, then Fisher's ideal index generates a "true" cost-of-living index. A practical attraction of F_p is that it is between L_p and P_p, and so avoids the extremes of overstating or understating "true" inflation. To measure Fisher's Ideal Index, information on consumption patterns is needed both in the base year and in the end year, which is impractical (or at least expensive) if one is constructing monthly price indexes, but it is feasible when comparing household surveys at two points in time.

4. The **Törnqvst index** weights the price increases of each good i by the budget share of the good averaged between the beginning and end period. This gives

$$T_p = \prod \left\{ \left(\frac{p_{it}}{p_{i0}} \right)^{(1/2)(s_0 + s_t)} \right\} \text{ where } s_{it} \equiv \frac{v_{it}}{\sum_i v_{it}}.$$

If the underlying utility function is logarithmic, then it can be shown that the Törnqvst index measures the true cost of living. Because many economists believe that the utility function is at least approximately (or locally) logarithmic, this is a strength of the index and explains why it is increasingly widely used. In practice, the Törnqvst index usually gives a measure of inflation that is close to the one generated by Fisher's ideal index. Both of these indexes have equally heavy data requirements.

reported officially, and is far more plausible too. Between 1987–88 and 1993–94 the official numbers show a modest reduction in poverty, whereas Deaton finds a more substantial drop (because he uses a price index that inflates the poverty line by less than the official one).

The official figures show a sharp drop in poverty between 1993–94 and 1999–2000. Deaton, using his price deflator, also finds a substantial drop (see the price-adjusted numbers in table 16.3), but he revises these upward somewhat to take into account the effect of changes in the questionnaire used. Deaton's preferred numbers, marked in boldface in table 16.3, show a relatively rapid fall in poverty between 1987–88 and 1999–2000, without any clear change in trend.

Review Questions

1. Sampling bias is common, but can be corrected for relatively easily.
o True   o False

2. Which of the following is correct?

- o A. The Laspeyres price index typically overstates inflation while the Paasche price index typically understates it.
- o B. The Laspeyres price index typically overstates inflation while the Törnqvst price index typically understates it.
- o C. The Laspeyres price index typically understates inflation while the Paasche price index typically overstates it.
- o D. The Laspeyres price index typically understates inflation while the Törnqvst price index typically understates it.

3. If households are asked to recall their spending levels over a longer period of time, then they will typically estimate annualized spending to be

- o Higher
- o Lower

4. We have the following information about household purchases of bread and milk in 2007 and 2008:

	Bread		Milk	
	Price	Quantity	Price	Quantity
2007	1.00	4	0.50	3
2008	1.30	3	0.50	4

Based on this information, inflation between 2007 and 2008 was 20.0 percent according to the

- o A. Laspeyres index.
- o B. Paasche index.
- o C. Fisher ideal index.
- o D. Törnqvst index.

Caution 5. Use Consistent Questions

When measuring changes in income or spending over time, it is important that the data come from surveys that used comparable questionnaires. The point is obvious enough, but it is worth emphasizing.

The first example comes from Honduras, where a 2003 survey found a headcount poverty rate of 13.8 percent, based on income. Naturally, one wants to compare this with data from previous surveys. The relevant numbers are shown in table 16.4. Are we to conclude that, between 1999 and 2003, poverty fell sharply from 26.3 percent? Or did it rise substantially from 10.7 percent? Or can we not tell? The answer depends on whether the income module used in 2003 was the same as "income module 1" (see table 16.4) or "income module 2." It turns out that the 2003 survey used "income

Table 16.4 Headcount Poverty Rates in Honduras, 1997, 1999, and 2003

	Income module 1	Income module 2	Which income module?
1997	24.1	12.0	
1999	26.3	10.7	
2003			13.8

Source: Shaohua Chen, personal communication.

Table 16.5 Income, Headcount Poverty, and Inequality, Ethiopia, 1999–2000

	Sample size	Mean expenditure per person (birr per month)	Headcount poverty index	Gini coefficient
Welfare Monitoring Survey (June–August 1999)	25,917	46.0	81.3	0.490
Household Income and Expenditure Survey (January–February 2000)	16,982	92.5	21.9	0.300

Sources: PovcalNet, at http://surveynetwork.org/home/?lvl1=activities&lvl2=catalog&lvl3=surveys&ihsn=231-2000-001; and Shaohua Chen, personal communication.

module 2" and thus poverty appears to have risen. It would be easy to make the wrong comparison, however, and erroneously conclude that poverty had fallen sharply.

Our second example comes from two surveys that were undertaken in Ethiopia in 1999–2000 (see table 16.5). According to the Welfare Monitoring Survey, undertaken in June-August 1999, expenditure per capita was relatively unequally distributed (a Gini coefficient of 0.49) and the headcount poverty rate rather high (at 81 percent). But the Household Income and Expenditure Survey (HIES), undertaken in January-February 2000, comes to a different conclusion, finding a remarkably even distribution of per capita expenditure (a Gini coefficient of 0.30) and a headcount poverty rate of just 22 percent.

Why do these results differ so much? Quite simply, the consumption modules used by the two questionnaires differed substantially. It would be necessary to examine each of them in some detail to determine which is more sensible, and which set of results more plausible. The World Bank's PovcalNet reports the data from the HIES, perhaps on the grounds that the expenditure data are more complete and extensive.

Caution 6. Adjust for Nonresponse Bias (if possible)

In very poor countries, compliance rates for surveys are typically high. But as countries become more affluent, it becomes more difficult to persuade people to respond to lengthy questionnaires or to keep diaries. For example, fewer than one in four people responds to a telephone survey in the United States, which naturally brings into question the representativeness of the results of such surveys.

As long as noncompliance is random, then the survey results are still usable in measuring poverty, income, or expenditure. But it is generally believed that compliance is nonrandom. Richer people are less likely to respond to a questionnaire for a number of reasons:

- Their time is more valuable, so they don't want to spend three hours answering questions.

- They may have more to hide, from the tax collector, for instance, or from prying neighbors.

- They are more likely to have multiple earners in their household, so the information on income is likely to be less reliable, because most surveys only question a single household member about income.

* They are more likely to be away from home.

Some poor people might also not respond to surveys (or be asked to participate), however, if they live in especially remote areas or if they are homeless (and so hard to find, or not on the roster of households), illiterate (especially a challenge when using a diary method to collect information), alienated from society, or illegal residents.

If compliance falls with income, then poverty is overestimated for all measures and poverty lines. It would be useful to be able to correct for noncompliance bias. Consider the basic example set out in table 16.6: a society has two groups of people, the poor (with a 90 percent response rate, constituting 81 percent of those surveyed) and the nonpoor (50 percent response rate, 19 percent of these surveyed). Given these figures, we may infer that 70 percent of the population is poor $(= (.81/.9)/(.81/.9 + .19/.5))$ and 30 percent nonpoor. Thus, we should weight each observation for the poor by 0.87 $(=.70/.81)$ and each observation for the nonpoor by 1.56 $(= .30/.19)$.

The main practical problem is estimating the response rate, because we do not now whether those who did not respond are rich or poor. An example of the implied correction to income that is needed to adjust for underreporting, for the United States, is shown in figure 16.3.

Table 16.6 Example of Correction for Nonresponse Bias

	"Poor"	"Nonpoor"
Estimated distribution (%)	81	19
But: Response rate (%)	90	50
So: True distribution of population	70	30
Memo: Correction factors	0.87	1.56

Source: Example generated by the authors.

Figure 16.3 Correction Factors for U.S. Income

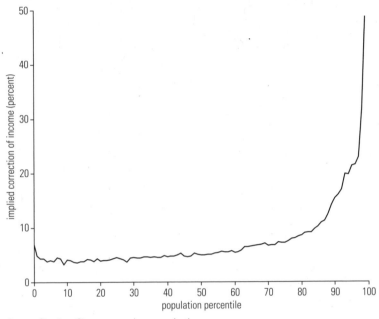

Source: Shaohua Chen, personal communication.

Caution 7. Define Expenditure Consistently

When making poverty or inequality comparisons, across countries or over time, it is essential that the way in which expenditure (or income) is defined remains unchanged. Yet this is frequently not the case.

Consider the information in table 16.7 for a number of countries in Eastern Europe and the former Soviet Union. The way in which the costs of durable goods and housing are treated varies sharply from one country to the next. It is simply not plausible that durable goods consumption represents 9.5 percent of expenditure in the Russian Federation but only 2.4 percent in neighboring Ukraine or 5.2 percent in Poland. And all of the figures on expenditure on rent appear to be too low—perhaps the imputed costs of housing have not been included. Certainly, it stretches credulity to believe that rent constitutes just 0.3 percent of expenditures in Romania; even the 3.5 percent figure for neighboring Moldova seems modest.

Faced with such faulty numbers, what is the analyst to do? Given enough time and resources, it might be possible to go back to the original data sets to recalculate expenditure for each country on a consistent basis, but rarely do researchers have such a luxury, and besides, this assumes that all of the questionnaires collected adequate information in the first place.

331

Table 16.7 Percentage of Reported Spending Devoted to Health, Durable Goods, and Rent, for Selected Eastern European and Former Soviet Union Countries, 2002–03

		Percent of consumption expenditure devoted to:		
	Survey year	Health	Durable goods	Rent
Armenia	2002	10.2	0.7	
Azerbaijan	2003	3.2	6.8	0.4
Belarus	2002	2.3	1.6	
Estonia	2003	3.6	6.4	1.1
Georgia	2003	5.3	1.2	0.3
Lithuania	2003	4.1	8.7	
Moldova	2003	5.5	5.1	3.5
Poland	2002	4.7	5.2	3.8
Romania	2003	3.0	1.6	0.3
Russian Federation	2002	2.1	9.5	0.7
Turkey	2002	2.4	7.8	3.3
Ukraine	2003	2.6	2.4	0.4

Source: Shaohua Chen, personal communication.

Table 16.8 Rates of Headcount Poverty and Inequality, with and without Spending on Health, Durable Goods, and Rent, for Selected Eastern European and Former Soviet Union Countries, 2002–03

		Including health, durables, rent		Excluding health, durables, rent	
	Survey year	Poverty rate (%)	Gini coefficient	Poverty rate (%)	Gini coefficient
Armenia	2002	31.1	0.338	33.8	0.292
Azerbaijan	2003	1.7	0.174	5.7	0.181
Belarus	2002	1.4	0.297	1.6	0.292
Estonia	2003	7.5	0.358	9.4	0.339
Georgia	2003	25.3	0.404	27.9	0.403
Lithuania	2003	7.8	0.360	8.7	0.332
Poland	2002	1.9	0.345	2.5	0.324
Romania	2003	12.9	0.311	13.8	0.299
Russian Federation	2002	12.1	0.399	13.6	0.364
Turkey	2002	20.1	0.434	22.7	0.400
Ukraine	2003	4.9	0.281	5.8	0.273

Source: Shaohua Chen, personal communication.
Note: Data use $2 per day standard in 1993 prices.

One approach is to exclude the doubtful expenditure headings entirely. The results of this exercise are shown in table 16.8, where expenditures on health, education, and rent are left out of the measures of consumption. Since no adjustment is made to the poverty line—the World Bank's old $2 per day standard—the reported poverty rates are now higher. In most cases, the Gini coefficient of inequality, which ranges from 0 for perfect equality to 1 for perfect inequality, falls, implying lower inequality.

In passing, one might note that there are other oddities in the numbers shown in table 16.8: it is strange that the poverty rate in Belarus should be so much lower than in nearby Estonia or Lithuania, which are much richer; and the reported inequality in Azerbaijan is implausibly low.

Is it better to ignore or use bad data? There is no simple answer, but if we are keen to make poverty comparisons, then it would be helpful to develop a set of research protocols that would help ensure consistency in measurement. These protocols would be especially useful in dealing with such problematic expenditure headings as durable goods and the cost of housing.

Caution 8. Value Own-Farm Income Properly

For poor people, a substantial fraction of income (and expenditure) comes from own-farm output. It is therefore important to measure the value of this output correctly if one is to get an accurate measure of poverty.

This is not a trivial point, as the experience with the China Rural Household Survey of 1990 makes clear. The traditional method of imputing income from own-farm consumption used official prices, which by 1990 were far lower than market prices. Using the old method, the headcount poverty rate was 38 percent (see table 16.9), but when own-farm consumption was valued at market prices the headcount rate was just 30 percent—that is, 60 million fewer poor people than had originally been thought!

Caution 9. Distinguish between Values That Are Zero and Those That Are Missing

It is important to distinguish between values that are zero and those that are missing, and it is not generally appropriate to substitute zeros for missing values. For instance, if a questionnaire does not record someone's age, one cannot assume that their age is zero.

Table 16.9 Levels of Income, Inequality, and Poverty in Rural China, 1990

	Mean income (yuan per capita p.a.)	Gini coefficient	Headcount poverty rate (%)
Old method	630	0.315	38
New method	686	0.299	30

Source: China Rural Household Survey 1990.

Note: The old method values own-farm production at official prices, while the new method values it at market prices.

The point might seem obvious, but it is sometimes overlooked. In a number of labor force surveys in Latin America and the Caribbean, zeros have been used when information on per capita income was missing. Figure 16.4 shows the cumulative distribution function of per capita income for Colombia for 2003, where 7 percent of the observations on income per capita were missing. When the missing values are included as zeros, one gets the upper curve, which understates the "true" distribution of income. However, the lower line—constructed by excluding the cases with missing values—is a reliable guide to the distribution of income in the population only if missing values are randomly distributed across those surveyed.

There are some occasions in which the use of zeros in the place of missing values may be justified, for instance, if a questionnaire asks the enumerator to fill in nonzero values (for example, for each item of consumption) and to skip an item if it is zero. In such cases, there would need to be a provision for a truly missing value, for instance, using a 99.

Sometimes it is possible to deal with missing values and outliers by going back to the original record to determine whether it is more reasonable to treat a value as zero or missing. This underscores the importance of keeping the original survey records and of putting in place a mechanism whereby the records may be consulted when questions arise about the accuracy of particular numbers.

Figure 16.4 Cumulative Distribution of Income per Capita, Colombia, 2003

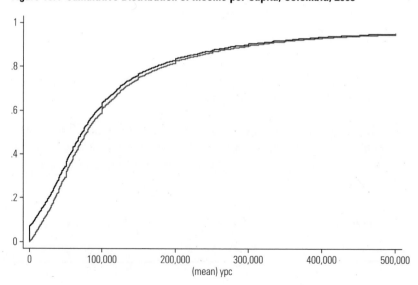

(mean) ypc

Source: Shaohua Chen, personal communication.

Note: The top line shows the distribution when missing values are set to zero; the bottom line excludes observations with missing values.

Caution 10. Use Expenditure per Capita, Not Expenditure per Household

Most surveys collect information on income and expenditure on the basis of the household, rather than on individuals. As discussed in chapter 2, if we are interested in the distribution of welfare, or the poverty rate, we need to rank households by income (or expenditure) *per capita* and not per household.

What happens if the wrong measure is used? Not surprisingly, we may end up drawing the wrong conclusions. This is illustrated in table 16.10, which first ranks individuals by per capita expenditure (correct), and then by per household expenditure (incorrect) based on the Benin Income/Expenditure/Household (IEH) survey of 2003. When ranked correctly, we see that more affluent households tend to be smaller than poor households; but if we mistakenly rank households by income per household, then we are left with the (incorrect) impression that richer households are larger.

Caution 11. Use Weights When They Are Needed

Few living standards surveys are based on simple random samples; most use a stratified cluster sampling design. The implication, as discussed in chapter 2, is that one must use weights when working with the data. The effects of ignoring weights can be striking: the simple average income of tax filers included in the U.S. Internal Revenue Service 1 percent Public Use Sample was $501,814 in 2001—an enormous amount, which reflects the fact that the data set oversamples high-income individuals. When weights are used to adjust for the sample design, one finds an average income, based on the 138,954 observations, of $26,840, which is entirely plausible.

Table 16.10 Household Size by Expenditure per Capita and Expenditure per Household Deciles, Benin, 2003

Households ranked by expenditure per capita		Households ranked by expenditure per household	
Decile	Mean household size	Decile	Mean household size
1 (poor)	8.54	1 (poor)	2.68
2	7.72	2	3.56
3	7.84	3	4.19
4	7.16	4	4.61
5	6.90	5	4.83
6	6.57	6	5.11
7	6.52	7	5.55
8	5.78	8	5.69
9	5.42	9	6.25
10 (rich)	4.33	10 (rich)	6.99

Source: Benin IEH survey of 2003.

Figure 16.5 **Cumulative Distribution of Expenditure per Capita, Benin, 2003**

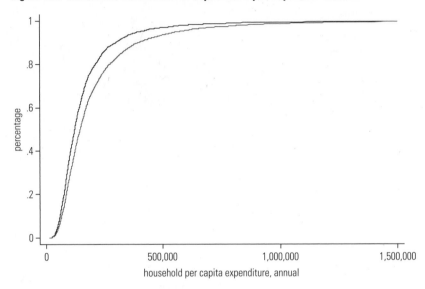

Source: Shaohua Chen, personal communication.

Note: Bottom line is incorrect because, unlike the top line, it does not apply sampling weights.

Another example comes from the Benin IEH survey of 2003. Figure 16.5 shows the cumulative density of expenditure per capita both using weights (the upper line, which is correct) and without weights (the lower line). In this particular example, low-income households were undersampled, so when weights were not used, the estimated poverty rate was too low. As shown in figure 16.5, an easy way to see this is to add a poverty line—which would be vertical—and ask which of the distribution curves would show the higher proportion of people in poverty.

Everyone who works with real survey data eventually has a set of stories to tell about the pitfalls that arise easily enough. While this chapter has highlighted some of the more important and obvious problems, there is no substitute for eternal vigilance when working with numbers. This chapter, indeed this entire book, is designed to help get started with data. The more one engages in data analysis using survey data, the more one finds that the topic is both important and fascinating. Enjoy it!

Review Questions

5. Richer people are less likely to respond to questionnaires for all of the following reasons *except*:

- ○ A. Their time is more valuable.
- ○ B. They have fewer members.
- ○ C. They are more likely to be away from home.
- ○ D. They have more to hide.

6. It does not matter what price is used to value own-consumption because it changes both consumption and the poverty line equally.

   ○ True
   ○ False

7. Which of the following statements, derived from the numbers in tables 16.7 and 16.8, is least implausible?

   ○ A. The Gini coefficient is 0.338 in Armenia and 0.174 in neighboring Azerbaijan.
   ○ B. The headcount poverty rate is 7.5 percent in Estonia and 12.1 percent in neighboring Russia.
   ○ C. The percentage of spending devoted to durable goods is 8.7 percent in Lithuania and 1.6 percent in neighboring Belarus.
   ○ D. Housing rental payments constituted 0.3 percent of consumption spending in 2003 in Romania.

8. Send us your own cautionary tale, if necessary with supporting graphs or data. (To Jonathan Haughton, at jhaughto@beaconhill.org.)

Note

1. The 55th round survey asked respondents to give expenditures both for the past 7 days and the past 30 days. But it is widely held that the presence of the question using a seven-day recall is likely to have pulled up reported expenditure levels.

References

Benin, Institut National de la Statistique et de l'Analyse Economique. 2003. "Income/Expenditure/Household Survey of 2003." Cotonou.

China: National Bureau of Statistics Rural Social and Economic Survey Team. Data from *China Rural Household Survey Yearbook 2000*. Beijing: China Statistics Press.

Deaton, Angus. 2001. "Computing Prices and Poverty Rates in India, 1999–2000." Research Program in Development Studies Working Paper, Princeton University, New Jersey.

———. 2002. "Is World Poverty Falling?" *Finance and Development* 39 (2).

Government of Malawi. 2006. *Malawi Growth and Development Strategy: From Poverty To Prosperity 2006–2011*.

PovcalNet. n.d. http://iresearch.worldbank.org/PovcalNet/jsp/CChoiceControl.jsp?WDI_Year=2007.

United Nations Statistics Division. 2006. "Price and Volume Measures." http://unstats.un.org/unsd/sna1993/toclev8.asp?L1=16&L2=3 (accessed December 14, 2006).

Data Introduction

In this appendix, we will be working extensively with Stata using a subset of information from the Household Survey 1998–99 that was conducted jointly by the Bangladesh Institute of Development Studies (BIDS) and the World Bank. The information was collected at individual, household, and community levels. A description of the data sets and file structure used for these exercises is given below. The data for the exercises are available at: http://mail.beaconhill.org/~j_haughton in ready-to-use Stata format.[1]

File Structure

We will use and generate a lot of files. There are mainly three types of Stata files. Some contain data sets (identified by the suffix .dta), others contain Stata programs (identified by the suffix .do), and yet others contain a record and output of the work we do in Stata (identified by the suffix .log). To keep these files organized, it is useful to create a well-structured set of directories. In what follows, we assume that you have created the following directory structure:

- c:\intropov
- c:\intropov\data
- c:\intropov\dofiles
- c:\intropov\logfiles

Four files should go into the directory c:\intropov\data:

- hh.dta includes 20 household level variables, such as household location, household business type, asset ownership, access to service, and so on.

339

- `ind.dta` includes 10 individual level variables, such as age, gender, education or schooling, marital status, main activity, working status, occupation, sector, relation to household head, and so on.

- `consume.dta` includes 30 categories of expenditure such as various food and nonfood items, rent or rental value of housing, and so on.

- `vprice.dta` includes village-level price information on the main food items.

The data files can be downloaded from: http://mail.beaconhill.org/~j_haughton.

Data Description

Table A1.1 Data Description

Variable	hh.dta
hhcode	household identification number
thana	thana code—a *thana* is an administrative center comprising a number of villages—ranging from 1 to 32, as there are 32 thanas in this sample
vill	village code—when combined with thana it uniquely identifies a village—ranging from 1 to 4, as a maximum of four villages are selected from a thana

region	region code
	    1. Dhaka (the capital)
	    2. Chittagong
	    3. Khulna
	    4. Rajshahi

weight	sampling weight for household
distance	distance to nearest paved road (km)
d_bank	distance to nearest commercial/agricultural bank (km)

toilet	type of latrine used in the household
	    1. sanitary
	    2. nonsanitary

hhelec	if household has electricity
	    1. yes
	    2. no

hassetg	household total assets (in *taka*)
famsize	household size

sexhead	gender of household head
	    1. male
	    2. female

agehead	age of household head (years)
educhead	years of schooling of household head
hhlandd	land (in *decimals*, that is, one-hundredth of an acre) owned by household

Variable	ind.dta
pid	household member identification number (unique for a household member, so becomes unique in the sample after being combined with household id)
indsave	individual savings (in *taka*)
snaghr	nonfarm self-employment working hours per month
sagrhr	farm self-employment working hours per month
wnaghr	nonfarm wage job working hours per month
waghr	farm wage job working hours per month
iemphr	total working hours per month
rel_hh	code for relation to household head

    1. Head himself/herself   8. Son-in-law/daughter-in-law
    2. Wife/husband   9. Spouse of brother or sister
    3. Son/daughter   10. Brother or sister of spouse
    4. Grandson/granddaughter   11. Father-in-law/mother-in-law
    5. Father/mother   12. Other relatives of head or spouse
    6. Sister/brother   13. Servant/maid servant
    7. Niece/nephew   14. Other _____ (specify)

Variable	ind.dta
educ	years of schooling completed
sex	gender
age	age (in years)

Variable	consume.dta
	10 items have been selected from the survey: rice, wheat, pulses, milk, oil, meat, fish, vegetables, fruits, sugar. Let X denote any items, so:
qX	quantity (kg) of item X consumed last week
eX	value of item X consumed last week (in *taka*)
expfd	household total food consumption per month (in *taka*)
expnfd	household total expenditure on regular nonfood items per month (in *taka*)

Variable	vprice.dta
	11 price items (vegetables in consume.dta now has two entries: potatoes and other vegetables) were selected from the survey. Again, denote an item by X:
pX	village price per kg

Note

1. The exercises use a subset of the complete data collected by 1991/92 and 1998/99 surveys conducted by the Bangladesh Institute of Development Studies and the World Bank. The full data sets, along with all the necessary documentation, are available at: http://econ. worldbank.org/WBSITE/EXTERNAL/EXTDEC/EXTRESEARCH/0,,conten tMDK:21470820~pagePK:64214825~piPK:64214943~theSitePK:469382,00.html. Another option for accessing the dataset is to go to: http://econ.worldbank.org. Under Research, select **Sustainable Rural and Urban Development** from the Research Programs menu. Select the **Datasets** link from the left. Select **Household Survey to Conduct Micro-Credit Impact Studies: Bangladesh.**

Stata Preliminary

Stata is a statistical software package that offers a large number of statistical and econometric estimation procedures. With Stata, we can easily manage data and apply standard statistical and econometric methods such as regression analysis and limited dependent variable analysis to cross-sectional or longitudinal data. Stata is widely used by analysts working with household survey data.

Getting Started

The next few subsections introduce the basics of starting up Stata, and reading and saving files.

Starting Stata

Start a Stata session by double-clicking on the Stata icon in your desktop. The Stata computing environment includes four main windows. The size and shape of these windows may be moved about on the screen. Their general look and description are shown in figure A2.1:

It is useful to have the **Stata Results** window be the largest so you can see a lot of information about your commands and output on the screen. In addition to these windows, the Stata environment has a menu and a toolbar at the top (to perform Stata operations) and a directory status bar at the bottom (that shows the current directory). You can use the menu and toolbar to issue different Stata commands (like opening and saving data files), although as you become proficient at Stata you

Figure A2.1 Stata Main Window

Source: Stata Corporation, Texas, US.

will find that most of the time it is more convenient to use the **Stata Command** window to perform those tasks. If you are creating a log file (see section on **Working with .log and .do Files** below for more details), the contents can also be displayed on the screen; this feature is sometimes useful if one needs to back up to see earlier results from the current session.

Opening a Data Set

You open a Stata data set by entering the following command in the **Stata Command** window:

   use hh

(or **use c:\intropov\data\hh,** depending on where Stata has opened up; details are given later in this section). You can also click on **File** and **Open** and then browse to find the file you need. Stata responds by displaying the following in the **Stata Results** window:

```
. use hh

.
```

The first line repeats the command you enter; when the second line is blank (no error message), the command has been executed successfully. In the remainder of this appendix, we will show only the **Stata Results** window to demonstrate Stata commands. The following points should be noted:

- Stata assumes the file to be in Stata format with an extension .dta. So, typing hh is the same as typing hh.dta.

- Only one data set can be opened at a time in Stata. So if we open another data set (for example, ind.dta), we will be replacing hh.dta with ind.dta. Fortunately, Stata does not allow you do to this without giving you a warning. You will not receive a warning, however, if you type something like **use ind.dta, clear.**

- The command above assumes that the file hh.dta is in the current directory (shown by the directory status bar at the bottom). If that is not the case, then you can do one of the following two things (assuming the current directory is c:\stata\data and the file hh.dta is in c:\intropov):

Type the full path of the data file:

```
. use c:\intropov\data\hh
```

Or make c:\intropov the current directory and then open the file as before:

```
. cd c:\intropov\data
. use hh

.
```

If the memory allocated to Stata (which is 10,000K or 10M by default) is too little for the data file to be opened, as is typically the case when working with large household survey data sets, you will receive an error message like the following:

```
. use hh
no room to add more observations
r(901);

.
```

345

The third line displays the code associated with the error message. All error messages in Stata have associated codes like this; further explanations are available in the Stata Reference Manuals. In this case, we have to allocate more memory to Stata. The following commands allocate 30M to Stata and then try again to open the file:

```
. set memory 30m
[This generates a table with information]
. use hh

.
```

Because the file opens successfully, allocated memory is sufficient. If you continue to receive error messages, you can use a larger amount of memory, although this may slow down your computer somewhat. Note that the set memory command works only if no data set is open. If a data set is open, you will get following error message:

```
. use hh
. set memory 10m
no; data in memory would be lost
r(4);
```

You can clear the memory using one of the two commands: clear or drop _all. The following demonstration shows the first command:

```
. use hh
. set memory 10m
no; data in memory would be lost
r(4);
. clear
. set memory 10m

.
```

Saving a Data Set

You can make changes in an open Stata data file and save those changes by using the Stata save command. For example, the following command saves the hh.dta file:

```
. save hh, replace
file hh.dta saved
```

You can optionally omit the filename here (just save, replace is good enough). If you do not use the replace option, Stata does not save the data and issues the following error message:

```
. save hh
file hh.dta already exists
r(602);
```

The replace option unambiguously tells Stata to overwrite the pre-existing original version with the new version. If you do NOT want to lose the original version, you have to specify a different filename in the save command, for instance, using the following:

```
. save hh1
file hh1.dta saved
```

Notice that there is no replace option here. However, if a file named hh1.dta already exists, then you have to either use the replace option or use a new filename.

Exiting Stata

An easy way to exit Stata is to issue the exit command. If you have an unsaved data set open and you try to exit, Stata will issue the following error message:

```
. exit
no; data in memory would be lost
r(4);
```

To exit without losing your data, you can save the data file and then issue the exit command. If you really want to exit Stata without saving the data file, you can first clear the memory (using clear or drop _all command as shown before) and issue the exit command. You can also simplify the process by combining two commands:

```
. exit, clear
```

Stata Help

Stata comes with an excellent multivolume set of manuals. However, the computer **help** facility in Stata is extensive and useful; and if you have access to the Web, an even larger set of macros and other useful information is available.

- From within Stata, if you know the command or keyword for which you need help, you can the issue the command help followed by the command name or keyword. This command only works if you type the full command name or keyword unabbreviated. For example, the following will not work,

```
. help mem
help for mem not found
try help contents or search mem
```

but this will:

```
. help memory
[output omitted]
```

- If you do not know or cannot remember the full command name or keyword, you can use the command lookup or search followed by the command name or keyword. So, the following will work:

```
. search mem
[output omitted]
```

This command will list all commands associated with this keyword and display a brief description of each of those commands. Then, you can select the relevant items and use help to obtain the specific reference.

- The Stata Web site (http://www.stata.com) has excellent help features, including an Online Tutorial, Frequently Asked Questions (FAQ), and other options.

Notes on Stata Commands

Here are some general comments about Stata commands:

- Stata commands are typed in lower case.

- All names, including commands or variable names, can be abbreviated as long as there is no ambiguity. So, for example, describe, des, or simply d do the same job.

- In addition to typing, some keystrokes can be used to represent a few Stata commands or sequences. The most important of them are the **Page-Up** and **Page-Down** keys. To display the previous command in the **Stata Command** window, you can press the **Page-Up** key. You can keep doing that until the first command of the session appears. Similarly, the **Page-Down** key displays the command that follows the currently displayed command in the **Stata Command** window.

- Clicking once on a command in the **Review** window will put it into the **Stata Command** window; double-clicking it will tell Stata to execute the command. This can be useful when commands need to be repeated, or edited slightly in the **Stata Command** window.

Working with Data Files: Looking at the Content

For the rest of this appendix, we primarily will list the commands and not the results. To go through this exercise, open the hh.dta file, as we will be using examples extensively from this data file.

Listing the variables

To see all variables in the data set, use the describe command (fully or abbreviated):

```
. describe
```

This command provides information about the data set (name, size, number of observations) and lists all variables (name, storage format, display format, label).

To see just one variable or list of variables, use the describe command followed by the variable name(s):

```
. d hhcode vill
  storage display value
variable name type format label variable label
-----------------------------------------------------------------------
hhcode double %7.0f COMPLETE HOUSEHOLD CODE
vill float %2.0f VILLAGE CODE
```

As you can see, the describe command shows the variable type, its length, and a short description of the variable (if available). The following points should be noted:

- You can abbreviate a list of variables by typing only the first and last variable names, separated by a hyphen (-); the **Variables** window shows the order in

349

which the variables are stored. For example, to see all variables from hhcode up to famsize, type the following command:

```
. describe hhcode-famsize
```

- The wildcard symbol (*) is helpful to save some typing. For example, to see all variables that start with "hh", type the following:

```
. describe hh*
```

In addition to describe, you can abbreviate a variable or variable list this way in any Stata command (for which it makes sense).

Listing Data

To see actual data stored in the variables, use the list command (abbreviated as l). If you type the command list by itself, Stata will display values for all variables and all observations, which is not desirable for any practical purpose (and you may need to use the **Ctrl-Break** combination to stop data from scrolling endlessly across the screen). We usually want to see the data for certain variables and for certain observations. We achieve this by typing a list command with a variable list and with conditions, as shown in the following examples.

The following command lists all variables of the first three observations:

```
. list in 1/3
```

In this example, Stata displays all observations starting with observation 1 and ending with observation 3. Stata can also display data as a spreadsheet. There are two icons in the toolbar called **Data Editor** and **Data Browser** (fourth and third from the right). By clicking either one of these icons, a new window will pop up and the data will be displayed as a table, with observations as rows and variables as columns. **Data Browser** will only display the data, whereas you can edit data with **Data Editor**. The commands edit and browse will also open the spreadsheet window.

The following command lists household size and head's education for households headed by a female who is younger than 45:

```
. list famsize educhead if (sexhead==0 & agehead<45)
```

Table A2.1 Stata Operators

Relational operators	Logical operators
> (greater than)	~ (not)
< (less than)	| (or)
== (equal)	& (and)
>= (greater than or equal)	
<= (less than or equal)	
!= or ~= (not equal)	

The statement above uses two relational operators (== and <) and one logical operator (&). Relational operators impose a condition on one variable, while logical operators combine two or more relational operators. The list in table A2.1 shows the relational and logical operators that are used in Stata:

In addition to the `list` command, you can use relational and logical operators in any Stata command (for which it makes sense). After an `if` statement, it is necessary to use a double equals sign to express equality; this is given by ==, which denotes "is identically equal to."

Summarizing Data

The very useful command `summarize` (which may be abbreviated as `sum`) calculates and displays a few of summary statistics, including means and standard deviations. If no variable is specified, summary statistics are calculated for all variables in the data set. The following command summarizes the household size and education of the household head:

```
. sum famsize educhead
```

Any observation that has a missing value for the variable(s) being summarized is excluded from this calculation by Stata (missing values are discussed later). If we want to know the median and percentiles of a variable, we need to add the `detail` option (abbreviated d), as shown here:

```
. sum famsize educhead, d
```

A great strength of Stata is that it allows for the use of weights. The `weight` option is useful if the sampling probability of one observation is different from another. In most household surveys, the sampling frame is stratified, where the first primary sampling units (often villages) are sampled, and conditional on the selection of primary sampling unit, secondary sampling units (often households) are drawn. Household surveys generally provide weights to correct for the sampling design differences and sometimes data collection problems. The implementation in Stata is straightforward:

```
. sum famsize educhead [aw=weight]
```

In this example, the variable `weight` has the information on the weight to be given to each observation and `aw` is a Stata option to incorporate the weight into the calculation. We will discuss the use of weights further in the chapter exercises given below. In passing, it is worth noting that one can add blank spaces without affecting the commands; the previous command could equally well have been written as:

```
. sum famsize educhead [ aw = weight ]
```

For variables that are strings, `summarize` will not be able to give any descriptive statistics except that the number of observations is zero. Also, for variables that are categorical (for example, illiterate = 1, primary education = 2, higher education = 3), it can be difficult to interpret the output of the `summarize` command. In both cases, a full tabulation may be more meaningful, which we will discuss next.

Many times we want to see summary statistics by group of certain variables, not just for the whole data set. Suppose we want to see mean family size, and education of household head, by region. We could use a condition in the sum command (for example, `sum famsize educhead if region == 1 [aw=weight]`), and so on for the other regions, but this is not convenient if the number of categories in the group is large.

There is a simpler solution. First, sort the data by the group variable (in this case, region). You can check this by issuing the `describe` command after opening each file. The `describe` command, after listing all the variables, indicates whether the data set is sorted by any variable(s). If there is no sorting information listed or the data set is sorted by a variable that is different from what you want it to be, you can use the `sort` command to sort as desired and then save the data set in this new form. The following commands sort the data set by `region` and show summary statistics of family size and education of household head by region:

```
. sort region
. by region: sum famsize educhead [aw=weight]
```

Frequency Distributions (Tabulations)

We often need frequency distributions and cross tabulations. We use the tabulate (abbreviated `tab`) command to do this. The following command gives the regional distribution of the households:

```
. tab region
```

The following command gives the gender distribution of household heads in region 1:

```
. tab sexhead if region == 1
```

In passing, note the use of the == (double equals) sign here. It indicates that if the regional variable is identically equal to 1, then do the tabulation.

We can use the `tabulate` command to show a two-way distribution. For example, we might want to check whether there is any gender bias in the education of household heads. We use the following command:

```
. tab educhead sexhead
```

To see percentages by row or columns, we can add options to the `tabulate` command:

```
. tab region sexhead, col row
```

Distributions of Descriptive Statistics (Table Command)

Another convenient command is `table`, which combines features of the `sum` and `tab` commands. In addition, it displays the results in a more presentable form. The following `table` command shows the mean of family size, and education of household head, by region:

```
. table region, c(mean famsize mean educhead)
```

region	mean(famsize)	mean(educhead)
Dhaka	5.23	2
Chittagon	5.82	3
Khulna	5.03	3
Ragfhahi	5.03	2

The results are as we expected. But note that the mean of `educhead` is displayed as an integer and not as a fraction. The results are displayed in this manner because the `educhead` variable is stored as an integer number, and Stata simply truncated numbers after the decimal. Look at the description of this variable.

```
. d educhead
storage  display  value
variable name type format label variable label
-----------------------------------------------------
educhead float %2.0f Education (years) of HH Head
```

We see that `educhead` is a `float` variable: its format (%2.0f) shows that its digits occupy two places, and it has no digit after the decimal. You can force Stata to reformat the display. Suppose we want the variable to display two places after the decimal, for a three-digit display. The following example shows this command as well as the subsequent `table` command:

```
. format educhead %3.2f
. table region, c(mean famsize mean educhead)
```

region	mean(famsize)	mean(educhead)
Dhaka	5.23	2.09
Chittagon	5.82	3.14
Khulna	5.03	2.91
Ragfhahi	5.03	2.15

This is much better. Formatting changes only the display of the variable, not the internal representation of the variable in the memory. The `table` command can display up to five statistics, and variables other than the mean (such as the sum, minimum, or maximum). It is also possible to display two-way, three-way, or even higher dimensional tables.

The following example illustrates a two-way table, which breaks down the education of the household head not just by region but also by sex of household head:

```
. table region sexhead, c(mean famsize mean
  educhead)
```

region	sex head 0	1=male 1
Dhaka	3.36	5.37
	0.18	2.24
Chittagon	4.17	6.08
	1.50	3.39
Khulna	4.18	5.11
	1.36	3.05
Ragfhahi	3.70	5.13
	0.00	2.31

Missing Values in Stata

In Stata, a missing value is represented by a dot (.). A missing value is considered larger than any number. The `summarize` command ignores the observations with missing values and the `tabulate` command does the same, unless forced to include missing values.

Counting Observations

We use the `count` command to count the number of observations in the data set:

```
. count
159
.
```

The `count` command can be used with conditions. The following command gives the number of households whose head is older than 50:

```
. count if agehead>50
159
.
```

Working with Data Files: Changing Data Sets

Generating New Variables

In Stata, the command `generate` (abbreviated `gen`) creates new variables, while the command `replace` changes the values of an existing variable. The following commands create a new variable called `oldhead`, then set its value to 1 if the household head is older than 32 years and to 0 otherwise:

```
. gen oldhead=1 if agehead>32
(98 missing values generated)

. replace oldhead=0 if agehead<=32
(98 real changes made)
```

In this example, for each observation, the `generate` command checks the condition (whether household head is older than 32) and sets the value of the variable `oldhead` to 1 for that observation if the condition is true, and to a missing value otherwise. The `replace` command works in a similar fashion. After the `generate`

355

command, Stata informs us that 98 observations failed to meet the condition and, after the `replace` command, Stata informs us that those 98 observations have been assigned new values (0 in this case).

There is actually a more elegant and compact way to create the `oldhead` variable, as follows:

```
. gen oldhead = (agehead>32)
```

Here the right hand expression is first evaluated; if it is true, then `oldhead` is set equal to 1, and if it is not true, then `oldhead` is set equal to zero.

The following points are worth noting:

- If a `generate` or `replace` command is issued without any conditions, that command applies to all observations in the data file.

- While using the `generate` command, care should be taken to handle missing values properly.

- The `replace` command can be used to change the values of any existing variable, independently of the `generate` command.

Stata provides many useful functions to be used in `generate` and `replace` commands, for example, `mean(.)` or `max(.)`. For example, in the `ind.dta` file, the following command calculates the maximum share of employment among four sectors for each household:

```
. gen maxhr=max(snaghr,saghr,wnaghr,waghr)
.
```

An extension of the `generate` command is `egen`. Like the `gen` command, the `egen` command can create variables to store descriptive statistics such as the mean, sum, maximum and minimum, or other statistics. For example, an alternative way to create the `maxhr` variable is as follows:

```
. egen maxhr = rmax(snaghr saghr wnaghr waghr)
```

Note the difference in syntax. The more powerful feature of the `egen` command is its ability to create statistics involving multiple observations. For example, the following command creates average individual employment hours for the data set:

```
. egen avgemphr = mean(iemphr)
```

All observations in the data set get the same value for `avgemphr`. The following command creates the same statistics, this time for males and females separately:

```
. egen avghrmf = mean(iemphr), by(sex)
```

Here, observations for males get the value that is average of male employment hours, whereas observations for females get the equivalent for female employment hours. In this particular example using Bangladesh data, women work a tenth as much as men (outside the home); you should check that you get this same result!

Labeling

Labeling Variables. You can attach labels to variables to give a description to them. For example, the variable `oldhead` currently does not have a label. You can attach a label to this variable by typing the following:

```
. label variable oldhead "HH Head is over 32"
```

In the `label` command, `variable` can be shortened to `var`. To see the new label, type the following:

```
. des oldhead
```

Labeling Data. We can create other types of labels. To attach a label to the entire data set, which appears at the top of our describe list, try the following:

```
. label data "Bangladesh HH Survey 1998/99"
```

To see this label, type the following:

```
. des
```

Labeling Values of Variables. Variables that are categorical, like those in `sexhead` (1=male, 0=female), can include labels that describe the categories. For example, using `hh.dta`, if we tabulate the variable `sexhead`, we see only 0 and 1 values:

```
. tab sexhead
```

To attach labels to the *values* of a variable, we have to do two things. First, we have to define a value label. Second, we have to assign this label to our variable(s). Using the new categories for sexhead,

```
. label define sexlabel 0 "Female" 1 "Male"
. label values sexhead sexlabel
```

To see the labels, type the following:

```
. tab sexhead
```

If you want to see the actual values of the variable sexhead, which are still stored as 0s and 1s, you can add an option to *not* display the labels assigned to the values of the variable. For instance, try the following:

```
. tab region, nolabel
```

Keeping and Dropping Variables and Observations

We can select variables and observations of a data set by using the keep or drop commands. Suppose we have a data set with six variables: var1, var2,..., var6. We would like to keep a file with only three of them, say var1, var2, and var3. You can use either of the following two commands:

```
. keep var1 var2 var3 (or keep var1-var3 if the
  variables are in this order)
. drop var4 var5 var6 (or drop var4-var6 if the variables
  are in this order)
```

Note the use of a hyphen (-) in both commands. It is good practice to use the command that involves fewer variables or less typing (and hence less risk of error). We can also use relational or logical operators. For example, the following command drops those observations where the head of the household is 80 years old or older:

```
. drop if agehead>=80
```

And this command keeps those observations where household size is six or less:

```
. keep if famsize<=6
```

In the examples above, the two commands `drop` or `keep` all variables based on the conditions. You cannot include a variable list in a `drop` or `keep` command that also uses conditions. For example, the following command will fail:

```
. keep hhcode famsize if famsize < = 6
invalid syntax
r(198);
```

You have use two commands to do the job:

```
. keep if famsize < = 6
. keep hhcode famsize
```

You can also use the keyword `in` in a `drop` or `keep` command. For example, to drop the first 20 observations, type the following:

```
. drop in 1/20
```

Producing Graphs

Stata is quite good at producing basic graphs, although considerable experimentation may be needed to produce really beautiful graphs. Version 8 of Stata introduced major changes in the way graphs are programmed. The following command shows the distribution of the age of the household head in a bar graph (histogram):

```
. histogram agehead
```

In many cases, the easiest way to produce graphs is by using the menus; in this case, click on **Graphics** in the toolbar at the top of the page, and then on **Histogram** and follow the prompts. An easy way to save a graph is to right click on the image, and use the command **Copy** to **Paste** it into Word or Excel.

Here is a command for a scatter plot of two variables. It must typed on a single **Stata Command** line.

```
twoway (scatter educhead agehead), ytitle (Education
of head) xtitle(Age of head) title(Education by Age)
```

Combining Data Sets

It is often necessary to combine data sets, and one of the strengths of Stata is that this can be done in a straightforward manner. There are two distinct operations, merging and appending, which are considered in turn.

Merging Data Sets. Stata can store only one data set in memory at a time. On many occasions, however, variables are spread over two or more files, and you may need to combine those files for the purpose of analysis.

For example, we want to see how an individual's education varies by the gender of the head of the household. Because the gender variable (sexhead) and the individual's education (educ) come from two different files (hh.dta and ind.dta), we have to merge these two files to do the analysis. We want to combine these two files at the household level, so the variable that is used for merging is hhcode (this is the *merge variable*). Before merging the data, both files must be sorted by the merge variable. The following command opens, sorts, and saves the ind.dta file:

```
. use ind,clear
. sort hhcode
. save, replace
```

Once both data sets have been sorted, they can be merged, as follows:

```
. use hh, clear
. sort hhcode
. merge hhcode using ind
```

In this context, hh.dta is called the *master file* (this is the one that remains in the memory before merging) and ind.dta is called the *using file*. To see how the merge operation went, we type the following command:

```
. tab _merge

_merge   |   Freq.    Percent    Cum.
---------+-------------------------------
3        |   2,767    100.00    100.00
---------+-------------------------------
Total    |   2,767    100.00
```

The variable _merge is created by Stata after each merge operation and it can have three possible values:

- 1—shows those observations from the master file that could not be merged

- 2—shows those observations from the using file that could not be merged

- 3—shows those observations that were successfully merged

The total number of observations in the resulting data set is the sum of these three _merge frequencies. A possible candidate for _merge=1 would be an observation in the hh.dta file with a hhcode value that cannot be found in the ind.dta file. Similarly, if the ind.dta file has a hhcode that is not found in the hh.dta file, that observation will appear with _merge=2. In the example above, however, each household in the hh.dta file has an exact match in the ind.dta file, which explains why we observed _merge=3 and not =1 or =2. If you keep only the matched observations, you can do so with the following command: keep if _ merge==3. After checking the _merge variable, it is good practice to drop it from the data set. To do so, use the command drop _merge or simply drop _m. Once we have merged the data sets, we can continue with our analysis:

```
. sort sexhead
. by sexhead: sum educ

----------------------------------------
-> sexhead = 0
    Variable │   Obs    Mean   Std. Dev. Min  Max
  -----------│---------------------------------------
        educ │   179  2.329609  3.424591   0   14
----------------------------------------
-> sexhead = 1
    Variable │   Obs    Mean   Std. Dev. Min  Max
  -----------│---------------------------------------
        educ │  2588  2.340417  3.324081   0   16
```

The result shows that there is not much difference in education by gender of household head.

Notice that to show the results by sexhead variable, we first have to sort the data by that variable, otherwise we will get an error message.

Appending Data Sets. Consider what would happen in the merging scenario above if we have _merge=1 and 2 only but no _merge=3 commands. This can happen if the individual data in ind.dta come from households that are completely different from the households in hh.dta. In this case, the resulting number of observations after merging is the sum of observations in the two files (observations with _merge=1 + observations with _merge=2). Stata in this case would actually append the two data sets; however, variables that are included only in one file will have missing values for all observations from the other file. Although this is not what we intend in the above example, appending is necessary when we need to combine two data sets that have the same (or almost the same) variables but are mutually exclusive. For example, suppose we had four regional versions of the hh.dta file: hhdhak.dta (has households only from Dhaka region), hhkhul.dta (has households only from Khulna region), hhraj.dta (has households only from

Rajshahi region), and `hhchit.dta` (has households only from Chittagong region). These data files have the same variables as `hh.dta` but represent four distinct sets of households. To combine them for an overall data set of the whole country, we use the `append` command:

```
. use hhdhak
. append using hhkhul
. append using hhraj
. append using hhchit
```

At this stage, we have a data set in the memory that has household information from all four regions. If we need this data set for subsequent use, we should save it after arranging it in a defined order (say, sorting by `hhcode`).

Working with .log and .do Files

Stata can work interactively, which is helpful in debugging commands and in getting a good "feel" for the data. You type one command line at a time, press Enter, and Stata processes that command, displays the result (if any), and waits for the next command.

You may want to save the results or perhaps print them out. This is done by creating a `.log` file. Such a file is created by issuing a `log using XXX.log` command, where XXX is the name you give to the file, and is closed by a `log close` command; all commands issued in between, as well as corresponding output (except graphs) are saved in the `.log` file.

Let us return to the example in the section "Merging Data Sets." Assume that we want to save only the education summary by household gender, not the merging outcomes. Here are the commands and associated output:

```
. log using educm.log
----------------------------------------------------
      log: C:\jhteaching\povertyonline\exercises\
           educm.log
 log type: text
opened on: 10 Dec 2008, 05:13:35

. by sexhead: sum educ
----------------------------------------------------
```

```
-> sexhead = 0
    Variable │  Obs    Mean    Std. Dev. Min  Max
        educ │  179  2.329609  3.424591   0   14
-> sexhead = 1
    Variable │  Obs    Mean    Std. Dev. Min  Max
        educ │ 2588  2.340417  3.324081   0   16

. log close
        log:  C:\jhteaching\povertyonline\exercises\
              educm.log
   log type:  text
  closed on:  10 Dec 2008,  05:13:45

---------------------------------------------------
```

In this example, Stata creates a text file named `educm.log` in the current directory and saves the summary output in that file. If you want the `.log` file to be saved in a directory other than current directory, you can specify the full path of the directory in the `.log` creation command. You can also use the **File** button in the toolbar at the top of the page, followed by **Log** and **Begin**.

If a `.log` file already exists, you could either replace it (with `log using educm. log, replace`) or append a new output to it (with `log using educm.log, append`). If you want to keep the existing `.log` file unchanged, then you can rename this file or the file in the `.log` creation command. In a `.log` file, if you want to suppress a portion of the output, you can issue the `log off` command, and then turn the log file back on again using the `log on` command when you want to record the output once again. You have to close a `.log` file before opening a new one, or you will get an error message.

If you use the same set of commands repeatedly, you can save those commands in a file and run them together whenever you need them. These very useful command files are called .do files, and they are the Stata equivalent of macros. There are at least three good ways to create .do files:

- Simply type the commands into a text file; label it `educm.do` (the .do suffix is important); and run the file using `do educm` in the **Stata Command** window.

- Right click anywhere in the **Review** window; this will save all the commands that were used interactively. The file in which they were saved can be edited, labeled, and used as a .do file.

- Use Stata's built-in .do editor. The editor is invoked by clicking on the icon (the fifth from the right, at the top of the page). Commands may be typed into the editor. These commands may be run by highlighting them and running them using the appropriate icon (the "Run current file" icon, which is the second from the right) within the .do editor. With practice, this becomes a quick and convenient way to work with Stata.

Here is an example of a .do file:

```
log using educm.log
use ind
sort hhcode
save, replace
use hh
merge hhcode using ind
tab _merge
sort sexhead
by sexhead:sum educ
log close
```

The main advantages of using .do files instead of typing commands line by line are their ability to be replicated and repeated. With a .do file, results can be replicated that were worked on weeks or months before. And .do files are especially useful when sets of commands need to be repeated—for instance, with different data sets or groups.

There are certain commands that are useful in a .do file. We will discuss these commands from the following sample .do file:

```
*This is a Stata comment that is not executed
/*****This is a do file that shows some very
useful commands used in do files. In addition,
it creates a log file and uses some basic Stata
commands ***/

#delimit ;
set more 1;
drop _all;
cap log close;
log using c:\intropov\logfiles\try1.log, replace;

use c:\intropov\data\hh.dta ;
describe ;
```

```
list in 1/3 ;
list hhcode famsize educhead if sexhead==2 &
agehead<45;
summarize famsize;
summarize famsize, detail;
sum famsize educhead [aw=weight], d;
tabulate sexhead;
tabulate educhead sexhead, col row chi;
tabulate educhead, summarize(agehead);
label define sexlabel 1 "MALE" 2 "FEMALE";
label values sexhead sexlabel;
tabulate sexhead;
label variable sexhead "Head Gender";
sort hhcode;
save temp, replace;
use c:\intropov\data\consume.dta, clear;
sort hhcode ;
#delimit cr
merge hhcode using temp
tabulate _merge
keep if _merge==3
drop _merge
log close
```

The first line in the file is a comment. Stata treats any line that starts with an aster-isk (*) as a comment and ignores it. You can write multiline comment by using a for-ward slash and asterisk (/*) as the start of the comment and end the comment with an asterisk and forward slash (*/). Comments are useful for documentation pur-poses. You should include at least the following information in the comment of a .do file: general purpose of the .do file and last modification time and date. You can include the following comments anywhere in the .do file, not just at the beginning.

#delimit ;   By default, Stata assumes that each command is ended by the carriage return (ENTER key press). If, however, a command is too long to fit on one line, you can spread it over more than one line. In this case, let Stata know what the command delimiter is. The command in the example says that a command is ended by a semicolon (;). Every command following the delimit com-mand has to end with a semicolon (;) until the file ends or a

`#delimit cr` command appears, which makes the carriage return again the command delimiter. Although for this particular .do file we don't need to use the `#delimit` command, it is done to explain the command.

`set more 1`   Stata usually displays results one screen at a time, and waits for the user to press any key. But this would soon become a nuisance if, after setting a .do file to run, you have to press a key every time this happens until the program ends. This command displays the whole output, skipping page after page automatically.

`drop _all`   This command clears the memory.

`cap log close` This command closes any open .log file. If no .log file is open, Stata ignores this command.

Exercise

1. Open the .do file editor.

2. Type the above code into the file and save it as `c:\intropov\dofiles\try.do`.

3. Click the **Do current file** icon and switch to the **Stata Results** window.

4. When you see `end of do file`, open `c:\intropov\logfiles\try11.log` in Word.

5. Check the results.

Follow-Up Practice

Now let's do some practice using all three data sets. Remember, do not overwrite these three data files.

1. Generate a new variable, `agegroup`, which categorizes individuals according to their age. For example, assign 1 to `agegroup` if the person is less than 30 years old. You can make your own categories as you consider appropriate. Label this variable and its categorical values, and then tabulate it.

2. Calculate the sex ratio of the sampled population, and the labor participation rates for both men and women.

3. Count the number of children younger than 15 years old and the number of adults older than 65. Compare the mean per capita staple food consumption (in kg) for households with no children, one child, and two or more children.

4. Calculate the mean per capita food consumption for those households whose heads are between 30 and 39 years old. Compare it with the mean per capita food consumption for those whose heads are between 50 and 59 years old.

5. Report the mean and median per capita food consumption for each education level of household head.

6. Calculate the food share in total household expenditure and compare the mean food share for households headed by men with that of households headed by women.

7. Tabulate mean household size and mean education level by region and area.

Exercises

Introduction

Working with household data sets requires a solid mastery of appropriate statistical and data management software, such as Stata or SPSS. This mastery comes from learning by doing. We have found that students who work though the exercises in this appendix acquire the necessary mastery, and are ready to tackle almost any challenge in working with household data. The exercises build on one another, so they should be done in the order given, and each completed fully before proceeding to the next one.

   Before beginning these exercises, it is important to prepare the data as set out in appendix 2. If you are new to Stata, you will want to work though appendix 2; if you once knew Stata, and have forgotten the details, a quick skim of Appendix 2 should suffice to bring back the fond memories.

Exercise 1. Chapter 2, Measuring Poverty

We first need to construct the data set that will be used in the later exercises.

Household Characteristics

Open c:\intropov\data\hh.dta, which consists of household-level variables. Answer the following questions:

1. How many variables are there? _____

2. How many observations (households) are there? _____

3. There are four regions. Household characteristics may vary by regions. Fill in the following table (Hint: use the `table` command).

	Dhaka	Chittagong	Khulna	Rajshahi
Total number of households	————	————	————	————
Total number of population	————	————	————	————
Average distance to paved road	————	————	————	————
Average distance to nearest bank	————	————	————	————
% Household has electricity	————	————	————	————
% Household has sanitary toilet	————	————	————	————
Average household assets	————	————	————	————
Average household land holding	————	————	————	————
Average household size	————	————	————	————

4. Are the sampled households very different across regions?

_____

_____

_____

5. The gender of the head of household may also be associated with different household characteristics:

	Male-headed households	Female-headed households
Average household size	————	————
Average years of schooling of head	————	————
Average age (years) of head	————	————
Average household assets (taka)	————	————
Average household land holding (acres)	————	———— (CAREFUL!)

(*For consideration:* How many decimal places should one report? As a general rule, do not provide spurious precision. Reporting the average household size as 5.35368 gives a false impression of accuracy; but reporting the size as 5 is too blunt. In such cases, 5.4 or 5.35 would be more appropriate, and is accurate enough for almost all uses.)

6. Are the sampled households headed by males very different from those headed by females?

_____

_____

_____

Individual Characteristics

Now open c:\intropov\data\ind.dta. This file consists of information on household members. Merge this data with the household level data (hh.dta) (see appendix 2 if you need a refresher on merging) and answer the following questions for individuals *who are 15 years old or older*:

1. Regional variation

	Dhaka	Chittagong	Khulna	Rajshahi
Average years of schooling	————	————	————	————
Gender ratio (% of household that is female)	————	————	————	————
% Working population (with positive working hours)	————	————	————	————
% Working population working on a farm	————	————	————	————

2. Are the sampled individuals very different across regions?

_____

_____

_____

3. We now examine some gender differences:

	For males	For females
Average schooling years (age ≥ 5)	————	————
Average schooling years (age < 15)	————	————
Average age	————	————
% Working population (with positive working hours)	————	————
% Working population working on a farm	————	————
Average working hours per month	————	————
Average working hours on farm, per month	————	————
Average working hours off farm, per month	————	————

4. Are the characteristics of the sampled women very different from those of the sampled men?

_____

_____

_____

Expenditure

Open c:\intropov\data\consume.dta. It has household level consumption expenditure information. Merge it with hh.dta.

1. Create three variables: per capita food expenditure (call it pcfood), per capita nonfood expenditure (call it pcnfood), and per capita total expenditure (call it pcexp). Now let's look at the consumption patterns.

Average per capita expenditure

	pcfood	pcexp
By region		
Whole		
Dhaka region		
Chittagong region		
Khulna region		
Rajshahi region		
By gender of head		
Male-headed households		
Female-headed households		
By education level of head		
Head has some education		
Head has no education		
By household size		
Large house hold (>5)		
Small household (≤5)		
By land ownership		
Large land ownership (>0.5 acres/person)		
Small land ownership or landless		

Summarize your findings on per capita expenditure comparison.

_____

_____

_____

2. Now add another measure of household size, which takes into account the fact that children consume less than adults. Assume that a child (age < 15) will be weighted as 0.75 of an adult. For instance, a household consisting of a couple with one child age 7 is worth 2.75 on this adult-equivalence scale, instead of 3. Go back to the ind.dta and create this variable (call it famsize2), then merge the revised file with the household data and the consumption data files. Create per-adult-equivalent expenditure variables (let's call them pafood and paexp) and repeat the exercise above.

Average per capita expenditure

	pcfood	pcexp
By region	_____	_____
Whole	_____	_____
Dhaka region	_____	_____
Chittagong region	_____	_____
Khulna region	_____	_____
Rajshahi region	_____	_____
By gender of head	_____	_____
Male-headed households	_____	_____
Female-headed households	_____	_____
By education level of head	_____	_____
Head has some education	_____	_____
Head has no education	_____	_____
By household size	_____	_____
Large household (>5)	_____	_____
Small household (<=5)	_____	_____
By land ownership	_____	_____
Large land ownership (>0.5 acres/person)	_____	_____
Small land ownership or landless	_____	_____

Compare your new results with those of per capita expenditure. In analyzing poverty, is it better to use adult equivalents?

_____

_____

_____

3. Besides looking at the mean or the median value of consumption, we can also easily look at the whole distribution of consumption using scatter. The following plots the cumulative distribution function curve of per capita total expenditure.

```
. cumul pcexp, gen(pcexpcdf)
. twoway scatter pcexpcdf pcexp if pcexp<20000,
  ytitle("Cumulative Distribution of pcexp") xtitle
  ("Per Capita total expenditure") title("CDF of
  Per Capita Total Expenditure") subtitle ("Exercise
  1.3") saving (cdf1, replace)
```

The cumul command creates a variable called pcexpcdf that is defined as the empirical cumulative distribution function (cdf) of pcexp; in effect, it sorts the data by pcexp, and creates a new variable that accumulates and normalizes pcexp, so that its maximum value is 1. To explore the variable, try

```
list pcexp pcexpcdf in 1/10
sort pcexp
list pcexp pcexpcdf in 1/10
list pcexp pcexpcdf in -10/-1
```

Then use the code shown here to graph the cdf. Feel free to experiment with the `scatter` command. The graph is also saved in a file called `cdf1.gph`. When you want to look at the graph later, just type "`graph use cdf1`".

The cumulative distribution function curve of a welfare indicator can reveal much information about poverty and inequality. For example, if we know the value of a poverty line, we can easily find the corresponding percentage value of people below the line. Suppose the poverty line is 5,000. Then the command

```
sum pcexpcdf if pcexp<5000
```

will give the poverty rate (under the "max" heading).

(*For consideration:* Why is the mean not the appropriate measure of poverty here?)

4. Keep `pcfood pcexp pafood paexp famsize2 hhcode`, merge with `hh.dta`, sort by `hhcode`, and save as `pce.dta` in the `c:\intropov\data` directory.

Household Weights

In most household surveys, observations are selected through a random process, but different observations may have different probabilities of selection. Therefore, we need to use weights that are equal to the inverse of the probability of being sampled. A weight of w_j for the jth observation means, roughly speaking, that the jth observation represents w_j elements in the population from which the sample was drawn. Omitting sampling weights in the analysis usually gives biased estimates, which may be far from the true values (see chapter 2).

Various postsampling adjustments to the weights are sometimes necessary. A household sampling weight is provided in the `hh.dta` file. This is the right weight to use when summarizing data that relate to households.

However, we are often interested in the individual, rather than the household, as the unit of analysis. Consider a village with 60 households; 30 households have 5 individuals each (with income per capita of 2,100), while the other 30 households have 10 individuals each (with income per capita of 1,200). The total population of the village is 450. Now suppose we take a 10 percent random sample of households, picking three 5-person households and three 10-person households. We would estimate the mean income per capita to be 1,650. While this properly reflects the nature of *households* in the village, it does not give information that is representative of *individuals*: the village has 150 people in 5-person households and 300 people in 10-person households. Weighted by individuals, per capita income in this village is in fact 1,500. (Try the calculation!) Such computations can be done easily in Stata.

In estimating individual-level parameters such as per capita expenditure, we need to transform the *household* sample weights into *individual* sample weights, using the following Stata commands:

```
. gen weighti = weight*famsize
. table region [pweight=weighti], c(mean pcexp)
```

Stata has four types of weights: `fweight`, `pweight`, `aweight`, and `iweight`. Of these, frequency weights and analytic weights are most important.

- **Frequency weights** (`fweight`) indicate how many observations in the population are represented by each observation in the sample. It takes integer values.

- **Analytic weights** (`aweight`) are especially useful when working with data that contain averages (for example, average income per capita in a household). The weighting variable is proportional to the number of persons over which the average was computed (number of members of a household, for instance). Technically, analytic weights are in inverse proportion to the variance of an observation (that is, a higher weight means that the observation was based on more information and so is more reliable in the sense of having less variance).

Further information on weights may be obtained by typing `help weight`. Now let's repeat some previous estimations with the newly created weights:

	Dhaka	Chittagong	Khulna	Rajshahi
Average household size	_____	_____	_____	_____
Average per capita food expenditure:	_____	_____	_____	_____
Average per capita total expenditure:	_____	_____	_____	_____

Are the weighted averages very different from unweighted ones?

_____

_____

_____

The Effects of Clustering and Stratification

If the survey under consideration has a complex sampling design, the standard errors of estimates (and sometimes even the means) will be biased if clustering and stratification are ignored.

Consider the following typical case of a multistage stratified random sample with clustering.

- First, the country is divided into regions (the ***strata***), and a sample size is selected for each region. Note that it is perfectly legitimate to sample some regions more heavily than others; indeed, one would typically want to sample a sparsely populated heterogeneous region more heavily (for example, one person per 300) than a densely populated, homogeneous region (for example, one person per 1,000).

- Within each region, communes are randomly picked, where the probability that a commune is picked depends on the population of the commune; in this case the commune is the primary sampling unit (the ***psu***). One may survey households in a cluster within the commune—for instance, picking 20 households in a single village. Cluster sampling is widespread because it is much cheaper than taking a simple random sample of the population. Let us assume that someone has also computed a weight variable (***wt***) that represents the number of households that each representative household "represents"; thus, the weight will be small for oversampled areas, and larger for undersampled areas.

Stata has a very useful set of commands designed to deal with data that have been collected from multistage and cluster sample surveys. Information must be provided on the structure of the survey using the `svyset` commands. Using our example we would have

```
svyset [pweight=weighti], strata(region) psu(thana)
clear(all)
```

where `region` is a variable that indicates the regions.[1] Having set out the structure of the survey, `svymean` can be used to give estimates of population means and their correct standard errors; and `svyreg` can be used to perform linear regression, taking survey design into account. Other commands include `svytest` (to test whether a set of coefficients are statistically significantly different from zero) and `svylc` (to test linear combinations, such as the differences between the means of two variables). Repeat the exercise from "Household Weights" and compare the results.

	Dhaka	Chittagong	Khulna	Rajshahi
Average household size	_____	_____	_____	_____
Average per capita food expenditure:	_____	_____	_____	_____
Standard deviation of per capita food expenditure:	_____	_____	_____	_____
Average per capita total expenditure:	_____	_____	_____	_____

Are the new weighted averages, adjusted for clustering and stratification, very different from the unweighted ones?

_____

_____

_____

Exercise 2. Chapter 3, Poverty Lines

To compare poverty measures over time, it is important that the poverty line itself represent similar levels of well-being over time and across groups. Three methods have been used to derive poverty lines for Bangladesh: direct caloric intake, food-energy intake, and cost of basic needs.

The following table gives a nutritional basket, in per capita terms, considered minimal for the healthy survival of a typical adult in a family in rural Bangladesh.

Direct Caloric Intake

The direct caloric intake method considers any household not meeting the nutritional requirement of 2,112 Calories per day per person as poor.[2] For this method, we need to know the quantity of every food item consumed by households and its calorie content. With that information, we calculate the total calorie content of the food actually consumed and derive an equivalent daily caloric intake per capita for each household. The data set `c:\intropov\data\consume.dta` includes the quantity of 10 food items consumed. ("Potatoes" and "other vegetables" listed in the table are combined into one item called "vegetables" in the survey; assume that the total per capita daily calorie provision of this combined item is 62 and the quantity is 177 grams.)

1. Use the quantity information from the data set and the calorie content information from the above table to calculate each household's per capita caloric intake (in Calories per day). (Hint: The unit in the data set is kilograms per week, and this needs to be converted into grams per day.)

Table A3.1 Bangladesh Nutritional Basket

Food items	Per capita normative daily requirements		Average rural consumer price (taka/kilogram)
	Calories	Quantity (gram)	
Rice	1,386	397	15.19
Wheat	139	40	12.81
Pulses	153	40	30.84
Milk (cow)	39	58	15.90
Oil (mustard)	180	20	58.24
Meat (beef)	14	12	66.39
Fish	51	48	46.02
Potatoes	26	27	8.18
Other vegetables	36	150	38.30
Sugar	82	20	30.49
Fruit	6	20	28.86
Total	2,112	832	

Source: Wodon 1997, 93.

2. Create a new variable `cpcap` to store this caloric intake variable. Now identify the households for which `cpcap` is less than 2,112. These households are considered "poor" based on the `direct` caloric intake method. Create a variable `directp` that equals 1 if the household is poor and 0 otherwise. What percentage of people are poor by this method?

	Bangladesh	Dhaka	Other regions
% poor using direct caloric intake method	<u>58.8</u>	____	_____

Food-Energy Intake

The food-energy intake method finds the value of per capita total consumption expenditures at which a household can be expected to fulfill its caloric requirement, and determines poverty based on that expenditure. Note that this expenditure automatically includes an allowance for both food and nonfood items, thus avoiding the tricky problem of determining the basic needs for those goods. This method does not need price data either, but as explained in chapter 3, it can also give very misleading results.

A simple way to implement this method is to rank households by their per capita caloric intakes and calculate the mean expenditure for the group of households that consume approximately the stipulated per capita caloric intake requirement. Proceed as follows:

1. Merge `cpcap` with `hh.dta` and calculate the average `pcexp` for the households whose per capita caloric intake is within 10 percent of 2,112, either above or below (see code in following box).

2. Call the average value `feipline` and identify the households for whom `pcexp` is less than `feipline`. These households are considered "poor" based on the food-energy intake method. Create a variable `feip` that equals 1 if the household is poor and 0 otherwise.

```
. sum pcexp [aw=weighti] if cpcap<2112*1.1 &
  cpcap>2112*.9
. gen feipline = r(mean)
. gen feip = (pcexp <= feipline)
```

Technical note: Stata commands that report results also save the results so that other commands can subsequently use those results; "r-class" commands, such as `summarize`, save results in `r()` in version 6.0 or higher. After any r-class commands, if you type "`return list`", Stata will list what was saved. (Try it!)

Another group—"e-class" commands such as `regress`—save results in `e()` and estimates list will list saved results. For example, `e(b)` and `e(V)` store the estimates of coefficients and the variance-covariance matrix, respectively. There is an easier way to access coefficients and standard errors: either `_b(varname)` or `_coef(varname)` contains the coefficient on `varname`, and `_se(varname)` refers to the standard error of the coefficient.

3. What percentage of people are poor by this method?

	Bangladesh	Dhaka	Other regions
% poor using food intake method	_____	_____	67.9

4. *Challenge:* A more sophisticated method is to regress per capita total expenditure on per capita caloric intake and then predict the expected per capita expenditure at the 2,112 Calorie level. Try this!

```
. regress pcexp cpcap [aw=weighti]
. gen feipline=_b[_cons] + _b[cpcap]*2112
```

5. Should there be separate regression for each region?

_____

_____

_____

Cost of Basic Needs

The idea behind the cost of basic needs method is to find the value of consumption necessary to meet minimum subsistence needs. Usually it involves a basket of food items based on nutritional requirements and consumption patterns, and a reasonable allowance for nonfood consumption.

1. According to the basket in table A3.1 and the average rural consumer prices, how much money does a household of four need each day to meet its caloric requirements?

2. One way to derive the nonfood allowance is simply to assume a certain percentage of the value of minimum food consumption. How much annual total expenditure does a family of four need if it is to avoid being poor, assuming that nonfood expenses amount to 30 percent of food expenses?

3. `vprice.dta` gives village-level price information on all 11 food items. Therefore, we can actually calculate a food poverty line (call it `foodline`) and a total poverty line (call it `cbnpline`) for each village using the cost of basic needs

method and merge this variable with `pce.dta`. (Hint: Here we need to `sort` both data sets and merge by `thana vill`.) Do this, and create a variable `cbnp` that equals 1 for the poor and 0 for the nonpoor.

4. What percentage of people are poor by this method?

	Bangladesh	Dhaka	Other regions
% poor by cost of basic needs method	_____	_____	_____

5. The percentage of people in poverty varies according to the three methods. Which method do you consider to be most suitable here? Why?

_____

_____

_____

6. Keep all imputed poverty lines and poverty indicators, merge with `pce.dta`, and save the file as `final.dta`.

Exercise 3. Chapter 4, Measures of Poverty

A Simple Example

In Stata, open the data file `example.dta` and browse the data using Stata "Data Browser" or type in the numbers shown here. You should see a spreadsheet listing information exactly as presented in the following table.

Stata Editor						
Preserve	Restore	Sort	<<	>>	Hide	Delete...

y_a[1] = **110**

	y_a	y_b	y_c
1	110	110	120
2	115	120	121
3	119	120	122
4	120	124	123
5	125	125	123
6	127	127	125
7	138	138	135
8	141	141	140
9	178	178	171
10	222	222	215

The data consist of information on consumption by all the individuals in three countries (A, B, and C). Each country has just 10 residents.

1. Summarize the consumption level for each of the three countries:

   _____

2. Assuming a poverty line of 125, calculate the following poverty rates for each country:

Country	A	B	C
a. Using the headcount index	____	____	____
b. Using the poverty gap index	____	____	____
c. Using the squared poverty gap index	____	____	____

(Hint: The relevant formulas are provided in chapter 4. Try programming the results in Stata rather than doing the computations by hand or using Excel.)

3. Which country has the highest incidence of poverty? Justify your answer.

   _____
   _____
   _____

Poverty Measures for Rural Bangladesh 1999

Now let's work with the per capita food expenditure and the per capita total expenditure (pcfood and pcexp in c:\intropov\data\final.dta) created in Exercise 1, and use cbnpline (the cost of basic needs poverty line derived in Exercise 2).

Technical note: Although it is possible to program the calculation of different measures of poverty, it is simpler to use programs that have been written by others. In Stata these programs are known as .ado programs. The basic version of Stata comes with a large library of such programs, but for specialized work (such as computing poverty rates) it is usually necessary to install .ado programs that have been provided on a diskette or obtained on the Web.

For computing poverty rates and their accompanying standard errors, a useful program is FGT.ado , which is based on poverty.ado written by Philippe Van Kerm; the standard error calculation follows Deaton (1997). The FGT.ado file should be put in your working directory; or into a directory given by c:\ado\plus\f (which you may need to create for this purpose). Two other useful .ado programs are SST.ado (for computing the Sen-Shorrocks-Thon poverty measure) and Sen.ado (for computing the Sen index of poverty). These files are available at: http://mail.beaconhill.org/~j_haughton. Other .ado programs are available on the Internet; for an example, and how to access them, see "Finding and Using .ado Files" below.

FGT.ado can calculate the headcount index (or FGT(0)), the poverty gap index (or FGT(1)), and the squared poverty gap index (or FGT(2)). For example,

```
. FGT y, line(1000) fgt0 fgt1 fgt2
```

will calculate the headcount ratio, the poverty gap ratio, and squared poverty gap index using a poverty line of 1,000 and welfare indicator y. Be careful: the command is case sensitive, and in this case FGT must be written in capital letters. After line, the brackets must contain a number. Instead of typing all three measures, one could specify the *all* option, or just some of the measures. If sd is typed, the command will also give standard errors for the estimates, which is very useful in determining the size of sampling error.

The command above works when there is a single poverty line. However, some researchers prefer to compute different poverty lines for each household (as a function of household size, local price levels, and the like). Assume that these tailor-made poverty lines are in a variable called povlines. Now the appropriate command becomes

```
. FGT y, vline(povlines) fgt0 fgt1 fgt2 sd
```

You can specify conditions, range, and weights with these commands. For example, the following command calculates the headcount ratio for the Dhaka region based on a poverty line of 3,000.

```
. FGT pcexp [aw=weighti] if region==1, line(3000)
    fgt0
```

Sen.ado and SST.ado calculate the Sen index and the SST index, respectively. The syntax follows the same format, but does not compute standard errors. So, for example, one could use

```
. Sen y, line(1000)
. SST y, line(1000)
```

An ambitious attempt to create a suite of programs to measure poverty and inequality within Stata has been undertaken by Abdelkrim Araar and Jean-Yves Duclos of Université Laval. After first creating stand-alone software for measuring poverty and inequality—the DAD (Distributive Analysis/Analyse Distributive) program—they then produced *DASP: Distributive Analysis Stata Package*; version 1.4 was published in December 2007, and may be downloaded from the DASP Web site (http://132.203.59.36/DASP/dmodules/madds14.htm). DASP is an add-in to Stata; once the program has been downloaded, every time Stata is opened it is possible to click on the User button at the top of the screen and then to click on DASP, which in turn provides a set of menu-driven options. In addition to basic measures of poverty and inequality, DASP can check for dominance, decompose inequality into components, and generate the Lorenz curve and other graphs; further details are given in the manual (Araar and Duclos 2007). By way of illustration, here are a couple of commands that can be used within Stata once DASP has been downloaded; the first measures the headcount index, producing the standard error of the estimate of the poverty rate, and lower and upper bounds of a 95 percent confidence interval, while the second computes the Gini index of inequality, again with a standard error and confidence interval.

```
Command
   ifgt pcexp, alpha(0) pline(3000)

Output
   Poverty index  : FGT index
   Sampling weight : weighti
   Parameter alpha : 0.00
--------------------------------------------------------------------
Variable |  Estimate     STD        LB        UB      Pov. line
---------+----------------------------------------------------------
pcexp    |  0.037168   0.011489   0.014597   0.059739   3000.00
--------------------------------------------------------------------


Command
   igini pcexp

Output
   Index : Gini index
   Sampling weight : weighti
--------------------------------------------------------------------
Variable       |  Estimate    STD        LB        UB
---------------+----------------------------------------------------
1: GINI_pcexp  |  0.266652  0.015956  0.235305  0.297999
--------------------------------------------------------------------
```

Now we are ready to turn to the measurement of poverty using the data from the Bangladesh Household and Expenditure Survey 1991/92.

1. Compute the five main measures of poverty (headcount, poverty gap, squared poverty gap, Sen index, and Sen-Shorrocks-Thon index) for per capita expenditure, using both the food poverty line and the total poverty line derived by the cost of basic needs method in the previous exercise.

	Food poverty line	Total poverty line
Headcount index	_____	_____
Poverty gap index	_____	_____
Squared poverty gap index	_____	_____
Sen index	_____	_____
Sen-Shorrocks-Thon index	_____	_____

2. Compute the headcount and poverty gap indexes for specific subgroups using the food poverty line.

	Headcount index	Poverty gap index
Dhaka region	_____	_____
Other three regions	_____	_____
Households headed by men	_____	_____
Households headed by women	_____	_____
Large households (>5)	_____	_____
Small households (≤5)	_____	_____

3. Repeat exercise 2 above using the total poverty line.

	Headcount index	Poverty gap index
Dhaka region	_____	_____
Other three regions	_____	_____
Households headed by men	_____	_____
Households headed by women	_____	_____
Large households (>5)	_____	_____
Small households (≤5)	_____	_____

Finding and Using .ado Files

There are a wealth of .ado files on the Web, and some of them are fairly easy to locate. For example, suppose one wants to compute the Sen index of poverty. From within Stata, type search Sen, which will yield the following:

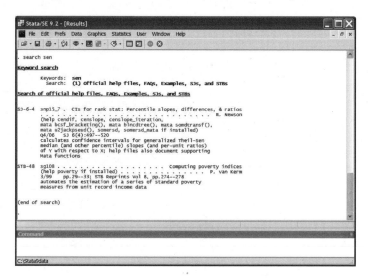

Now by double-clicking on sg108, you will obtain the following page, assuming that your computer is connected to the Internet.

Double-click again, this time on `click here to install`, and the relevant `.ado` file will be found, downloaded, and placed in the appropriate folder on your computer. Once this has been done successfully, you will get a screen like this one:

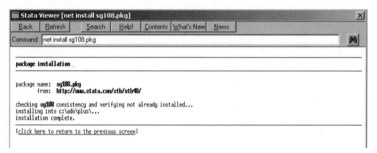

This file is called `poverty.ado`. To find out more about it, simply type `help poverty`. This program generates many measures of poverty (but not, unfortunately, their standard errors). For a sampling of the output, try

```
. poverty pcexp [aw=weighti], line(5000) all
```

Exercise 4. Chapter 5, Poverty Indexes: Checking for Robustness

The robustness of poverty measures is important because if poverty measures are not accurate, many conclusions about poverty comparisons between groups and over time may not be warranted.

Sampling Error

For example, the fact that poverty calculations are based on a sample of households rather than the population implies that calculated measures carry a margin of error. When the standard errors of poverty measures are large, small changes in poverty may well be statistically insignificant and should not be interpreted for policy purposes.

As noted above, FGT also computes the standard errors of its poverty measures if option *sd* is specified:

```
.  FGT y, line(1000) fgt0 fgt1 sd
```

1. Now let's recompute the headcount index and poverty gap index for Dhaka, and for the rest of the country, using the total poverty line, and compute the standard errors of the two measures as well.

	Headcount index	Poverty gap index
Dhaka region: Poverty rate	_____	_____
Standard error of poverty rate	_____	_____
Other three regions: Poverty rate	_____	_____
Standard error of poverty rate	_____	_____

2. Does the factor of standard errors change any conclusion about the poverty comparison between Dhaka and other regions?

_____

_____

_____

Measurement Error

Another reason we need to be very careful in poverty comparisons is because the data collected are measured incorrectly. This could be due to recall error on the part of respondents while answering survey questions, or because of enumerator error when entering the data into specific formats. Let us simulate measurement error in per capita expenditure, and then investigate what effect this error has on basic poverty measures. Try the following:

```
.  sum pcexp [aw=weighti]
.  gen mu = r(sd)*invnorm(uniform())/10
.  gen pcexp_n1 = pcexp + mu
```

Here we assume that the measurement error is a random normal variable with a standard error as big as one-tenth of the standard error of observed per capita expenditure. Let us assume that the measurement error, mu, is additive to observed per capita expenditure. Note that, by design, this error is independent of observed per capita expenditure and of any other household or community characteristics.

1. Now recompute the headcount ratio and poverty gap ratio using this new per capita expenditure.

	pcexp	pcexp_n1
Headcount index	_____	_____
Poverty gap index	_____	_____

2. Are these measures different for the headcount index? For the poverty gap index?

_____

_____

_____

3. Now consider the following situation. If the measurement error is correlated with a household characteristic—for example, if subsistence farmers usually underreport their consumption of own production—will the measurement error problem be more or less severe?

_____

_____

_____

Sensitivity Analysis

Apart from taking standard errors into account, it is also important to test the sensitivity of poverty measures to alternative definitions of consumption aggregates and alternative ways of setting the poverty line. For example, some nonfood items are excluded from the expenditure aggregate on the basis that those items are irregular and do not reflect a household's command over resources on average. Also, a 30 percent allowance for nonfood expenditure is arbitrary.

1. Create a new measure of total expenditure that includes the previously excluded irregular nonfood expenditure (expnfd2), compute the three FGT poverty measures of per capita expenditure (pcexp_n2), and compare the results with those based on the original definition of expenditure (pcexp).

	pcexp	pcexp_n2
Headcount index	_____	_____
Poverty gap index	_____	_____
Squared poverty gap index	_____	_____

The nonfood allowance can be estimated from data. Two methods have been considered (see chapter 4).

• The first finds the average nonfood expenditure for households whose *total* expenditure is equal (or close) to the food poverty line. The nonfood expenditure for this group of households must be necessities because the households are giving up part of minimum food consumption to buy nonfood items.

- The second finds the nonfood expenditure for households whose *food* expenditure is equal (or close) to the food poverty line.

Because the second is more generous than the first, the two are usually referred to as the "lower" and the "upper" allowances and the poverty lines constructed using them are called "lower" and "upper" poverty lines, respectively.

2. Try the following, then compare the results of using the two poverty lines:

```
. sum pcnfood [aw=weighti] if pcfood<foodline*1.1
  & pcfood>foodline*.9
. gen line_u = foodline + r(mean)
. sum pcnfood [aw=weighti] if pcexp<foodline*1.1
  & pcexp>foodline*.9
. gen line_l = foodline + r(mean)
```

Poverty line	lower	upper
Headcount index	_____	_____
Poverty gap index	_____	_____

3. *Challenge:* Compare poverty measures when using per-adult-equivalence scale expenditure (paeexp), with those of using per capita expenditure.

_____

_____

_____

Stochastic Dominance

One may also explore the robustness of poverty comparisons by using stochastic dominance tests. The first-order stochastic dominance test compares the cumulative distribution functions of per capita expenditure. Let's compare the cumulative distributions for Dhaka with those of the rest of Bangladesh.

1. First, generate the cumulative distribution function for Dhaka region. (Note: You may need to use the hh.dta file and merge it with the consume.dta file; you might also need to create weighti as the product of weight and famsize.)

```
. * Note the double equal signs to represent
the identity
. keep if region == 1
. sort pcexp
. * Now create a running sum of the weighti
variable
```

```
. gen cump1 = sum(weighti)
. * This normalizes cump1 so it varies between 0
and 1
. replace cump1 = cump1/cump1[_N]
. keep cump1 pcexp
. save temp, replace
```

2. Now generate the cumulative distribution cump2 for the rest of Bangladesh. Keep cump2 and pcexp, and append temp.dta by

```
. append using temp
. label variable cump1 "Dhaka"
. label variable cump2 "other regions"
. scatter cump1 cump2 pcexpscatter
  intcump1 intcump2 pcexp if pcexp<20000, c(l l)
  m(i i) title("CDFs for Dhaka and other
  regions") clwidth(medthick thin)
```

3. Does one distribution dominate another?

_____

_____

_____

4. If the two lines cross at least once, then we may need to test for second-order stochastic dominance. The *poverty deficit curve* is the integral of the cumulative distribution up to every per capita expenditure value. After creating cump1, it may be obtained by

```
. gen intcump1 = sum(cump1)
. keep intcump1 pcexp
. save temp, replace
```

Create intcump2 for the rest of Bangladesh. After combining variables and labeling them properly,

```
. label variable intcump1 "Dhaka"
. label variable intcump2 "Other regions"
. scatter intcump1 intcump2 pcexp if pcexp<20000,
  c(l l) m(i i) title("Poverty Deficit Curves for
  Dhaka and other regions") clwidth(medthick thin)
```

5. Does one distribution dominate another here?

_____

_____

_____

Challenge: Bootstrapping Standard Error for the SST Index

The bootstrapping technique can be used to calculate standard errors of poverty measures, and is especially helpful in cases where the standard errors are impossible to solve analytically (for example, with the SST index of poverty). The idea is quite simple. Repeat the calculation of the poverty measure many times, each time using a new random sample drawn from the original one with replacement. For this purpose, it is necessary to use macros and loops in Stata. The following code is an example; it could be copied or typed into the do-file editor and executed.

```
set more 1
local i = 1
while 'i'<=100 {
        use c:\intropov\data\final.dta, clear
        keep pcexp weighti cbnpline
        bsample _N
  SST pcexp [aw=weighti], line(5000)
        drop _all
        set obs 1
        gen sst = $S_6
        if 'i' ==1 {
                save temp, replace
        }
        else {
                append using temp
                save temp, replace
        }
  local i = 'i' + 1
}
sum sst
```

The code above repeats the calculation of the SST index 100 times; the sum command provides the standard error of these 100 estimates.

Exercise 5. Chapter 6, Inequality Measures

Lorenz Curve

The Lorenz curve can give a clear graphic interpretation of the Gini coefficient. Let's make the Lorenz curve of per capita expenditure distribution for rural Bangladesh.

First, we need to calculate the cumulative shares of per capita expenditure and population: (Reminder: information on pcexp is in `consume.dta`.)

```
. sort pcexp
. gen cumy = sum(pcexp*weight)
. gen cump = sum(weight)
. quietly replace cumy = cumy/cumy[_N]
. quietly replace cump = cump/cump[_N]
```

Second, we need to plot the cumulative share of expenditure against the cumulative share of population. It is also helpful to have a 45-degree line (the line of perfect equality) as a point of reference. Some of the following commands are not strictly necessary, but they do help produce a nice graph.

```
. sort pcexp
. gen equal = cump
. label variable equal "Line of Perfect Equality"
. label variable cump "Cumulative proportion
  of population"
. label variable cumy "Lorenz curve"
. scatter cumy equal cump, c(l l) m(i i)
  title("Lorenz Curve for Bangladesh")
  clwidth(medthick thin) ytitle("Cumulative
  proportion of income per capita")
```

Now repeat this exercise for Dhaka region and compare its Lorenz curve with the Lorenz curve for the whole rural area. What conclusions emerge?

_____

_____

_____

Inequality Measures for Rural Bangladesh

There is a very useful program called `ineqdeco.ado` that computes the Gini coefficient, generalized entropy family, and Atkinson family of inequality measures. By typing search ineqdeco within Stata and following the instructions it is straight-forward to load this .ado file onto your computer. As in Exercise 3, you can use these programs just like other Stata commands. The syntax is

```
. ineqdeco y [if...][w=weight], [by(...)]
```

When the by option is used, this program decomposes inequality into the within-group and between-group components, which is often very helpful. Here is a more concrete example of the command at work:

```
. ineqdeco rlpcex1 [w=hhsizewt], by(urban98)
```

In this example, we get several measures of inequality for real per capita expenditure (rlpcex1), adjusted for weights (given by hhsizewt), and separated into urban and rural components.

Another helpful program is fastgini, which calculates the Gini coefficient along with jackknife standard errors. For example, the command fastgini rlpcex1 [w=hhsizewt], jk would generate the Gini coefficient and its standard error for real per capita expenditure rlpcex1.

Let's continue using per capita total expenditure to calculate inequality measures:

1. Compute the Gini coefficient, the Theil index, and the Atkinson index with inequality aversion parameter equal to 1 for the four regions.

	Gini	Theil	Atkinson
All regions	_____	_____	_____
Dhaka region	_____	_____	_____
Other three regions	_____	_____	_____

2. Now repeat the above exercise using decile dispersion ratios, and the share of consumption of the poorest 25 percent. Stata command xtile is good for dividing the sample by ranking. For example, to calculate the consumption expenditure ratio between the richest 20 percent and the poorest 20 percent, you need to identify those two groups.

```
. xtile group = y, nq(5)
```

The command xtile will generate a new variable group that splits the sample into five groups according to the ranking of y (from smallest to largest, that is, the poorest 20 percent will have group==1, while the richest 20 percent will have group==5). Similarly, to identify the poorest 25 percent, you need to split the sample into four groups.

	top 20% ÷ bottom 20%	top 10% ÷ bottom 10%	Percentage of consumption of poorest 25%
All Bangladesh	_____	_____	_____
Dhaka region	_____	_____	_____
Other regions of Bangladesh	_____	_____	_____

3. *Challenge*: Many inequality indexes can be decomposed by subgroups. Decompose the Theil index by region and comment on the results.

_____

_____

_____

Exercise 6. Chapter 7, Describing Poverty: Poverty Profiles

In the previous exercises we computed poverty measures for various subgroups, such as regions, gender of head of household, household size, and so on. Another way to present a poverty profile is by comparing the characteristics of the "poor" with those of the "nonpoor."

Characteristics of the Poor

Complete the following table, where "poor" and "nonpoor" are defined by cbnp in Exercise 2.

	poor	nonpoor
% of all households	_____	_____
% of total population	_____	_____
Average distance to paved road	_____	_____
Average distance to nearest bank	_____	_____
% of households with electricity	_____	_____
% of households with a sanitary toilet	_____	_____
Average household assets (taka)	_____	_____
Average household land holding (decimals) [Reminder: a decimal is 0.01 of an acre.]	_____	_____
Average household size	_____	_____
% of households headed by men	_____	_____
Average schooling of head of household (years)	_____	_____
Average age of head (years)	_____	_____
Average head of household working hours on nonfarm activities (per year)	_____	_____

More Poverty Comparisons across Subgroups

Calculate the headcount and poverty gap measures of poverty for the following subgroups, using `cbnpline` to define poverty.

	Headcount index	Poverty gap index
Household head has no education		
Household head has a primary education only		
Head had secondary or higher education		
Large land ownership (>0.5 ha/person)		
Small land ownership or landless		
Large asset ownership (>50,000 taka)		
Small asset ownership (≤50,000 taka)		

Combined with the poverty measures computed in Exercise 3, describe the most significant poverty patterns in Bangladesh.

_____

_____

_____

Exercise 7. Chapter 8, Understanding the Determinants of Poverty

Develop and estimate a model that explains $\log(\text{pcexp/cbnpline})$ using available data. The regressors may include demographic characteristics such as gender of head and family structure; access to public services such as distance to a paved road; household members' employment such as working hours on farm and off farm; human capital such as average education of working members of the household; asset positions such as land holding; and so forth. You need to identify potentially relevant variables and the direction of their effect. Then put all those variables together and run the regression. Report the result and discuss whether it matches your hypothesis. If not, give possible reasons.

```
. gen y = log(pcexp/cbnpline)
. reg y age age2 workhour x1-x3 [aw=weighti]
```

The expression `x1-x3` represents other explanatory variables that you want to include; don't feel confined to just three variables!

Note that if you want to include categorical variables, you need to convert them into dummy ("binary") variables if the ranking of categorical values does not have any meaning. For example,

```
. tab region, gen(reg)
```

will generate four variables, labeled `reg1`, `reg2`, `reg3`, and `reg4`. The variable `reg1` takes on a value of 1 for Dhaka and zero otherwise, and so on. When using a set of such dummy variables in a regression, one must be left out, to serve as a reference area. So, for instance,

```
.  reg y age age2 workhour x1-x3 reg2-reg4
   [aw=weighti]
```

would include dummy variables for the regions, with Dhaka serving as the point of reference.

After the regression, it is usually a good idea to plot the residuals against the fitted values to ensure that the pattern appears sufficiently random. This could be done by adding, right after the regression command,

```
.  predict yhat, xb
.  predict e, residuals
.  scatter e yhat
```

Exercise 8. Chapter 10, International Poverty Comparisons

The World Bank estimates the extent and evolution of world poverty with the help of PovcalNet, a software interface that is available on line at http://iresearch.world bank.org/PovcalNet/jsp/index.jsp. This exercise represents an exploration of world poverty using PovcalNet. To answer this exercise you will need to use a browser such as Explorer and log in to PovcalNet.

1. Assume a poverty line of $1.25 per person per day (in 2005 prices). Create a table that shows the headcount poverty rate for the six main regions (East Asia and Pacific, Europe and Central Asia, Latin America and the Caribbean, the Middle East and North Africa, South Asia, and Sub-Saharan Africa) for 1981, 1993, and 2005.

2. Repeat 1, but for a poverty line of $2 per person per day.

3. Based on 1 and 2, which are the world's poorest regions? And which regions have seen the biggest reduction in poverty over the past two decades?

4. Pick a country. Graph the evolution of its headcount poverty rate over time (that is, for every year available: 1981, 1984, 1987, 1990, 1993, 1996, 1999, 2002, and 2005). On the same graph, show the headcount poverty rate for the region in which the country is located. Relative to the region, has the country you chose done relatively well, or poorly, in reducing poverty over time?

5. Pick any two countries. Compute the headcount poverty rate for each country at a dozen different poverty lines ($1.00 a day, $1.25 a day, $1.50 a day, and so on) and graph these curves. The horizontal axis will show the poverty line and the vertical axis will show the headcount poverty rate. These are poverty incidence curves. Which country has the higher poverty rate? Explain

Exercise 9. Chapter 11, Panel Data

The goal in this exercise is to create a panel of data. The Bangladeshi data come from a panel of households surveyed in 1991 and 1998. The relevant data are hh91.dta, hh98.dta, etc. (or hh91v7s.dta, and so on, if one is using Stata version 7). Each household has a single id called nh ("number of household").

1. Download the household data for 1998 and rename the variables (except for nh). For instance:

```
rename sexhead sexhead98
```

This is done so that when the data from the two surveys are merged, it will still be possible to distinguish the 1998 numbers from the 1991 numbers.

2. Sort the file using nh and save it with a name like hh98newlabels.dta.

3. Now open the household data file for 1991, sort it by nh, and merge it with hh98newlabels.dta.

4. Check that the villages are comparable (for example, using `compare vill vill98`).

5. Use a paired t-test to determine whether there was a significant change in the education level of heads of household between 1991 and 1998. Do the same for land holdings and access to toilets.

6. Repeat step 5, but use an unpaired t-test.

Exercise 10. Chapter 11, Transition Matrix

In this exercise, you will create a transition matrix that shows the extent to which households moved into or out of poverty.

1. Open consume98.dta, rename the expenditures by suffixing 98. Merge with consume91.dta (using nh to link the files). Save as consume9198.dta.

2. Create poverty lines for 1991 and 1998 using the vprice91.dta and vprice98.dta files, as set out in the Exercise 2 for chapter 3. Food needs are as shown in

table A3.1; assume the cost of basic needs poverty line is the food poverty line times 1.3. Call the poverty lines `foodline91`, `cbnpline91`, `foodline98`, and `cbnpline98`. Merge this information using thana and vill to create a single file with all the poverty lines. Call it povlines91and98.dta.

> Remember: `gen fpovline = pveg*3.4 + pfish*8.7 + ...`
>
> `gen cbnpline = 1.3*fpovline`

3. Construct a poverty indicator (1=poor) for 1991 and for 1998, and show the poverty transition matrix—that is, a simple table showing who was poor in both years, in neither year, in 1991 only, or in 1998 only.

Exercise 11. Chapter 11, Quintile Transition Matrix

In this exercise, you will construct a quintile transition matrix and generate measures of chronic, persistent, and transient poverty using data from Bangladesh.

Preparatory Steps

1. Open consume98.dta, keep `nh hhexpfd hhexpnfd` and `hhexpnfd2`, rename each of these by appending `98`, sort by `nh`, and save under a new name such as rconsume98.dta.
2. Open consume91.dta, keep the same variables, sort by `nh`, merge with rconsume98, check that the merge has worked (using `tab _merge`), drop the `_merge` variable, sort by `nh`, and save as rconsume9198.dta.
3. If you have not already done so, open hh98big7bs.dta and rename each variable (except nh) by suffixing 98. For example:

> `rename vill vill98.`

This file has information on income. Sort using `nh` and save under a new name such as revhh98.dta.
4. Now open hh91.dta, sort by `nh`, and merge using revhh98.dta. As usual, check that the two files have merged, by examining _merge, and then delete this variable.
5. Sort by `nh` and merge using rconsume9198.dta. Save this file, which is the file with which you will now work.

Note that prices in 1998 were 47 percent higher than in 1991, so before incomes or expenditures can be compared, they must be adjusted for the price difference. We will do this in the following exercises.

3

Exercises

1. Construct a measure of household expenditure per capita for 1991 and multiply it by 1.47 to get the equivalent in 1998 prices. Call it pce91in98.
2. Use the `xtile` command to create quintiles for this variable and call them qex91in98. [You may need to look up the `xtile` command from within Stata to get the precise syntax.]
3. Construct a measure of household expenditure per capita for 1998. Call it `pce98`.
4. Use the `xtile` command to create quintiles for this variable and call them `qex98`.
5. Construct a transition matrix (using a simple tabulation) to show how people moved from quintile to quintile between 1991 and 1998.
6. Let the poverty line be 5,500. Work out the proportions of the households in the sample who are
   a. Chronically poor (that is, average expenditure per capita is below the poverty line)
   b. Persistently poor (that is, expenditure per capita is always below the poverty line)
   c. Transiently poor (that is, were poor in one of the two years, but have average expenditure per capita above the poverty line)
   d. Never poor.

Exercise 12. Chapter 12, Basic Measurement of Vulnerability

In this exercise, you will calculate the basic measurement of vulnerability. For this exercise, the following information is available on the income of five households.

To complete this exercise, fill in the blanks. [Hint: Use Excel for this.]

Income	Poverty line	SD of income	Probability of poverty next year	Vulnerability[a]	Probability of poverty at least once in next two years
100	125	10			
120	125	12			
130	125	22			
160	125	20			
220	125	30			

- Highly vulnerable: 1. If probability of poverty next year is >0.5.
- Somewhat vulnerable: 2. If probability of poverty next year is > P_0 but <=0.5
- Not vulnerable: 3. If probability of poverty next year is <=P_0.

Note: SD = standard deviation.

398

a. Indicate here whether individual is highly vulnerable, somewhat vulnerable, or not vulnerable.

Exercise 13. Chapter 12, Measuring Vulnerability in Bangladesh

In this exercise, you will measure the proportion of households in Bangladesh who were "highly vulnerable to poverty" in 1998. Complete the following steps:

1. Use the 1998 Bangladesh data to construct and estimate a regression model where the dependent variable is the log of consumption per capita. [Use final.dta or pce.dta for the numbers.]

2. Keep the predicted output (yhat) and residuals (resid).

3. Regress the square of the residuals on the same variables as in step 1 and save the predicted value (estvar).

4. Construct a variable (call it flessc) that is (log of food poverty line – estimated log of consumption)/(square root of estimated variance).

5. Compute the probability of poverty for each household using norm(flessc).

6. Construct a variable called vul1 that is equal to 1 if the household has at least a 50 percent probability of being poor next year.

7. Time permitting, redo the exercise on the assumption that the age of the household head has risen by five years and the household assets have increased by 20 percent.

Exercise 14. Chapter 13, Simple Impact of Thai Village Fund

In this exercise, you will determine the impact of the Thailand Village Fund. The 2004 socioeconomic survey undertaken in Thailand included a module that asked questions about who borrowed funds from the Thailand Village Fund—a program that provides 1 million baht (US$25,000) per village, which villagers administer in the form of loans.

1. Open Stata and open the data file, which is called tvf.dta (available at http://mail.beaconhill.org/~j_haughton). This is a fairly large file, but is only a subset of the full data from the 2004 socioeconomic survey (and so cannot be used to make inferences about the effect of the program in Thailand; we are using it for teaching purposes only). The questions, and responses to them, are fairly well labeled, so you should be able to navigate your way through this data set without too much difficulty.

2. Answer the following questions based on the data in tvf.dta. [Note: the variable a30 is a weight variable and should be used when answering these questions.]

a. What proportion of households participated as borrowers?

b. Why reasons did people give for not participating? In what proportions?

c. How large was the average loan requested? Received?

d. What interest rates were charged?

e. For what purposes did people say they used the loans?

f. What was the default rate on the loans?

g. What fraction of borrowers had to borrow money from elsewhere in order to repay their Village Fund loan?

h. How did the Village Fund affect households "economic situation"?

i. What changes would households like to see in the Village Fund? Distinguish between the responses of participants and nonparticipants. Summarize the data.

3. How would you evaluate the impact of the Village Fund? Write a 200-word proposal. [This may seem like a narrow question, but it is really asking you to think about how you might go about measuring the impact of any program or project.]

Exercise 15. Chapter 13, Impact of Agricultural Extension

In this exercise, you will determine the impact of agricultural extension. Download hh98big7bs.dta. This file has familiar data from Bangladesh, but we have now added a new variable called agextend that indicates whether a household was chosen to participate in a program of agricultural extension that provides advice and support. [Note: The variable is invented, but the rest of the data set is real.] We now want to ask a basic question: what was the impact of the agricultural extension program?

1. First, let us look at the raw numbers.

a. Load hh98big7bs.dta, sort by the variable nh, and save.

b. Now load consume98v72.dta (or equivalent), sort by nh, and merge nh using hh98big7bs.

c. Check that the merge worked correctly by looking at the _merge variable.

2. Now compare income and consumption levels for households that did, and did not, get agricultural extension help.

a. Hint 1. First create measures of total income per capita, and total consumption per capita.

b. Hint 2. Sort by agextend and then use the syntax by agextend: sum hh* or equivalent.

c. Specifically, are households that got agricultural extension poorer? Richer? Larger? Are they more reliant on farm income?

3. Next, let us assume that agricultural extension was provided randomly, once other variables are held constant, and then ask what effect the program had.

   a. Create dummy variables for each district ("thana"). The `tab   thana, gen(than)` command will do this nicely.

   b. Run a regression of per capita income (or consumption or farm income) on the `agextend`, individual variables (such as gender, age, education, family size), and district dummy variables. The coefficient on the `agextend` variable measures the impact of the program. You will probably want to run a few regressions, one for each output variable (such as income per capita) that is of interest.

   c. Are the effects measured in 3(b) larger or smaller than in 2?

4. Finally, let us run a propensity score analysis. The idea is first to create a "propensity score" that measures the probability that a household will get agricultural extension; and then to use this score to match each "treated" household (that is, a household that gets agricultural extension) with an untreated household that is otherwise similar (that is, has a similar propensity score). Here is how it might work:

   a. From within Stata, use the search command to find "pscore" and "attnd" and download the relevant *.ado files. This is mainly an issue of following the instructions.

   b. Estimate the propensity score equation. This will look something like this:

```
pscore agextend sexhead ... [other variables, including
       district dummies] ... , pscore(fhat1) comsup
```

   c. Now make the comparison, using nearest-neighbor matching, using

```
       attnd xxx agextend, pscore(fhat1) comsup
```

   where xxx refers to the outcome variable (for example, consumption per capita) that is of interest.

Notes

1. These commands were substantially revised in Stata version 8, and the syntax differs significantly from earlier versions of Stata.
2. A calorie is the energy required to heat one gram of water by one degree Celsius. A Calorie is 1,000 calories.

References

Araar, Abdelkrim, and Jean-Yves Duclos. 2007. *USER MANUAL: DASP version 1.4.* Université Laval, PEP, CIRPÉE, and World Bank. [DASP stands for Distributive Analysis Stata Package.]

Deaton, Angus. 1997. *The Analysis of Household Surveys: A Microeconometric Approach to Development Policy.* Baltimore, MD: Johns Hopkins University Press for the World Bank.

Wodon, Quentin T. 1997. "Food Energy Intake and Cost of Basic Needs: Measuring Poverty in Bangladesh." *Journal of Development Studies* 34 (2): 66–101.

Answers to the Review Questions

Here are the answers to the review questions.

Chapter 1.   1-D. 2-C. 3-False.

Chapter 2.   1-B. 2-False. 3-B. 4-A. 5-D. 6-A. 7-A. 8-B. 9-False. 10-C. 11-D.

Chapter 3.   1-D. 2-D. 3-A. 4-C. 5-True. 6-C. 7-True. 8-A. 9-B. 10-True. 11-B. 12-False. 13-C.

Chapter 4.   1-C. 2-B. 3-False. 4-B. 5-True. 6-B. 7-C.

Chapter 5.   1-D. 2-C. 3-D. 4-B. 5-B. 6-True. 7-A.

Chapter 6.   1-D. 2-True. 3-C. 4-D. 5-A. 6-D. 7-True. 8-B.

Chapter 7.   1-True. 2-D. 3-False. 4-D. 5-A. 6-D. 7-B. 8-B.

Chapter 8.   1-False. 2-D. 3-B. 4-True. 5-D. 6-Yes. 7-No. 8-No.

Chapter 9.   1-B. 2-C. 3-False. 4-C. 5-C.

Chapter 10.   1-C. 2-C. 3-True. 4-B. 5-C. 6-D. 8-A. 9-True. 10-True. 11-A. 12-B. 13-True.

Chapter 11.   1-A. 2-True. 3-C. 4-False. 5-D. 6-A. 7-A. 8-B. 9-D. 10-True.

Chapter 12.   1-C. 2-False. 3-D. 4-B. 5-C. 6-D. 7-C. 8-D.

Chapter 13.   1-D. 2-False. 3-A. 4-True. 5-B. 6-D. 7-C. 8-C. 9-False. 10-D.

Chapter 14.   1-C. 2-D. 3-B. 4-D. 5-True. 6-B. 7-B. 8-D. 9-D.

Chapter 15.   1-True. 2-C. 3-B. 4-Progressive. 5-B. 6-D. 7-C. 8-True. 9-A.

Chapter 16.   1-False. 2-A. 3-Lower. 4-D. 5-B. 6-False. 7-B.

Index

Boxes, figures, notes, and tables are indicated by b, f, n, and t, respectively.